1 MONTH OF
FREE
READING

at
www.ForgottenBooks.com

By purchasing this book you are eligible for one month membership to ForgottenBooks.com, giving you unlimited access to our entire collection of over 1,000,000 titles via our web site and mobile apps.

To claim your free month visit:
www.forgottenbooks.com/free875392

ISBN 978-0-265-61019-0
PIBN 10875392

FIRST GREEK BOOK;

ON THE PLAN OF THE

FIRST LATIN BOOK.

BY THOMAS KERCHEVER ARNOLD, M. A.
RECTOR OF LYNDON,
AND LATE FELLOW OF TRINITY COLLEGE, CAMBRIDGE.

CAREFULLY REVISED AND IMPROVED

BY REV. J. A. SPENCER, M. A.
PROFESSOR OF LATIN AND ORIENTAL LANGUAGES
IN BURLINGTON COLLEGE, N. J.

NEW YORK:
D. APPLETON & CO., 443 & 445 BROADWAY.
1868.

597646

C

PREFACE.

In presenting a new and improved edition of the FIRST GREEK BOOK, the American Editor takes great pleasure in acknowledging the very gratifying success of the "Arnold Series," as issued under his supervision. He has not spared labor on his part, nor have the Publishers expense on their's, to render the various volumes of the series even still more worthy of the confidence and support of the public; and he ventures to express the opinion that the present "First Greek Book" will be found to be admirably adapted to the grounding of the young student in the fundamental principles of the noble language of Greece, as well as a very considerable improvement on former editions of the same book.

In this, as in the "First Latin Book," Mr. Arnold has prepared with great care, in both Greek and English, such Exercises as serve to illustrate those portions of the Grammar which are needful at the outset. Grammatical apparatus is supplied according as it is wanted; difficulties are elucidated; peculiarities of the Greek language are pointed out; differences of idiom between the two languages are specially noted; and, in accordance with the plan pursued by Ollendorff in his excellent works on education, *frequent repetition* of principles learned, and of things already acquired, impresses them upon the memory with surprising distinctness and force.

It may not be deemed amiss here to say, that the educational works of Mr. Arnold require activity and energy on the part of the teacher as well as the scholar. They are *not* meant to supersede the necessity of a competent and faithful instructor, who can take occasion to enlarge upon, render more full (as boys now and then need), and impress upon his classes, the admirably arranged and clearly and logically drawn out course of instruction contained in these volumes. On the contrary, the teacher must be active and hard-working as well as his boys: if he be so, it is really surprising how rapid and yet how solid is their progress ; if he be not, this as well as every other good school-book will be of comparatively little service in carrying forward the student toward the goal of his wishes and his efforts. It *ought* not to be necessary, in these days, to remind any one that there is no royal road to learning, and that the best of books and best of systems will not make thorough scholars, without good teachers, and studious, hard-working pupils.

The American Editor has endeavored to do all in his power to improve the present volume : he has amplified the earlier Lessons and Exercises ; added simple and clear explanations where they seemed to be needed ; inserted " Ques-

tions," rather as suggestive of what may be, than as express-
ive of all that should be, asked ; has referred frequently to
Kühner's valuable Grammar for fuller elucidation of difficulties or peculiarities, &c.   He hopes, ere long, to be able
to go still further, and in a "Second Greek Book" to carry
the pupil through the Verb in μι (which is not fully treated
of in this volume), the Irregular Verbs, and the principal
rules of the Syntax.   In that event, the apparatus supplied
would be full and complete in all respects ; and by a faithful
use of these works, the foundation would be laid, broad and
deep, of sound classical scholarship in our country.

J. A. S.

BURLINGTON COLLEGE,
   Sept. 20th, 1850.

CONTENTS.

LESSONS AND EXERCISES.

NOTES.

PARADIGMS, &c.

CONTENTS.

NOTANDA.

1. The small numerical references *above the line of words* refer to the Differences of Idiom, &c., at the end of the work (p. 237).

2. The pupil should be constantly practised in the *Paradigms* given at the end of the work.

3. He should be required from the beginning (i. e. from the *sixth* Exercise) to *accentuate* his Greek. The rules for changing the accents in the declensions are given after each declension. Those for the Verbs will be found at p. 206.

4. The references to Kühner are to the "Grammar for High Schools and Colleges," translated by Messrs. Edwards and Taylor: Andover, 1844. 8vo.

FIRST GREEK BOOK.

LESSON I.

The Alphabet.

1. The Greek Alphabet consists of twenty-four letters: seven of these are vowels, and seventeen consonants.

Forms.		Roman Letters.	Names.		Numeral Power.
A	*a*	a (ah)	Alpha	Ἄλφα	1
B	*β ϐ*	b	Beta	Βῆτα	2
Γ	*γ*	g (hard)	Gamma	Γάμμα	3
Δ	*δ*	d	Delta	Δέλτα	4
E	*ε*	ĕ (short)	Epsilon	Ἔ ψῑλόν	5
Z	*ζ*	z	Zeta	Ζῆτα	7
H	*η*	ē (long)	Eta	Ἤτα	8
Θ	*ϑ, θ*	th	Theta	Θῆτα	9
I	*ι*	i (et)	Iota	Ἰῶτα	10
K	*κ*	k	Kappa	Κάππα	20
Λ	*λ*	l	Lambda	Λάμβδα	30
M	*μ*	m	Mu	Μῦ	40
N	*ν*	n	Nu	Νῦ	50
Ξ	*ξ*	x	Xi	Ξῖ	60
O	*ο*	ŏ (short)	Omicron	Ὄ μῑκρόν	70
Π	*π*	p	Pi	Πῖ	80
P	*ρ*	r	Rho	Ῥῶ	100
Σ	*σ, ς*	s	Sigma	Σίγμα	200
T	*τ*	t	Tau	Ταῦ	300
Υ	*υ*	u	Upsilon	Ὕ ψῑλόν	400
Φ	*φ*	ph	Phi	Φῖ	500
X	*χ*	ch	Chi	Χῖ	600
Ψ	*ψ*	ps	Psi	Ψῖ	700
Ω	*ω*	ō (long)	Omega	Ὤ μέγα	800

1

LESSON II.

The Sounds of the Letters.

2. The Greek being a dead or *unspoken* language, we cannot determine how the ancients pronounced their words; hence modern nations adopt a system of pronunciation suited to their own peculiarities. In English, we usually give the vowels and consonants the following sounds:

3. a^* has the sound of *a* in *far*, or like *a* in *hat*.

4. ϵ "   "   *e* in *met*.

5. η "   ··   *a* in the words *same, fame,* &c., as $\mu\acute{\eta}\nu$ (*mane*); others give it the sound of *ee* in *meet*.

6. ι "   ··   *i* in *machine*, or like *i* in *bit*.

7. o "   ··   *o* in *not, dot*, &c.

8. υ "   "   *u* in *tube, crude*, &c.

9. ω ··   "   *o* in *hope, note, devote*, &c.

REM. E-*psilon*, U-*psilon :* Ψιλόν means *simple*, that is, *unaspirated* (ϵ or υ)*:* the character H having been also used originally to mark the rough breathing (our *h*); and Υ to mark another breathing, that of the *Digamma*, or Latin *Vau*.

O-*micron*, O-*mĕga :* μικρός, μικρόν, *little;* μέγας, μέγα, *great*.

10. Sigma (σ) at the end of a word takes the form of ς, as σεισμός, πρός, &c.

This form is now sometimes used in the middle of compound words, when the first word in the compound ends in σ, as προσφέρω, for προσφέρω. This is contrary to ancient authority.

---

* In classifying the vowels, note that two of them are always *short ;* two always *long ;* and three *doubtful*, being sometimes long, sometimes short :

short vowels,	ϵ, o.
long "	η, ω.
doubtful "	a, ι, υ.

11. γ before a vowel is sounded like *g* hard, as γῆ (gĕ, like the English *gay*); when before another γ and also before κ, χ, ξ, it is sounded like *ng* in *ring*. Thus ἄγγελος must be pronounced *ang-gelos* (Latin *angelus*); συγκοπή, *sŭng-kŏpĕ*; Ἀγχίσης, *Ang-chīses*; λάρυγξ, *larūngx*; &c.

12. ζ has the sound of *dz* (nearly), as in the English *adze*; as ζέω, *dzeo*; μελίζω, *melid-zo*.

13. θ has the sharp sound of *th* in *thin*, *thick*; never the sound of *th* in *this*, as θεολογία, *theology*.

14. τ always retains its proper sound of *t* and is never pronounced like *sh*, as in some English words (*propitiation*, *condition*, &c.); thus, Κριτίας, *Krit-i-as* (not *Krish-i-as*); αἰτία, *ait-i-a*; &c. So, too, σ never has the sound of *sh*, as Ἀσία, *As-i-a* (not *Ash-i-a*).

15. χ has the hard, guttural sound, as *ch*, in *chemist*, *chaos*, *loch*, &c.

Exercise 1.

16. Give the *names* and *sounds* of the following letters:

α	η	δ	ζ	ρ	ψ	ω	ξ
ι	β	ξ	λ	φ	μ	ζ	ν
π	κ	γ	σ	ρ	γ	ν	υ
χ	ρ	λ	δ	ζ	η	ξ	σ
γ	ψ	ς	μ	ε	γ	δ	τ
τ	η	ω	τ	ν	ζ	υ	ν
φ	π	χ	ρ	υ	ξ	η	ρ
γ	ψ	θ	ν	χ	θ	ο	ς
Α	Η	Δ	Ζ	Ρ	Ψ	Ω	Ξ
Ι	Β	Ξ	Λ	Φ	Μ	Ζ	Ν
Π	Κ	Γ	Σ	Ρ	Γ	Ν	Υ
Χ	Ρ	Λ	Δ	Ζ	Η	Ξ	Σ
Γ	Ψ	Σ	Μ	Ε	Γ	Δ	Τ
Τ	Η	Ω	Τ	Ν	Ζ	Υ	Ν
Φ	Π	Χ	Ρ	Υ	Ξ	Η	Ρ
Γ	Ψ	Θ	Ν	Χ	Φ	Ο	Θ

17. Write the *names* of the letters in Greek : also write in Greek *capitals* these words, Xĕnŏphōn, Paulŏs, Matthaiŏs.

---

18. QUÉSTIONS.—How many letters are there in the Greek alphabet? How many and which are vowels? How many and which consonants? What do you mean by *ĕ-psilon?* *u-psilon?* Which is short or little *ŏ?* Which long or great *ō?* When does *γ* have the sound of *ng?* Give an example. Do you ever give *σ* or *τ* the sound of *sh?* Does the same rule apply to the English?

LESSON III.

The Diphthongs.—Breathings.

19. There are *twelve* diphthongs in Greek ; *six* of these are termed *proper, six improper* diphthongs.

1) Proper diphthongs are :

αι	pronounced like *ai* in *aisle,*	e. g.	αἴξ
αυ	"	ου	*sound,*	ναῦς
ει	"	ei	*height,*	δεινός
ευ	"	eu	*neuter,*	Ζεύς
οι	"	oi	*boil,*	κοινός
ου	"	ou	*youth,*	οὐρανός

Some prefer to sound *αυ* as *au* in *laud,* and *ου* as *ou* in *sound.*

2) Improper diphthongs are :

ᾳ	pronounced like the simple vowel *a.*		
ῃ	"	"	*η.*
ῳ	"	"	*ω.*
ηυ	*eu* in *feudal,* or like the diphthong *ευ.*		
υι	"	*whee* in *wheel.*	
ωυ	"	the diphthong *ου.**	

---

* The following example will show how the Romans sounded

REM. ᾳ, ῃ, ῳ have the second vowel (ι) of the diphthong written underneath. This is called *Iota subscriptum*, and is generally so written after α, η, ω. But when *capital* letters are used the ι is still written *as a letter;* thus ΔΕΣΠΟΤΗΙ = δεσπότῃ, 'Αΐδης = ᾅδης, 'Ωιδή = ᾠδή. Iota is then said to be *adscribed*.

· 20. Every word in Greek that begins with a vowel or diphthong, has a mark over this initial vowel or diphthong termed a *breathing :* it is placed over the *second* vowel of a diphthong; as ἔχω, αἴξ, &c.

21. The *rough* breathing or *aspirate* (spiritus asper) is a *comma turned the wrong way*, and is sounded · like an *h* before a vowel; as, ὁ, *ho ;* οἱ, *hoi ;* "Εκτωρ, *Hector;* εὑρίσκω, *heurisko.*

22. The *smooth* breathing (spiritus lenis) is a *comma*, and has no effect on the pronunciation; thus, ἀνήρ is pronounced *anēr,* ὄρος, *ŏrŏs,* &c.

23. Every word that begins with υ has, in Attic Greek, the rough breathing, as ὑπέρ, *huper ;* ὑφέν, *huphen* (hyphen).

24. The *consonant* ρ has also the rough breathing over it, when it stands at the beginning of a word, as 'Ρέα, *Rhea.*

25. In the *middle* of a word a *single* ρ has no breathing over it: of two ρ's, the first has the smooth, the second the rough breathing: ἔρρωσο! (In some modern editions the breathings over ρρ are omitted.)

these diphthongs, and how they are represented in English : α is expressed by the diphthong *æ*, ει by *i* and *ē*, υ by *y*, οι by *œ*, ου by *u* m.ē.g.

Φαῖδρος, Phædrus,	Μοῦσα, Mūsa,
Γλαῦκος, Glaucus,	Εἰλείθυια, Ilithyia,
{ Νεῖλος, Nilus,	Θρᾷκες, Thrāces,
{ Λυκεῖον, Lycēum,	Θρῇσσα, Thrēssa,
Εὖρος, Eurus,	τραγῳδός, tragœdus.
Βοιωτία, Bœotia,	

Exercise 2.

26. Write (with the proper *breathings*) the following words in Greek characters.

☞ Note that ē, ō stand for η, ω : ĕ, ŏ for ε, o : also that the *h* represents the *rough* breathing.

hĕn	hŏmoiŏs	rhabdŏs	rhinos	arrhabōn
hois	hōn	hikanoi	adunatŏs	ĕsti
ĕgō	hōs	agathŏs	houtoi	ĕchousin
ēn	aneu	hōspĕr	hēdu	hŏti
hun	an	hēgĕmŏna	rheuma	rhachŏs
anēr	anggelós	rhiptō	hŏ	rhētōr
hagia	hōstĕ	ŏmbrŏs	tŏdĕ	arrhētŏs
hē	hōn	hēbē	alōpēx	ĕchō
ĕchō	autŏs	hĕautŏn	ĕrō	haima
huiŏs	auriŏn	angkura	hĕn	hŏs

hŏ	hĕ	tŏ	tō	ta	tō	hoi	hai	ta	
tou	tĕs	tou	toin	tain	toin	tōn			
tōi	tēi	tōi *				tois	tais	tois	
tŏn	tēn	tŏ				tous	tas	ta	

27. Read (and write down in English characters) the following words :

οὗτος. αὐτος. Τις. ποτε. πωποτε. τυπτει. χην. ἐξει. ἐχω. Ἐστιν. αὐτον. αὐτον. ῥιμφα. βλεφαρον. σωμα. χειρες. τυπτουσι. γιγαντες. δορυ. λαμβανειν. Νυν. ἡμερα. νυξ. Χειμων. νεφελη. ἐτος. Γαρ. ἐνιαυτος. ἀξιουν. φαιδρος. ψηφισμα. μερος. κατα. φιλος. σοφος. Μων. ὁ. Ῥους. τουτων. τοσουτος. Φευ. Ποθεν. παλαιος. γερας. οὐδεπωποτε.

☞ This exercise should be lengthened and varied according to circumstances, till the pupil is thoroughly acquainted with the breathings and their proper places.

---

* The *iota* is here to be *subscript*, [see 19. 2) REM.]

28. QUESTIONS.—How many diphthongs are there in Greek ? How do you distinguish them ? Name the proper diphthongs, and give their pronunciation. Name also the improper diphthongs with their sounds. What do you call the little straight mark under ᾳ, ῃ, ῳ ? Why ? When is iota written by the side of the preceding letter ? What do you call it then ? Which words in Greek take a *breathing* ? Where is it placed when the word begins with a diphthong ? What is the rough breathing ? What is its equivalent in English ? What effect does the smooth breathing have on the pronunciation ? What do words that begin with υ always take ? When does ρ have the rough breathing ? When not ? How is it when two ρ's come together ?

LESSON IV.

Classification of the Consonants.

29. The consonants are divided into *semi-vowels* and *mutes*.

1) Semivowels ⎨ liquids λ, μ, ν, ρ.
⎩ sibilant σ.
2) Mutes   π, β, φ : κ, γ, χ : τ, δ, ϑ.
3) Double Letters   ζ, ξ, ψ.

30. The mutes are divided,

a) according to their fundamental sound :
1) π, β, φ, P-mutes.
2) κ, γ, χ, K-mutes.
3) τ, δ, ϑ, T-mutes.

b) according to the breathing or aspiration with which they are pronounced :
1) π, κ, τ, *smooth.*
2) β, γ, δ, *middle.*
3) φ, χ, ϑ, *aspirate.*

REM. The P-sounds are termed *labials*, because the lips (*labium*, lip) are principally concerned in uttering them ; the K-sounds are termed *palatals* or *gutturals*, because formed by the palate or throat (*palatum*, *guttur*, palate, throat) ; and the T-sounds are termed *linguals*, because formed by the tongue (*lingua*, tongue).

31. In the following table the mutes correspond, both when taken *horizontally*, and when taken *perpendicularly*.

		Smooth.	Middle.	Aspirates.
P-sounds	. . .	π	. . . β	. . . φ
K-sounds	. . .	κ	. . . γ	. . . χ
T-sounds	. . .	τ	. . . δ	. . . ϑ

32. The three *double letters* arise from the blending of the mute consonants with σ :—

ζ = δς (or σδ).

ξ = *any* k sound with σ (= κσ, γσ, or χσ).

ψ = *any* p sound " σ (= πσ, βσ, or φσ).

33. A pure Greek word can end only in one of the three liquids, *ν, σ, ρ*. It will be remembered that ψ = πσ, βσ, or φσ, and ξ = κσ, γσ, or χσ, and so fall under the rule. The two words, οὐκ, *not*, and ἐκ, *out of*, form only an apparent exception, since they incline so much to the following word as to become, as it were, a part of it. (See 54.)

This law of euphony (says Kühner, § 25. 5) occasions either the omission of all other consonants, or it changes them into one of the three liquids just mentioned ; hence, σῶμα (gen. σώματ-ος) instead of σῶματ, γάλα (gen. γάλακτ-ος) instead of γάλακτ, λέων (gen. λέοντ-ος) instead of λέοντ, ἐβούλευον, instead of ἐβούλευοντ; τέρας (gen. τέρατ-ος) instead of τέρατ, κέρας (gen. κέρατ-ος) instead of κέρατ, μέλι (gen. μέλιτ-ος) instead of μέλιτ.

Hence it follows that we find Greek words always ending in a vowel or one of the semi-vowels, ν, ρ, σ.

Exercise 3.

34. 1) Name and distinguish the *vowels, diphthongs, semivowels* and *mutes*, in the Greek words following.

2) In the case of the *mutes* distinguish them according to what you have learnt in 30, 31.

3) Point out the *double letters* and show how they arise.

1. φρένες ἀγαθαί. 2. εὐωδία καὶ μῦρον γυψὶν εἰσιν
αἰτία θανάτου. 3. τὸ ξίφος. 4. ζωῆς ἀρχή. 5. ἐν τῇ
λάρνακι Δανάης καὶ Περσέως. 6. βουλεύω. 7. ὁ λόγος
τοῦ ἀνθρώπου. 8. ἡ φλόξ. 9. δὸς ποῦ στῶ, καὶ τὸν
κόσμον κινήσω.

QUESTIONS.—How many consonants are there ? How are they
divided ? Name the semivowels; the mutes; the double letters.
How are the mutes divided ? (*Ans.* In two ways, according to their
fundamental sound, and according to the aspiration with which they
are pronounced.) Name them according to the former way; according to the latter. Which are the labials ? Why so called ? Which
the palatals or gutturals ? Why so called ? Which the linguals ?
Why so called ? Which are the double consonants ? What does ς
arise from ? What ξ ? What ψ ? What letters do Greek words
always end in ? (*Ans.* Vowels, and the liquids ν, ρ, σ.) What two
words are exceptions to this rule ?

LESSON V.

Syllables.—Quantity.

35. A vowel, when uttered by itself, or in connection with one or more consonants, is termed a syllable ;
as, ἤ, δή, πρός, ἀρχή, &c.

36. A word is composed of one or more syllables.
No syllable or monosyllabic word contains more than
six or seven consonants; as, in στράγξ. A word of *one*
syllable is termed a *monosyllable ;* of *two*, a *dissyllable ;*
of *three*, a *trisyllable*, of more than three, a *polysyllable ;* as, μήν, πόλις, βραχίων, προσδέχομαι.

37. The *last* syllable of a word is called the *ultima ;* the one next to the last, the *penultima ;* the one
preceding the penult (or the last but two) the *antepenultima ;* thus in the word κάτοπτρον, πτρον is the
ultima, το the *penultima*, κα the *antepenultima*.

1*

38. DIVISION OF SYLLABLES.*—The fundamental rule is that syllables end with a vowel and begin with a consonant. When, therefore, a consonant stands between two vowels, it belongs to the following syllable; as, πο-τα-μός, ὄ-ψο-μαι, ἔ-σχον, ἔ-βλα-ψα.

Exception.—A compound word is best divided according to the elements of the compound; as, συν-εκ-φώνησις, προ-στά-της, προσ-στείχω.

39. In the case of *a consonant doubled* (ππ, λλ, γγ, &c.) *a smooth and aspirate mute* (πφ, κχ, τθ, see 31) and *a liquid before one or more consonants* (the combination μν excepted), the first consonant ends a syllable, the second begins one; as, τάτ-τω, ἄν-θρω-πος, Βάκ-χος, ἄλ-γος, ἔρ-γον, ἰ-μνός. In all other cases, of course the general rule applies; as κλέ-πτης, Κά-δμος, &c.†

40. By *quantity* is meant the *time* which is taken to utter a syllable. Syllables are either *long* or *short;* the long are regarded as having *double* the time of the short.

41. A syllable is *short by nature* when it contains a short vowel (ε, ο, ᾰ, ῐ, ῠ) followed by a *vowel* or *simple consonant;* as, ἐνόμῐσᾰ, ἐπῠθετὄ. (See 3, note *.)

42. A syllable is *long by nature* when it contains either a *simple long vowel* (η, ω, ᾱ, ῑ, ῡ), or a *diphthong;* as, ἥρως, κρῑνῶ, γέφῡρα, ἰσχῡροῦς, παιδευῇς. Hence those syllables are *always long*, in which two vowels are *contracted* into one; as, ἄκων (from ἀέκων), βότρῡς (from βότρυας).

43. A syllable with a short vowel becomes long by *position*, (i. e. by the *place* of the vowel) if two or more consonants, or a double consonant (ζ, ξ, ψ) follow the

---

* See Note 1. (The "Notes" are to be found immediately after the Lessons and Exercises.)

† A more important distinction, however, is that which is made between the stem-syllables and the syllables of inflection or derivation. The stem-syllables express the essential idea of the word, the syllables of inflection or derivation, the relations of the idea. Thus, e. g. in

short vowel; as, ᾿Εκστέλλω, τύψαντες, κόραξ (κόρᾰκος) τράπεζα.

> REM. The position of *a mute with a liquid* generally leaves a *short* vowel *short*; as, ἄτεκνος, ἄπεπλος, ᾿ἀκμή, βότρυς, δίδρᾰχμος, γενέσλη, &c. Note, however, that in compounds, and when middle mutes (β, γ, δ) stand before λ, μ, ν, the general rule holds good in respect to the lengthening of a short vowel by position; as, ᾿ἐκνέμω, βίβλος, εὔσδμος, πέπλᾰγμαι.

[☞ The pupil may omit, for the present, from 40 to 43 inclusive.]

Exercise 4.

44. 1) Divìde the following Greek words into syllables (38, 39.)

2) Name each word according to the number of syllables of which it is composed.

1. πηγή. 2. ἐστίν. 3. ἀναμφισβήτητος. 4. πράσσω. 5. Σαπφώ. 6. ἔχω. 7. Επίδαμνος. 8. ᾿Ατθίς. 9. συντρέχω. 10. ἵππος. 11. ναύκραρος. 12. ἅπτω. 13. μοῖρα. 14. παλίγκοτος. 15. συνεμβάλλω. 16. πάγχριστος. 17. παθητικός. 18. Μελέαγρος. 19. χαράδρα. 20. τέκνον. 21. πότμος. 22. μαργίτης. 23. ὄπτομαι. 24. συνέχω. 25. αἴξ. 26. ποδός. 27. πρός. 28. νεανίας.

---

45. QUESTIONS.—What is a syllable? What do you call a word of *one* syllable? Of *two*? Of *three*? Of more than three? What name do you give to the *last* syllable of a word? The last but one? The last but two? What do you call a letter or syllable at the beginning of a word? (*Ans.* An *initial* letter or syllable.) What at the end of a word? (*Ans.* A *final* letter, &c.) What in the body of a word? (*Ans.* A *medial* letter, &c.) Give the fundamental rule for the division of syllables. How do you divide the words πότᾰμος, ἔβλαψα, ἔσχον? State the exception to the rule. What is the rule in 39?

γέ·γραφ·α, the middle syllable is the stem-syllable, the two others syllables of inflection; in πρᾶγ·μα, the first is the stem-syllable, the last the syllable of derivation. See Kühner's *Gr. Gram.* § 26. 2.

How do you divide into syllables ἵππος, ἀμνός, ᾽Ατθίς, Κάδμος, ἔλγος? What is the more important distinction quoted from Kühner in the note?

LESSON VI.

Accents, Enclitics, &c.

46. *a)* The Greek accents are the *acute* (´) and the *circumflex* (ˆ).

b) The acute stands on *one* of the *last three* syllables. It cannot, however, stand on the *antepenult* (*last but two*), unless the final is *short*; as ποιήσω, ἔδωκε, ἀρχή, ἄνθρωπος.

c) The *circumflex* can stand on either of the *last two* syllables: but it stands only over *long vowels* and *diphthongs*, and not over the *penult* (*last but one*), unless the final is *short*; as, ἡμᾶς, ταῦτᾰ.

47. In comparison with the sharply accented syllable, the other syllables of a word have a depressed tone, which *used* to be called the *grave* accent, and marked by a stroke drawn to the *right*: Θεὸδὼρὸς, i. e. Θεόδωρος.

48. From the *acute* and the *grave* (`) arose the *circumflex*. Thus ᾶ from άὰ; ῶ from όὰ; ῆ from έὰ; &c.

But ὰά, ὸά, (the *acute* being on the *second* vowel or diphthong) would be contracted into ά, ώ, with the acute.

49. When the *penult* is the *tone-syllable*,* and has a *long vowel* or *diphthong*, then, if the *final* is *short*, the accent is the *circumflex*: φεύγω· but φεῦγε.

50. When a tone-syllable has also a breathing, the acute and grave are placed after the breathing, the circumflex above it. They stand over the vowel (ῆ, ὢ, ὅ); being, however, for convenience, placed a *little before* a capital (῍Η, ᾽Ω). For a (*proper*) *diphthong* their place is over the second vowel (Οὔτε, Οὖν, οὔτε, οὖν): but an *improper* one, even when it is a capital, and, as sucl , takes its ι into the line of the etters, is treated as a single vowel: ῞Αιδης = ᾅδης. (19. REM.) **In**

---

* i. e. the *accented* syllable.

diærēsis,* the acute accent stands *between,* and the circumflex *above* the points; as: ἀΐδιος, κληῖδι.

51. Words receive the following appellations according to the accentuation of the final syllables :—

Oxytones†	⌢	*acute* on the last syllable; as, τετυφώς, κακός, Ͽήρ.
Par-oxytones	"	"	last syllable but one; as, τύπτω, ἀνϽρώπου.
Pro-par-oxytones	"	"	last syllable but two; as, ἄνϽρωπος, τυπτόμενος.
Peri-spōmena, circumflex	"		last syllable; as, κακῶς, ἐλϽεῖν.
Pro-peri-spōmena	"	"	last syllable but one; as, πρᾶγμα, φιλοῦσα.

52. ☞ A *non-oxytone* is called a *barytone,†* because it has, *not* the acute, but the supposed *grave accent* (47) on its final syllable; as, λύω, πρᾶγμα, πράγματα.

53. An *oxytone* is written as a *barytone* (i. e. the *acute* of an *oxytone* is written as the *grave*) when the word is in a sentence, except when it is the last word of a sentence, or immediately precedes a stop; as, εἰ μὴ μητρυιὴ περικαλλὴς Ἡερίβοια ἦν. μενοῦμεν αὐτούς. ὁ μὲν Κῦρος ἐπέρασε τὸν ποταμόν, οἱ δὲ πολέμιοι ἀπέφυγον.

Rem. The accent thus written over oxytones in connected discourse is generally termed the *softened acute.*

54. A few small words are without an accent: these are called *atonics,* from *a,* which means *not,* and τόνος, 'tone' or 'accent.*

Obs. The atonics (or *proclitics*) are the following: ὁ, ἡ, οἱ, αἱ: ἐν, εἰς (ἐς), ἐκ (ἐξ): ὡς, εἰ: οὐ (οὐκ, οὐχ).

The word οὐ = 'not,' takes the acute, when it stands as the last word of a sentence.

---

* When two vowels, which regularly form a diphthong, are to be pronounced separately, two points (called *puncta diærēsis,* 'points of separation' [διαίρεσις]) are placed over the second vowel (ι, υ), as: εΐ, οΐ, αΰ.

† Ὀξύς, *acutus*: περισπώμενος, *circumflexus*: Βαρύς, *gravis*: τόνος, *accentus*.

55. Certain other *small* words (of *one* or *two* sylla
bles) are called *enclitics*. They are so closely joined
with the preceding word, that *their accent* is generally
placed upon *it*, they themselves being pronounced without any *tone ;* as, φίλος τις (pronounced as if written
φιλοστίς).

* Σέ, '*thee*,' '*you*,' (*sing.*), is one of these enclitics.

Μέ, '*me*,' is another : but the longer form for '*me*' (ἐμέ) is not
enclitic.

'Εστίν, '*is*,' is another *enclitic.**

56. 1) When an enclitic follows a *proparoxytone*
or *properispomenon* (51), the enclitic loses its accent,
which is written over the *last syllable* of the preceding
word.

κρύπτουσί σε, *they hide you.* | φιλοῦσί με, *they love me.*

2) When an enclitic follows a *paroxytone,*
　a *monosyllable* enclitic *loses* } its accent.
　a *dissyllable* enclitic *retains* }

κρύπτε με, *hide me.* | φίλος ἐστὶν, *he is friendly.*

3) When an enclitic follows a *perispomenon,* it
.oses its *accent,* whether it is a monosyllable or a dis-
:yllable.

φιλεῖ με, *he loves me.* | ἁπλοῦς ἐστιν, *he is simple.*

4) When an enclitic follows an *oxytone,* the enclitic
loses its accent, but the *acute* of the *oxytone* is then *not*
written as the *grave.*

καλός ἐστιν, *he is beautiful.*

Ͽήρ τις, (τὶς, '*a certain*,' is an enclitic.)

REM. As the correct pronunciation of the Greek language is unknown (see 2), we are not able to determine the precise use

---

* The other enclitics are mostly contained in the following list:
the pres. indic. of εἰμί and φημί (except εἶ and φής) ; the personal pronouns, μοῦ, μοί, σοῦ, σοί, οὗ, &c. ; the indef. pron. τὶς, τὶ ; the indef.
adverbs, πός, πό, πή, πού, ποτέ, &c. ; the particles, τέ, τοί, γέ, νύν, &c.

of the accents: their principal value to us is in their serving to distinguish words; thus νόμος, *law*; νομός, *pasture-ground.* βίος, *life*; βιός, *bow.* δῆμος, *people*; δημός, *fat.* τίς, *who?* τὶς, *some one.* εἰσί, *they are*; εἶσι, *he goes.* δόλος, *a dome*; δολός, *mud.* ὦμος, *shoulder*; ὠμός, *cruel*; &c.

57. Beside the accents, the Greeks have several other marks to assist the reader, some of which refer to words alone and others to the members of the sentence only. These are

a) The *apostrophe*, which marks the cutting off (elision) of a vowel at the end of a word when the following word begins with a vowel; as, ἀπ᾽ ἄλλων for ἀπὸ ἄλλων, κατ᾽ ἐμέ for κατὰ ἐμέ, ἀφ᾽ ἑαυτοῦ for ἀπὸ ἑαυτοῦ, &c.

The *coronis*, which marks the blending (crasis) of two words, one ending the other beginning with a vowel, into one word; as, τοὔνομα for τὸ ὄνομα, τἀγαθά for τὰ ἀγαθά, ταὐτά for τὰ αὐτά, &c.

The *diæresis* which marks a division between two vowels; as, ἀΐσσω, ὄϊς, &c.

b) The punctuation marks—

The comma	[,]	as in English; τοῦτο, κ. τ. λ.
The colon (and semicolon)	[·]	a point above the line; με·
The interrogation	[;]	like the English semicolon; τίς;
The period	[.]	as in English; πρᾶγμα.

Exercise 5.

58. Name the accents in the following sentences; show whether they are placed according to the rules above given; and point out the *enclitics* and *atonics.*

1. Ὁ δειλός ἐστι τῆς πατρίδος προδότης. 2. Ὄρτυγές εἰσιν ἡδύφωνοι καὶ μαχητικοὶ ὄρνιθες. 3. ὅπως δὲ εἰδῶ μάλιστα, ὁποῖός τίς ἐστι τὴν ὄψιν; 4. Ῥάδιον εὑρεῖν ἀπό γε τούτων. 5. τό τε τῶν Τριτώνων γένος.

6. ἀλλὰ δίελέ μου τὴν κεφαλὴν ἐς δύο κατενεγκών.
7. τῷ ἐλέφαντι ἐστὶ δράκοντος ὀῤῥωδία. ὦ κακοδαῖμον υἱὲ τοῦ κακοδαίμονος Πριάμου.   8. Τυφὼν ὑπὸ Ζηνὸς ἐκολάσθη.   9. Σαρδανάπαλος, ἐν βασιλείοις κατακε κλεισμένος, οὐδὲν ἄλλο ἐδίωκεν ἢ ἡδονήν.

59. Are the accents rightly or wrongly placed in the examples following? if wrongly, then make the correction required.

1. βλάπτει τόν ἐχθρὸν. (46, c; 53.)   2. τήν τοῦ γεώμετρου σοφίαν θαύμαζομεν. (46, b.)   3. ἤλειφες τόν δέσποτην.   4. ἔπειθε τοὺς ξένους.   5. πεῖσομὲν σέ.
6. ἐχθρός ἐστίν.   7. ῥῖπτει τόν δίσκον.   8. φιλεῖ σέ.
9. καλός ἐστίν.   10. βλάπτουσι σε.

☞ This exercise may profitably be lengthened according to the necessities of the learner, until he is thoroughly acquainted with the accents, their right places, the enclitics, &c. ·

●

LESSON VII.

Parts of speech.   Inflection, &c.

60. The parts of speech in Greek are,—the article, the noun, the adjective, the pronoun, the verb, the adverb, the preposition and the conjunction.   The interjection is commonly ranked among the adverbs.

61. The first five of these (viz., article, noun, adjective, pronoun, verb) are susceptible of variation or modification in order to indicate their different relations. · This is properly termed *inflection.*

62. The inflection of the article, nouns, adjectives and pronouns is termed *declension;* the inflection of the verb *conjugation.*

63. The other parts of speech (viz., adverbs, prepositions and conjunctions) do not admit of inflection.

64. The Greek, like our own language, has *three* genders, viz., the *masculine*, the *feminine* and the neuter ; as, ὁ ἄνθρωπος, *the man ;* ἡ μήτηρ, *the mother ;* τὸ σῦκον, *the fig.**

Obs. To mark the genders of substantives in Greek, the different forms of the article are employed; as ὁ for the masculine, ἡ for the feminine, τό for the neuter, &c. (See 89.)

Some nouns are both masculine and feminine, and are said to be of the *common* gender ; as ὁ, ἡ θεός, *god* or *goddess ;* ὁ, ἡ τρόφος, *nurse ;* ὁ, ἡ ἄνθρωπος, *human being ;* &c.

65. The Greek has *three* numbers, the *singular*, the *plural*, and the *dual* which denotes *two*, or a pair.

66. It has also *five* cases, viz., the *nominative*, the *genitive*, the *dative*, the *accusative* and the *vocative*.

Obs. 1. There is no *ablative*, the place of that case being supplied mostly by the *dative*, sometimes by the *genitive*.

Obs. 2. The nominative, accusative, and vocative neuter have the same form in all numbers, and in the plural they always end in α. The nominative, accusative, and vocative dual are alike ; the genitive and dative dual are also alike. The nominative and vocative plural are always alike. The dative singular always ends in ι, but in the first two declensions it is *subscript* [see 19. 2) Rem.]

67. There are *three* Declensions in Greek, the *First*, *Second*, and *Third*.

---

* The gender of nouns is determined partly by their meaning ; the following general rules may be noted to advantage :

1) Names of *males*, of *nations*, *winds*, *months*, *mountains*, and most *rivers*, are masculine.

2) Names of *females*, of *countries*, *islands*, most *cities*, most *trees* and *plants*, are feminine.

3) The names of the *letters* and *fruits*, *infinitives*, *diminutives* in -ον (except the proper names of females, e. g. ἡ Λεόντιον), all *indeclinable* words, and finally every word considered as simply *that word* (e. g. τὸ μήτηρ, 'the word *mother*'), are neuter.

General Table of the Declensions.

	I.	II.	III.
Sing. Nom.	{ ης, ᾱς, *masc.* { η, ᾰ, ᾱ, *fem.*	ος, *m.* et *f.* ον, *neut.*	{ α, ι, υ, *neut.* { ω, *fem.* { ν, ξ, ρ, σ, ψ, *of all* *genders.*
Gen.	ου), ης, *or* ας,	ου,	ος (ως), *increases* *in gen.*
Dat.	ῃ, *or* ᾳ,	ῳ,	ι,
Acc.	ην, *or* αν,	ον,	α, *or* ν,
Voc.	η, *or* α,	ε, ον, *neut.*	*various ; neut. as* *nom.*
Plural. Nom.	αι,	οι, ᾰ, *neut.*	ες, ᾰ, *neut.*
Gen.	ῶν,[1]	ων,	ων,
Dat.	αις,	οις,	σι (σιν),
Acc.	ᾱς,	ους, ᾰ, *neut.*	ᾰς, ᾰ, *neut.*
Voc.	αι,	οι, ᾰ, *neut.*	ες, ᾰ, *neut.*
Dual. N. A. V.	ᾱ,	ω,	ε,
G. D.	αιν,	οιν,	οιν,

[1] Contracted from *άων*, and therefore circumflexed (48). In repeating tho table, let the pupil say " *ων* circumflexed."

---

68. QUESTIONS.—Name the parts of speech in Greek. How many and which admit of inflection ? What do you mean by inflection ? What term is applied to the inflection of nouns, adjectives, &c. ? What to that of the verb ? What parts of speech do not admit of inflection ? How many genders are there in Greek ? How are they generally marked ? What is the common gender ? How many numbers are there in Greek ? What does the dual denote ? How many cases ? Is there any ablative ? Name the cases which are alike. Repeat the table of declensions. What are the terminations of the nominative of the first declension ? What of the second ? Of the third ? What of the genitive of the first ? Of the second ? Of the third ? (And so on, through all the table.)

LESSON VIII.

The Verb. Present and Future Active.

69. Greek Verbs are of two kinds, those ending in ω and those in μι.*

70. There are *three. Voices*, the *Active*, the *Passive* and the *Middle;* as, τύπτω, *I strike* (act.); τύπτομαι, *I am struck* (pass.); τύπτομαι, *I strike myself.*

REM. For the present we use only verbs in ω in the active voice.

71. The *Moods* of Greek Verbs are, the *Indicative*, the *Imperative*, the *Subjunctive*, the *Optative* and the *Infinitive.*

72. The *Tenses* are, 1) PRINCIPAL TENSES, the *Present*, the *Perfect*, the *Future;* 2) HISTORICAL TENSES, the *Imperfect*, the *Pluperfect*, the *Aorist.*

73. The Mutes, as we have seen (30, 31), are divided into three sets of three :—

	Smooth.	Middle.	Aspirate.
p-sounds	π	β	φ
k-sounds	κ	γ	χ
t-sounds	τ	δ	ϑ

1) For *any p*-sound with σ (πσ, βσ, φσ), you must write ψ.

2) For *any k*-sound with σ (κσ, γσ, χσ), you must write ξ.

3) For *any t*-sound with σ (τσ, δσ, ϑσ), you must write σ only :

That is, the *t*-sound is *thrown away.*

4) Also for ππ-σ you must write ψ: for κτ-ς, ξ.

---

* They are so called from the ending of the first person singular of the Present Indic., as γράφω, λέγω, ἔχω, &c. (verbs in ω), and τίθημι, ἵστημι, &c. (verbs in μι).

74. Thus : 1) βλεπ-ς becomes βλεψ

τριβ-ς " τριψ

ἀλειφ-ς " ἀλειψ

τυπτ-ς " τυψ

2) πλεκ-ς " πλεξ

λεγ-ς λεξ

ἀρχ-ς ἀρξ

3) πειθ-ς πεις

σπευδ-ς " σπευς

75. The Infinitive (of the Pres. Act.) ends in ειν ; as, λέγειν, βλέπειν, &c.

76. The *root of the Present* (Active) is got,

a) By throwing away the ειν of the Pres. Infin.; as, τύπτειν, root, τυπτ. ἄρχειν, root, ἀρχ.

b) By throwing away the ω of the first sing. of the Present ; as, ἄρχω, ἀρχ. βλέπω, βλεπ.

77. The root of the Future is got from the root of the Present (or Infinitive) by *sigmating* it ; that is, by adding ς ; thus, βλεπ, add ς, βλεπς = βλεψ.

78. The Greek language (see 65) has a form called the *Dual*, to denote *two*. The Active Voice has no *dual* form for the *first person*.

79. In the Indicative, both the *Present* and the *Future* of the *Active Voice* end in ω, and the *terminations* of the Persons are :

	1.	2.	3.		EXAMPLE.		
					Present.		
S.	ω	εις	ει	S.	τύπτω	τύπτεις	τύπτει
				P.	τύπτομεν	τύπτετε	τύπτουσι
P.	ομεν	ετε	ουσι	D.		τύπτετον	τύπτετον
					Future.		
				S.	τύψω	τύψεις	τύψει
D.		ετον	ετον	P.	τύψομεν	τύψετε	τύψουσι
				D.		τύψετον	τύψετον.

* See Note 2.

80. The second person sing. of the Imperative ends in ε added to the root of the *Present* (or *Infinitive*). Γράφ-ω, *I write.* Γράφ-ε, *write (thou).*

81. VOCABULARY 1.

To write, γράφ-ειν	To say, to tell, λέγ-ειν
To look, βλέπ-ειν	To rule, ἄρχ-ειν (governs
To rub, τρῑβ-ειν	gen.)
To strike, τύπτ-ειν	To persuade, πείϑ-ειν
To anoint, ἀλείφ-ειν	To cheat, } ψεύδ-ειν.
To weave, πλέκ-ειν	To beguile, }

Exercise 6.

82. a) *Read and translate into English.*

[*You*, in what follows, is to be considered *sing.* unless *pl.* is added.]

1. Γράψω. 2. Γράφετον. 3. Βλέπομεν. 4. Τρί-βουσι. 5. Τρίψουσι. 6. Λέγετε. 7. Λέγε. 8. Τύπτει. 9. Ἄρξει. 10. Πείσουσι. 11. Ψεύσεις. 12. Βλέψω. 13. Ἀλείφεις. 14. Ἀλείψουσι. 15. Λέγεις. 16. Λέγομεν. 17. Πείϑετε. 18. Πεῖϑε. 19. Πείϑετον. 20. Λέ-ξετον. 21. Πλέξω. 22. Τρίβεις. 23. Τρίψετον.

b) *Translate into Greek.*

1 You * anoint. 2. He anoints. 3. We will anoint. 4. You (*pl.*) anoint. 5. You (*two*) will say. 6. He will tell. 7. He will look. 8. You will beat. 9. They look. 10. You (*pl.*) look. 11. You (*pl.*) will cheat. 12. They will persuade. 13. He will persuade. 14. Persuade. 15. Tell. 16. Look. 17. They (*two*) look. 18. They will rub. 19. You (*two*) will weave. 20. You will persuade.

* As in Latin, the nom. of the *personal pronouns* is not expressed except for the sake of *distinction* or *emphasis.* They are to be left untranslated here.

The pupil ought to write out, plainly and distinctly, his translations from Greek into English, and from English into Greek. In the latter case, too, he should accentuate the Greek words, bringing to bear, as far as he is able, the rules for accentuation, 46, &c.

LESSON IX.

The Verb, continued.

83. If a root ends in ε, the terminations of the Present (79) will be contracted thus (see 48):

S.	έ-ω	έ-εις	έ-ει	ῶ	εῖς	εῖ
P.	έ-ομεν	έ-ετε	έ-ουσι	οῦμεν	εῖτε	οῦσι
D.		έ-ετον	έ-ετον		εῖτον	εῖτον

84. When a root ending in ε is *sigmated* (i. e. is increased by an added sigma, 77), the ε is changed into η. Thus,

$$\left.\begin{array}{l}\phi\iota\lambda\epsilon\text{-}ς\\\pi o\iota\epsilon\text{-}ς\end{array}\right\}\quad\text{becomes}\quad\left\{\begin{array}{l}\phi\iota\lambda\eta\text{-}ς\\\pi o\iota\eta\text{-}ς\end{array}\right.$$

ποιέω, *I make ;* ποιήσω, *I will make.*

φιλέω, *I love ;* φιλήσω, *I will love.*

85. The pupil will recollect that—

1) A verb agrees with its nominative case in *number* and *person ;** as,

Κῦρος τύπτει, *Cyrus strikes.*

τὰ ζῷα τρέχει, *The animals run.*

ἡμεῖς σε φιλοῦμεν, *We love you.*

2) A transitive verb is followed by the *accusative ;* as,

Κύνες τοὺς ἐχθροὺς δάκνουσιν, *Dogs bite their enemies.*

---

* But a *dual nominative* is often joined with a *plural* verb; and a *neuter plural* generally takes a *singular* verb.

Λύκος ἄμνον ἐδίωκεν, *A wolf was pursuing a lamb.*

Γυνή τις ὄρνιν εἶχε, *A woman had a hen.*

86. VOCABULARY 2.

To love, (φιλέ-ειν =) φιλεῖν		To hide, κρύπτ-ειν.	
To make, (ποιέ-ειν =) ποιεῖν			
Nom. *I,* ἐγώ.	*Thou,* σύ.	*We,* ἡμεῖς.	*You,* ὑμεῖς.
Acc. *Me,* ἐμέ or μέ.	*Thee,* σέ.	*Us,* ἡμᾶς.	*You,* ὑμᾶς.
Him, αὐτόν.		*Them,* αὐτούς.	
This (neut. sing.), τοῦτο.		*These things,* ταῦτα.	
Not, οὐ, (with the imperative, μή.)			

☞ Μέν—δέ are *indeed—but.* The μέν is, however, mostly *not translated* in English. They cannot stand as the *first word* of a sentence or clause.

Exercise 7.

87. *a) Translate into English.*

1. Φιλοῦσιν αὐτόν. 2. Φιλήσουσι. 3. Φιλεῖ. 4. Ποιοῦσι ταῦτα. 5. Ποιεῖς. 6. Ποιήσεις. 7. Κρύπτεις. 8. Κρύψομεν. 9. Ἐγὼ* μὲν κρύπτω ταῦτα, σὺ δὲ οὐ κρύπτεις. 10. Ἡμεῖς μὲν φιλοῦμεν αὐτόν, ὑμεῖς δὲ οὐ φιλεῖτε. 11. Σὺ μὲν ψεύσεις αὐτόν, ἐγὼ δὲ οὐ ψεύσω. 12. Ἡμᾶς μὲν πείσεις, αὐτὸν δὲ οὔ.

b) Translate into Greek.

(Words to which * are prefixed are not to be translated.)

1. You love him. 2. I indeed love him, but you do not love (*him). 3. You*†† will love him, but I *shall not. 4. They will love them. 5. You love him. 6. You (*pl.*) love him. 7. They are doing these things. 8. He is doing this. 9. We*†† are doing these

---

* See note * on p. 21.

† These numerals refer to the Table of "Difference of Idioms," &c. immediately preceding the Indexes.

things, but you (*pl.*) are not doing *them.   10. I will do this.   11. I will do this, but you shall not do *it. 12. We will hide this.   13. Ye shall weave.

---

88. QUESTIONS.—What accent has φιλοῦσιν? [48.] What hence called? [51.] Why is αὐτόν written as an *oxytone*? [53.] Why are ἐγώ, μέν, σύ, δέ written thus, and not ἐγό, μέν, σύ, δέ? Why has σί no accent in several places, but has the acute in the last sentence above? [54, OBS.] What case is ταῦτα? By what rule? [85, 2.] What cases are ἐγώ, σύ and ἡμεῖς? Give the rule for the agreement of a verb with its nominative case. [85, 1.] How is αὐτόν governed? What case is ἡμᾶς? Why? Parse the verb ψεύσεις (thus: ψεύσεις is the fut. act. 2d pers. sing. from ψεύδω, root ψευδ: the root of the fut. is got from the root of the pres. by adding ς, which makes ψευδς: but by 73, 8, for any *t*-sound with ς you must write ς only, which makes ψευς, root of the fut.) What is the root of ποιεῖς? [84, 77.] If the root of ποιεῖς is ποιε, why do you write ποιήσεις in the fut.? [84.] What is the place of μέν and δέ in Greek sentences? Do you translate μέν in the sentences above? In translating the English into Greek, do you insert the μέν, or not, in 2, 8, 9, 11? (*Obs.* Imitate the order of the words in the Greek sentences.)

LESSON X.

The Article.

89. The Article in Greek is prefixed to nouns in order to ascertain or define them; as, ὁ ποιητής, "*the* poet;" ἡ κόρη, "*the* maiden;" τὸ γόνυ, "*the* knee."

REM. The Greeks have no indefinite article, answering to our "*a*" or "*an.*"

PARADIGM OF THE ARTICLE.

ὁ, ἡ, τό, "*the.*"

	SINGULAR.			PLURAL.			DUAL.		
	m.	f.	n.	m.	f.	n.		m.	f.	n.
N.	ὁ	ἡ	τό	οἱ	αἱ	τά	N. A.	τώ	τά	τώ
G.	τοῦ	τῆς	τοῦ	τῶν	τῶν	τῶν				
D.	τῷ	τῇ	τῷ	τοῖς	ταῖς	τοῖς	G. D.	τοῖν	ταῖν	τοῖν
A.	τόν	τήν	τό	τούς	τάς	τά				

90. The pupil will observe that ὁ, ἡ, οἱ, αἱ are **atonic** (54); the genitives and datives *perispomena* (51); and the other cases *oxytone* (51).

REM. In the dual the feminine is more commonly τώ, τοῖν, than τά, ταῖν. Τά (as *fem. dual*) is very uncommon.

91. The Article is often equivalent to a weakened possessive; and is translated by *my, your, his, her, their*; as, κύνες τοὺς ἐχθροὺς δάκνουσιν, ἐγὼ δὲ τοὺς φίλους, ἵνα σώσω, "*Dogs bite* their *enemies, but I* my *friends, that I may save them.*"

REM. "The chief employment of the definite article is to distinguish the subject from the predicate; for, from the nature of the case, the subject is considered to be something definite, of which something general is predicated or denied." (*Donaldson.*)

92. VOCABULARY 3.

Poet, ποιητής, ὁ (acc. ποιητήν).
Letter, epistle, ἐπιστολή, ἡ (acc. ἐπιστολήν).
Young man, youth, νεανίας, ὁ (acc. νεανίαν).
Tent, σκηνή, ἡ (acc. σκηνήν).
Sea, θάλασσα, ἡ (acc. θάλασσαν).

Exercise 8.

93. *a) Translate into English.*

1. Ὁ ποιητὴς τὴν ἐπιστολὴν γράψει. 2. Τὸν νεανίαν φιλοῦμεν. 3. Μὴ γράφε ἐπιστολήν. 4. Ἡμεῖς μὲν πείσομεν αὐτούς, ὑμεῖς δὲ οὐ πείσετε. 5. Ποιήσετε σκηνήν. 6. ὁ νεανίας λέξει ταῦτα. 7. Ἐγὼ μὲν οὐ φιλέω τὴν θάλασσαν, σὺ δὲ φιλεῖς. 8. Κρύψει τὴν ἐπιστολήν. 9. Ἀλείφομεν τὸν νεανίαν. 10. Ποιητής. 11. Ὁ ποιητής. 12. Ὑμεῖς με φιλεῖτε. 13. Ταῦτα αὐτοὺς πείσει. 14. Λέξετον τοῦτο. 15. Σκηνὴν ποιεῖ. 16. Πείσομέν σε. 17. Ὁ νεανίας λέξει τὴν ἐπιστολήν. 18. Σὲ μὲν

πείσουσιν,* ἐμὲ δὲ οὔ.　19. Κῦρος γράφειν ἐπιστολὴν φιλήσει.

b) Translate into Greek.

1. The young man will persuade the poet. 2. He will hide the letter. 3. Do not strike the poet. 4. He loves us. 5. They are doing these things. 6. We will love them, but you will not love (⁹ them). 7. The young man weaves. 8. These things beguile the poet. 9. Do not persuade the youth to love the sea. 10. He loves a youth. 11. We will make a tent. 12. The poet does not love the sea. 13. Write your letters.

94. QUESTIONS.—What is the use of the article in Greek? Is there any thing answering to our indefinite article? Which portions of the article are *atonic?* Which *perispome?* Which *oxytone?* Which are the most usual forms in the dual? What is the article often equivalent to? Give the Greek for "Dogs bite *their* enemies." In the Exercise (sentence 8, Greek), how do you translate ἐπιστολήν, without the article? 4. Account for the acute on αὐτούς. 10, 11. Point out the difference. 12. What is με? 13. What rule applies? [85, 1.] 14. Parse λέξετον. 16. Account for the two accents on πείσομέν. 18. What do you call the ν in πείσουσιν? To what words is it added? In sentence 8 (English), do you use μή or οὐ? 8. Is the verb singular or plural? 13. How do you translate "your"?

LESSON XI.

First Declension of Nouns.

95. As we have seen above (67), there are in Greek three different ways of inflecting substantives, distinguished as the *first, second,* and *third* declensions.

---

* The third singular and the third plural of verbs in σι, ε, or ι, have sometimes an ν added, when a word beginning with a vowel follows. This ν is also added to the dative plur. in σι, and to some adverbs of place, &c. It is called ν ἐφελκυστικόν. But in reality, the ν which is thus said to be added belonged to the original form of the word.

96. Nouns of the first declension end in *a* and *η*, *feminine ; as* and *ης, masculine.*

TERMINATIONS OF THE FIRST DECLENSION.

	SINGULAR.					PLURAL.	DUAL.
N.	ă,	ā or η		ās or ης		αι	ā
G.	ης	ᾱs	ης	ου	ου	ῶν	αιν
D.	ῃ	ᾳ	ῃ	ᾳ	ῃ	αις	αιν
A.	ᾰν	ᾱν	ην	ᾱν	ην	. ᾱς	ā
V.	ă	ā	ṛ	ā	η, ă	αι	ā

REM. The gen. *as* and dat. *ᾳ* belong to nouns that end in *ρα*, or in *a* preceded by a *vowel* (*a pure*), together with ἀλαλά, and some proper namés in *ā*: Ἀνδρομέδᾱ, Λήδᾱ, &c. The rest in *a* take *ης, ῃ*. The termination *a*, gen. *ης*, is *always short ;* *a*, gen. *ας*, is *mostly long.**

PARADIGMS OF FEMININE NOUNS.

		Muse.	Shadow.	Country.	Honor.	Justice.
Sing.	N.	ἡ Μοῦσᾰ	σκιά (ᾱ)	χώρᾱ	τιμή	δίκη
	G.	τῆς Μούσης	σκιᾶς	χώρας	τιμῆς	δίκης
	D.	τῇ Μούσῃ	σκιᾷ	χώρᾳ	τιμῇ	δίκῃ
	A.	τὴν Μοῦσᾰν	σκιάν (ᾱ)	χώραν	τιμῆν	δίκην
	V.	Μοῦσᾰ	σκιά (ᾱ)	χώρᾱ	τιμή	δίκη
Plur.	N.	αἱ Μοῦσαι	σκιαί	χῶραι	τιμαί	δίκαι
	G.	τῶν Μουσῶν	σκιῶν	χωρῶν	τιμῶν	δικῶν
	D.	ταῖς Μούσαις	σκιαῖς	χώραις	τιμαῖς	δίκαις
	A.	τὰς Μούσᾱς	σκιάς (ᾱ)	χώρας	τιμάς	δίκας
	V.	Μοῦσαι	σκιαί	χῶραι	τιμαί	δίκαι
Dual.	N. A. V.	τὰ Μούσᾱ	σκιά (ᾱ)	χώρᾱ	τιμά	δίκα
	G. D.	ταῖν Μούσαιν	σκιαῖν	χώραιν	τιμαῖν	δίκαιν

97. *On the accentuation.*] The accent remains, as long as the general rules (46, *b, c*) will let it, on the same syllable ; with the exception of the gen. plural, which in this declension is always *perispŏmenon.*

1) If the accent is on the last syllable, it remains indeed on that syllable, but is changed into the *circumflex* in the *gen.* and *dat.* of all numbers. Thus, τιμή, τιμῆς, τιμῇ, τιμῶν, τιμαῖς, τιμαῖν.

2) In the nom. plural, *αι* is considered *short* with respect to *accentuation :* hence if the penult has a *diphthong* or *long vowel,* an acute

---

* See Note 3.

on that syllable is changed into the circumflex. For instance, γνώμη has nom. plural γνῶμαι, χώρᾱ has nom. plural χῶραι.

3) When the final syllable becomes long, the *circumflex* cannot stand on the penult (46, c): σφαῖρᾱ cannot have σφαῖρᾱς. Hence the accent must be the *acute,* since that accent *can* stand on the penult, whatever the quantity of the final may be: σφαῖρα, gen. σφαίρας, Μοῦσᾰ, gen. Μούσης.

4) If the word be proparoxytone (which it cannot be, unless the final ᾱ is short), no accent *can* stand on the antepenult when the final becomes long. It is necessary therefore to move the acute one place to the right: ἔχιδνα, gen. ἐχίδνης.

98. The pupil will observe that—

1) *Abstract* substantives (e. g. the names of *virtues, vices, &c.)* often take the article, which is not to be translated into English.

2) *Proper names* often take the article when they have been lately mentioned; or when they are the names of *well known* persons or places.

EXAMPLES.

φιλοῦμεν τὴν σοφίαν, *we love wisdom.*

ἡ μέθη μικρὰ μανία ἐστίν, *drunkenness is a brief madness.*

βλάπτουσι τὴν Ἐρέτριαν, *they are injuring Eretria.*

ὁ Σωκράτης ἦν φιλόσοφος, *Socrates was a philosopher.*

Κῦρον μεταπέμπεται· ἀναβαίνει οὖν ὁ Κῦρος, *He sends for Cyrus; Cyrus thereupon goes up.*

99. VOCABULARY 4.

Eretria, Ἐρέτρια, ας.	*Pleasure,* ἡδονή, ῆς.
Philosophy, φιλοσοφία, ας.	*Wisdom,* σοφία, ας.
The soul, the mind, ψυχή, ῆς.	*Slavery,* δουλείᾱ, ας.
Virtue, ἀρετή, ῆς.	*Ignorance* (brutish), ἀμαθία, ας.
Benefit, profit; a blessing, ὠφέλεια, ας.	*Madness,* μανία, ας.
	Calamity, συμφορά, ᾶς.

Loss, injury, penalty; a cala-
mity, ζημία, *as* (damnum).
Hurt, βλάβη, ης.
Fate, μοῖρα, *as.*
'Injustice, ἀδικία, *as.*
Justice (as habit), δικαιοσύνη, ης.

Necessity, compulsion ἀνά-
γκη, ης.
Damsel, κόρη, ης.
Force, violence, βία, *as.*
Anger, ὀργή, ῆς.
Ball, σφαῖρα, *as.*

To hurt, injure, βλάπτ-ειν.
To flee or *fly from, shun,* φεύγ-
ειν.
To pursue, διώκ-ειν.

To yield, εἴκ-ειν, (governs the *da-*
tive.)
To throw, ῥίπτ-ειν.
Is, ἐστί (ἐστίν); *are,* εἰσί, (εἰσίν.)

Both—and, καί—καί; τὲ καί (τέ is enclitic, 55), or τέ . . . καί
(with a word or words between). Τὲ καὶ often = 'and' only.
Himself, ἑαυτόν or αὐτόν.   *Who?* τίς;
Towards, πρός (with *accusative*).

Obs. 1) αὐτόν (with *smooth* breathing) = *him.*
αὑτόν (with *rough* breathing) = *himself.*
2) Τίς; '*who?*' retains its *acute* accent even in a sentence.

Exercise 9.

100. *a) Translate into English.*

1. Μὴ βλάπτε τὴν Ἐρέτριαν. 2. Οὐ βλέπει πρὸς
φιλοσοφίαν. 3. Ἄρχε τῆς ψυχῆς. 4. Ἡ ἀρετὴ οὐ
βλέψει πρὸς ὠφέλειαν. 5. Ῥίψω τὴν σφαῖρνν. 6. Ἡ
μοῖρα ἄρχει βλάβης τε καὶ ὠφελείας. 7. Φεῦγε τὴν ἀδικίαν. 8. Τὴν μὲν ἀδικίαν φεῦγε, τὴν δὲ δικαιοσύνην
δίωκε. 9. Εἶκε τῇ βίᾳ. 10. Μὴ εἶκε ταῖς ἡδοναῖς.
11. Φεῦγε τὴν τῶν ἡδονῶν δουλείαν. 12. Τῇ μὲν σοφίᾳ
εἶκε, τῇ δὲ ἡδόνῇ μὴ εἶκε. 13. Ἡ μὲν ἀρετὴ σοφία ἐστίν,
ἡ δὲ ἀδικία ἀμαθία τε καὶ μανία. 14. Ταῖς συμφοραῖς
εἴκομεν. 15. Μὴ βλάπτε τὰ (or τὼ) κόρᾱ. 16. Ἡ δικαιοσύνη ἀρετή ἐστι. 17. Σωκράτης αὐτὸν φιλεῖ, ἐμὲ
δὲ οὔ. 18. Τίς τὴν σκηνὴν ποιήσει; 19. Ἑαυτὸν κρύψει. 20. Ζημία ἐστίν. (See 56, 2.)

b) *Translate into Greek.*

1. We yield to force and necessity. 2. Pursue virtue. 3. You will look to profit. 4. Pursue both justice and virtue. 5. We will yield to necessity, but not to force. 6. Rule over your (*say* 'the') anger. 7. We will yield to the compulsion of calamities. 8. Do not yield to the slavery of pleasure. 9. Who will hide me? 10. He loves himself. 11. Who is looking towards the young man? 12. They are throwing the ball. 13. It is a ball. 14. Virtue and justice are wisdom. 15. This is a loss to the poet.

101. QUESTIONS.—How many declensions are there in Greek? What are the terminations of the first declension? Which are *feminine*? Which *masculine*? Which nouns have gen. *as*, dat. ᾳ? What is the quantity of *a*, gen. *ης*? Of *a*, gen. *as*? Go through with Μοῦσα, σκιά, χώρα, τιμή, δίκη. What is the general statement as to the accent? How is the gen. pl. always accented? If a noun is oxytone in the nom., what is the accent of the gen. and dat.? What is the quantity of *αι* with respect to accentuation? Suppose then the penult have a diphthong or long vowel, with an acute on it, what is that acute changed into when the termination becomes *αι*? Can the circumflex stand on the penult when the last syllable becomes long? If the final of a proparoxytone becomes long, what accent do you give it? Give the rules for the use of the article in 98. In the Exercise (sentence 3, Greek) account for the genit. [81, 99.] 7, 8, 9, &c, account for the article. [98, 1.] 15. Which is better, τά or τὰ κόρα? [90, REM.] Sentence 9 (English), what is the Greek for *who*? Does it retain its accent in a sentence? 10. Give the Greek for *himself*. 13. How do you express "it is" &c. in Greek? (By ἐστίν simply.)

LESSON XII.

Contracts. Masculines of the First Declension.

102. Some feminines of the first end in ῆ, ᾶ contracted from *έα, άα*. They are declined regularly as if from η, a; but every case is a *perispomenon*. (Συκέα

=) συκῆ, συκ-ῆς, συκ-ῇ, &c.: (μνάα =) μνᾶ, μνᾶς, μνᾷ, &c.

PARADIGMS OF MASCULINE NOUNS.

			Citizen.	Persea.	Youth.	Fowler.
Sing.	N.	ὁ	πολίτης	Πέρσης	νεανίας	ὀρνιϑοϑήρας
	G.	τοῦ	πολίτου	Πέρσου	νεανίου	ὀρνιϑοϑηρᾶ
	D.	τῷ	πολίτῃ	Πέρσῃ	νεανίᾳ	ὀρνιϑοϑηρᾷ
	A.	τὸν	πολίτην	Πέρσην	νεανίαν	ὀρνιϑοϑηραν
	V.		πολῖτᾰ	Πέρση	νεανία	ὀρνιϑοϑήρα
Plur.	N.	οἱ	πολῖται		νεανίαι	ὀρνιϑοϑῆραι
	G.	τῶν	πολιτῶν		νεανιῶν	ὀρνιϑοϑηρῶν
	D.	τοῖς	πολίταις		νεανίαις	ὀρνιϑοϑήραις
	A.	τοὺς	πολίτας		νεανίας	ὀρνιϑοϑήρας
	V.		πολῖται		νεανίαι	ὀρνιϑοϑῆραι
Dual. N. A. V.		τὼ	πολίτᾱ		νεανία	ὀρνιϑοϑήρᾱ
	G. D.	τοῖν	πολίταιν		νεανίαιν	ὀρνιϑοϑηραιν

103. Masculine nouns in ης have the vocative in η, except the following, which have ᾰ:

1) Those in της.

2) Those compounded of a substantive and a verb, that simply append ης to the verbal root; as γεωμέτρης, geometer; ἀρτοπώλης, breadseller, baker.

3) National names; as Πέρσης, a Persian, voc. Πέρσα,—but Πέρσης, Perses, voc. Πέρση.

104. The rules of accentuation are the same as for feminines (97).—Δεσπότης irregularly throws back its accent in vocat. (ὦ δέσποτα), and χρήστης, usurer, has gen. pl. χρήστων.*

105. Some nouns in ῆς, contracted from εας, are declined regularly, but every case is *perispomenon*. ('Ερμέας =) 'Ερμῆς, οὗ, ῇ, ῆν, &c.

106. Several masculines in ᾱς have the Doric gen. in ᾱ: viz. πατραλοίας, a parricide, μητραλοίας, a matricide, ὀρνιϑοϑήρας, a fowler or *bird-catcher*: also several proper names; as Σύλλας, gen. Σύλλα, and contracts in ᾶς, Βοῤῥᾶς (from Βορέας), gen. Βοῤῥᾶ.

---

* Three other nouns of the first declen. are paroxytone in the gen. pl.; as ἀφύη, anchovy; ἐτησίαι, Etesian winds; χλούνης, wild boar; which have gen. pl. ἀφύων, ἐτησίων, χλούνων.

107. A few proper names have the Ionic genit. in εω, even in the Attic dialect; as Τήρης, Θάλης, Τήρεω, Θάλεω. (Note the *irregular* accent.)

108. VOCABULARY 5.

Persian, Πέρσης.

Perses (proper name), Πέρσης.

Land, earth, γῆ.

Domestic, οἰκέτης.

Baker, ἀρτοπώλης.

Bookseller, βιβλιοπώλης.

Geometer, γεωμέτρης.

Master, δεσπότης (see 104).

Laborer, cultivator, ἐργάτης.

Desire, ἐπιθυμία.

Disciple, pupil, μαθητής.

Citizen, πολίτης.

Sailor, ναύτης.

Minerva, Ἀθηνᾶ (ᾶ = άα, Athēnē).

Mercury, Ἑρμῆς (Hermes).

Boreas, the north wind, Βορρᾶς (106).

The Gelas, (a river in Sicily,) Γέλᾱς, ᾱ (106).

Poet, ποιητής.

Mina, (a coin,) μνᾶ (= μνάα).

Weasel, γαλῆ (= γαλέη).

Fig-tree, συκῆ (ῆ = έα).

To chastise, κολάζειν.

To have, ἔχειν (takes *rough* breathing in the future.)

To plant, φυτεύειν.

To hunt, θηρεύειν.

To admire, θαυμάζειν.

One ought; we ought, χρή (= oportet.)

Hail! χαῖρε (imperat. of χαίρω).

"By," in swearing by a deity, νή (with accus.)

Not even, οὐδέ (ne ... quidem).

Five, πέντε.

Was, ἦν: *were,* ἦσαν.

To speak ill (or *evil*) *of,* κακῶς λέγειν, (with acc. of person.)

109. The Infinitive Mood with the article answers to our participial substantive: τὸ λέγειν, *to say,* or *(the)* *saying;* τοῦ λέγειν, *of saying;* τῷ λέγειν, *by saying,* or (with governed case interposed) τῷ ταῦτα λέγειν, *by saying these things.* It may be governed by prepositions, &c., just like any other substantive: ἀπὸ τοῦ λέγειν· τῇ τοῦ λέγειν ῥώμῃ, &c.

Exercise 10.

110. *a) Translate into English.*

1. Ὁ Πέρσης ἄρχει· τῆς τε γῆς καὶ τῆς θαλάσσης.

2. Οὐδ' οἰκέτας χρὴ ὀργῇ κολάζειν. 3. Ὁ ἀρτοπώλης

πέντε μνᾶς ἔχει. 4. Ὁ Προμηθεὺς⁰ κλίπτει Ἀθηνᾶς
τὴν σοφίαν. 5. Ὦ Πέρση, μὴ εἶκε τῇ. τοῦ ἄρχειν ἐπιθυμίᾳ. 6. Φεῦγε, ὦ Πέρσα. 7. Ὁ ἐργάτης συκᾶς φυ-
τεύει. 8. Οἱ Πέρσαι γῆς ἐργάται εἰσίν. 9. Θηρεύσομεν
τὰς γαλᾶς. 10. Τὴν τοῦ γεωμέτρου σοφίαν θαυμάζομεν.
11. Νὴ τὴν Ἀθηνᾶν ποιήσω ταῦτα. 12. Χαῖρε, ὦ δέσποτα. 13. Χαῖρε καὶ σύ, ὦ βιβλιοπῶλα. 14. Τὸ ὄνο-
μα⁰ ἦν ἀπὸ τοῦ Γέλᾱ. 15. Τὴν τοῦ ὀρνιθοθήρα⁴ τέχνην
θαυμάζομεν. 16. Οὐδὲ δεσπότας χρὴ κακῶς λέγειν.

⁰ 81.   ᵇ *Prometheus.* (98, 2.)   ᶜ τὸ ὄνομα, a name; ἀπὸ, from, (with gen.).   ᵈ 106.

b) Translate into Greek.

1. The disciples of the geometer have five minæ.
2. The Persians are masters of the sea. 3. The labor-
ers are planting a fig-tree. 4. O laborer, plant the fig-
tree. 5. By Hermes, I will not do this. 6. They yield
to the desire of having disciples. 7. The geometers
have pupils. 8. O Geometer, do not yield to the desire
of talking. 9. Do not speak-evil of the citizens.
10. Hail! O baker. 11. By Athēnē, I will have the
sphere. 12. By Hermes, I will plant the fig-trees.
13. One-ought not to plant even a fig-tree.

111. QUESTIONS.—How are femin. contracts declined? Go through
with πολίτης, Πέρσης, νεανίας, ὀρνιθοθήρας. What is the vocat. of masc.
nouns in ης? Name the exceptions. What are the rules of accentuation? Give the vocat. of δεσπότης and gen. pl. of χρήστης. How
are nouns in ῆς declined? What peculiarity have several masculines
in ᾶς? What is the genit. of such nouns as Τήρης, Θάλης, &c.? How
is the infin. mood with the article used? In the Exercise (sentence
1, Greek), why has τε no accent? 2. Why is ὀργῇ perispomenon?
[97, 1.] 8. Why is γῆς without the article? (Common nouns omit
the article under certain circumstances, as here, γῆ being used of the
particular country of the Πέρσαι.) Why does εἰσίν retain its accent
after ἐργάται? [56, 2.] 10. What is the order of the words? Is it to
be imitated? 13. What is the quantity of the α in βιβλιοπῶλα? Son-

tence 1 (English), how do you translate "have?" Give the rule
[85, 1]. 2. What case do you put "masters" in? (The nom. after
the verb.) 6. What case does εἴκειν govern? 9. What case do you
put "citizens" in?

LESSON XIII.

Second Declension of Nouns.

112. Nouns of this declension end in *os*, *masculine*,
often *feminine*, and *ov neuter*.

REM. Fem. diminutive proper nouns in *ov* are an exception, e. g.
ἡ Γλυκέριον. (See 64, note *.)

TERMINATIONS OF THE SECOND DECLENSION.

	SINGULAR.		PLURAL.		DUAL.
N.	ος	ον	οι	ᾰ	ω
G.	ου		ων		οιν
D.	ῳ		οις		οιν
A.	ον		ους	ᾰ	ω
V.	ος, ε	ον	οι	ᾰ	ω

PARADIGMS.

		Word.	Disease.	God.	Fig.
SING.	N.	ὁ λόγος	ἡ νόσος	ὁ θεός	τὸ σῦκον
	G.	τοῦ λόγου	τῆς νόσου	τοῦ θεοῦ	τοῦ σύκου
	D.	τῷ λόγῳ	τῇ νόσῳ	τῷ θεῷ	τῷ σύκῳ
	A.	τὸν λόγον	τὴν νόσον	τὸν θεόν	τὸ σῦκον
	V.	λόγε	νόσε	θεός	σῦκον
PLUR.	N.	οἱ λόγοι	αἱ νόσοι	οἱ θεοί	τὰ σῦκα
	G.	τῶν λόγων	τῶν νόσων	τῶν θεῶν	τῶν σύκων
	D.	τοῖς λόγοις	ταῖς νόσοις	τοῖς θεοῖς	τοῖς σύκοις
	A.	τοὺς λόγους	τὰς νόσους	τοὺς θεούς	τὰ σῦκα
	V.	λόγοι	νόσοι	θεοί	συκᾶ
DUAL. N.A.V.		τὼ λόγω	τὼ νόσω	τὼ θεώ	τὼ σύκω
G. D.		τοῖν λόγοιν	ταῖν νόσοιν	τοῖν θεοῖν	τοῖν σύκοιν

113. The vocative of words in *os* (as will be observed) sometimes
ends in *os*: as ὦ φίλε and ὦ φίλος: always ὦ θεός.

114. *On the accentuation.*]—The accent remains on the syllable
which is accented in the nominative, as long as it can: except in the
vocative ἄδελφε, from ἀδελφός, *a brother.* The termination οι in the

plural, like αι in the first declension, is considered *short* with reference to accentuation. The change of the accent is like that in the first declension (97), except that it is only *oxytones* (not *all* words, as in the first declension) that become *perispomena* in the genitive plural (ἰατρός· ἰατρῶν). The rest are *paroxytones*.

115. VOCABULARY 6.

Lecythus, Λήκυθος, ἡ (a fortress in Macedonia near Torōne).

A temple, ἱερόν, τό, (prop. neut. adj. from ἱερός, *holy.*)

A gift, δῶρον, τό.

God, θεός, ὁ.

Word, speech, reason, λόγος, ὁ.

Judge, juror, δικαστής, ὁ.

Work, action, ἔργον, τό.

Man, human being, ἄνθρωπος, ὁ.

Stranger, host, guest, ξένος, ὁ.

Physician, ἰατρός, ὁ.

Sorrow, λύπη, ἡ.

Plain, πεδίον, τό.

Targeteer, πελταστής, ὁ.

An enemy, πολέμιος (prop. adj., *hostile*); ἐχθρός, ὁ.

Way, road, ὁδός, ἡ.

Army, στρατία, ἡ.

Running, race-course, δρόμος, ὁ.

To run, θεῖν (= θέειν.) Δρόμῳ θεῖν is stronger; *to run at full speed; to run to the charge* (of soldiers).

Quoit, discus, δίσκος, ὁ.

Slave, δοῦλος, ὁ.

Drug, poison, φάρμακον, τό.

Tale, legend, μῦθος, ὁ.

Garland, στέφανος, ὁ.

Stadium, στάδιον, (= 606¾ English feet) pl. στάδιοι or στάδια.

Rock, πέτρα, ἡ.

Stone, λίθος, ὁ.

Silver, ἄργυρος, ὁ.

Gold, χρυσός, ὁ.

Mere talk, mere stuff, nonsense, λῆρος, ὁ.

Fear, φόβος, ὁ.

Horse, ἵππος, ὁ.

Ass, ὄνος, ὁ.

To care for, φροντίζειν, (governs the gen.)

To lead forward; to march forward; to advance (trans.) προάγειν.

To sow, σπείρειν.

To restrain, κατέχειν.

Ten, δέκα.

As (as it were =) about, ὡς.

That, ὅτι.

116. When a substantive with the article has a dependent genitive, the genitive usually either (1) stands between the article and its substantive, or (2) follows the substantive with a second article: thus,

1. ἡ τῶν παλαιῶν σοφία. | τὸ τῆς ἀρετῆς κάλλος.
2. ἡ σοφία ἡ τῶν παλαιῶν. | τὸ κάλλος τὸ τῆς ἀρετῆς.

a) In the first order (ἡ τῶν παλαιῶν σοφία) neither notion has any preponderance of emphasis over the other; the order with the repeated article (ἡ σοφία ἡ τῶν παλαιῶν), is used, when the speaker wishes *to dwell upon* the notions separately. The reason *may* be, to add an *ironical* or *contemptuous* meaning to one of them.—β) The following are rarer orders :—3. Ἡ σοφία τῶν παλαιῶν. 4. Τῶν παλαιῶν ἡ σοφία.

117. Words that modify a substantive are interposed, in Greek, *between* it and the article; or *follow it* with the article repeated.

English.	Greek.
The guards *from the city.*	1. οἱ ἀπὸ τῆς πόλεως φύλακες.
	2. οἱ φύλακες οἱ ἀπό τῆς πόλεως.
The guards *summoned to attend the king.*	1. οἱ τῷ βασιλεῖ ἀκολουθεῖν παρακεκλημένοι φύλακες.
	2. οἱ φύλακες οἱ τῷ βασιλεῖ ἀκολουθεῖν παρακεκλημένοι.

☞ Let the pupil note carefully and imitate the Greek order in the Exercises following.

Exercise 11.

118. a) *Translate into English.*

1. Ἔστιν· ἐν τῇ Ληκύθῳ Ἀθηνᾶς ἱερόν. 2. Δῶρα θεοὺς πείθει[b]. 3. Πείσει τοῖς λόγοις τοὺς δικαστάς. 4. Δίωκε τὴν ἀρετήν τε καὶ σοφίαν. 5. Οἱ θεοὶ τῶν ἀνθρώπων φροντίζουσιν. 6. Χαῖρε, ὦ ξένε. 7. Λύπης ἰατρός ἐστιν ἀνθρώποις λόγος. 8. Οἱ ἐκ τοῦ πεδίου πελτασταὶ δρόμῳ θέουσιν, οἱ δὲ πολέμιοι οἱ ἐπὶ τῇ ὁδῷ φεύγουσι. 9. Προάγε. ὁ Χειρίσοφος τὴν στρατιὰν ὡς δέκα σταδίους πρὸς πολεμίους. 10. Εἰς πέτρας τε καὶ λίθους[25] μὴ σπεῖρε. 11. Μὴ εἶκε τῇ τοῦ χρυσοῦ τε καὶ ἀργύρου ἐπιθυμίᾳ. 12. Λέγομεν ἔργοις, ὅτι λῆρος πρὸς[21] χρυσόν τε καὶ ἄργυρόν ἐστιν ἡ ἀρετή. 13. Πλέξομεν τοὺς στεφάνους. 14. Τὰς ἐπιθυμίας οὐ λόγῳ κατέχει, ἀλλ' ἀνάγκῃ καὶ φόβῳ. 15. Βλάπτει τὸν ἐχθρόν. 16. Πλέξουσι τὸν στέφανον. 17. Ὁ δοῦλος τρίβει τὸ

φάρμακον. 18. Τὸν μὲν δίσκον ῥίψω, τὴν δὲ σφαῖραν
οὔ. 19. Δοῦλός ἐστιν. 20. Ὁ ἰατρος τῶν τοῦ πελταστοῦ δώρων οὐ φροντίζει.

^a *There is.* In this sense ἐστιν (at the head of a sentence) keeps
its accent.   ^b Neuter plurals usually take a sing. verb. See 85.

b) Translate into Greek.

1. The horse is pursuing the ass.   2. Do not yield
to the enemy.   3. Restrain the desires of the soul by
reason.   4. The citizens do not care-for the strangers.
5. We will march- the army -forward^c about five stadia.
6. The enemy fly through fear.^d   7. Yield not to the
fear of the enemy.   8. In our words^e pleasure is mere-
nonsense to^f virtue, but by our actions we declare that
virtue is mere-nonsense to pleasure.   9. Gifts persuade
the souls of men.   10. The young-man will anoint
himself.   11. Who is weaving the garland?   12. It is
a discus.   13. They will throw the ball, but not the
discus.⁴¹   14. There are ten men in^g the temple of
Minerva.   15. O Persian, restrain the desire of speak-
ing evil of man.

^c These hyphens mean that *march-forward* is translated by one
word.   ^d Use the dative of the noun.   ^e Dative of the
noun, as in 12 (Greek) above.   ^f "To" (= compared with). See
29, "Diff. of Idiom."   ^g ἐν with dat.

119. QUESTIONS.—What are the terminations of the second de-
clens.?   Go through with the table.   Decline λόγος, νόσος, κῆπος,
θεός, σῦκον.   What is the vocat. of nouns in *os*?   What the rules with
respect to accentuation?   What is the order of the words when a
noun with the article has a dependent genit.?   Discriminate the
meaning, according to the order of the words.   What are rarer orders?
Where do you place words that modify a substantive?   Give the Greek
(both ways) for "the guards *from the city*;" "the guards *summoned to
attend the king*."   Can you point out any illustrations in the Greek
sentences following?   Sentence 14, (English) will the verb in the
sense of "there are," be accented or not?   (It retains its accent when
it stands at the beginning of a sentence.)

LESSON XIV.

Contracts of Second Declension.   Imperfect Tense.
Augment.

120. Some few nouns in εος, οος, εον, οον are contracted throughout.

PARADIGMS.

SING.	Mind.		Circumnavigation.		Bone.	
N.	ὁ νόος	νοῦς	ὁ περίπλοος	περίπλους	τὸ ὀστέον	ὀστοῦν
G.	τοῦ νόου	νοῦ	τοῦ περιπλόου	περίπλου	τοῦ ὀστέου	ὑστοῦ
D.	τῷ νόῳ	νῷ	τῷ περιπλόῳ	περίπλῳ	τῷ ὀστέῳ	ὀστῷ
A.	τὸν νοον	νοῦν	τὸν περίπλοον	περίπλουν	τὸ ὀστέον	ὀστοῦν
V.	νόε	νοῦ	περίπλοε	περίπλου	ὀστέον	ὀστοῦν
PLUR.						
N.	οἱ νόοι	νοῖ	οἱ περίπλοοι	περίπλοι	τὰ ὀστέα	ὀστᾶ
G.	τῶν νόων	νῶν	τῶν περιπλόων	περίπλων	τῶν ὀστέων	ὑστῶν
D.	τοῖς νόοις	νοῖς	τοῖς περιπλόοις	περίπλοις	τοῖς ὀστέοις	ὀστοῖς
A.	τοὺς νόους	νοῦς	τοὺς περιπλόους	περίπλους	τὰ ὀστέα	ὀστᾶ
V.	νόοι	νοῖ	περίπλοοι	περίπλοι	ὀστέα	ὀστᾶ
DUAL						
N.A.V.	τὼ νόω	νώ	τὼ περιπλόω	περίπλω	τὼ ὀστέω	ὀστώ
G. D.	τοῖν νόοιν	νοῖν	τοῖν περιπλόοιν	περίπλοιν	τοῖν ὀστέοιν	ὀστοῖν

121. Obs. 1) The *dual ὼ* is (irregularly) *oxytone*. Neuters contract εα into ᾶ (not ῇ) to preserve the *distinctive a* of a neuter plural. The gen. pl. from εον is generally open; ὀστέων (not οστῶν, The substantive κάνεον is accented κανοῦν (though *regularly* it should be κάνουν).

2) The compounds of νοῦς, πλοῦς are *paroxytone* throughout.

122. The Imperfect tense is formed from the root of the Present by adding ον and prefixing the *augment ;* as, λεγ (root of pres.) λεγ-ον (by adding ον), ἔ-λεγ-ον (by prefixing the augment); τυπτ, τυπτ-ον, ἔ-τυπτ-ον; &c.

123. If the verb begins with a consonant, the augment is ε prefixed; this is called the *syllabic* augment, because it forms a *syllable.*   Λύ-ω, Imperf. ἔ-λυ-ον. Τύπτ-ω, Imperf. ἔ-τυπτ-ον.

REM. The Imperfect, besides its usual meaning, expresses *continued* or *repeated actions*, taking place in past time; as, "I was wri-

ting" (at some time past and while something else was goingon): ἐν ᾧ
σὺ ἔπαιζες, ἐγὼ ἔγραφον, "while you *were playing*, I *was writing*."

124. If the verb begins with a vowel, this vowel is
changed (the *changed vowel* being called the *temporal
augment*);

1) ε, α, ο, are changed into the corresponding long
vowels η, η, ω.*

2) The diphthongs αυ, αι, οι become ηυ, ῃ, ῳ; ᾳ
becomes ῃ.

3) ῐ, ῠ, are lengthened into ῑ, ῡ.

4) ει, ευ, ου, and the long vowels ῑ, ῡ, η, ω, are
unaugmented;† P is *doubled* after the augment; as,
ῥίπτω, ἔρριπτον.

125. The terminations of the persons are :

			EXAMPLE.		
S. ον,	ες,	ε	S. ἔ-τυπτ-ον,	ἔ-τυπτ-ες,	ἔ-τυπτ-ε
P. ομεν,	ετε,	ον	P. ἐ-τύπτ-ομεν,	ἐ-τύπτ-ετε,	ἔ-τυπτ-ον
D.	ετον,	έτην	D.	ἐ-τύπτ-ετον,	ἐ-τύπτ-έτην.

126. VOCABULARY 7.

Voyage, πλοῦς.

Stream, ῥοῦς.

Mind, reason, νοῦς.

A passage (across), διάπλους
(121, 2.)

A sailing round, a voyage round,
περίπλους.

Grandson, υἱδοῦς.

Entrance (into a port), ἔσπλους.

Athens, Ἀθῆναι, ῶν.

Cenæum, Κήναιον.

Eubœa, Εὔβοια.

A Lacedæmonian, Λακεδαιμόνιος.

The Nile, Νεῖλος, ὁ.

Egypt, Αἴγυπτος, ἡ.

Munychia, Μουνυχία (a poet at
Athens).

Mob; crowd, ὄχλος, ὁ.

Love, ἀγάπη.

Country, χώρα.

To reign; to be king, βασιλεύειν,
(takes the gen.)

To be distant from, ἀπέχειν (with
gen.)

* There are eleven verbs which change ε into ει instead of η: as,
ἔχω, εἶχον; ἕλκω, εἶλκον; ἐθίζω, εἴθιζον; ἔπομαι, εἱπόμην; &c.

† Sometimes, however, ευ is augmented into ηυ, and ει is sometimes augmented in εἰκάζω, Imperf. (sometimes) ἤκαζον.

Æetes, Αἰήτης.
The Phasiani, Φασιανοί.
Sicily, Σικελία.

To bar (a passage), ἐμφράττειν.
To colonize, οἰκίζειν.
Eight, ὀκτώ (indeclin.).

Exercise 12.

127. a) Translate into English.

1. Ἐξ Ἀθηνῶν βραχύς· ἐστιν ὁ διάπλους πρὸς τὸ
Κήναιον τῆς Εὐβοίας. 2. Αἰήτου υἱδοῦς ἐβασίλευε[b] τῶν
Φασιανῶν. 3. Σικελίας περίπλους ἐστὶν ὡς ὀκτὼ ἡμερῶν[c]. 4. Ἡ Μουνυχία οὐ τῶν Ἀθηνῶν ἀπέχει. 5. Ὁ
Θεὸς ἀγάπη ἐστίν. 6. Ἡ Αἴγυπτος δῶρόν ἐστι τοῦ
Νείλου. 7. Οἱ Λακεδαιμόνιοι ἦρχον[d] τοῦ ἐς Μουνυχίαν
ἔσπλου. 8. Οἱ Λακεδαιμόνιοι ἐν νῷ ἔχουσι τοὺς ἐς τὴν
Μουνυχίαν ἔσπλους ἐμφράττειν. 9. Ἔρριπτε τὸν δίσκον. 10. Ἔπειθε τοὺς ξένους. 11. Ἐτύπτετε τοὺς
οἰκέτας. 12. Οἱ Γελῶνοι ᾤκιζον τὴν χώραν. 13. Ἤλειφες τὸν δεσπότην. 14. Ὁ Πέρσης ὄχλον φιλεῖ, οὐκ ἔχει
δὲ νοῦν. 15. Τὸν τοῦ ῥοῦ διάπλουν οἱ νεανίαι ἐποίουν[e].
16. Ὁ τοῦ ἰατροῦ δοῦλος δῶρα ἐφίλει. 17. Ὁ δικαστὴς
τὸν τοῦ πελταστοῦ φόβον κατεῖχεν[f]. 18. Ἡ ἀμαθία ἡ
τῶν ἀνθρώπων[g] Αἴγυπτον ἔβλαπτεν[h]. 19. Οἱ Πέρσαι
τῆς Σικελίας ἀπέχουσι. 20. Ἔβλεπον πρὸς τὴν θάλασσαν.

[a] *Short* (masc. adj.)   [b] See Kühner, 275. 1.   [c] The genit. is
used of the time *within which* any thing happens or has not happened.
K. 274, 3, b.   [d] See 124, 1): from ἄρχειν.   [e] Impf. from ποιεῖν.
[f] From κατέχειν. For augment, see 124, 1) note.* It is taken between
the preposition and the verb.   [g] See 115, a.   [h] On the added ν,
see 93, note.*

b) Translate into Greek.

1. We are barring the entrance into the Munychia.
2. He was telling the legend. 3. We shall be masters
of the entrance. 4. You (*pl.*) were masters of the
entrances into the Munychia. 5. Ye will hurl the

quoits.   6. The two-young-men were hurling quoits.
7. You (*pl.*) were looking towards profit.   8. We will
not yield to the desire of looking after (πρός) profit.
9. You (*pl.*) were reigning over the Persians.   10. You
(*pl.*) were colonizing the country of the Geloni.   11. I
was admiring the temple of Minerva.   12. The gods
of the Egyptians rule over the country.   13. By
Hermes, I will chastise the Phasiani.   14. They restrained the desire of speaking ill of (the city of)
Athens.   15. O stranger, the slave had ten minæ.
16. The domestic was caring-for the horses and the
asses of his master.   17. O brother, march- the army
-forward about eight stadia.   18. The young-men were
hunting weasels.   19. The targeteers were running (at
full speed) towards the plain.   20. The physician's
grandson loves gold and silver.   21. Do not yield to
the desire for gold.   22. There is in Sicily a temple of
Mercury.

LESSON XV.

Adjectives.

128. Adjectives are words which describe a property
supposed to belong already to the object spoken of (as,
" a *red* rose "), or distinctly assert such property to belong to the object (as, "the rose is *red* ").

129. Adjectives agree with substantives in *gender,*
number, and *case :* they are declined like substantives
and are of *three* declensions.

1) The *first* comprises adjectives of *three termina-*
tions.

REM. Most of the adjectives belong to this class.

2) The *second*, those of *two terminations*.

3) The *third*, those of *one termination*.

130. Adjectives of three terminations in ος, η, ον, and ος, a, ον are declined in the *masc.* and *neut.* like nouns of the *second* declension, and in the·*femin.* like a noun of the *first* declension. Other adjectives of three terminations are declined like nouns of the *third* declension.*

PARADIGMS.

		ἀγαθός, ή, όν, "good."			ἄξιος, a, ον, "worthy."		
SING.	N.	ἀγαθ-ός	-ή	-όν	N. ἄξι-ος	-α	-ον
	G.	ἀγαθ-οῦ	-ῆς	-οῦ	G. ἀξί-ου	-ας	-ου
	D.	ἀγαθ-ῷ	-ῇ	-ῷ	D. ἀξί-ῳ	-ᾳ	-ῳ
	A.	ἀγαθ-όν	-ήν	-όν	A. ἄξι-ον	-αν	-ον
	V.	ἀγαθ-έ	-ή	-όν	V. ἄξι-ε	-α	-ον
PLUR.	N.	ἀγαθ-οί	-αί	-ά	N. ἄξι-οι	-αι	-α
	G.	ἀγαθ-ῶν	-ῶν	-ῶν	G. ἀξί-ων	-ων	-ων
	D.	ἀγαθ-οῖς	-αῖς	-οῖς	D. ἀξί-οις	-αις	-οις
	A.	ἀγαθ-ούς	-άς	-ά	A. ἀξί-ους	-ας	-α
	V.	ἀγαθ-οί	-αί	-ά	V. ἄξι-οι	-αι	-α
DUAL.	N. A. V.	ἀγαθ-ώ	-ά	-ώ	N. A. V. ἀξί-ω	-α	-ω
	G. D.	ἀγαθ-οῖν	-αῖν	-οῖν	G. D. ἀξί-οιν	-αιν	-οιν

131. Obs. 1.) Adjectives in ος have feminine a if the ος follows a *vowel* or ρ: if not, the feminine is η: e. g.

ἴδιος, ἰδία, ἴδιον.   δῆλος, δήλη, δῆλον.

ἱερός, ἱερά, ἱερόν.   σοφός, σοφή, σοφόν.

ἀθρόος, ἀθρόα, ἀθρόον.   καλός, καλή, καλόν.

2) But οος, when not preceded by ρ, forms the femin. in η, e. g.

ὄγδοος, ὀγδόη, ὄγδοον.   ἁπλόος, ἁπλόη, ἁπλόον.

---

* Table of the different terminations of Adjectives of three endings.

1.	{ ος	η	ον }	ἀγαθ-ός	ή	όν
	{ ος	α	ον }	ἐχθρ-ός	ά	όν
2.	ας	αινα	αν	μέλ-ας	αινα	αν
3.	εις	εσσα	εν	χαρί-εις	εσσα	εν
4.	ην	εινα	εν	τέρ-ην	εινα	εν
5.	υς	εῖα	υ	γλυκ-ύς	εῖα	ύ
6.	ών	οῦσα	όν	ἐκ-ών	οῦσα	όν

132. Vocabulary 8.

Base, disgraceful, αἰσχρός.
Wise, clever, σοφός.
Friendly, dear, φίλος.
Empty, κένος.
Strong, ἰσχυρός.
Long, μακρός.
Bad, κακός.

Beautiful, καλός.
Worthy, ἄξιος.
Good, ἀγαθός.
Sacred, ἱερός.
Plain, evident, δῆλος.
Human, ἀνθρώπινος.
Divine, θεῖος.

Exercise 13.

133. *a*) *Translate into English.*

1. Ἡδονὴ κακὴ οὐκ ἔστι μακρά.　2. Οἱ πολῖται ἦσαν σοφοί, καὶ καλὴ ἦν ἡ χώρα.　3. Καλὰ[a] δῶρα τῆς σοφίας. 4. Ἡ τοῦ ποιητοῦ τοῦ ἀγαθοῦ σοφία πείσει τὸν ἄξιον γεωμέτρην.　5. Ὁ λόγος ἐστὶν αἰσχρός.　6. Ἔστι ἱερὸν[b] καλὸν ἐν Ἀθήναις.　7. Μὴ δίωκε τὰ αἰσχρά[c].　8. Τὼ νεανία ἐτριβέτην τὸ φάρμακον.　9. Προμηθεὺς οὐκ ἦν φίλος τοῖς θεοῖς.　10. Ἡ ἀγαπὴ τοῦ Θεοῦ πείσει ἀνθρώπους.　11. Χαῖρε, ὦ δέσποτα, μὴ εἶκε τῇ τοῦ ἄρχειν κένῃ ἐπιθυμίᾳ.　12. Δῆλόν ἐστιν ὅτι ὁ λόγος ἰσχυρός τε καὶ μακρός.　13. Ἰσχυρὸν[d] ὄχλος ἐστίν, οὐκ ἔχει δὲ νοῦν.　14. Τίς τὼ κόρα[e] βλάψει;　15. Αἱ καλαὶ κόραι τὸν σοφὸν ἰατρὸν πείσουσι.　16. Ὁ στέφανος ὁ τοῦ ποιητοῦ ἐστιν ἱερός.　17. Τῷ[f] ταῦτα λέγειν, ἔψευδον αὐτόν.　18. Ἡ σοφία ἐστὶν καλὴ καὶ θεία.

[a] The copula ἐστί is often omitted.　[b] a temple.　[c] base (things).
[d] nom. sing. neut. (after the verb).　[e] See 90, Rem.　[f] See 66, Obs.

b) *Translate into Greek.*

1. Look, O Persian, towards the beautiful sea. 2. Empty wisdom will persuade the citizens. 3. The poet was admiring the two-wise-geometers. 4. O young man, do not yield to base pleasures. 5. Who will hide base (things)? 6. Sicily is beautiful and dear

to its citizens. 7. The two young men were telling the legend. 8. Bad men admire bad (things). They do not love good (things). 9. The clever geometer will anoint himself. 10. They were weaving garlands in the garden of the good laborer. 11. We ought admire the strong mind of Æetes's grandson. 12. Wh, is colonizing the country of the Geloni? 13. The Lacedæmonians were looking towards profit by barring the entrance into the Munychias. 14. The way is long and not good. 15. The long legend of the poet is empty and mere nonsense. 16. The good (man) is dear to God.

LESSON XVI.

Adjectives (continued). *Future from verbs in ζω, εω, αω, οω.*

134. In the case of adjectives in εος, εα, εον, and οος, οη, οον, contraction takes place, which in some instances deviates from the general rules (see Note 6), the distinctive terminations (as *a* in the neut. plur., *as* in the accus., and *αις* in the dat. plur.) being always left unchanged in contraction. From χρύσεος the contracted forms are (irregularly) *perispomena ;* except (probably) ώ of the dual (as in ὀστώ).

135. If another vowel or ρ precedes εος, the feminine is contracted, not into ῆ, but into ᾶ; e. g.

(ἐρέεος =) ἐρεοῦς, ἐρεᾶ, ἐρεοῦν, *woollen*
(ἀργύρεος =) ἀργυροῦς, ἀργυρᾶ, ἀργυροῦν, *silver.*

136. Such compound adjectives in (οος) ους as are formed from contracted substantives of the second declension (νοῦς, πλοῦς), are accented throughout on the *penult* [εὔνους, εὔνου, &c. ; nom. pl. *m.* εὖνοι] undergo no contraction in the three similar cases of the neut.

plur.; e. g. ἄνοα (from ἄνους), ἄπλοα (from ἄπλους, *not seaworthy*) ;
but ἁπλᾶ, from ἁπλοῦς. (*simplex*).

PARADIGMS

χρύσε-ος, χρυσέ-α, χρύσε-ον, *golden.*			ἁπλό-ος, ἁπλό-η, ἁπλό-ον, *simple*		
M.	**F.**	**N.**	**M.**	**F.**	**N.**
χρύσε-ος	χρυσέ-α χρύσε-ον		ἁπλό-ος	ἁπλό-η	ἁπλό-ον
SING.	contracted into			contracted into	
N. χρυσοῦς	χρυσῆ	χρυσοῦν	ἁπλοῦς	ἁπλῆ	ἁπλοῦν
G. χρυσοῦ	χρυσῆς	χρυσοῦ	ἁπλοῦ	ἁπλῆς	ἁπλοῦ
D. χρυσῷ	χρυσῇ	χρυσῷ	ἁπλῷ	ἁπλῇ	ἁπλῷ
A. χρυσοῦν	χρυσῆν	χρυσοῦν	ἁπλοῦν	ἁπλῆν	ἁπλοῦν
PLUR.					
N. χρυσοῖ	χρυσαῖ	χρυσᾶ	ἁπλοῖ	ἁπλαῖ	ἁπλᾶ
G. χρυσῶν	χρυσῶν	χρυσῶν	ἁπλῶν	ἁπλῶν	ἁπλῶν
D. χρυσοῖς	χρυσαῖς	χρυσοῖς	ἁπλοῖς	ἁπλαῖς	ἁπλοῖς
A. χρυσοῦς	χρυσᾶς	χρυσᾶ	ἁπλοῦς	ἁπλᾶς	ἁπλᾶ
DUAL					
N. A. V. χρυσώ	χρυσᾶ	χρυσώ	ἁπλῶ	ἁπλᾶ	ἁπλώ
G. D. χρυσοῖν	χρυσαῖν	χρυσοῖν	ἁπλοῖν	ἁπλαῖν	ἁπλοῖν

137. From verbs whose root ends in ζ the *sigmated*
root is generally formed by changing ζ into ς: as θαυ-
μαζ, θαυμᾶς.

> REM. From verbs in αζω, ιζω, the futures ασω, ισω have the penult
> *short.*

138. For verbs whose roots end in ε, α, ο, these
vowels are lengthened into η, η, ω, before ς is added
(84). A root ending in a *doubtful* vowel usually has it
long in the fut.: λύ-ω, λῡ-σω.

Simple Root.	Sigmated Root.	Present.	Future.
φιλε-	φιλη-σ	φιλέω	φιλήσω
τιμα-	τιμη-σ	τιμάω	τιμήσω
ὀχυρο-	ὀχυρω-σ	ὀχυρόω	ὀχυρώσω.

139. Vocabulary 9.

Simple, ἁπλόος, ἁπλοῦς.
Double, διπλόος, -οῦς.
Golden; of gold, χρύσεος, -οῦς.

Brazen, (*of*) *brass* or *bronze,*
χάλκεος, -οῦς.
(*Of*) *iron,* σιδήρεος, -οῦς.

(Of) silver, ἀργύρεος, -οῦς.
Bowl; (shallow) cup, φιάλη (= patera).
Cup, goblet, κύπελλον.
Barbarian, βάρβαρος (a term used of all who were *not* Greeks).
Door, θύρα.
Truth, ἀλήθεια.
Gate, πύλη.
Bolt, bar, κλεῖθρον.
Ring, δακτύλιος, ὁ.
Hoof, ὁπλή
Prick, goad, κέντρον.

Death, θάνατος, ὁ.
House; small house, οἰκίδιον.
Hollow, κοῖλος, η, ον.
Senseless, ἄνοος, ἄνους.
Well disposed (towards); well affected (towards), εὔνοος, εὔνους.
Ill disposed, ill affected, δύσνοος, δύσνους.
To honor, τιμάειν (= τιμᾶν).
To love, φιλέειν (= φιλεῖν).
To make-fast, ὀχυρόειν (= ὀχυροῦν).
To kick (at), λακτίζειν.

Exercise 14.

140. a) *Translate into English.*

1. Ἁπλοῦς ἐστιν ὁ τῆς ἀληθείας λόγος. 2. Τὸ κύπελλόν ἐστιν ἀργυροῦν. 3. Ὁ θάνατος λέγεται* χαλκοῦς ὕπνος. 4. Φιάλας ἔχει χρυσᾶς τε καὶ ἀργυρᾶς. 5. Οὐκ ἐχθροὺς τοὺς Θεσσαλοὺς διώκομεν ἀλλ' εὔνους. 6. Τοῖς μὲν εὔνοις τῶν βαρβάρων δύσνους ἡμᾶς ποιοῦσιν, τοῖς δὲ πολεμίοις ὠφελίμους. 7. Ὁ νεανίας ἐθαύμαζεν ἵππον χαλκοῦν κοῖλον καὶ χρυσοῦν δακτύλιον. 8. Τὰς πύλας σιδηροῖς κλείθροις ὀχυρώσομεν. 9. Οἱ ἵπποι λακτίζουσιν ἀλλήλους[b] σιδηραῖς ὁπλαῖς. 10. Τοῖς Ἀθηναίοις[c] οὔτε αἰσχροί ἐσμεν[d] οὔτε δύσνοι. 11. Ὁ δοῦλος ἐλάκτιζε πρὸς τὰ κέντρα. 12. Τὴν τοῦ βιβλιοπώλου θύραν λακτίσομεν. 13. Διπλοῦν ἐστι τὸ οἰκίδιον. 14. Ἄνοά ἐστι* τὰ παιδία. 15. Τιμήσομεν τοὺς δικαστάς. 16. Φιλήσω τὸ παιδίον. 17. Ὁ δοῦλος τρίβει τὸ φάρμακον. 18. Ἡ Αἴγυπτός ἐστι φίλη τοῖς βαρβάροις. 19. Διπλᾶ ἀγαθα ἐστιν· τὰ μὲν ἀνθρώπινα, τὰ δὲ θεῖα.

* is called.   b one another, each other.   c the Athenians
d we are (first pl. pres. of εἶναι).   e see 85, 1, note.

b) Translate into Greek.

1. The bowl is silver. 2. The cup is of gold, but the bowl not. 3. He has both gold and silver cups. 4. You shall make-fast the gate with an iron bar. 5. The horse will kick the ass. 6. We are ill-affected towards' the Persians, but well-affected towards the Athenians. 7. They are not ill-affected either to the Athenians or the Lacedæmonians (*Say :* 'neither to the Athenians nor to the Lacedæmonians are they ill-affected'). 8. You will honor neither geometrician nor the judge. 9. O young man, admire the simple words of truth and justice. 10. By Minerva, I will march the army forward ten stadia. 11. There are eight golden goblets in the Nile. 12. The house of the poet has five doors. 13. O man, it is hard⁵ for thee* to kick against¹ the pricks.

f say, *to* (dat.)   ᵍ σκληρόν.   ₕ σοι, dat. of pron. σύ.   ᵢ πρός.

LESSON XVII.

First Aorist Active.

141. The first Aorist of the Active is formed by adding ᾰ to the *sigmated* root * (or root of future), and prefixing the augment (123, 124):

Root.	Sigmated Root.	Aorist.
ῥιπτ-	ῥιψ-	ἔῤ-ριψ-ᾰ
βλεπ-	βλεψ-	ἔ-βλεψ-α
λεγ-	λεξ-	ἔ-λεξ-α
πειϑ-	πεισ- (for πειϑs)	ἔ-πεισ-α
ἀρχ-	ἀρξ-	ἦρξ-α

142. The Aorist expresses actions, *independently,*

---

* i. e. root with *s* added. . See 77.

as *completed* in past time ; as, "the Greeks *conquered* (ἐνίκησαν) the Persians."

REM. Thus the aorist is used of actions conceived as *single* and *definite* (often *momentary*) actions, without any reference to their *duration*. The aorist is a *narrative*, the imperf. a *descriptive* tense.

143. TERMINATIONS.

S.	ᾰ	ᾰς	ε
P.	ᾰμεν	ᾰτε	ᾰν
D.		ᾰτον	ᾰτην

144. The accent is as far back as possible. It will therefore be on the *antepenult* of *hyperdissyllables*, except in *ἄτην*.

145. VOCABULARY 10.

Orestes, Ὀρέστης.
Friendly ; (as subst. *a friend*,) φίλος.
Marrow, μυελός, ὁ.
Some, ἔνιοι, ἔνιαι, ἔνια (pl.).
A natural philosopher, φυσικός, ὁ (physicus).
War, πόλεμος, ὁ.
Enemies, the enemy, πολέμιοι (hostes).
Resident-alien, resident-foreigner, μέτοικος, ὁ.

General, στρατηγός, ὁ.
Soldier, στρατιώτης.
Animal, ζῶον, τό.
Head, κεφαλή.
Tongue, γλῶσσᾰ.
Queen, βασίλισσα.
To pay attention to; to attend to, τὸν νοῦν προσέχειν (with dat.) = animum applicare.
To steal, κλέπτ-ειν.
To whet, to sharpen, θήγ-ειν.
To hide, κρύπτ-ειν.*

At all (after a negative), ὅλως (omnino).

Not only ... but also, οὐ μόνον ... ἀλλὰ καί (non solum ... sed etiam).

The one ... the other, ὁ μέν ... ὁ δέ.

These ... those
Some ... others } οἱ μέν ... οἱ δέ.

The article ὁ is here a *pronoun,* as it originally was in all cases.

Αὐτός (ipse) : the oblique cases usually answer to *his, him, their, them*: αὐτοῦ = ejus : ἑαυτοῦ (sui =) suus ipsius, or suus.

---

* Hence the *crypt* of a church.

Exercise 15.

146. a) Translate into English.

1. Λέγετε πρὸς αὐτὸν τί (= what) ἐν νῷ ἔχετε, ὡς φίλον τε καὶ εὔνουν. 2. Τὰ τοῦ Ὀρέστου ὀστᾶ ἐκ Τεγέας ἔκλεψε. 3. Τῶν ὀστῶν τὰ μὲν ἔχει μυελόν, τὰ δὲ οὐκ ἔχει· ἔνια δὲ ζῷα* οὐδὲ ἔχειν ὅλως μυελὸν ἐν τοῖς ὀστοῖς λέγουσιν οἱ φυσικοί. 4. Ὁ στρατηγὸς οὐ μόνον τοῖς πολεμίοις τὸν νοῦν προσέχει, ἀλλὰ καὶ τοῖς ἑαυτοῦ στρατιώταις. 5. Ἡ ὀργὴ ἔδηξε τὰς ψυχάς. 6. Ὁ Πέρσης ἔκρυψε τὴν τοῦ ἄρχειν ἐπιθυμίαν. 7. Οἱ στρατηγοὶ τὰς τῶν στρατιωτῶν ψυχὰς εἰς πόλεμον ἔδηξαν. 8. Ἠλείψατε τὴν τῆς βασιλίσσης κεφαλήν. 9. Οἱ Πέρσαι ἔκρυψαν τὰ χρυσᾶ κύπελλα ἐν τῷ τοῦ Χειρισόφου κήπῳ. 10. Οἱ ἀγαθοὶ τὸ καλὸν φιλοῦσιν. 11. Ὁ ἀρτοπώλης ὁ σοφὸς πέντε ἵππους ἔχει.

* Acc. c. Infin. is used nearly as in Latin: though λέγειν is usually followed by ὅτι (that).

QUESTIONS.—1. Why has τε no accent? 2. Why is ἔκλεψε proparoxytone? 3. Why is the accent on the final of φυσικοί not written as the grave accent? 7. Why is στρατιωτῶν perispomenon?

b) Translate into Greek.

1. You were throwing the quoit. 2. They threw the balls. 3. Anger sharpened his tongue. 4. This will sharpen the young-man's anger. 5. I injured Eretria, but I did not injure the country of the Geloni. 6. The just judge did not look to [29] his own advantage 7. You said by your deeds, that justice °is idle-talk to [29] profit; but with your tongues you did not say this. 8. They injured not only the resident-foreigners, but also the citizens. 9. You persuaded not only the resident-foreigners, but also the judges. 10. The two maidens admired the silver goblets in the poet's little

house. 11. Some (men) love good (things), others base
(things). 12. Who planted the fig-trees in the baker's
garden? 13. We ought not to admire the citizen's bad
desire of ruling. 14. O Persian, it is a base thing to
strike a maiden.

LESSON XVIII.
Attic Second Declension.

147. Several substantives have the endings ως
(masc. and fem.) and ων (neut.) instead of ος and ον,
and retain the ω through all the cases instead of the regular vowels and diphthongs (112), *subscribing* ι where
the regular form has ῳ or οι.

PARADIGMS.

		People.	Rope.	Dining-Room.
Sing.	N.	ὁ λε-ώς	ἡ κάλ-ως	τὸ ἀνώγε-ων
	G.	τοῦ λε-ώ	τῆς κάλ-ω	τοῦ ἀνώγε-ω
	D.	τῷ λε-ῷ	τῇ κάλ-ῳ	τῷ ἀνώγε-ῳ
	A.	τὸν λε-ών	τὴν κάλ-ων	τὸ ἀνώγε-ων
	V.	λε-ώς	κάλ-ως	ἀνώγε-ων
Plur.	N.	οἱ λε-ῴ	αἱ κάλ-ῳ	τὰ ἀνώγε-ω
	G.	τῶν λε-ών	τῶν κάλ-ων	τῶν ἀνώγε-ων
	D.	τοῖς λε-ῴς	ταῖς κάλ-ῳς	τοῖς ἀνώγε-ῳς
	A.	τοὺς λε-ώς	τὰς κάλ-ως	τὰ ἀνώγε-ω
	V.	λε-ῴ	κάλ-ῳ	ἀνώγε-ω
Dual.	N.A.V.	τὼ λε-ώ	τὰ κάλ-ῳ	τώ ἀνώγε-ω
	G. D.	τοῖν λε-ῷν	ταῖν κάλ-ῳν	τοῖν ἀνώγε-ῳν

148. Some adjectives follow this declension, having
ως masc. and fem., ων neut. Such are ἵλεως, *propi·
tious*, ἔμπλεως, *full*, &c.

Obs.—Some of these substantives drop ν in the acc. So the regular acc. of ἕως (ἡ), *dawn*, is ἕω. Λαγώς (*hare*) has more frequently ω
than ων, so Ἄθως, Κέως Κῶς, Τέως; the adjective ἀγήρως has ων or ω
in *acc. masc.* and *fem.*

149. ACCENTUATION.—*Proparoxytones* in εως, εων retain the accent upon the *antepenultimate* through all the cases of all the numbers ; the two syllables εως, εων, &c., being reckoned as one.

Oxytones in ώς remain such, even in the *genitive* singular, as λεώ (against 97, 1).

150. VOCABULARY 11.

Halo, Ἅλως, ἡ.

Temple, νεώς, ὁ.

Peacock, ταώς, ὁ.

Hare, λαγώς, ὁ.

Minos, Μίνως, ὁ.

Androgeus, Ἀνδρόγεως, ὁ.

Dawn, ἕως, ἡ.

Propitious, ἵλεως.

Full, ἔμπλεως.

Undying, (prop. *not subject to old age,*) ἀγήρως.

Circle, κύκλος, ὁ.

Sun, ἥλιος, ὁ.

Moon, σελήνη.

Heavenly body ; star, ἄστρον, τό.

Praise, ἔπαινος, ὁ.

Juno, Ἥρα.

Delphi, Δελφοί, ῶν (pl.).

Egg, ὠόν, τό.

Ætolia, Αἰτωλία.

Roman, Ῥωμαῖος.

Trojan, Τρωϊκός.

Palladium, Παλλάδιον, τό.

Quirinus, Κυρῖνος.

Son, υἱός, ὁ.

Eagle, ἀετός, ὁ.

Sepulchre, tomb, τάφος, ὁ.

Vine, ἄμπελος, ἡ.

Tree, δένδρον, τό.

Whole, ὅλος, η, ον.

Often, πολλάκις.

Bright, λαμπρός, ά, όν.

A little, ὀλίγον.

Of every kind, παντοδαπός, ή, όν.

To come in being, to become, γίγν-εσθαι (fieri)

To appear, to be seen, φαίν-εσθαι.

To set out, πορεύ-εσθαι (proficisci.)

To plot against, lie in wait for, ἐνεδρεύ-ειν (insidiari).

To receive, λαμβάν-ειν.

To build (a house), οἰκοδομέ-ειν (= -εῖν).

To lay (of eggs), τίκτ-ειν (parĕre).

To disembark, ἀποβαίν-ειν.

To rob, συλά-ειν (=-ᾶν).

To nourish, feed (of birds), *to keep,* τρέφ-ειν.

To come, ἥκ-ειν.

151. ☞ *Deponent* verbs.*] Some verbs have, like the Latin Deponents, a passive form (with some exceptions, to be afterwards

---

* In Greek grammar such verbs are said to belong to the *Middle Voice.* The explanation of this term will be given afterwards. (See 269, &c. *infra.*)

2) The *second*, those of *two terminations.*

3) The *third*, those of *one termination.*

130. Adjectives of three terminations in ος, η, ον, and ος, α, ον are declined in the *masc.* and *neut.* like nouns of the *second* declension, and in the *femin.* like a noun of the *first* declension. Other adjectives of three terminations are declined like nouns of the *third* declension.*

PARADIGMS.

		ἀγαθός, ή, όν, "good."			ἄξιος, α, ον, "worthy."		
SING.	N.	ἀγαθ-ός	-ή	-όν	N. ἄξι-ος	-α	-ον
	G.	ἀγαθ-οῦ	-ῆς	-οῦ	G. ἀξί-ου	-ας	-ου
	D.	ἀγαθ-ῷ	-ῇ	-ῷ	D. ἀξί-ῳ	-ᾳ	-ῳ
	A.	ἀγαθ-όν	-ήν	-όν	A. ἄξι-ον	-αν	-ον
	V.	ἀγαθ-έ	-ή	-όν	V. ἄξι-ε	-α	-ον
PLUR.	N.	ἀγαθ-οί	-αί	-ά	N. ἄξι-οι	-αι	-α
	G.	ἀγαθ-ῶν	-ῶν	-ῶν	G. ἀξί-ων	-ων	-ων
	D.	ἀγαθ-οῖς	-αῖς	-οῖς	D. ἀξί-οις	-αις	-οις
	A.	ἀγαθ-ούς	-άς	-ά	A. ἀξί-ους	-ας	-α
	V.	ἀγαθ-οί	-αί	-ά	V. ἄξι-οι	-αι	-α
DUAL.	N. A. V.	ἀγαθ-ώ	-ά	-ώ	N. A. V. ἀξί-ω	-α	-ω
	G. D.	ἀγαθ-οῖν	-αῖν	-οῖν	G. D. ἀξί-οιν	-αιν	-οιν

131. OBS. 1.) Adjectives in ος have feminine α if the ος follows a *vowel* or ρ: if not, the feminine is η: e. g.

ἴδιος,   ἰδία,   ἴδιον.   δῆλος,   δήλη,   δῆλον.

ἱερός,   ἱερά,   ἱερόν.   σοφός,   σοφή,   σοφόν.

ἁθρόος,   ἁθρόα,   ἁθρόον.   καλός,   καλή,   καλόν.

2) But οος, when not preceded by ρ, forms the femin. in η, e. g.

ὄγδοος,   ὀγδόη,   ὄγδοον.   ἁπλόος,   ἁπλόη,   ἁπλόον.

---

* Table of the different terminations of Adjectives of three endings.

1.	{	ος	η	ον }	ἀγαθ-ός	ή	όν
	{	ος	α	ον }	ἐχθρ-ός	ά	όν
2.		ᾶς	αινα	ᾶν	μέλ-ας	αινα	αν
3.		εις	εσσα	εν	χαρί-εις	εσσα	εν
4.		ην	εινα	εν	τέρ-ην	εινα	εν
5.		ῦς	εῖα	ῦ	γλυκ-ύς	εῖα	ύ
6.		ών	οῦσα	όν	ἐκ-ών	οῦσα	όν

132. Vocabulary 8.

Base, disgraceful, αἰσχρός.	Beautiful, καλός.
Wise, clever, σοφός.	Worthy, ἄξιος.
Friendly, dear, φίλος.	Good, ἀγαθός.
Empty, κένος.	Sacred, ἱερός.
Strong, ἰσχυρός.	Plain, evident, δῆλος.
Long, μακρός.	Human, ἀνθρώπινος.
Bad, κακός.	Divine, θεῖος.

Exercise 13.

133. *a) Translate into English.*

1. Ἡδονὴ κακὴ οὐκ ἔστι μακρά. 2. Οἱ πολῖται ἦσαν σοφοί, καὶ καλὴ ἦν ἡ χώρα. 3. Καλὰ* δῶρα τῆς σοφίας. 4. Ἡ τοῦ ποιητοῦ τοῦ ἀγαθοῦ σοφία πείσει τὸν ἄξιον γεωμέτρην. 5. Ὁ λόγος ἐστὶν αἰσχρός. 6. Ἔστι ἱερὸν ᵇ καλὸν ἐν Ἀθήναις. 7. Μὴ δίωκε τὰ αἰσχρά ᶜ. 8. Τὼ νεανία ἐτριβέτην τὸ φάρμακον. 9. Προμηθεὺς οὐκ ἦν φίλος τοῖς θεοῖς. 10. Ἡ ἀγαπὴ τοῦ Θεοῦ πείσει ἀνθρώπους. 11. Χαῖρε, ὦ δέσποτα, μὴ εἶκε τῇ τοῦ ἄρχειν κένῃ ἐπιθυμίᾳ. 12. Δῆλόν ἐστιν ὅτι ὁ λόγος ἰσχυρός τε καὶ μακρός. 13. Ἰσχυρὸν ᵈ ὄχλος ἐστίν, οὐκ ἔχει δὲ νοῦν. 14. Τίς τὼ κόρα ᵉ βλάψει; 15. Αἱ καλαὶ κόραι τὸν σοφὸν ἰατρὸν πείσουσι. 16. Ὁ στέφανος ὁ τοῦ ποιητοῦ ἐστιν ἱερός. 17. Τῷ ᶠ ταῦτα λέγειν, ἔψευδον αὐτόν. 18. Ἡ σοφία ἐστὶν καλὴ καὶ θεία.

ᵃ The copula ἐστί is often omitted.   ᵇ a temple.   ᶜ base (things).
ᵈ nom. sing. neut. (after the verb).   ᵉ See 90, Rem.   ᶠ See 66, Obs.

b) Translate into Greek.

1. Look, O Persian, towards the beautiful sea. 2. Empty wisdom will persuade the citizens. 3. The poet was admiring the two-wise-geometers. 4. O young man, do not yield to base pleasures. 5. Who will hide base (things)? 6. Sicily is beautiful and dear

οντσι, εντσι, αντσι, υντσι, become ουσι, εισι, ᾱσι, ῦσι.
The *P-* and *K-* sounds with ς become ψ, ξ, respectively:

For example: λεόντσι becomes λέουσι (dat. pl. of λέων, *lion*); λειφϑέντσι becomes λειφϑεῖσι (dat. pl. of 1 aor. pass. part. of λείπω); γίγαντσι becomes γίγᾱσι (dat. pl. of γίγας, *giant*); ζευγνύντσι becomes ζευγνῦσι (dat. pl. of part. ζευγνύς). Root λαιλαπ with ς becomes λαῖλαψ; Αραβ with ς becomes Ἄραψ; κατηλιφ with ς becomes κατῆλιψ; κορακ with ς becomes κόραξ; λαρυγγ with ς becomes λάρυγξ, &c.

157. *Terminations of the Third Declension.*

	SINGULAR.	PLURAL.	DUAL.
N.	various, (α, ι, υ : ω: ν, ξ, ρ, σ, ψ)	ες, ᾰ, *neut.*	ε,
G.	ος (ως),	ων,	οιν,
D.	ι,	σιν *or* σι,	οιν,
A.	α *or* ν,	ας, ᾰ, *neut.*	ε,
V.	various, (*neut.* as *nom.*)	ες, ᾰ, *neut.*	ε,

158. PARADIGMS.

		Raven.	Child.	Mouth.	Vein.
SING.	N.	ὁ κόραξ*	ὁ, ἡ παῖς	τὸ στόμα	ἡ φλέψ
	G.	κόρακ-ος	παιδ-ός	στόματ-ος	φλεβ-ός
	D.	κόρακ-ι	παιδ-ί	στόματ-ι	φλεβ-ί
	A.	κόρακ-α	παῖδ-α	στόμα	φλέβ-α
	V.	κόραξ	παῖ	στόμα	φλέψ
PLUR.	N.	κόρακ-ες	παῖδ-ες	στόματ-α	φλέβ-ες
	G.	κοράκ-ων	παίδ-ων	στομάτ-ων	φλεβ-ῶν
	D.	κόραξι(ν)	παισι(ν)	στόμασι(ν)	φλεψί(ν)
	A.	κόρακ-ας	παῖδ-ας	στόματ-α	φλέβ-ας
	V.	κόρακ-ες	παῖδ-ες	στόματ-α	φλέβ-ες
DUAL.	N.A.V.	κόρακ-ε	παῖδ-ε	στόματ-ε	φλέβ-ε
	G.D.	κοράκ-οιν	παῖδ-οιν	στομάτ-οιν	φλέβ-οιν

*Roots: κορακ, παιδ, στοματ, φλεβ. Cf. 156.

159. *Accentuation in Third Declension.*

a) The tone syllable remains unchanged, as long as the general rules allow it to be so; as: τὸ πρᾶγμα, *an action*, πράγματος (but πραγμάτων); ὁ ἡ χελιδών, *a swallow*, χελιδόνος. (The occasional exceptions will be given as they occur.)

b) *Monosyllables* are accented on the *last syllable* in the *genitive* and *dative* of all numbers; and the long syllables ων and οιν are then circumflexed; as: ὁ Ͽήρ, *a wild animal*, Ͽηρ-ός, Ͽηρ-ί, Ͽηρ-οῖν, Ͽηρ-ῶν, Ͽηρσί (ν): but Ͽῆρα, Ͽῆρες, &c.

Exceptions. δᾴδων, δμώων, παίδων, Ͽώων, } So in G. D. dual (παιδοῖν, &c.)
φῴδων, φώτων, ὤτων, Τρώων.* }

160. In addition to these may be mentioned the adjective πᾶς, *all, every*, G. παντός, D. παντί, but πάντων, πᾶσι (ν); ὁ Πάν, G. Πανός, but τοῖς Πᾶσι (ν).

161. VOCABULARY 12.

Paid-laborer, Ͽής, Ͽητ-ός, ὁ.
Old man, γέρων, γέροντ-ος, ὁ.
Boy, παῖς, παιδ-ός, ὁ.
A written character; pl. (= literæ) *a letter*; *an epistle*, γράμμα, γράμματ-ος, τό.
Elephant, ἐλέφας, ἐλέφαντ-ος, ὁ.
Honey, μέλι, μέλιτ-ος, τό.
Talon; *claw*, ὄνυξ, ὄνυχ-ος, ὁ.
Fox, ἀλώπηξ, ἀλώπεκ-ος, ἡ.
Chest; *coffin*, λάρναξ, λάρνακ-ος, ἡ.
Trunk (of an elephant), μυκτήρ, μυκτῆρ-ος, ὁ.
Hand, χείρ,† χειρ-ός, ἡ.
Neck, αὐχήν, αὐχέν-ος, ὁ.
Statue, ἀνδριάς, ἀνδριάντ-ος, ὁ.
Fire, πῦρ, πυρ-ός, τό.

Hireling, mercenary, μισϽωτός, ὁ.
Beginning; commencing point, ἀρχή.
Fodder, χόρτος, ὁ.
Kite, ἰκτῖνος, ὁ.
Bull, ταῦρος, ὁ.
Wagon, ἅμαξα.
Twice, δίς.
More powerful, κρείττων.
Of cypress, κυπαρίσσινος, η, ον.
Willing (masc. adj., to be rendered *willingly*), ἑκών, ἑκόντ-ος.
An insect, ἔντομον, τό.
I perform a service; minister, ὑπηρετέω (with *dat.*).
To send, πέμπ-ειν.
To dip, βάπτ-ειν.

Exercise 17.

162. *a*) *Translate into English.*

1. Ἡ καρδία ἐστὶν ἀρχὴ τῶν φλεβῶν. 2. Οἱ μισϽωτοὶ καὶ Ͽῆτες πᾶσιν ὑπηρετοῦσιν. 3. Τῷ νῷ δὶς παῖδες οἱ γέροντες γίγνονται·. 4. Ὁ Ἀλκιβιάδης πέμπει γράμ-

---

* From ἡ δᾴς, *a torch*; ὁ δμώς, *a slave*; ὁ ἡ παῖς, *a child*; ἡ δᾴς, *a jackal*; ἡ φῴς (G. φῳδός), *a blister caused by burning*; τὸ φῶς (G. φωτός), *light*; τὸ οὖς (G. ὠτός), *the ear*; ὁ ἡ Τρώς, *a Trojan.*

† This word has χερ- for root in χερ-οῖν, and χερ-σί.

ματα ἐς τὴν Σάμον. 5. Τὸν τοῦ ἐλέφαντος χόρτον εἰς
μέλι ἔβαψαν. 6. Τοῦ κόρακος κρείττων [b] ἐστὶν ὁ ἰκτῖνος
τοῖς ὄνυξι [c]. 7. Λύκος ὄνῳ καὶ ταύρῳ καὶ ἀλώπεκι πολέμιος [d]. 8. Λάρνακας κυπαρισσίνας ἄγουσιν ἅμαξαι.
9. Τοῖς ἐλέφασιν ὁ μυκτὴρ ἀντὶ [e] χειρῶν· τῶν δ᾽ ἐντόμων
ἐνίοις ἀντὶ στόματος ἡ γλῶττα. 10. Ὁ παῖς μακρὸν
ἔχει τὸν αὐχένα [36]. 11. Ἀνεὺ πυρὸς οὐχ οἷόν τ᾽ [38] ἐστὶν
ἀνδριάντα χρυσοῦν [f] ἐργάσασθαι [g]. 12. Τοῖς γέρουσιν
ἑκόντες εἴκομεν.

a become. b comparatives govern the *gen.* which, of course, is to
be rendered by *than.* c See 66, Obs. 1. d Supply *ἐστί.* e ἀντί,
prep. with gen. = *instead of;* hence as good, εἶναι ἀντὶ χειρῶν (*to be for
hands* =) 'to *serve* for hands.' f χρυσοῦς. g Inf. aor. to *work;*
to *make.*

b) Translate into Greek.

1. You (*pl.*) did not honor even the old-men.
2. Yield to old men [37], but not to boys [37]. 3. The boys
wondered-at the elephant's trunk. 4. Elephants [37]
have long trunks. 5. The boy wonders-at both the
eagle's talons and the lion's mane, and especially [h]
the elephant's trunk. 6. Camels [37] have long necks.
7. The Persians threw the quoit. 8. They were injuring the good resident-foreigners by their speeches [i].
9. Who will say that [k] one ought not to minister to old
men? 10. Boys love honey. 11. By Hermes, Androgeus, the son of Minos, is willingly an enemy to me.
12. Restrain, O general, the desires of (your) soldiers
by reason. 13. Not only the son of the baker but
Orestes also was looking towards the sea. 14. By Minerva, O boy, the paid-laborers and the hirelings do
not perform-service-for the old man.

h καὶ ... δέ, with a *word* between. i Use the *dat.* See also 91.
k ὅτι. See 146 a) note a.

LESSON XX.

Present and Future of Verbs in άω. Present Participle.

163. The Infinitive *Present* Active of verbs in άω is contracted thus: *a'-ειν* = *ᾶν*. The terminations of the *Present Indicative* are:

ά-ω	ά-εις	ά-ει	ῶ	ᾷς	ᾷ
ά-ομεν	ά-ετε	ά-ουσι	ῶμεν	ᾶτε	ῶσι
	ά-ετον	ά-ετον		ᾶτον	ᾶτον

(Observe the *ι subscript* where the *uncontracted form has* ει.

164. In the *sigmated root*, the *a* is mostly changed into *η*. Hence Fut. not *τιμάσ-ω*, but *τιμήσ-ω*. Aor. *ἐτίμησα.*

165. The *Present Participle* of the Act. Voice ends in *m. ων, f. ουσα, n. ον.* The *masc.* and *neut.* have Gen. *οντ-ος,* and are declined regularly after the third. The Fem. is declined regularly after the *first.*

166. Thus, from *τύπτ-ω* the root of Present Participle is *τύπτοντ-* for masc. and neut.: the *nominatives* being *masc. τύπτων* (compare *λέων, λέοντ-ος*), and *neut. τύπτον.*

167. ☞ With the *article* the participle is usually translated by a relative clause with *he, they,* &c. Ὁ *πράττων* = *he who does; τοῦ πράττοντος, of him who does,* &c.—Ὁ *ταῦτα πράττων* = *he who does this.* Οἱ *ταῦτα πράττοντες* = *those who do these things.*

168. VOCABULARY 13.

To *leap-down,* κατα-πηδᾷν (= -άειν).

To *end, to die,* τελευτᾷν (= -άειν).

To *honor,* τιμᾷν (= -άειν).

Phalanx, φάλαγξ, φάλαγγ-ος, ἡ.

To *praise,* ἐπαινεῖν (= -έειν).

To *be separated by an interval, to be distant* (from), διέχ-ειν.

To *sing the Pæan* (the Greek war song), παιανίζ-ειν.

When, ἡνίκα.

3*

To cast into (literally), ἐμβάλλειν; to charge, ἐμβάλλειν εἰς
(= ἐμβάλλειν τὸ στράτευμα
εἰς . . . to cast his men into =
to charge.)

To offer, make an offer of, ὑπο-
φέρειν.

To belong to, to be the due of,
προσήκ-ειν.

Goat, αἴξ, αἰγ-ός, ἡ.

Coin, money, νόμισμα, νομίσματ-
ος, τό.

Greek, Ἕλλην, Ἕλλην-ος, ὁ.

Other, ἄλλος, η, ο.

Chariot, ἅρμα, ἅρματ-ος, τό.

Not yet, not still, no longer, now-
not, οὐκέτι.

Ether, αἰθήρ, αἰθέρ-ος, ὁ.

Herald, κῆρυξ (or κήρυξ), κήρυκ-
ος, ὁ.

A truce, (prop. libations), a peace
(because ratified with libations,
σπένδειν), σπονδαί, pl.

Attempt, ἐπιχείρημα, ἐπιχειρήματ-ος, τό.

Stroke, πληγή.

Wound, τραῦμα, τραύματ-ος, τό

Exercise 18.
169. a) Translate into English.

1. Τὸ νόμισμα τὸ τῶν Περσῶν ὁ στρατηγὸς ἐφίλει.
2. Ἡ δικαιοσύνη ἀρετή ἐστιν. 3. Ὁ Κῦρος καταπηδᾷ
ἀπὸ τοῦ ἅρματος. 4. Οὐκέτι τρία· ἢ τέτταρα· στάδια
διέχουσιν τὼ φάλαγγε ἀπ᾿ ἀλλήλων, ἡνίκα παιανίζουσιν
οἱ Ἕλληνες. 5. Ὁ στρατηγὸς εἰς τὴν τῶν Αἰγυπτίων
φάλαγγα ἐμβάλλει. 6. Τὸν οὐρανὸν οἱ ποιηταὶ αἰθέρα
ὀνομάζουσιν. 7. Οἱ Ἀργεῖοι ἔπεμψαν δύο κήρυκας ᵇ ὑπο-
φέροντας σπονδάς. 8. Αἶγας αἰγῶν ἄρχοντας ᶜ οὐ ποιοῦ-
μεν. 9. Τοῖς τῆς γῆς ἄρχουσι τὴν προσήκουσαν τιμὴν
ἀποδίδομεν ᵈ. 10. Ὁ τοῦ γεωμέτρου λόγος οὕτω τελευτᾷ.

ᵃ Paradigms 36. ᵇ Observe that the *dual* is not necessarily used
when *two* are meant. For δύο see Paradigm 36. ᶜ *rulers*: properly
participle, *ruling*. ᵈ *we give* or *pay*.

b) Translate into Greek.

1. The Persians leap-down from their chariots.
2. You (*pl.*) honor those who rule the land. 3. We
honor him who rules the land with the honor that
belongs to him. 4. We praise and honor him who
rules well and justly. 5. The attempts of the Scy-
thians will end in ¹⁹ this. 6. One ought to yield to

those who rule. 7. He calls the attendant who is
pounding* the poison. 8. The assistants honor him.

  * Use pres. partic. of τρίβ-ειν.

LESSON XXI.

Third Declension.   Adjectives in ᾶς, εις.

170. PARADIGMS.

SING.	Xenophon.	Lion.	Bait.	Nectar.
N.	ὁ Ξενοφῶν	ὁ λέων	τὸ δέλεαρ	τὸ νέκταρ
G.	Ξενοφῶντ-ος	λέοντ-ος	δελέατ-ος	νέκταρ-ος
D.	Ξενοφῶντ-ι	λέοντ-ι	δελέατ-ι	νέκταρ-ι
A.	Ξενοφῶντ-α	λέοντ-α	δέλεαρ	νέκταρ
V.	Ξενοφῶν	λέον	δέλεαρ	νέκταρ
PLUR.				
N.	Ξενοφῶντ-ες	λέοντ-ες	δελέατ-α	νέκταρ-α
G.	Ξενοφῶντ-ων	λεόντ-ων	δελεάτ-ων	— νεκτάρ-ων
D.	Ξενοφῶ-σι	λέου-σι	δελέα-σι	νέκταρ-σι
A.	Ξενοφῶντ-ας	λέοντ-ας	δελέατ-α	νέκταρ-α
V.	Ξενοφῶντ-ες	λέοντ-ες	δελέατ-α	νέκταρ-α
DUAL				
N.A.V.	Ξενοφῶντ-ε	λέοντ-ε	δελέατ-ε	νέκταρ-ε
G. D.	Ξενοφῶντ-οιν	λεόντ-οιν	δελέατ-οιν	νεκτάρ-οιν

171. PARADIGMS.

μέλας, μέλαινα, μέλαν, *black.*			χαρίεις, χαρίεσσα, χαρίεν, *lovely.*		
SINGULAR.			**SINGULAR.**		
N. μέλας	μέλαινα	μέλαν	χαρίεις	χαρίεσσα	χαρίεν
G. μέλανος	μελαίνης	μέλανος	χαρίεντος	χαριέσσης	χαρίεντος
D. μέλανι	μελαίνῃ	μέλανι	χαρίεντι	χαριέσσῃ	χαρίεντι
A. μέλανα	μέλαιναν	μέλαν	χαρίεντα	χαρίεσσαν	χαρίεν
V. μέλας	μέλαινα	μέλαν	χαρίεν	χαρίεσσα	χαρίεν
PLURAL.			**PLURAL.**		
N. μέλανες	μέλαιναι	μέλανα	χαρίεντες	χαρίεσσαι	χαρίεντα
G. μελάνων	μελαινῶν	μελάνων	χαριέντων	χαριεσσῶν	χαριέντων
D. μέλασι	μελαίναις	μέλασι	χαρίεσι	χαριέσσαις	χαρίεσι
A. μέλανας	μελαίνας	μέλανα	χαρίεντας	χαριέσσᾶς	χαρίεντα
V. μέλανες	μέλαιναι	μέλανα	χαρίεντες	χαρίεσσαι	χαρίεντα
DUAL.			**DUAL.**		
N.A.V. μέλανε	μελαίνα	μέλανε	χαρίεντε	χαρίεσσα	χαρίεντε
G. D. μελάνοιν	μελαίναιν	μελάνοιν	χαρίεντοιν	χαριέσσαιν	χαρίεντοιν

172. VOCABULARY 14.

Bad, wicked, κακ-ός, ή, όν.

Demagogue, δημαγωγός, ὁ (δῆμος, people, ἄγ-ω, lead).

People, δῆμος, ὁ.

Flatterer, κόλαξ, κόλακ-ος, ὁ.

Orator, ῥήτωρ, ῥήτορ-ος, ὁ.

Nightingale, ἀηδών, ἀηδόν-ος, ἡ.

Swallow, χελιδών, χελιδόν-ος, ἡ.

Day, ἡμέρα.

Night, νύξ, νυκτ-ός, ἡ (nox).

Vulture, γύψ, γυπ-ός, ὁ.

Cuckoo, κόκκυξ, κόκκῦγ-ος, ὁ.

Color, χρῶμα, χρώματ-ος, τό.

Foot, πούς, ποδ-ός;* ὁ.

Rock, πέτρα.

Difference, (of colors,) a shade, διαφορά.

Poor man, πένης, πένητ-ος, ὁ.

Continuously, without ceasing, συνεχῶς (σύν & ἔχω).

Even (opposed to odd), of an even number, ἄρτιος, α, ον (par).

The aspalathus, (a prickly shrub,) ἀσπάλαθος, ὁ.

White, λευκός, ή, όν.

Black, μέλας, μέλαινα, μέλαν. (τὸ μέλαν, black; τὸ λευκόν, white; used as substant.)

Opposite, contrary (to), ἐναντίος, α, ον.

To sing, ᾄδ-ειν (= ἀείδειν).

To change, μεταβάλλ-ειν.

To hatch (its) young, to breed, to build its nest, νεοττεύ-ειν.

Exercise 19.

173. a) Translate into English.

1. Οἱ κακοί, τὴν ἡδονὴν ὡς δέλεαρ ἔχοντες, θηρεύουσιν ἡμῶν* τὰς ψυχάς. 2. Ὁ δημαγωγός ἐστι τοῦ δήμου κόλαξ. 3. Τοὺς σοφούς τε καὶ ἀγαθοὺς ῥήτορας ἐπαινοῦμεν καὶ τιμῶμεν. 4. Ἡ ἀηδὼν ᾄδει μὲν συνεχῶς ἡμέρας καὶ νύκτας δεκαπέντε·[b] μετὰ δὲ ταῦτα ᾄδει μέν, συνεχῶς δ' οὐκέτι. 5. Μεταβάλλει καὶ[c] ὁ κόκκυξ τὸ χρῶμα. 6. Οἱ πένητες πολλάκις τοῖς πένησι ὑπηρετοῦσιν. 7. Πάντα τὰ ζῷα ἀρτίους ἔχουσι τοὺς πόδας[36]. 8. Ὁ ἀσπάλαθος μέλαιναν ἔχει τὴν ῥίζαν[36]. 9. Τὸ μέλαν χρῶμά ἐστι· καὶ τοῦ μέλανος πολλαὶ[d] διαφοραί. 10. Ὁ γὺψ νεοττεύει ἐπὶ πέτραις ἀπροσβάτοις.[e] 11. Μὴ ἄνοα λέγε, ὦ Ξενοφῶν. 12. Τίς λέξει τὸν Πέρσην κρύπτειν

* Grimm's law shows this to be the same word as the Gothic fot, English foot; π or p being changed into the cognate f; δ (d) into t.

τὴν τοῦ ἄρχειν ἐπιθυμίαν;   13. Ὁ ταῦτα πράττων ἐστὶν ἄξιος τοῦ ἐπαίνου.

ᵃ (*of us* =) *our.*   ᵇ *fifteen* (indeclinable). Acc. denotes *duration*
of time.   ᶜ *also* (i. e. as well as *some other* birds).   ᵈ *many*, fem.
pl. from πολύς: supply the verb εἰσίν (*there are*).   ᵉ *inaccessible* (adj.
of two terminations).

b) *Translate into Greek.*

1. Vultures[37] lay two eggs[38].   2. One (μία) swallow does not make a spring.   3. We admire the swallow's young-ones.   4. We call demagogues flatterers
of the people.   5. Virtue renders life happy.   6. White
(ᵃ is) opposite to black.   7. I will tell you ᶠ the whole ᵍ
truth.   8. He rules-over a l l s e n s u a l p l e a s u r e s ʰ.
9. The gods rule-over all things ⁱ.

ᶠ ἐρῶ ὑμῖν.   ᵍ Put the proper case of πᾶς *before* the article.
ʰ Say: '*all the pleasures about the body*' (πᾶσαι αἱ περὶ τὸ σῶμα ἡδοναί).
Verbs of ruling, &c. *take genit.*   ⁱ *all things* are πάντα.

LESSON XXII.

Πᾶς, ἅπας. *Aorist Participle.*

174. Πᾶς = quisque, unusquisque (*every*).

175. Πᾶς ὁ —; ὁ πᾶς = totus (*the whole:* ὁ πᾶς
adds emphasis to *the whole* as opposed to its *constituent
parts*).

176. Πάντες· πάντες οἱ —· = omnes (the latter
especially when there is reference).

177. Οἱ πάντες = (1) omnes simul (*all together,
altogether*); (2) in universum (*in all*).

178. Πᾶσα πόλις, *every city:* πᾶσα ἡ πόλις, ἡ πόλις πᾶσα, *the
whole city* (also ἡ πᾶσα πόλις, *the whole city together*)· πάντα ἀγαθά·
πάντα τὰ ἀγαθά (the article is *usually* expressed, when a definite

class of things is meant) ; πᾶσαι αἱ καλαὶ πράξεις· τὰ πάντα μέρη, all the parts (together)· τοῖς πᾶσιν ὀργίζεται· τ ὰ π ά ν τ α εἴκοσι (in universum viginti), twenty in all.

179. Ἄπας = every (in the Sing.), is without the article; but in the sense of the whole, ἅπας (= ἅμα πᾶς) and σύμπας or ξύμπας (= all together), universus, are naturally more frequently without the article than πᾶς is in the sense of whole. Sometimes, too, σύμπαντες = in all is without the article [ξύμπαντες ἑπτακόσιοι ὁπλῖται, Th.].

180. PARADIGM.

πᾶς, πᾶσα, πᾶν, every, all.								
SING.			**PLUR.**			**DUAL.**		
m.	f.	n.	m.	f.	n.	m.	f.	n.
N. πᾶς	πᾶσα	πᾶν	πάντες	πᾶσαι	πάντα	πάντε	πάσα	πάντε
G. παντός	πάσης	παντός	πάντων	πασῶν	πάντων	πάντοιν	πάσαιν	πάντοιν
D. παντί	πάσῃ	παντί	πᾶσι(ν)	πάσαις	πᾶσι(ν)	πάντοιν	πάσαιν	πάντοιν
A. πάντα	πᾶσαν	πᾶν	πάντας	πάσας	πάντα	πάντε	πάσα	πάντε
V. πᾶς	πᾶσα	παν	πάντες	πᾶσαι	πάντα	πάντε	πάσα	πάντε

181. The participle of the Aorist Active appends ας to the sigmated root (λύσ-ας, τύψ-ας).

N. ᾱς,   ᾱσα,   ᾰν

G. αντος,   αοης,   αντος, &c.

(See Paradigm 17.) It is Englished by having —ed. But for verbs signifying emotions or states of mind, it is often Englished by pres. participle, the emotion having been felt and continuing to be felt: e. g. πιστεύσας (= confisus), trusting, relying on.

182. VOCABULARY 15.

Zeal, earnestness, eagerness, σπουδή.

Life, βίος, ὁ.

Leader, ἡγεμών, ἡγεμόν-ος, ὁ, ἡ.

Temperance, sobriety of mind, σωφροσύνη.

Absence of government, anarchy, licentiousness, ἀναρχία.

To grow old, γηράσκ-ειν. -

Lawlessness, ἀνομία.

River, ποταμός, οῦ, ὁ.

Innocence, ἀβλάβεια.

Danger, κίνδυνος, ὁ.

Low estate, ταπεινότης, ταπεινό-τητ-ος, ἡ.

Extreme, ἔσχατος, η, ον.

Obscurity, ἀδοξία.

To trust, πιστεύ-ειν (dat.).

Hoplite (heavy-armed soldier), ὁπλίτης, ὁ.	To do, πράττ-ειν (fut. πράξ-ω), to commit a murder, πράττειν φόνον.
To be the slave of, to serve, δουλεύ-ειν (dat.).	I am come, ἥκω (= veni).
To complete, διατελεῖν (= έειν).	To dissolve, to dismiss (an assembly), break (a treaty, &c.),
To bid, order, tell (to do any thing), κελεύ-ειν.	repeal (a law), λύ-ειν.

Exercise 20.

183. a) Translate into English.

1. Σπουδὴ πᾶσα ἔσται (= erit) διὰ παντὸς τοῦ βίου. 2. Ἥδιστον᾽ πάντων ἐστὶν ἀλύ᾽πως διατελεῖν τὸν βίον ἅπαντα. 3. Δεῖ βλέπειν πρὸς τὴν τῆς συμπάσης ἡγεμόνα ἀρετῆς σωφροσύνην. 4. Ἐν πάσῃ ἀναρχίᾳ καὶ ἀνομίᾳ διατελεῖ τὸν βίον. 5. Πάντα ἄνθρωπον χρὴ φεύγειν τὸ σφόδρα φιλεῖν αὐτόν. 6. Ὁ Νεῖλος γλυκύτατός ᵇ ἐστι πάντων τῶν ποταμῶν. 7. Ἦσαν οἱ πάντες ἑπτακόσιοι ὁπλῖται. 8. Ὁ Σωκράτης πιστεύσας τῇ αὑτοῦ᾽ ἀβλαβείᾳ ἐκινδύνευσε τὸν ἔσχατον κίνδυνον ᵈ. 9. Δύο στρατιῶται, τὰ αἰσχρὰ πράξαντες, φεύγουσιν. 10. Ἥκω δεῦρο σὺν τοῖς πολίταις τοῖς ἀγαθοῖς. 11. Τοὺς νόμους τοὺς ἐς τὸ παρὸν᾽ βλάπτοντας ὑμᾶς ἐλύσατε. 12. Κολάσομεν τοὺς τὴν εἰρήνην λύσαντας. 13. Πᾶν ζῷον ἀναγκαῖον ᶠ ἀρτίους ἔχειν τοὺς πόδας.

ᵃ most pleasant; superl. of ἡδύς.　　ᵇ sweetest; superl. of γλυκύς. ᶜ (of himself =) his.　　ᵈ κινδυνεύειν κίνδυνον = to incur (risk, expose oneself to) a danger, K. 278, 2.　　ᵉ for the present; at the present. ᶠ Supply ἐστί.

b) Translate into Greek.

1. The man is growing-old in extreme (say ʿall') obscurity and low-estate. 2. Every man ought to fly - from being - the - slave - of anger. 3. Through the whole of life we ought to pursue virtue. 4. We are-pursuing virtue with all eagerness. 5. From ¹³ being-

the-slave of s e n s u a l [173, *b*, note *h*,] pleasures he will be a slave for his whole life. 6. The wagons •w e r e in all seven-hundred. 7. We are angry with those who are breaking the peace. 8. We a r e e n r a g e d a g a i n s t ꞓ those who have broken the truce. 9. The geometer p l a c e s h i m s e l f b e f o r e ʰ all the Greeks.

ꞓ *To be enraged against—*, ἐν ὀργῇ ἔχειν (acc. of person).
ʰ *To place oneself before*, προτάσσειν αὑτὸν πρό (with gen.).

LESSON XXIII.
*Nouns that suffer Syncope.**

184. To this class belong the following substantives in ηρ: πατήρ, *father*, μήτηρ, *mother*, θυγάτηρ, *daughter*, ἡ γαστήρ, *the belly*, Δημήτηρ, *Ceres*, and ἀνήρ, *man;* which have this peculiarity, that they omit ε in the *gen.* and *dat. sing.* and *dat. plural.* They have voc. ερ (ἀνήρ, πατήρ throwing back the accent), and insert ά (*cum acuto*) before σι in *dat. plur.* Ἀνήρ, *a man* (root ἀνερ), drops the ε in all its cases except the voc. sing., but inserts a δ to soften the pronunciation.

PARADIGMS.

		Mother.	Man.	Father.
SING.	N.	ἡ μήτηρ	ὁ ἀνήρ	ὁ πατήρ
	G.	μητρός	ἀν-δ-ρός	πατρός
	D.	μητρί	ἀν-δ-ρί	πατρί
	A.	μητέρα	ἄν-δ-ρα	πατέρα
	V.	μῆτερ	ἄνερ	πάτερ
PLUR.	N.	μητέρες	ἄν-δ-ρες	πατέρες
	G.	μητέρων	ἀν-δ-ρῶν	πατέρων
	D.	μητράσι	ἀν-δ-ράσι	πατράσι
	A.	μητέρας	ἄν-δ-ρας	πατέρας
	V.	μητέρες	ἄν-δ-ρες	πατέρες
DUAL.	N. A. V.	μητέρε	ἄν-δ-ρε	πατέρε
	G. D.	μητέροιν	ἀν-δ-ροῖν	πατέροιν

* *Syncope* = the taking away of one or more letters from the body of a word. Cf. Paradigm 19.

185. Words of this class have several peculiarities of accent.
(1) The *dat. pl.* and the forms that *retain* the ε, are always *paroxytone*: (2) the forms that *reject* the ε have all the accent on the *last* syllable, with (3) the exception of voc. sing. in which the tone-syllable is thrown as far back as possible. (Δημήτηρ (see 186) is an exception to these rules.)

186. Ὁ ἀστήρ, έρος, *a star*, has its dative plural ἀστράσι, but is not syncopated in any other case. Δημήτηρ (*Demeter* or *Ceres*) has a varying accentuation, viz. Δήμητρος, Δήμητρι, Voc. Δήμητερ, but Acc. Δημητέρα.

187. Obs. For '*many great men*' the Greeks usually said '*many* and *great* men :' and so in similar combinations of two adjectives.

188. Vocabulary 16.

Bad, *worthless*, φαῦλος, η, ον.
Happiness, εὐδαιμονία.
Most disgraceful, basest, αἴσχιστος, η, ον.
Worthy, ἄξιος, a, ον (with gen.).
Liberty, ἐλευθερία.
Insolent, ὑβριστικός, ή, όν.
(Small) tunic, χιτώνιον, τό.
Three, τρεῖς, neut. τρία (Pdm. 36).
Nurse, τροφός, ἡ.
(Native) country, πατρίς, πατρίδος, ἡ.
Slaughter, φόνος, ὁ.
Dice, κύβος, ὁ.

Arms, ὅπλα, τά (arma).
Absolute prince, tyrant, τύραννος, ὁ.
To measure, μετρεῖν (= -έειν).
To love, στέργ-ειν.
To exclude, to keep away from, εἴργ-ειν.
To desire, ἐπιθυμεῖν (= -έειν) with gen.
To follow, attend (of a consequence), ἔπεσθαι, with dat.
To kill, to put to death, ἀπο-κτείνειν.
To drag away from, ἀποσπᾶν (= -άειν).

Exercise 21.

189. a) Translate into English.

1. Οἱ φαῦλοι τῇ γαστρὶ μετροῦσι καὶ τοῖς αἰσχίστοις τὴν εὐδαιμονίαν. 2. Ἄνδρες εἰσὶν ἀγαθοὶ καὶ ἄξιοι τῆς ἐλευθερίας. 3. Ὁ νέος, τοὺς τοῦ πατρὸς ὑβριστικοὺς καὶ μὴ σοφοὺς λόγους ἀκούων, ὑψηλόφρων[a] τε ἔσται (= erit) καὶ φιλότιμος[b] ἀνήρ. 4. Ἔστιν υἱοῦ γε[13] ἢ θυγατρὸς ὁ πατὴρ

· πατήρ. 5. Ταῖς Κέβητος θυγατράσι χιτώνια δώσω· (= dabo) τρία. 6. Εἰσί μοι τρεῖς θυγάτερες. 7. Τὴν γῆν ἀνδρῶν μητέρα τε καὶ τροφὸν ὀνομάζομεν. 8. Οἱ ἀγαθοὶ ὥσπερ ὑπὲρ [17] μητρὸς ὑπὲρ τῆς πατρίδος κινδυνεύουσιν. 9. Τῇ Δήμητρι πολλοὶ καὶ καλοὶ νεῴ ἦσαν. 10. Ὦ φίλη θύγατερ, στέργε τὴν μητέρα.[d] 11. Ὦ ἄνδρες Ἕλληνες, νομίζω σοφούς τε καὶ ἀξίους τῆς εὐδαιμονίας ὑμᾶς εἶναι. 12. Οἱ βάρβαροι τὰ αἰσχρὰ φιλοῦσιν. 13. Τοῦ σπουδὴ Σωκράτους ἀξία ἄπαντος τοῦ ἐπαίνου. 14. Ὦ Πέρσα, τίς ταῦτα λέξει Ξενοφῶντι; 15. Ἐν τῷ τοῦ ἀγαθοῦ. κήπῳ ἐστὶν οἰκίδιον.

[a] high minded.   [b] (fond of honor =) ambitious.   [c] I will give.
[d] See 91.

b) Translate into Greek.

1. Fathers [37] keep-away their sons from bad men. 2. There •was much• slaughter of men, and (δέ) much din of arms. 3. The enemy's camp •was unoccupied (say: 'void of men'). 4. Man differs from the othe1 animals in desiring honor. 5. Love (pl.) your father and your mother. 6. Be- not -the-slave-of the belly. 7. Great honor attends good men [37]. 8. Cyrus puts-to-death his mother's father. 9. Tyrants [37] drag children from •their fathers and mothers. 10. The man will spend his life in great glory. 11. The men are performing many great [52] •actions. 12. The many[f] will measure happiness by gain. 13. Bad (men) love anarchy and lawlessness. 14. Who will say that great honor does not attend good men? 15. There is a temple of Ceres in Cilicia. 16. Many great men love not only the Greeks but also the Persians.

[e] πολύς.   [f] οἱ πολλοί.

LESSON XXIV.

Adjectives of two terminations. Κέρας, &c.

190. Adjectives of two terminations have only *one form* for the *masculine* and *feminine,* as ὁ, ἡ ἔνδοξος, τὸ ἔνδοξον. They are declined like nouns of the third declension (except ος, ος, ον, which is like the second declension).

191. PARADIGMS.

σαφής, σαφές, *clear.*			εὐδαίμων, εὔδαιμον, *happy.*	
SING.			**SING.**	
m. f.		n.	m. f.	n.
N.	σαφής	σαφές	N. εὐδαίμων	εὔδαιμον
G.	σαφέ-ος / σαφοῦς		G. εὐδαίμον-ος	
D.	σαφέ-ῑ / σαφεῖ		D. εὐδαίμον-ι	
A.	σαφέ-α / σαφῆ	σαφές	A. εὐδαίμον-α	εὔδαιμον
V.	σαφές	σαφές	V. εὔδαιμον	εὔδαιμον
PLUR.			**PLUR.**	
N.	σαφέ-ες / σαφεῖς	σαφέ-α / σαφῆ	N. εὐδαίμονες	εὐδαίμονα
G.	σαφέ-ων / σαφῶν		G. εὐδαιμόνων	
D.	σαφέσι(ν)		D. εὐδαίμοσι(ν)	
A.	σαφέ-ας / σαφεῖς	σαφέ-α / σαφῆ	A. εὐδαίμονος	εὐδαίμονα
V.	σαφέ-ες / σαφεῖς	σαφέ-α / σαφῆ	V. εὐδαίμονες	εὐδαίμονα
DUAL.			**DUAL.**	
N. A. V.	σαφέ-ε / σαφῆ		N. A. V. εὐδαίμονε	
G. D.	σαφέ-οιν / σαφοῖν		G. D. εὐδαιμόνοιν	

* Table of Adjectives of Two Endings.

	m. f.	n.	m. f.	n.
1.	ος	ον	κόσμιος	κόσμιον
2.	ων	ον	πέπων	πέπον
3.	ης	ες	ἀληθής	ἀληθές (the most usual form)
4.	ην	εν	ἄρσην	ἄρσεν (the only adj. of this form)
5.	ις	ι	ἴδρις	ἴδρι

192. The *nominative plural* of τέρας usually drops the τ, and is contracted into τέρα, G. τερῶν. Τὸ γέρας, *reward*, τὸ γῆρας, *old age*, τὸ κρέας, *flesh*, and τὸ κέρας, *horn*, omit the τ in all the numbers, and suffer contraction in the genitive and dative singular, and throughout the dual and plural (except the dative plural): in κέρας, however, the regular forms with the τ are found as well as the contracted.

193. PARADIGMS.

τὸ κέρας, *the horn.*			τὸ κρέας, *the flesh.*		
SINGULAR.			**SINGULAR.**		
N. κέρας			κρέας		
G. κέρατ-ος	κέρα-ος	κέρως	κρέατ-ος	κρέα-ος	κρέως
D. κέρατ-ι	κέρα-ε	κέρᾳ	κρέατ-ι	κρέα-ῑ	κρέᾳ
A. κέρας			κρέας		
V. κερας			κρεας		
PLURAL.			**PLURAL.**		
N. κέρατ-α	κέρα-α	κέρα	κρέατ-α	κρέα-α	κρέα
G. κεράτ-ων	κερά-ων	κερῶν	κρεάτ-ων	κρεά-ων	κρεῶν
D. κέρα-σι(ν)			κρέασι(ν)		
A. κέρατ-α	κέρα-α	κέρα	κρέατ-α	κρέα-α	κρέα
V. κέρατ-α	κέρα-α	κέρα	κρέατ-α	κρέα-α	κρέα
DUAL.			**DUAL.**		
N.A.V. κέρατ-ε	κέρα-ε	κέρα	κρέατ-ε	κρέα-ε	κρέα
G.D. κεράτ-οιν	κερά-οιν	κερῷν	κρεάτ-οιν	κρεά-οιν	κρεῷν

194. VOCABULARY 17.

Horn, wing of an army, κέρας, κέρατ-ος, τό.

Honorary privilege, γέρας, γέ-ρατ-ος, τό.

Old age, γῆρας, γήρατ-ος, τό.

Prodigy, portentous-monster, τέ-ρας, τέρατ-ος, τό.

Alone, only, μόνος. η, ον.

Stag, ἔλαφος, ὁ.

The bonassus, wild ox, βόνασ-σος, ὁ.

Again, πάλιν.

On both sides, ἐκατέρωθεν.

Horse = cavalry, ἵππος, ἡ.

(Of) twenty thousand, δισμύριοι α, ον.

Already, ἤδη.

Fruit, καρπός, ὁ.

Child, τέκνον, τό.

Monument, μνημεῖον, τό.

Weakness, ἀσθένεια, ἡ.

Best, ἄριστος, η, ον.

At once, ἅμα.

Most, πλεῖστος, η, ον.

Solid, στερεός, ά, όν.

Throughout, διόλου.

To put to flight, to rout, τρέπεσθαι.

To cast away, to shed (horns), ἀποβάλλ-ειν.

To bear, φέρ-ειν.

| |
| To put forth (some natural product, as *horns, leaves,* &c.), φύ-ειν. |
| To butt, κυρίττ-ειν. |
| Much divided, branching, πολυσχιδής, ες (πολύς, σχίζω). |

Exercise 22.

195. a) Translate into English.

1. Τῷ ἀριστερῷ κέρᾱτι τρέπονται τοὺς πολεμίους. 2. Ἀποβάλλει τὰ κέρατα μόνος ὁ ἔλαφος κατ᾽ ἔτος [15], καὶ πάλιν φύει. 3. Ἐπὶ κέρως [25] ἑκατέρωθεν ἡ ἵππος, δισμυρία οὖσα [a]. 4. Κυρίττουσιν ἀλλήλους σιδηροῖς κέρασιν. 5. Ὁ ἀνὴρ ἐν πύλαις ἤδη γήρως ἐστίν. 6. Οὔτε γῆ καρποὺς φέρει, οὔτε μητέρες τέκνα τίκτουσιν, ἀλλὰ τέρᾰτα. 7. Οἱ ὑπὲρ τῆς πατρίδος [17] καλῶς τελευτήσαντες [b] τάφων τε καὶ τῶν ἄλλων μνημείων μέγιστα ἔχουσι γέρα.

[a] Ὤν, οὖσα, ὄν, pres. part. of εἰμί, *I am.*   [b] τελευτήσαντες, first aor. part. of τελευτάω.

b) Translate into Greek.

1. •It is necessary to yield to the weakness of old-age. 2. The geometer died of [23] old-age, not (*say:* 'but not') of disease. 3. This (τοῦτό γε) is the best remedy for [17] old-age. 4. The bonassus has at once both a mane and two horns [30]. 5. With •our right wing we are conquering the enemy's hoplites. 6. Most horns (*say:* 'the most of horns') are hollow, and those (τὰ δὲ) of stags alone are solid throughout and branching [a]. 7. The citizens have honors and panegyrics from one another, and honorary-privileges.

[a] πολυσχιδῆ (= πολυσχιδέα).

LESSON XXV.·

196. *Substantives in* ης, ος.—*Adjectives in* ης.

SINGULAR.		PLURAL.	
·N. **ης** :	.*ος, (neut.)*	N. .**εες, εις** :	**εα, η, (neut.)**
G. **εος, ους**		G. **εων, ων**	
D. **εῖ, ει**		D. **εσι(ν)**	
A. **εα, η** }	*ος, (neut.)*	A. **εας, εις** :	**εα, η, (neut.)**
V. **ες** ·}		V. **εες, εις** :	**εα, η, (neut.)**
DUAL.			
N. A. V. **εε, η.**		G. D. **έοιν, οῖν.**	

197. *a*) In Attic prose the *open* form occurs only in *dual* εε from adjectives in ης, and *gen. pl.* εων from ος.

b) Τριήρης (properly an *adj.*), with the adj. αὐτάρκης, and compound adjectives in ήϑης (from ῆϑος) remain *paroxytone* in gen. pl. It is not certain whether we should write τριήρες, τριήροιν ; or τρίηρες, τριηροῖν. K. adopts the former; see his *Gramm.* 59.

(Learn Paradigm 21.)

198. ☞ Observe that most adjectives in ης are *oxytone ;* αὐτάρκης, εὐήϑης, συνήϑης, πλήρης, are exceptions.

199. VOCABULARY 18.

One who pursues gain by base means, αἰσχροκερδής, ές.

Gain, κέρδος, κέρδε-ος, κέρδους, τό.

Reproach, ὄνειδος (-εος, ους), τό.

Character, disposition, ῆϑος (ῆεος, ους), τό (mores).

Simple, εὐήϑης, ες (εὐ and ῆϑος).

Disobedient, ἀπειϑής, ές.

Obedient, εὐπειϑής, ές.

Summer, ϑέρος (-εος, ους), τό.

Year, ἔτος (-εος, ους), τό.

Multitude, πλῆϑος (-εος, ους); hence = democratical constitution.

Mountain, ὄρος (-εος, ους), τό.

Wall, τεῖχος (-εος, ους), τό.

Kind, γένος (-εος, ους), τό.

False, ψευδής, ές.

True, ἀληϑής, ές.

Dicer, κυβευτής, οῦ, ὁ.

Footpad, (prop. *a filcher of clothes,*) λωποδύτης, ου, ὁ.

Robber, λῃστής, οῦ, ὁ.

Gentleness, πραότης, πραότητος, ἡ.

Tameness, ἡμερότης, ἡμερότητος, ἡ.

Want of intelligence, stupidity, ἄνοια, ας, ἡ.

Courage, ἀνδρία, ας, ἡ (ἀνήρ).

Cowardice, δειλία, ας, ἡ (δειλός).

Sheep, πρόβατον, ου, τό.

Unintelligent, stupid, ἀνόητος, ον (ἀ and νοέω, νοῦς).

Trireme, τριήρης (-εος, ους), ἡ.

Useless, ἄχρηστος, ον.

I suppose, (opinor,) δήπου.

Army, στράτευμα, στρατεύματ-ος, τό.

Chase, hunting-expedition, ϑήρα, ας, ἡ.

Winter, χειμών, χειμῶν-ος, ὁ.

Alike, ὁμοίως.

To endure, ὑπομέν-ειν.

To differ, διαφέρ-ειν.

To plot against, ἐπιβουλεύ-ειν (with dat.).

To value before or above, to prefer, προτιμᾶν (= -άειν) with acc. and gen.

To show sobriety or sense of mind, σωφρον-εῖν (= -έειν).

Less, ἐλάττων.

Little, μικρός, ά, ον : μικρῷ, (by) a little (with comparative).

Safety, σωτηρία, ας, ἡ.

Poetical, ποιητικός, ή, όν.

Of earth; hence, of brick, γήϊ-νος, ον.

More than, rather than, μᾶλλον ἤ.

Exercise 23.

200. a) Translate into English.

1. Ὁ κυβευτὴς καὶ ὁ λωποδύτης καὶ ὁ λῃστὴς αἰσχρο-κερδεῖς εἰσι. 2. Οἱ κυβευταὶ κέρδους ἕνεκα ὀνείδη ὑπο-μένουσι. 3. Τὰ ἤϑη τῶν ζώων διαφέρει (85, 1) κατά τε δειλίαν καὶ πραότητα καὶ ἀνδρίαν καὶ ἡμερότητα καὶ νοῦν τε καὶ ἄνοιαν. 4. Τὸ τῶν προβάτων ἦϑος εὔηϑες καὶ ἀνόητονª. 5. Ἐνταῦϑα Ἀλκιβιάδης ἧκεν ἐκ τῶν Κλα-ζομενῶν σὺν πέντε τριήρεσι. 6. Ἄχρηστον δήπου καὶ οἰκέτης καὶ στράτευμα ἀπειϑές. 7. Θήραν ποιοῦνται ᵇ ὁμοίως ϑέρουςᶜ καὶ χειμῶνος. 8. Ὁ ταὼς ἅπαξ τοῦ ἔτους ᵈ τίκτει μόνον· τίκτει δὲ ᾠὰ δώδεκα ἢ μικρῷ ἐλάτ-τω ᵉ. 9. Ὁ Πέρσης ἐπιβουλεύει τῷ πλήϑει τῷ ὑμετέρῳ. 10. Σωφρονοῦσι τὴν σωτηρίαν τοῦ κέρδους προτιμῶντες (= προτιμάοντες). 11. Ὁ βόνασσος γίγνεται ἐν τῇ Παιωνίᾳ, ἐν τῷ ὄρει τῷ Μεσσαπίῳ. 12. Κατὰ τὸν ποιητικὸν λόγον, χαλκᾶ καὶ σιδηρᾶ δεῖ εἶναι τὰ τείχη μᾶλλον ἢ γήϊνα.

* Supply the *copula* ἐστίν.   ᵇ ποιοῦνται (= ποιέ-ονται) θήραν (*lit.* faciunt sibi venationem), *go out a hunting; hunt.*   ᶜ K. 273. 4. *b.*   ᵈ the partitive genitive stands with adverbs of *time* and *place:* e. g. *thrice a day,* τρὶς τῆς ἡμέρας.   ᵉ For ἐλάττονα, cf. Paradigm 12 (μείζων).

b) *Translate into Greek.*

1. There are two kinds of lions. 2. He conceals the truth by a false tale. 3. Do not trust (*pl.*) to walls and gates. 4. You (*pl.*) trusted to the bravery of the citizens, and not (*say:* 'but not') to walls and gates. 5. The general of the Persians has well-disciplined soldiers ᵃᵈ. 6. O boys, you are pursuing false pleasures, and not true ones. 7. The wicked for the most part ᶠ delight in ¹⁹ false pleasures, but good men (*say:* 'the good of men') in true ones.

ᶠ τὰ πολλά.

LESSON XXVI.

Ἡρακλῆς, &c.

201. When a vowel stands before the terminations ης, ες, and ος, the Attics contract εα of the acc. sing. and neut. plur., not into η, but *a*; e. g. κλέος (*glory*), plur. κλέεα—κλέᾱ.

202. Proper names in κλέης, contr. κλῆς, undergo (in Attic Greek) a double contraction in the dative sing.; e. g. έ-εῖ (= έ-ει) = εῖ.

N.	(Ἡρακλέης)		Ἡρακλῆς
G.	(Ἡρακλέεος)	Ἡρακλέους	
D.	(Ἡρακλέεϊ)	(Ἡρακλέει)	Ἡρακλεῖ
A.	(Ἡρακλέεα)	Ἡρακλέᾱ [sometimes Ἡρακλῆ *]	
V.	(Ἡράκλεες)	Ἡράκλεις	(Ἡρακλες, in *exclamations*.)

* *Plat. Phæd.* 89.

203. VOCABULARY 19.

Sophŏcles, Σοφοκλῆς (see note 5).
Ameinŏcles, Ἀμεινοκλῆς.
Eucles, Εὐκλῆς.
Euthycles, Εὐθυκλῆς.
Unwritten, ἄγρᾰφος, ον.
Written, γεγραμμένος, η, ον.
The Antigone (a play of Sopho-
  cles), ἡ Ἀντιγόνη.
Law, νόμος, ου, ὁ.
Accurate, ἀκρῐβής, ές.
Full, πλήρης, ες.
Fair, reasonable, ἐπιεικής, ές.
Expensive, costly, πολυτελής, ές.
Human, natural to man, hence
  (of sins) venial, ἀνθρώπινος
  η, ον.
A sin, a fault, ἁμάρτημα, ἁμαρτή-
  ματ-ος, τό.
Procession, πομπή, ἡ.
Sacrifice, θυσία, ἡ.
Strong, ἰσχῦρός, ά, όν.
Fifth, πέμπτος, η, ον.
Straight, right, ὀρθός, ή, ον
  (rectus).

It befits, is becoming, πρέπει,
  (decet,) with dat.
To think, οἴεσθαι.
Not to transgress, (lit. to remain
  within,) to observe (a law),
  ἐμμέν-ειν (with dat).
It is fitting or expedient, συμφέρει (= expedit), τὸ συμφέρον,
  (= id quod expedit, or utile
  est), the expedient.
To pardon, συγγιγνώσκ-ειν (with
  dat.).
To accept, ἀποδέχ-εσθαι.
To court, to consult a thing,
  e. g. expediency, θεραπεύ-ειν.
To give in evidence, bear witness, μαρτυρ-εῖν (= -έειν).
Test, proof, mode of examination,
  (of a witness, e. g. by torture,)
  ἔλεγχος, ου, ὁ.
Judge, κριτής, οῦ, ὁ.
Healthy, sound, ὑγιής, ές.
(There) were, ἦσαν, imp. 3d. pl.
  from εἰμί.

REM. By 201, ὑγιέα (from ὑγιής, ὑγιέ-ος) is contracted into ὑγιᾶ, but
ὑγιῆ is also found in Plato.

Exercise 24.

204. a) Translate into English.

1. Ταῦτα οὐκ οἴονται⁵³ Θεμιστοκλεῖ πρέπειν. 2. Οἱ
μὲν ἄγραφοι νόμοι οὐδέποτε μεταβάλλουσιν, οἱ δὲ γε-
γραμμένοι πολλάκις, ὥσπερ εἴρηται· ἐν τῇ τοῦ Σοφο-
κλέους Ἀντιγόνῃ. 3. Τὸ δίκαιόν ᵇ ἐστιν ἀληθές τι· καὶ
συμφέρον. 4. Βελτίονος ἀνδρὸς ᵈ τὸ τοῖς ἀγράφοις νόμοις
ἢ τοῖς γεγραμμένοις ἐμμένειν. 5. Τὸ τοῖς ἀνθρωπίνοις
ἁμαρτήμασι συγγιγνώσκειν ἐπιεικές·. 6. Οἱ θεοὶ οὐκ
4

ἀποδέχονται τὰς πολυτελεῖς πομπάς τε καὶ θυσίας.
7. Ἦσαν κῶμαι πολλαὶ πλήρεις πολλῶν ἀγαθῶν ἐν τῷ
πεδίῳ τῷ παρὰ τὸν Τίγρητα ποταμόν. 8. Οἱ Συρακού-
σιοι στρατηγοὺς ἔχουσιν Ἡρακλείδην καὶ Εὐκλέα καὶ
Τελλίαν. 9. Στρατηγὸς ἦν Κορινθίων Ξενοκλείδης ὁ
Εὐθυκλέους, πέμπτος αὐτός⁴². 10. Τἀληθὲς ᵇ (= τὸ
ἀληθὲς) ἰσχῦρόν ἐστι. 11. Οἱ πολλοί, τοῦ ὀρθοῦ ᵇ οὐκ
ἀληθεῖς κριταὶ ὄντες,ᶜ τὸ συμφέρον μᾶλλον θεραπεύου-
σιν. 12. Ἡγοῦμαι⁵ παντάπᾱσί γε⁴³ ἀληθῆ εἶναι καὶ
ὑγιᾶ (or ὑγιῆ) καὶ πιστὸν τὸν ἄνθρωπον.

ᵃ 'has been said.'　ᵇ 'justice, right.' See K. 244, 8.　ᵉ 'something.'　ᵈ the gen. with ἐστί is construed as in Lat.: it is the part,
duty, &c. of; it is characteristic of, &c.　ᵉ supply ἐστί.　ᶠ ὄντες
(εἰμί).　ᵍ = ἡγέομαι, I think.

b) Translate into Greek.

1. We praise those who speak the truth (say:
'the true •things'). 2. You (pl.) all gave false
witness (say: 'gave-in-evidence the false •things').
3. We will give-in-evidence what is true, not⁴⁶ what
is false (say: 'the true •things;' 'the false •things').
4. You see the faithlessness of Tissaphernes. 5. Their
general is Dercyllidas, the (son) of Eucles, with two
others⁴². 6. Who avoids such (say: 'so') accurate
methods-of-examination? 7. I will give these things
to Ameinŏcles the Samian.

LESSON XXVII.

Substantives in εύς.　(Paradigm 27.)

205. The termination εύς (oxytone) takes ω in the
genitive sing.; and in the dat. sing. and nom. and acc.

plur. admits of regular contraction. The voc. is *εῦ*
(*perispomenon*); dat. pl. *εῦσι(ν)*. (Observe the accent.)

SINGULAR.	PLURAL.	DUAL.	
N. *εύς*	*εῖς*	N.	
G. *έως*	*έων*	A.	*έε*
D. *εῖ*	*εῦσι(ν)*	V.	
A. *έᾱ*	*έας (εῖς)*	G.	*έοιν*
V. *εῦ*	*εῖς*	D.	

206. Besides *εῖς* the old Attic dialect possesses a collateral form
in *ῆς* (contracted from the Epic *ῆες*) for the nom. and voc. plur.;
e. g. Πλαταιῆς for Πλαταιεῖς.

207. Most substantives which have a vowel before the termina-
tion *ευς*, contract *έως* into *ῶς*, *έα* into *ᾱ*, *έας* (seldom) into *ᾶς*; e. g.
Εὐβοεύς (*an inhabitant of Eubœa*), gen. Εὐβοῶς, acc. Εὐβοᾶ, acc.
plur. Εὐβοᾶς. So sometimes G. plur.; e. g. Ἐρετριῶν, Δωριῶν.

208. *Future Participle.*] The *fut. participle* is formed by adding
ων to root of Future, βλάπτω, fut. βλάψω, participle βλάψων (-ουσα,
-ον). It is declined like a participle of the Present (Pdm. 16).

209. The future participle is often used to denote a
purpose

(*Eng.*) I am come *to do* this.
(*Greek*) *I am come* about-to-do this (*ἥκω π ο ι ή σ ω ν ταῦτα*)
(Eng.) I sent a man *to do* this.
(Greek) *I sent (a man)* about to do this (*ἔπεμψα π ο ι ή σ ο ν τ α*
ταῦτα [or, *τὸν ποιήσοντα*]).

210. VOCABULARY 20.

Interpreter, ἑρμηνεύς, ὁ.
King, βασιλεύς, ὁ.
Painter, γραφεύς, ὁ.
Priest, ἱερεύς, ὁ.
Horseman, ἱππεύς, ὁ.
Scribe, γραμματεύς, ὁ.
Parent, γονεύς, ὁ.
Abundant, ἄφθονος, ον, (ἀ, *not*,
φθόνος, *envy, there being so
much that none need envy
another.*)

The Piræus (port of Athens),
Πειραιεύς, ὁ.
Mart, custom-house (at Athens),
ἐμπόριον, ου, τό.
Superintendent, inspector, ἐπι-
μελητής, οῦ, ὁ (ἐπιμ. ἐμπορίου
= *custom-house officer*).
Foot soldier, πεζός, οῦ, ὁ (*pedes*).
Higher up, more inland, beyond,
ἄνω (adv. with *gen.*).
To dig down, κατασκάπτ-ειν

Twenty thousand, δισμύριοι, αι, α.

Together with (dat.), ἅμα; ἅμα τῇ ἡμέρᾳ, at day-break.

To sacrifice, θύ-ειν.

An offering, a sacrifice, θῦμα, θύματ-ος, τό.

To put into the hands, to hand over, ἐγχειρίζ-ειν.

Priestess, ἱέρεια, ἡ.

Holy, ὅσιος, α, ον.

To disobey, ἀπειθ-εῖν (= -έειν), with dat.

To make a likeness of, to copy, to draw, ἀπεικάζ-ειν.

To imitate, μιμέ-εσθαι (μιμεῖ-σθαι).

Serious or earnest in character, good, worthy, σπουδαῖος, α, ον.

I am come, ἥκω (= veni, adsum).

To go away, ἀπέρχ-εσθαι.

Exercise 25.

211. a) Translate into English.

1. Ξενοφῶν διελέγετο αὐτοῖς* δι' ἑρμηνέως περὶ σπονδῶν. 2. Οὐκ ἔστι χρήματα ἡμῖν[b], τοῖς δὲ πολεμίοις ἄφθονα παρὰ βασιλέως. 3. Λαμβάνει τὸ ἀργύριον ὁ γραμματεὺς ὁ τοῦ ἐμπορίου ἐπιμελητῶν Εὐθύδημος. 4. Ἅμα τῇ ἡμέρᾳ ὁρῶμεν ἱππέας πολλούς, πεζοὺς δ' ἄνω τῶν ἱππέων ὡς δισμυρίους. 5. Ἥκω θύσων. 6. Θύσοντες[10] τοῖς ἱερεῦσί τε καὶ ἱερείαις ἐγχειρίζομεν τὰ θύματα. 7. Οὐχ ὅσιον τοῦτό γε[13] τὸ τοῖς γονεῦσιν ἀπειθεῖν. 8. Αἰσχρὸν τοὺς μὲν γραφεῖς ἀπεικάζειν τὰ καλὰ τῶν ζώων, τοὺς δὲ παῖδας μὴ μιμεῖσθαι τοὺς σπουδαίους τῶν γονέων. 9. Πέμπομεν κατασκάψοντας τὰ τείχη.

* 'conversed with them.'   b like est (sunt) mihi = 'I have' in Latin.

b) Translate into Greek.

1. It is •the mark of a bad boy to disobey his parents. 2. The painter will draw the insects. 3. O dear boy, you ought to imitate your parents. 4. The clerks receive money from [18] the Lacedæmonians. 5. We are come to sacrifice [50] to Athene (= Minerva). 6. The Persian, having handed-over his offering to the

priest, is-going-away.   7. Many of the cavalry fly.
8. Many of the men from the Piræus are digging-down
the wall. · 9. Those from the city are coming to aid ⁵⁸
those in the Piræus.   10. We admire not only the city
but also the Piræus.

LESSON XXVIII.

Words in ις, ι, υς, υ.

212. A considerable number of words with the terminations *ις, ι, υς, ὐ,* retain their proper vowel only in
the acc. and voc. sing., substituting ε for it in all the
other cases.   Words in *ις* and *υς* take ω in the genitive
(i. e. *ως* for *ος*), which, however, in reference to the
accent, is considered as short, like ω in the gen. plur.
of these words.   The neuters in *ι* and *υ* form their
genitive in the usual manner.

SING.				
	N.	ις	υς	υ
	G.	εως	εως	εος
	D.	ει	ει ·	ει
	A.	ιν	υν	
	V.	ι	υ	
PLUR.	N. V.	εις	εις	η
	G.	εων	εων	εων
	D	εσι(ν)	εσι(ν)	εσι(ν)
	A.	εις	εις	
DUAL.	N. A. V.	εε	εε	εε
	G. D.	έοιν	έοιν	έοιν

213. VOCABULARY 21.

Intelligence, σύνεσις, ἡ.
Intellectual act, intellect, νόησις, ἡ.
Elbow, fore-arm, πῆχυς, ὁ.
Prophet, μάντις, ὁ.
Insolence, ὕβρις, ἡ ; ὕβρεως νό-

Articulation of a joint, joint, δι-
     άρθρωσις ἡ.
Hatchet, axe, πέλεκυς, ὁ.
     μος = *the law of assault.*
Power, δύναμις, ἡ.

Gift, present, δόσις, ἡ.

Nature, φύσις, ἡ.

Seeing (the sense of sight), sight, ὄψις, ἡ.

Smelling (the sense of) smell, ὄσφρησις, ἡ.

(The sense of) hearing, ἀκοή, ἡ.

Limb, μέλος, μέλε-ος (-ους), τό.

Between, μεταξύ (adv. with gen.).

Wrist, καρπός, οῦ, ὁ.

Elbow, ἀγκών, ἀγκῶν-ος, ὁ.

Hunting-knife, cutlass, μάχαιρα, ας, ἡ.

Sword, ξίφος, ξίφε-ος (-ους), τό.

Axe, ἀξίνη, ης, ἡ.

House, οἰκία, ας, ἡ.

Saw, πρίων, πρίον-ος, ὁ.

Low-bred, ignoble, ἀγεννής, ές.

Tail, οὐρά, ᾶς, ἡ.

Breadth, πλάτος, πλάτε-ος (-ους), τό.

Unbearable, ἀφόρητος, ον. (Comparat. ἀφορητότερος.)

Prisoner of war, αἰχμάλωτος, ον (αἰχμή, cuspis, ἀλίσκειν, capere).

To cut off, ἀποκόπτ-ειν.

To surpass or be superior, ὑπερέχ-ειν, (with gen.).

To contemplate, behold, ϑεωρ-εῖν (-έειν).

To read, ἀναγιγνώσκ-ειν.

Low, base, ταπεινός, ή, όν.

Exercise 26.

214. a) *Translate into English.*

1. Ὁ ἄνϑρωπος συνέσει τε ὑπερέχει τῶν ἄλλων ζώων καὶ δίκην καὶ ϑεοὺς νομίζει⁴⁴. 2. Πολλὰ πολλάκις νοήσει ἀλλ' οὐκ⁴⁸ ὄμμασιν ϑεωροῦμεν. 3. Πῆχυς καλεῖται* καὶ τὸ σύμπαν μέλος, ὅσον ᵇ ἐστὶ μεταξὺ τῆς τε κατὰ καρπὸν καὶ τῆς κατ' ἀγκῶνα διαρϑρώσεως°. 4. Πολλὰς μὲν μαχαίρας ἔχουσι, πολλὰ δὲ ξίφη, πολλοὺς δὲ πελέκεις καὶ ἀξίνας· 5. Λυκοῦργος ἐκέλευε ᵈ τὰς οἰκίας ποιεῖν ἀπὸ πελέκεως καὶ πρίονος μόνον. 6. Φεῦγε ἔκγονον ὕβρεως ἀδικίαν. 7. Τοῖς σοφοῖς ὥσπερ μάντεσι πιστεύομέν τισι⁵¹. 8. Οἱ κόλακες φύσιν ἀγεννῆ καὶ ταπεινὴν ἔχουσιν. 9. Οἱ ἐκεῖ* καὶ ὄψει⁴⁸ καὶ ἀκοῇ καὶ ὀσφρήσει καὶ πᾶσι τοῖς τοιούτοις ᶠ πολὺ τῶν ἐνϑάδε ᵍ διαφέρουσιν. 10. Ἐν τῇ Συρίᾳ τὰ πρόβατα τὰς οὐρὰς ³⁴ ἔχει τὸ πλάτος πήχεως⁴⁵. 11. Οἱ ἐκ τοῦ ἄστεος φεύγουσι.

ᵃ '*is called*' (= καλέ-εται). ᵇ ὅσον (= quantum) '*as much (of it as*'). ᵉ ἡ κατὰ καρπὸν διάρθρωσις (*the articulation at the wrist =*) *the wrist joint:* so ἡ κατ' ἀγκῶνα διάρθρωσις. ᵈ sc. *the Lacedaemonians.* ᵉ K. 244. 10. ᶠ τοιοῦτος = *talis:* understand '*things.*'

b) Translate into Greek.

1. The man takes-his-estimate of ᶠ Alexander, not from ¹⁰ Alexander's •own nature, but from his own cowardice. 2. Nothing is more unbearable than insolence. 3. Read me ʰ the law of assault. 4. The power of the city is (K. 241. 2) great ‖ .* 5. By his power of speaking he conquered his opponents. 6. We will aid the god with foot, hand, voice, and all our power •of every kind ⁴⁷. 7. Themistocles courted him with a present of money. 8. The soldiers cut-off (*pres.*) the necks of their prisoners-of-war with an axe. 9. The walls of the city are beautiful ‖. 10. Insolence, and pleasure, and all •manner of senselessness, rules-over those (•who dwell) in cities ‖.

ᶠ θεωρ-εῖν (= ἕειν), i. e. to *contemplate* him. *Alexander,* Ἀλέξανδρος. ʰ μοί, enclit.

LESSON XXIX.

ἠχώ, αἰδώς.

215. The terminations of nouns in ώ and ώς are as follows:

	SINGULAR.		PLURAL.	DUAL.
N.	ώ	ώς	οί, &c. as 2d Declension.	ώ, &c. as 2d Declension.
G.	(όος), οῦς			
D.	(όι), οῖ			
A.	(όα), ώ			
V.	οῖ			

Obs. Note the peculiar *vocat.* οῖ.

* This mark ‖ means that *this* notion is to stand first in the sentence.

216. VOCABULARY 22.

Shame, reverence, αἰδώς, ἡ.

Persuasion, obedience, πειθώ, ἡ.

Goddess, θεά, ας, ἡ.

Shamelessness, ἀναίδεια, ἡ.

The inspector of boys (at Sparta), παιδονόμος, ὁ.

A taxiarch (the commander of a τάξις or division), ταξίαρχος, ὁ.

Device, contrivance, ἐπίνοια, ας, ἡ.

Endurance, patience, καρτερία, ἡ.

Toil, labor, πόνος, ου, ὁ.

Lover, ἐραστής, οῦ, ὁ.

Opinion, glory, δόξα, ης, ἡ.

Maker, author, hence (impro-prie) of a thing, the instrument, δημιουργός, οῦ, ὁ.

Oratory, ῥητορική, ἡ, (τέχνη, art, understood,) prop. fem. adj. oratorical.

To receive, λαμβάν-ειν.

To take one's work easily, to be lazy or idle, ῥᾳδιουργ-εῖν (= -έειν).

To supply, to bestow, παρέχεσθαι.

Exercise 27.

217. a) Translate into English.

1. Οἱ Λακεδαιμόνιοι θεὰν οὐ τὴν Ἀναίδειαν ἀλλὰ τὴν Αἰδῶ νομίζουσι. 2. Ὁ κόλαξ πολλὰ χρήματα παρὰ[18] Ἀμεινοκλέους* πειθοῖ λαμβάνει. 3. Ἐν Λακεδαίμονι ὁ παιδονόμος τοὺς παῖδας τοὺς ῥᾳδιουργοῦντας (= ῥᾳδιουρ-γέ-οντας) ἰσχυρῶς κολάζει, ὥστε πολλὴν μὲν αἰδῶ, πολλὴν δὲ πειθὼ ἐκεῖ συμπαρεῖναι.[b] 4. Ὁ Κῦρος τοῦ μὲν ταξι-άρχου τὴν ἐπίνοιαν, τῶν δὲ στρατιωτῶν τὴν πειθὼ ἐπαι-νεῖ. 5. Οὕτως χρὴ καὶ τὸ λοιπὸν[c] ἄνδρας ἀγαθοὺς εἶναι, γιγνώσκοντας, ὅτι τὰς μεγάλας[d] ἡδονὰς καὶ τὰ ἀγαθὰ τὰ μεγάλα ἡ πειθὼ καὶ ἡ καρτερία καὶ οἱ ἐν τῷ καιρῷ πόνοι καὶ κίνδυνοι παρέχονται. 6. Τιμῆς ἐρασταί εἰσιν μετὰ σωφροσύνης τε καὶ αἰδοῦς καὶ ἀληθινῆς δόξης. 7. Γιγνώ-σκω ὅτι πειθοῦς δημιουργός ἐστιν ἡ ῥητορική.

* Ἀμεινοκλῆς, 207.   b = simul adesse, to be present there at the same time : ὥστε, so that, with infin. (to be rendered by a finite verb). c = in posterum; for the future, henceforth : καὶ, also ; i. e. as you have hitherto been.   d μέγας.

b) Translate into Greek.

1. Deem that Persuasion, not Force[46], is a goddess.

2. Hermes (= Mercury) conducts to[20] mankind Rever-

ence and Justice.   3. The bad call shame silliness.
4. Tellias, the son of Eucles, called reverence and
shame a divine fear.   5. We ought to surpass others
in ₁₀justice and reverence.   6. Bad masters teach the
young not by * persuasion, but by violence.   7. Nearly ꜜ
all will yield to persuasion, but very few to force.

       * ὑπό with gen.   ꜜ σχεδόν τι.

LESSON XXX.
Imperative.   Adjectives in υς.
218. The terminations of the Imperative are :

PRESENT.		AORIST.	
S. ε ἐτω		S. ον ατω	
P. ετε ἐτωσαν, or (more		P. ατε . ατωσαν	
commonly) ὁντων.		or αντων.	
D. ετον ἐτων		D. ατον ατων	

219. EXAMPLES.

PRESENT.		AORIST.	
S. λῦ-ε λυ-έτω		S. λῦσ-ον λυσ-άτω	
P. λύ-ετε λυ-έτωσαν		P. λύσ-ατε λυσ-άτωσαν	
or λυ-όντων.		or λυσ-άντων.	
D. λύ-ετον λυ-έτων		D. λύσ-ατον λυσ-άτων	

220. *a)* The Imperative of the *Present* is used as
in other languages, in requests, commands, exhortations, permissions, and the like.

It is used in *general precepts*, and when the action *commanded* or
advised, against which *we are warned*, &c. is either considered as
continuing (*lasting*, that is, for *some time*) or *being repeated* from time
to time.

b) The Imperative of the Aorist is used when the
action *commanded, advised, permitted*, &c. is considered
as a *single, definite* action (not as being *continued* for
any length of time, or being repeated).   Thus παῦσον

4*

τὸν λόγον, *end your speech* (by a single effect of the will, &c.).

221. This distinction is often but small: and it disappears when the verb has only one of the forms in use.—The *Aorist Imperative* may be used of an action that *really has* (and *must* have) *duration*, but then it does not *indicate* this: it speaks of it simply as *one, definite* action.

222. The negative with an Imperative is μή, but the *Aorist Imperative* is *hardly ever* used with μή (the *Aorist Subjunctive* being used, as we shall see) instead of it.

223. Adjectives in υς are contracted in the dat. sing. and the nom. accus. and vocat. plural.*

224. PARADIGMS.

γλυκύς, γλυκεῖα, γλυκύ, *sweet.*		
SINGULAR.		
m.	f.	n.
N. γλυκύς	γλυκεῖα	γλυκύ
G. γλυκέ-ος	γλυκείας	γλυκέ-ος
D. { γλυκέ-ῐ / γλυκεῖ }	γλυκείᾳ	{ γλυκέ-ῐ / γλυκεῖ }
A. γλυκύν	γλυκεῖαν	γλυκύ
V. γλυκύ	γλυκεῖα	γλυκύ
PLURAL.		
m.	f.	n.
N. { γλυκέ-ες / γλυκεῖς }	γλυκεῖαι	γλυκέα
G. γλυκέων	γλυκειῶν	γλυκέων
D. γλυκέσι(ν)	γλυκείαις	γλυκέσι
A. { γλυκέας / γλυκεῖς }	γλυκείας	γλυκέα
V. { γλυκέ-ες / γλυκεῖς }	γλυκεῖαι	γλυκέα
DUAL.		
m.	f.	n.
N.A.V. γλυκέε	γλυκεία	γλυκέε
G.D. γλυκέοιν	γλυκείαιν	γλυκέοιν

* ☞ Nor γλυκ-έε, nor γλυκ-έα,
Nor γλυκ-έοιν contract you may:
So γλυκ-έος and γλυκ-έων
Contraction ever let alone.

225. Vocabulary 23.

Sweet, pleasurable, ἡδύς.

Quick (also mentally), ὀξύς.

Slow, βραδύς.

Short, small, βραχύς.

Appetite, ὄρεξις, εως, ἡ.

Ready-witted, clever, shrewd, ἀγχίνους (see 136).

Having a good memory, of a retentive memory, μνήμων, μνήμονος (see 191).

Prone (to) ὀξύῤροπος, ον (from ὀξύς and ῥέπειν).

Fond of gain, φιλοκερδής, ές.

Part, μόριον, ου, τό.

Again, πάλιν.

Confession, ὁμολογία, ας, ἡ.

Confidently, boldly, ϑαρρῶν, (partic. of ϑαρρεῖν : lit. "feeling confidence.")

Sycophant, informer, συκοφάντης, ου, ὁ.

Otherwise, ἄλλως.

To commit injustice, ἀδικεῖν (= -έειν.)

To deliberate, to decide, βουλεύειν.

To hear, to listen to, ἀκού-ειν (with gen.)

To abide by, ἐμμέν-ειν (with dat.)

To wail, μέν-ειν.

To make to cease, put a stop to, παύ-ειν : παύειν τινὰ τῆς ἀρχῆς, to stop a man from his government or magistracy = to deprive him of his magistracy.

To define, ὁρίζ-ειν. (Hence the horizon = the boundary-line of earth and sky.)

To test, prove, δοκιμάζ-ειν.

To examine, ἐξετάζ-ειν.

Participation, κοινωνία, ας, ἡ.

To snatch at, to seize, ἁρπάζ-ειν (rapere).

Exercise 28.

226. a) Translate into English.

1. Ἡ ἐπιϑυμία τοῦ ἡδέος ἐστὶν ὄρεξις.   2. Οἱ ὀξεῖς καὶ ἀγχίνοι καὶ μνήμονες ὡς τὰ πολλὰ καὶ πρὸς τὰς ὀργὰς ὀξύῤροποί εἰσιν.   3. Οἱ φιλοκερδεῖς ἕνεκα κέρδους βραχέος ἀδικοῦσι.   4. Ἐν βραχεῖ μορίῳ ἡμέρας περὶ πολλῶν σωμάτων καὶ χρημάτων καὶ πόλεων καὶ δόξης βουλεύομεν.   5. Πρὸς τοὺς Ἀϑηναίους πέμπετε περὶ᾽ Ποτιδαίας.   6. Λέγε τὸν νόμον (Æsch.).   7. Ὅτι ἀληϑῆ λέγω,ᵇ ἀκούσατε τῶν ψηφισμάτων (Æsch.).   8. Λέγε δὴ πάλιν ὃ (= quod) Δημοσϑένης κατὰ Δημοσϑένους ἔγραψε· προσέχετε, ὦ ἄνδρες.   9. Μὴ λεγέτω τὸ ὄνομα ἀλλὰ τὸ πρᾶγμα.   10. Τὴν μάχην μοι, ἔφη

ὁ Κῦρος, λέξον ἑκάστων, ἥτις ἐστί.ᵃ 11. Βοηθήσατέ
μοι, καὶ μὴ διδάσκετε τοὺς συκοφάντας μεῖζον ὑμῶν
αὐτῶν δύνασθαι.ᵈ 12. Θαρρῶν ἐμμενέτω τῇ ὁμολογίᾳ. 13. Ἐμμενόντων·ᵉ τοῖς ὅρκοις.

ᵃ ' on the subject of:' lit. about. · ᵇ a sentence with ' that' (ὅτι)
often depends on a suppressed notion; such as, to see, to convince yourselves, &c. ᶜ the Aorist implies one definite statement. λέξον μοι
τὴν μαχ. ἑκάστων ἥτις ἐστι = ἥτις ἐστὶν ἡ μάχη ἑκάστων. The acc. is
here placed as the object of λέξον, instead of as the subject (nom. case)
to ἐστί. ἥτις is fem. of ὅστις (quæ, qualis), what, of what kind.
ᵈ μεῖζον δύνασθαι (= plus posse or valere), to have more power, to be
stronger. ᵉ see 218.

b) Translate into Greek.

1. Stay, and do not do otherwise. 2. Of boys, some
are quick, and others slow. 3. Hear, O Athenians, the
decrees against Æschines. 4. Remove him from ¹⁸ his
command. 5. Define for me (μοί, enclit.) up to ᶠ how
many years we ought to consider men young.
6. Prove your friends by their participating ᵍ with
you in danger. 7. Bring them hither ᵍ, and examine what ʰ they say. 8. Do not snatch-at the honors of the state.

ᶠ μέχρι, c. gen. (quot = πόσοι, -αι, -α, -ων). Define single definite
act. ᵍ to bring ... hither, δεῦρο παράγειν. Say: 'bringing
them hither ... examine.' ʰ τί = quid (it retains the acute).

LESSON XXXI.

Subjunctive of the Present and Aorist Active.

227. The Subjunctive, like the Principal Tenses
(242), has third dual ον; third plural σι·

It has the long e and o sounds (η, ω) where the Indicative has the short ones (ε, ο).

Terminations of the *Subjunctive.*

S.	ω	ης	$\eta\ (=\eta\text{-}i\varsigma,\ \eta\text{-}i)$
P.	ωμεν	ητε	ωσι
D.		ητον	ητον.

EXAMPLES.

(Subjunctive Present.)

S.	τύπτ-ω	τύπτ-ης	τύπτ-η
P.	τύπτ-ωμεν	τύπτ-ητε	τύπτ-ωσι
D.		τύπτ-ητον	τύπτ-ητον

(Subjunctive Aorist.)

S.	τύψ-ω	τύψ-ης	τύψ-η
P.	τύψ-ωμεν	τύψ-ητε	τύψ-ωσι
D.		τύψ-ητον	τύψ-ητον.

228. The *Subjunctive* of the *Aorist* does not (like the *Indicative*) *denote past time,* but a *single, definite action* considered as standing alone : whereas the Subjunctive of the Present denotes a *continued* or *repeated* * action.

229. Thus with ὅπως, ἵνα = *ut* ('*in order that*'), the Present Subjunctive is used of *general purposes,* and the like, and wherever *duration* is to be pointed out.—It must, however, be remembered, that the *Aorist Subj.* may be used of an action that *really does* and *must* continue for a considerable time ; but then the tense *does not imply this,* but considers it as one action, complete in itself.

230. On the other hand, the *Present Subj.* cannot be used of a *single, definite* action, *performed once.*

231. But with those particles of *time* that are compounded with ἄν (e. g. ὅταν, quum, quoties, ἐπειδάν, postquam) the *Subj. Aor.* = the Latin *futurum exactum.*

---

* By a *repeated* action is meant an action spoken of *indefinitely,* such an action, *whenever* it takes place; *such* a state, *whenever* it exists.

232. Examples (for imitation).

a. *Temporal Particles.*

ὅταν ποιῇς = *quum (quoties) facias, when (whenever) you do* (of a habit, general truth, &c.).

ὅταν ποιήσῃς, *quum (quoties) feceris, when you shall have done ; when you have done.* Often = *when you do* (from the difference of our English idiom).

ἐπειδὰν ποιήσῃς = *postquam feceris.*

b. *Final Particles.* -

ἵνα (ὅπως) ποιῇς, *ut facias ; that you may do* (habitually).

ἵνα (ὅπως) ποιήσῃς, *ut facias, that you may do* (once).

c. *Conditional Particle.* ·

ἐὰν ποιῇς, *si facias ; si quando facias.*

ἐὰν ποιήσῃς, *si feceris : si quando facias* (semel).

d. ☞ All these particles take μή, not οὐ, for *not*; μηδείς, not οὐδείς, for *nobody.*

233. VOCABULARY 24.

In the way of, ἐμποδών, (adv. with *dat.*)

Any wild animal that is hunted, θηρίον, ου, τό : τὰ θηρία = *game.*

Young animal, σκύμνος, ου, ὁ : οἱ σκύμνοι, *the young* (ones).

Dog, κύων, κυν-ός, ὁ et ἡ.

Female, θῆλυς, εια, υ.

Young bird, νεόττιον, ου, τό.

Viviparous, ζωοτόκος, ον. (ζωός, *vivus ;* τεκ, root of τίκτειν, pa-rĕre.)

Four-footed, τετράπους, τετρά-πουν, (gen. τετράποδος, &c.)

Herb, grass, πόα, ας, ἡ.

At any other time, ἄλλοτε.

Wax, κηρός, οῦ, ὁ.

Pitch, πίττα (Attic for πίσσα).

Oil, ἔλαιον, ου, τό.

Healthy, ὑγιεινός, ή, όν.

Water, ὕδωρ· ὕδατ-ος, τό.

Without pleasure, ἀηδῶς.

To hinder, κωλύ-ειν (fut. ύσω).

To counsel, advise, συμβουλεύ-ειν, (with *dat.*)

To make plain, to show, δηλό-ειν.

Right time, καιρός, οῦ, ὁ. *Op-portunely, at the right time,* εἰς καιρόν.

To bind, to tie up, δέ-ειν.

To cease, leave off, παύ-εσθαι (= *to stop oneself*).

To sing, ᾄ-δειν (= ἀείδειν).

To sit (of a bird), ἐπωάζ-ειν.

To dream, ἐνυπνιάζ-ειν.

To be suffering, to be ill, κάμν-ειν
(laborare).

To eat, ἐσθί-ειν.

To be in pain, ἀλγεῖν (= έειν).

Less, ἧττον.

To be strong, ἰσχύ-ειν.

Fit, ἱκανός, ή, όν (idoneus).

To collect (in a heap), ἀθροίζ-ειν.

Dung, manure, κόπρος, ου, ὁ.

To dine, δειπνεῖν (= έειν).

To drink, πίν-ειν.

Being present, παρών (= praesens, part. pres. of παρεῖναι).

Exercise 29.

(Learn Paradigms 29, 32: βοῦς, οἷς.)

234. a) Translate into English.

1. Δέομεν* τὸν κύνα, ὅπως μὴ ἁρπάζῃ τοὺς τῶν θηρίων σκύμνους. 2. Ἡ θήλεια ἀηδὼν παύεται ᾄδουσα,ᵇ ὅταν ἐπωάζῃ καὶ τὰ νεόττια ἔχῃ. 3. Ἐνυπνιάζειν φαίνονται οὐ μόνον ἄνθρωποι, ἀλλὰ καὶ ἵπποι καὶ κύνες καὶ βόες· ἔτι δὲ πρόβατα καὶ αἶγες καὶ πᾶν τὸ τῶν ζωοτόκων καὶ τετραπόδων γένος. 4. Οἱ λύκοι πόας ἄλλοτε μὲν οὐκ ἐσθίουσιν, ὅταν δὲ κάμνωσι.ᶜ 5. Οἱ βόες τοὺς πόδας ἧττον ἀλγοῦσιν,ᵈ ἐάν τις τὰ κεράτια ἀλείφῃ κηρῷ ἢ πίττῃ ἢ ἐλαίῳ. 6. Ὑγιεινότεραι ὄιες τῶν αἰγῶν· ἰσχύουσι δὲ μᾶλλον αἱ αἶγες τῶν ὄιων. 7. Τοὺς λύκους φασὶν, ὅταν πεινῶσιν,ᵉ ἐσθίειν τινὰ γῆν. 8. Ἐπειδὰν ἅπαντα ἀκούσητε, κρίνατε.ᶠ 9. Αὖθίς σοι συμβουλεύσομεν, ἐὰν μὴ κωλύσῃ με τὸ γῆρας. 10. Εἰς καιρὸν ἥκεις, ὅπως τῆς δίκης ἀκούσῃς παρὼν τῆς ἀμφὶ τοῦ πατρός. 11. Ποιήσω ταῦτα, ἵνα δηλώσω τοὺς ἐμποδὼν ὄντας τῇ τῶν Ἑλλήνων εὐδαιμονίᾳ.

* In the Present Indic. dissyllables in έω do not contract έομεν and έουσι.   ᵇ παύομαι ποιῶν τι = I leave off doing any thing. But in English doing is participial subst. in acc.; in the Greek it is a present participle agreeing with subj. 'I doing it' (= who am doing it) leave-off.   ᶜ Supply 'then they do,' or prefix 'only' to ὅταν, when.   ᵈ ἀλγεῖν τοὺς πόδας, to feel pain as to their feet = feel pain in their feet.   ᵉ = πεινά-ωσι, from πεινάειν, esurire.   ᶠ ἔκρινα, Aor. of κρίνω, to judge. Imperat. κρῖ'νον, άτω, &c.

b) .Translate into Greek.

1. Speak, that I may h e a r (*single action*). 2. 1 say this, that you may r e m o v e (*one definite act*) Tellias from his command. 3. We say this, that nobody. may trust those ·who have done such things. 4. When (= *after*) you have made him fit to govern, let him govern. 5. A good husbandman is c a r e f u l **ꜱ** to collect (*say:* 'p r o v i d e s h o w [ὅπως] he m a y c o l l e c t,' i. e. *habitually*) his manure. 6. When you havᵉ collected the manure, you shall dine. 7. Do not think that they drink without-pleasure, when (= *whenever, if at any time*) they drink water. 8. It is a custom with the P e r s i a n s (*dat.*) to kiss relations, when' **ᵉ** t h a t is (γέ) they see **ʰ** them after a l o n g t i m e.ᵉ

ꜱ ἐπιμελεῖται (= ἐπιμελέ-εται).   ʰ The subj. of ὁράω is (irregularly) ἴδω, -ῃς, -ῃ, &c.

LESSON XXXII.

*First Future and Aorist of Liquid Verbs.**

235. *Short root.*]   Many verbs are *strengthened forms* of *simpler* roots.—To obtain the *short* from the *strengthened* root, we must retrace the step or steps by which the strengthening was effected :

1) By changing the radical vowel or diphthong into the short vowel from which it arose.

αι becomes ᾰ.

ει before a *mute* must be changed into ι.

ει before a *liquid* must be changed into ε.

ου becomes ο.

η (when it has arisen from *a*) becomes ᾰ.

---

* i. e. verbs whose root ends in a *liquid.*

EXAMPLES.

φαιν	φαν	λειπ	λιπ	τειν	τεν
ἀκου	ακο	ληϑ	λαϑ	φϑειρ	'φϑερ

2) By rejecting the latter of two consonants : τεμν, τεμ.

a) Since ππ = *any* P-sound + τ, the short root *may* end in π, β, or φ.

b) From ζ (= σδ) the *former* is ejected : φραζ, φραδ.

c) But a strengthened root in ζ has sometimes arisen from a short root ending in γ : οἰμωζ, οἰμωγ.

d) Σσ, ττ, are mostly strengthened roots from short roots that end in a *K-sound* (κ, γ, or χ): but sometimes from roots that end in a *T-sound :* πρασσ, πραγ. φρισσ, φρικ. πτυσσ, πτυχ.—— ἐρεσσ, ἐρετ. κορυσσ, κορυϑ.

236. In the Active Voice, *liquid* verbs have only what is called the *Second Future*. It is formed by adding ῶ to the short root.

237. The *Aorist Act.* of liquid verbs is without σ : it lengthens the vowel of the Future; and for that purpose changes

ε into ει } σπερῶ, ἔσπειρα
a into η } φανῶ, ἔφηνα.*

PRESENT.	FUTURE.	AORIST.
σφάλλ-ω, to trip up	σφᾰλ-ῶ	ἔ-σφηλ-α
φαίν-ω, to show	φᾰν-ῶ	ἔ-φην-α
μέν-ω, to remain	μεν-ῶ	ἔ-μειν-α
σπείρω, sow	σπερ-ῶ	ἔ-σπειρ-α
τίλλ-ω, to pluck	τῐλ-ῶ	ἔ-τιλ-α
ἀμύν-ω, to defend	ἀμῠν-ῶ	ἤμῡν-α.

* But the following take *Aor.* 1. in ανα :—

a) All in ραίνω, ιαίνω (except τετραίνω, μιαίνω).

b) ἰσχναίνω, κερδαίνω, κοιλαίνω, λευκαίνω, ὀργαίνω, πεπαίνω.

c) σημαίνω, σαίνω, have -ηνα or -ανα. καθαίρω has -ηρα, or -αρα.

The terminations of the *Future of liquid verbs* are ῶ, εῖς, εῖ |
οῦμεν, εῖτε, οῦσι(ν) | εῖτον, εῖτον.

238. Τί ποιῶ = *What am I to do? what shall I
do?* (called the 'deliberative subjunctive.')

239. Οὐ μή with *Fut.* and *Aor. Subj.*]

a) Οὐ μὴ γράψεις; (cum interrogatione), *Will you
not not-write?* = '*don't write:*' '*don't write*, I tell you.'

b) Thus οὐ μή, *used interrogatively* with the *Second Person* of the Future, is virtually a *strong prohi-
bition:* but *without interrogation* it is (with any Person of the *Future* or (more commonly) the *Subjunctive*
of the *Aorist*) a *strong denial:*

οὐ μὴ γράψω (*fut.*),   -εις, -ει, &c. } *I (you, he) will
οὐ μὴ γράψω (*aor. subj.*), -ῃς, -ῃ, &c. }   not write.*

c) The last idiom is explained by an ellipse of δέος ἐστί (*metus
est*) or δεινόν ἐστι (*verendum est*). So that οὐ μὴ γράψεις, or γράψῃς = οὐ (δέος ἐστὶ) μὴ γράψεις or γράψῃς, [*there is no fear lest*]
you should write = you will certainly not write.

d) Sometimes instead of the simple οὐ μή, there is a *compound*
of one or both (e. g. οὔτοι, οὐδείς, οὔποτε· μηδείς, μήποτε). Render
as if it were οὐ μή, adding the *additional force* of the *compound.*

240. VOCABULARY 25.

To sow, σπείρ-ειν.

To wait, and (*like* manere) to
wait for (a person, acc.) μέν-ειν.

To distribute, allot, νέμ-ειν.

To gain, κερδαίν-ειν.

To reap (a harvest), gather fruit,
&c. θερίζ-ειν.

To fear, δείδ-ειν.

To insult, ὑβρίζ-ειν.

To scoff, jeer at, σκώπτ-ειν.

To talk nonsense, ληρεῖν (= έειν.)

Laid waste, (of cities, &c.) ruined, ἀνάστᾰτος, ον.

To disagree (lit. *to sound differ-
ently*), to dissent, to make a
different statement, διαφωνεῖν
(= έειν.)

What kind of, ποῖος, ποία, ποῖον
(qualis). Ποῖός τις has nearly
the same force, but adds a notion of *indefinite magnitude* to
it.

Assuredly not, οὔτοι (non sane).

Who in the world? τίς ποτε
(= quis quidem.)

More, πλείων, (compar. adj.)

Exercise 30.

(Learn τίς, τὶς, Paradigms 37, 38.)   •

241. *a) Translate into English.* •

1. Ταῦτα ποιῶν, οὐ μὴ δείσῃς τοὺς πολεμίους. 2. Οὗτοι σ' Ἀχαιῶν μή τις ὑβρίσῃ. 3. Οὐ μὴ σκώψεις; 4. Οὐ μὴ ληρήσεις; 5. Οὐ μή σε κρύψω· ταῦτα. 6. Τοὺς πονηροὺς οὐ μήποτε βελτίους ποιήσετε. 7. Δέκα ἔτη μείναντες Ἀχαιοὶ τὴν Τροίαν ἀνάστατον ἐποίησαν. 8. Μενοῦμεν αὐτούς. 9. Τῇ ὁμολογίᾳ πότερον[d] ἐμμενοῦμεν ἢ διαφωνήσομεν; 10. Ποῖόν τινα ἐλπίζεις καρπὸν ὧν[b] ἔσπειρας θερίσειν; 11. Ἄλλων σπειράντων καὶ φυτευσάντων, τὸν καρπὸν ὑμεῖς ἐθερίσατε. 12. Ἆρ' οὐχ[c] οἱ θεοὶ πολλοῖς ἀγαθοῖς δυστυχίας τε καὶ βίον κακὸν ἔνειμαν; 13. Τί ποιῶμεν; 14. Πότερον[d] κερδανοῦσιν οἱ κακοὶ τοιαῦτα ποιήσαντες, ἢ οὔ; 15. Οἱ φιλοκερδεῖς ἐπιθυμοῦσιν ἄρχειν, ἵνα πλείω[e] κερδαίνωσι.

ᵃ K. 280. 4.   ᵇ Gen. pl. of ὅς, *qui* (Pdm. 49): καρπὸν ... ὧν = καρπὸν ... τούτων, ἅ; the relative being put in the case of the antecedent τούτων (= *eorum*) by attraction.   ᶜ ἆρ' οὐ or ἆρ' οὐχ.   ᵈ πότερον — ἤ.   ᵉ for πλείονα, neut. plur. (*more things* =) *more* Pdm. 12.

b) Translate into Greek.

1. What am I to do? 2. They will not remove him from his command. 3. Did they remove him from his magistracy, or not? 4. Who in-the-world will remove them from their command? 5. He will not reap the fruit of what[f] he sowed. 6. Who in-the-world will sow on[25] rocks and stones? 7. Will you sow on[25] the water? [•No.]ᵍ 8. What am I to say? 9. Will you abide-by your oaths, or not?ʰ

ᶠ ὧν by attraction for ἅ. 910.   ᵍ ἄρα μή.   ʰ πότερον ... ἤ.

LESSON XXXIII

The Tenses.

242. The *Tenses* are divided into *principal* and *historical* tenses.

Principal Tenses.   *Historical Tenses.*

PRESENT.   IMPERFECT.

PERFECT.   PLUPERFECT.

FUTURE.   AORIST.

243. After ἵνα, ὅπως, ὡς (= *ut*), '*that*,' '*in order that*,' the Subjunctive answers to the Latin *Present Subjunctive,** and follows the *principal tenses.* (See 229.)

Μὴ κλέπτ-ε, *do not steal* (forbids stealing *generally*).

Μὴ κλέψ-ῃς τοῦτο, *do not steal* this (forbids stealing in a *particular instance*).

244. As a general rule, in *prohibitions* with μή, the *Imperative* of the *Present* is used, or the *Subjunctive* of the *Aorist*.   The *Present Imperative* is used in *general precepts*, and whenever the *action forbidden* is considered as *continuing* or *being repeated.*—The *Subjunctive* of the *Aorist* (whether with μή, or after ἵνα, &c.) does not denote *past time* (like the *Indicative* of the *Aorist*), but a *single definite* action ; an *action done once*, without *any reference* to *duration* or *repetition.*† Cf. 229.

---

* The *present subjunctive* denotes *continuance* or *repetition.*

† Such an action (as has been observed in 229) may *have duration* (even *necessarly*), but then the Aorist Subj. considers it as *one action*, without any *reference* to this (necessary) *duration.*

245. Vocabulary 26.

To reproach, ὀνειδίζ-ειν.

Calamity, misfortune, συμφορά, ᾶς, ἡ.

To blot out, expunge, ἐξαλείφ-ειν.

To cut off, ἐκκόπτ-ειν.

A vexatious information, συκοφαντία, ας, ἡ.

Nourishment, food, τροφή, ῆς, ἡ (τρέφ-ειν, nutrire).

Juice, χυμός, οῦ, ὁ (χέω, fundo).

Experience, ἐμπειρία, ας, ἡ.

Strength, ἰσχύς, ἰσχύ-ος, ἡ.

To be strong, to avail, ἰσχύ-ειν (valere).

To diversify, to relieve, to decorate, ποικίλλ-ειν.

Wall of a house, τεῖχος, ου, ὁ (= paries).

I am here, πάρειμι.

Spirit, εὐψυχία, ας, ἡ.

Being lifted up (= with pride, with exultation), ἐπαιρόμενος, η, ον (participle).

Capable of being taught, that can be taught, διδακτός, ή, όν : also ός, όν.

To grudge, to envy, φθονεῖν (= -έειν).

Unseen, invisible, ἀόρᾱτος, ον.

The future, what is to be, τὸ μέλλον (= quod futurum est).

(*Eng.*)   To reproach a man *with any thing.*

(*Greek.*)   To reproach *any thing to a man,* (ὀνειδίζειν τί τινι : cf. *exprobrare alicui paupertatem,* &c.)

Exercise 31.

246. *a) Translate into English.*

1. Μηδενὶ συμφορὰν ὀνειδίσῃς· κοινὴ γὰρ ἡ τύχη, καὶ τὸ μέλλον ἀόρατον.   2. Ἐξαλείψομεν τὸν νόμον, ἵνα τὰς συκοφαντίας ἐκκόψωμεν.   3. Ἡ μέλιττα χρῆται* τροφῇ οὐδεμίᾳ ἀλλ᾽ ἢ[b] τῇ γλυκὺν ἐχούσῃ χυμόν.   4. Μὴ ποιήσῃς τοῦτο.   5. Τὸν δῆμον μὴ ἀπολύσητε.   6. Ἄνευ εὐψυχίας οὐδεμία τέχνη πρὸς τοὺς κινδύνους ἰσχύει.   7. Μὴ τοῖς ἐξ Εὐβοίας καὶ Σπάρτης λίθοις τοὺς τοίχους ποίκιλλε.   8. Ὅταν λέγῃς ἐπαιρόμενος, ὅτι[c] ἵππον καλὸν ἔχω, ἠλίθιος εἶ.   9. Εἰ ἔχεις[d] ἡμῖν ἐπιδεῖξαι* ὡς διδακτόν ἐστιν ἡ ἀρετή, μὴ φθονήσῃς ἀλλὰ ἐπίδειξον.[e]

---

* = χρά-εται, from χρῆσθαι (= χρά-εσθαι), *uti,* which contracts *ae* into η instead of *a*.   It governs the *dat.* : χρῆσθαι τροφῇ (literally) (*cibo uti =*) *to take* (any) *food.*   [b] ἀλλ᾽ ἤ (*literally* 'but than')

= *nisi* or *præter* after *οὐδεὶς ἄλλος*, or *οὐδεὶς* only.   * *ὅτι* (*that*)
precedes the *quoted* words of another person, and is then not to be
translated.   d have = *have it in your power'; can.*   * *ἐπίδειξον* is
Imper. Aorist (2nd person), and *ἐπιδεῖξαι, Infin. Aorist* of *ἐπιδεικνύναι,*
to show ; to prove.

b) Translate into Greek.

1. Do not wonder-at the strength of the giant.   2.
Do not reproach the just man with the misfortunes
• sent from the gods.   3. Do not admire external f
goods.   4. The soldier's spirit will avail against d dan-
gers.   5. The arts of the general availed nothing against
the spirit and experience of the enemy.   6. I am here
to remove (*say :* 'that I may remove') them from
their command.

f *ὁ (ἡ, τό) ἔξω = external. ἔξω,* adv. *without ; outwardly.*

LESSON XXXIV.

Optative of Present and Aorist.

247. In these tenses, the Optative (like the *other*
moods) drops the augment of the *Indicative*.

	Subjunctive.			Optative.			Infin.
PRESENT	ω	ης	η	οιμι	οις	οι	ειν
	ωμεν	ητε	ωσι	οιμεν	οιτε	οιεν	
		ητον	ητον		οιτον	οίτην	
AORIST	(as Present)			αιμι	αις	αι	αι *
				αιμεν	αιτε	αιεν	
					αιτον	αίτην	

248. Besides the *Aorist Optative* in *αιμι*, another is
n use (called the *Æolic Aorist*) in *εια*.   In the *second*
and *third sing.* and *third plur.* this is far more common than the other form.—*ειας, ειε.*—plur. *ειαν.*

* *With accent on* penult.

249. EXAMPLES.

PRESENT.		AORIST.	
Subjunctive.	**Optative.**	**Subjunctive.**	**Optative.**
λύ-ω	λύ-οιμι	λύ-σω	λύ-σαιμι
λύ-ῃς	λύ-οις	λύ-σῃς	λύ-σαις (λύ-σειας)
λύ-ῃ	λύ-οι	λύ-σῃ	λύ-σαι (λύ-σειε[ν])
λύ-ωμει	λύ-οιμεν	λύ-σωμεν	λύ-σαιμεν
λύ-ητε	λύ-οιτε	λύ-σητε	λύ-σαιτε
λύ-ωσι(ν)	λύ-οιεν	λύ-σωσι(ν)	λύ-σαιεν (λύ-σειαν)
λύ-ητον	λύ-οιτον	λύ-σητον	λύ-σαιτον
λύ-ητον	λυ-οίτην	λύ-σητον	λυ-σαίτην

Subjunctive.			Optative.		
So,		PRESENT.			
τύπτ-ω,	ῃς,	ῃ, &c.	τύπτ-οιμι,	οις,	οι, &c.
λέγ-ω,	ῃς,	ῃ, &c.	λέγ-οιμι,	οις,	οι, &c.
πείθ-ω,	ῃς,	ῃ, &c.	πείθ-οιμι,	οις,	οι, &c.
θαυμάζ-ω,	ῃς,	ῃ, &c.	θαυμάζ-οιμι,	οις,	οι, &c.
		AORIST.			
τύψ-ω,	ῃς,	ῃ, &c.	τύψ-αιμι,	αις,	αι, &c.
λέξ-ω,	ῃς,	ῃ, &c.	λέξ-αιμι,	αις,	αι, &c.
πείσ-ω,	ῃς,	ῃ, &c.	πείσ-αιμι,	αις,	αι, &c.
θαυμάσ-ω,	ῃς,	ῃ, &c.	θαυμάσ-αιμι,	αις,	αι, &c.
τιμήσ-ω,	ῃς,	ῃ, &c.	τιμήσ-αιμι,	αις,	αι, &c.

(Opt. Aor. also τύψ-εια, ᾰς, &c. λέξ-εια, ας, &c.)

250. *a*) In the *Optative* (as in the *Subjunctive*, 244), the *Present* refers to a *continued* or *repeated* action ; the *Aorist* to a *single, definite* one.

b) The *Optative* (like the Latin *Imperfect Subjunctive*) follows ἵνα, ὅπως, ὡς (= *ut*) when they depend on an *historical* tense (242).

c) ☞ Ἵνα, ὅπως, ὡς are followed by μή (not οὐ), μηδείς (not οὐδείς), &c.

251. VOCABULARY 27.

Talked about every-where, περιβό-ητος, ον : περιβόητον εἶναι, *to be the common talk.*

Quietness, rest, ἡσυχία, ας, ἡ : ἡσυχίαν ἄγειν, *to keep quiet.*

Recompense, punishment, τιμωρία, ας, ἡ.

Act of impiety, an impiety, ἀσέβημα, ἀσεβήματ-ος, τό.

Manifest, evident, δῆλος, η, ον.

Place, τόπος, ου, ὁ.

Destitute of, ἐρῆμος, η, ον (with gen.) : it may be translated 'without.'

Possessing a right, κύριος, a, ον : κύριός εἰμι ποιεῖν τι, I have the right to do any thing.

Windy, full of wind, ὑπηνέμιος, ον : ὑπηνέμιον ᾠόν, a wind-egg, which produces no chicken.

Yesterday, χθές (adv. cĩas).

Lycurgus, Λυκοῦργος, ου, ὁ.

Tυ bid, tell, order, κελεύ-ειν.

To remain (in a country, &c.), καταμέν-ειν.

Hither, here (= hither), δεῦρο.

To perceive, to discover, κατανοεῖν (= -έειν).

To be present, παρεῖναι (Imperf. παρῆν, ἦς, ἦ, ἦμεν, ἦτε, ἦσαν, ἦτον, ἤτην. Partic. παρών, οὖσα, όν. Gen. παρόντος, &c.).

To call, καλεῖν (= -έειν) : fut. and aor. with ε, not η : καλέσω ; ἐκάλεσα.

Dinner, δεῖπνον, ου, τό : καλεῖν ἐπὶ δεῖπνον, to invite to dinner.

To hope, ἐλπίζ-ειν.

To commit a fault, sin, ἁμαρτάν-ειν.

To seek, to look for, ζητεῖν (= -έειν).

252. PARADIGMS.

PRESENT.—Εἰμί, I am.								
Indicative.			Subjunctive.			Optative.		
S. εἰμί	εἶ	ἐστί(ν)	ὦ	ῆς	ῆ	εἴην	εἴης	εἴη
P. ἐσμέν	ἐστέ	εἰσί(ν)	ὦμεν	ῆτε	ὦσι(ν)	εἴημεν	εἴητε	εἴησαν and εἶεν
D.	ἐστόν	ἐστόν		ῆτον	ῆτον		εἴητον	εἰήτην

IMPERFECT.—Ἦν, I was.								
Sing.			Plur.			Dual.		
ἦν	ἦσθα	ἦν	ἦμεν	ῆτε	ῆσαν or ῆστε	ῆστον	ῆστην or ῆτον or ἤτην

Exercise 32.

(Learn Paradigms 41, 42, 43, 45.)

253. a) *Translate into English.*

1. Ἐγὼ τότε, ἵνα μὴ περιβόητος εἴην, ἡσυχίαν ἦγον.

2. Ἡ ψυχὴ ἡγεῖται τιμωρίαν οἱ (= sibi) ἥξειν τῶν ἀσεβημάτων.　3. Μένων ὁ Θετταλὸς δῆλός ἐστιν[18] ἐπιθυμῶν[a] ἄρχειν, ὅπως πλείω[b] λαμβάνῃ.　4· Μένων ὁ Θετταλὸς δῆλος ἦν ἐπιθυμῶν τιμᾶσθαι,[c] ἵνα πλείω κερ-

δαίνοι. 5. Σεύθης πέμπει τὸν ἑαυτοῦ ἑρμηνέα πρὸς Ξενοφῶντα, κελεύων αὐτὸν καταμεῖναι,ᵈ παρ' ἑαυτῷ χιλίους ὁπλίτας ἔχοντα.ᵗᵛ 6. Οἱ πέρδικες οὐκ ἐν τῷ αὐτῷ τίκτουσι καὶ ἐπωάζουσι, ἵνα μή τις κατανοήσῃ τὸν τόπον. 7. Λυκοῦργος, ὅπως μὴ ἔρημοί ποτε· οἱ παῖδες εἶεν ἄρχοντος, ἐποίησε τὸν ἀεὶ παρόντα τῶν πολιτῶν ᶠ κύριον εἶναι κολάζειν, εἴ τι ᵍ ἁμαρτάνοιεν. 8. Ὦ Ἀριστόδημε, καὶ χθὲς ἐζήτουν ʰ σε, ἵνα καλέσαιμι δεῦρ' ἐπὶ δεῖπνον. 9. Ἅπερ· (Pdm. 49) αὐτοὶ σφᾶς αὐτοὺς οὐκ ἔπεισαν, ὑμᾶς ἐλπίζουσι πείσειν (fut. infin.). 10. Παρῆσαν καὶ οἱ ῥήτορες ἵνα τὸν δῆμον τοῖς σοφοῖς λόγοις πείσειαν.

ᵃ = ἐπιθυμέ-ων, pres. particip. (nom. m.)   ᵇ Note 7.   ᶜ = τιμάεσθαι, to be honoured.   ᵈ to remain (Aor. Infin.): παρά (by) here = with.   ᵉ ποτέ (ever), indefinite, is enclitic. ἔρημος, gen.   ᶠ τὸν τῶν πολιτῶν ἀεὶ παρόντα = illum ex civibus, qui quovis tempore praesens esset. In this way ἀεὶ (semper) = at any given time. Hence ὁ ἀεὶ παρὼν τῶν πολιτῶν = any citizen who happened to be present at the time. ᵍ Neut. of τὶς. ἁμαρτάνειν τι = to commit any fault.   ʰ = ἐζήτε-ον.

b) Translate into Greek.

1. They expunged the law, that they might cut-off the vexatious-informations. 2. The young-man is admiring *his* (own) horse. 3. The boy evidently admires⁴⁸ the Hoplite. 4. The orators had evidently not persuaded even themselves. 5. The orator was-there, that he might persuade the people of the Athenians. 6. The generals were-there, that they might sharpen the passions of the people. 7. The peacocks lay wind-eggs. 8. Who saw the men from the Piræus? 9. Most men (*say:* 'the most of men') love honors and honorary-privileges.

LESSON XXXV.

Some of the Passive Tenses.

254. Passive.

Present.	*Imperfect.*	*Future.*	*Aorist.*
ομαι	όμην	3ήσομαι	3ην

255. The Imperfect and Aorist take the augment; the terminations beginning with Ꝺ will affect the final consonant of a *mute root*, because ☞ *when two mutes come together, they must be of the same order of breathing* (i. e. both *smooth* mutes, both *middle*, or both *aspirate*). Hence *to retain the* Ꝺ, we must change the *final consonant* of the root (called the *characteristic*) into the corresponding aspirate. Thus

$$\textit{any p-sound with } \; \Theta = \phi\Theta,$$
$$\textit{any k-sound with } \; \Theta = \chi\Theta.$$

256. Hence, (*a*) τριβ-3ήσομαι = τριφ3ήσομαι : πεμπ-3ήσομα == πεμφ3ήσομαι.—Ἀλειφ-3ήσομαι requires no change.

b) Πλεκ-3ήσομαι = πλεχ-3ήσομαι : φλεγ-3ήσομαι = φλεχ-3ήσομαι.—Βρεχ-3ήσομαι requires no change.

c) A *t*-sound before Ꝺ is changed into *s*. Hence ψευδ-3ήσομαι = ψευσ-3ήσομαι : πειϑ-3ήσομαι, πεισ-3ήσομαι.

257. *a*) Verbs whose root ends in ππ, κτ, ζ, σσ, ττ, are lengthened forms from simpler roots. The final consonant of that *simpler root* is called the *true characteristic.*

b) The true characteristic of verbs in ππ is a *p*-sound (π, β, or φ).

c) The true characteristic of verbs in κτ is a *k*-sound (κ, γ, or χ).

d) The true characteristic of verbs in ζ is *usually* δ (a *t*-sound) : but sometimes a *k*-sound (235. 2. *c*).

e) The true characteristic of verbs in σσ, ττ, is *usu-*

ally a *k*-sound : but sometimes a *t*-sound (235. 2. *d*).—
Hence

258. *a*) Verbs in ππ follow the *p*-sounds, and have
fut. and aor. φ-θησομαι, φ-θην.

b) Verbs in κτ, and *usually* those in σσ, ττ, follow
the *k*-sounds, and have χ-θησομαι, χ-θην.

c) Verbs in ζ *usually* follow the *t*-sounds, and have
σ-θησομαι, σ-θην.

d) Verbs in αω, εω, οω, lengthen the *characteristic*
vowel, as in the Future Active, by (usually) changing
a, ε, o, into η, η, ω, respectively.

259. EXAMPLES.

	Present.	Imperfect.	Future.	Aorist.
p-sounds	τρίβ-ομαι	ἐ-τριβ-όμην	τριφ-θήσομαι	ἐ-τρίφ-θην
	πέμπ-ομαι	ἐ-πεμπ-όμην	πεμφ-θήσομαι	ἐ-πέμφ-θην
	τύπτ-ομαι	ἐ-τυπτ-όμην	τυφ-θήσομαι	ἐ-τύφ-θην.
k-sounds	πλέκ-ομαι	ἐ-πλεκ-όμην	πλεχ-θήσομαι	ἐ-πλέχ-θην
	λέγ-ομαι	ἐ-λεγ-όμην	λεχ-θήσομαι	ἐ-λέχ-θην
	ἄρχ-ομαι	ἠρχ-όμην	ἀρχ-θήσομαι	ἤρχ-θην.
t-sounds	ψεύδ-ομαι	ἐ-ψευδ-όμην	ψευσ-θήσομαι	ἐ-ψεύσ-θην
	πείθ-ομαι	ἐ-πειθ-όμην	πεισ-θήσομαι	ἐ-πείσ-θην.
ζ.	θαυμάζ-ομαι	ἐ-θαυμαζ-όμην	θαυμασ-θήσομαι	ἐ-θαυμάσ-θην
σσ, ττ	τάσσ-ομαι	ἐ-τασσ-όμην	} ταχ-θήσομαι	ἐ-τάχ-θην.
	τάττ-ομαι	ἐ-ταττ-όμην	}	

260. *Pure Verbs :*

φιλέ-ω	φιλοῦμαι*	ἐ-φιλούμην	φιλη-θήσομαι	ἐ-φιλή-θην
τιμά-ω	τιμῶμαι†	ἐ-τιμώμην	τιμη-θήσομαι	ἐ-τιμή-θην
δουλό-ω	δουλοῦμαι‡	ἐ-δουλούμην	δουλω-θήσομαι	ἐ-δουλώ-θην
λύω	λύ-ομαι	ἐ-λυ-όμην	λυ-θήσομαι	ἐ-λύ-θην.

261. NOTE. The verbs whose characteristic is a *liquid*, have
more peculiarities, and will be treated of separately.

262. Terminations: ομαι, both in *Present* and *Fut.*,
as in Pres. of deponent verbs (η, εται, &c.). Cf. 151.

---

* = φιλέ-ομαι, ἐ-φιλε-όμην.　　　† = τιμά-ομαι, ἐ-τιμα-όμην.

‡ = δουλό-ομαι, ἐ-δουλο-όμην.

IMPERF. ὀμην, ου, ετο	ὀμεϑα, εσϑε, οντο	ὀμεϑον, εσϑον, ἐσϑην
AOR. ην, ης, η	ημεν, ητε, ησαν	ητον, ἠτην

263. NOTE. The other persons of the *contracted* forms (οὐμην **ὠμην**) will not be used at present.

264. The terminations of the participles are :

Pres.   Fut.   Aor.

ὀμενος ϑησόμενος ϑείς (*cum acuto*)

(ϑης-)ό-μενος, -μένη, -μενον, regular

-ϑείς, -ϑεῖσα, -ϑέν, G. -ϑέντος, &c. (Pdm. 34.)

265. *On the augment of verbs compounded with a preposition.*

a) The general rule is, that the augment *follows the preposition.*

b) The final vowel of the prepositions that end in a vowel, is elided, except in περί and πρό. Προ-ἐ is often changed by what is called *crasis* [Note 11] into προὐ (the breathing being marked over the υ): ἀπο-βάλλω, ἀπ-έ-βαλλον : but περι-βάλλω, περι-έ-βαλλον, προ-βάλλ-ω, προ-έ-βαλλον = προὒ-βαλλον.

c) The prepositions ἐν, σύν, have often undergone a change by being *assimilated* to the initial consonant of the verb according to the following laws :

ν before a *p*-sound, or ψ, becomes μ.

ν before a *k*-sound, or ξ, becomes γ.

ν before a liquid becomes that liquid.

266. When ἐν, σύν, have been thus *assimilated,* they will resume their *natural* form before ε.

	(by assimilation)	(Imperf.)
ἐν-βάλλω	= ἐμ-βάλλω	ἐν-έ-βαλλον
συν-βάλλω	= συμ-βάλλω	συν-έ-βαλλον
ἐν-κλείω	= ἐγ-κλείω	ἐν-έ-κλειον
ἐν-χέω	= ἐγ-χέω	ἐν-έ-χεον
ἐν-μένω	= ἐμ-μένω	ἐν-έ-μενον
ἐν-λείπω	= ἐλ-λείπω	ἐν-έ-λειπον.

d) 'Ἐκ will become ἐξ before a vowel : ἐκ-βάλλ-ω, ἐξ-έ-βαλλον.

267. Vocabulary 28.

To educate, παιδεύ-ειν.

Mars's hill, the hill of the Areopagus, Ἄρειος πάγος (Ἄρειος = Martius).

Kindly, εὐμενῶς.

To receive, ὑποδέχ-εσθαι.

To worst, κακίζ-ειν.

The Mede (= Xerxes), ὁ Μῆδος.

Retreat, ἀναχώρησις, εως, ἡ.

Circuit (of walls, &c.), περίβολος, ου, ὁ.

Every-where, on all sides, πανταχῇ (or χῇ).

To carry farther out, to extend. ἐξάγ-ειν.

To send down (to a country nearer the coast), καταπέμπ-ειν.

Satrap, σατράπης, ου, ὁ.

To torture, put to the rack, βασανίζ-ειν : (βάσανος, touch-stone, test ; torture.)

Marriage, γάμος, ου, ὁ.

To keep silence, hold one's tongue, σιωπᾶν (= ἄειν).

To dissolve, to destroy (i. e. a form of government), καταλύ-ειν.

Democracy, δημοκρατία, ας, ἡ.

Oligarchy, ὀλιγαρχία, ας, ἡ.

To slay, to murder, φονεύ-ειν.

Tyrant, τύραννος, ου, ὁ. (In the Greek sense, one who ruled by his own will, not by law ; usually after having obtained absolute power in a state that ought to be free.)

Teacher, διδάσκαλος, ου, ὁ.

To be tempest-tossed, to be tossed by a storm, χειμάζ-εσθαι.

To put in at, land at, προσμίσγ-ειν (with dat.).

Tarentum, Τάρας, -αντος, ὁ.

More quickly, more easily, θᾶττον.

To acquit, ἀπολύ-ειν.

Exercise 33.

268. a) Translate into English.

1. Ὁ Κῦρος ἐπαιδεύθη ἐν τοῖς Περσῶν νόμοις. 2. Ἀπὸ τοῦ Ἰλισσοῦ· λέγεται ὁ Βορέας τὴν Ὠρείθυιαν ἁρπάσαι·ᵇ λέγεται αὖ καὶ ὁ λόγος, ὡς ἐξ Ἀρείου πάγου ἡρπάσθη. 3. Κακισθέντας ὑμᾶς οὐδεὶς εὐμενῶς ὑποδέξεται. 4. Μετὰ τὴν τοῦ Μήδου ἀναχώρησιν μείζων ὁ περίβολος πανταχῇ ἐξήχθη· τῆς τῶν Ἀθηναίων πόλεως 5. Κῦρος κατ-ε-πέμφθη ὑπὸ τοῦ πατρὸς σατράπης Λυδίας τε καὶ Φρυγίας καὶ Καππαδοκίας. 6. Ἀρ' οὐκ ἐβασανί-

σθησαν οἱ δοῦλοι ;   7. Τὴν ἐν Ἐρετρίᾳ ὀλιγαρχίαν τὴν
τῶν ἱππέων Διαγόρας·δὴ¹² κατέλυσεν ἀδικηθεὶς περὶ γά-
μον.   8. Ὁ κριτὴς ὑβρισθεὶς ὑπὸ τούτου οὐ σιωπᾷ.   9.
Ὁ Ἕκτωρ ὑπὸ τοῦ Ἀχιλλέως ἐφονεύθη.   10. Τὼ ἀδελ-
φὼ ὑπὸ τοῦ αὐτοῦ διδασκάλου ἐπαιδευθήτην. .11. Πολλαὶ δημοκρατίαι ὑπὸ τῶν τυράννων κατελύθησαν.   12.
Ψευσθήσομαι τῶν ἐλπίδων.   13. Ὁ Γύλιππος χειμα-
σθεὶς ἐς τὰ μάλιστα[d] τῷ Τάραντι προσμίσγει.   14.
Εἰ νυνὶ σοῦ[e] ἀκούσας ἐλθεῖν[f] πεισθήσομαι, πολὺ θᾶττον
ὑπ’ αὐτοῦ καὶ πάλιν ἐλθεῖν πεισθήσομαι.   15. Οἱ τοῦ
βιβλιοπώλου δοῦλοι ἐβασανίζοντο.

* The *Ilissus*, a river in Attica.   For the fable of *Boreas* and *Ori-
thyia*, see Keightley's Mythol.   b = *to have carried off.*   c μείζων ἐξήχθη, lit. *was carried out larger*, i. e. *was carried further out*, and
so became *larger*.   Hence μείζων is a *proleptic* (= *anticipative*) predicate ; as in μέγας ηὐξήθη ('*he was increased great*' =) *he grew great.*
  d The adv. μάλιστα (= *maxime*) is here used *adverbially* with the
article and *prep.* Translate, '*with extreme violence,*' '*most violently.*'
* σοῦ, gen. after ἀκούειν = *to listen to* (an adviser).   f ἐλθεῖν, *to go.*

b) Translate into Greek.

1. O slaves, you will be examined-by-torture. 2.
His slaves having been examined-by-torture, he will be
acquitted. 3. You were both taught by the same master. 4. You will all be insulted by these persons. 5.
I will not be persuaded to do this.' 6. The Mede was
disappointed of his expectation. 7. Gylippus, being
seized by the wind, is carried-out to sea. 8. The garlands shall be woven. 9. The slaves of Xenophon
were insulting the wise geometer. 10. We were all
taught wisdom by the same teacher.

LESSON XXXVI.

Middle Voice.

269. Besides the *Active* and *Passive Voices*, the Greek language has a *Middle Voice*, which denotes an action (1) *done* by the agent *to himself;* or (more commonly) one which (2) he *does for his own benefit;* or (3) *gets done for his own benefit.*

The relation, however, to *oneself* is often much more distant and obscure.

Middle verbs may be considered *Deponents*, when their *middle force* is so slight, that they appear to have the simple meaning of *active* verbs.

OBS. The *Middle Voice* does not belong to all the verbs that are capable of receiving the meanings just mentioned.—The pupil must never *assume* its existence without authority.

270. ☞ It is only for the *Futures* and *Aorists* that the *Middle Voice* has forms of its own. For the *Present, Imperfect, Perfect,* and *Pluperfect*, it does not differ *in form* from the *Passive.*

271. Such *Middle Verbs* as may be considered *Deponents*, are divided into

   1. *Deponents Middle* = those with *Future* and *Aorist* of the *middle* form.

   2. *Deponents Passive* = those whose *Aorist* is of the *passive form;* their *Future* is mostly of the *middle* form.

272. The terminations of the *Future* and *Aor. Middle* are (for all but *liquid* verbs : see 274) :

	FUT.	AOR.
Indic.	σομαι	σάμην
Infin.	σεσθαι	σασθαι
Particip.	σόμενος	σάμενος

273. These terminations are appended like σω, σα, in the *Active* (141) ; the *Aor.* taking the augment (123, 124) in the *Indicative*, but not in the Moods and Participle.

μετα-πέμπομαι	μετα-πέμψομαι	μετ-ε-πεμψάμην
δέχομαι	δέξομαι	ἐ-δεξάμην
ἀλείφομαι	ἀλείψομαι	ἠλειψάμην
δουλό-ομαι	δουλώσομαι	ἐ-δουλωσάμην
λούομαι	λούσομαι	ἐ-λουσάμην

Both for *Act.* and *Mid.* a after any of the letters in ρει (i. e. ρ, ε, or ι) is lengthened into ā (not η) ; but χράομαι, χρήσομαι, is an exception. Ἀκροάομαι makes ἀκροάσομαι.

274. Verbs whose roots end in a *liquid*, have for the terminations of the *Fut.* and *Aor. Mid.* οῦμαι and άμην, the *radical* vowel being shortened in the *Future* and lengthened in the *Aorist*, as in the Active Voice (237).

275. The terminations of the Fut. Indic. (except for *liquid* verbs) are the same as those of the Present *Indic.* (151).

IMPERF.	όμην	ου	ετο
	όμεθα	εσθε	οντο
	όμεθον	εσθον	έσθην
AOR.	(σ)άμην	(σ)ω	(σ)ατο
	(σ)άμεθα	(σ)ασθε	(σ)αντο
	(σ)άμεθον	(σ)ασθον	(σ)άσθην

276. The Fut. of the liquid verbs is :

οῦμαι	ῇ or εῖ	εῖται
ούμεθα	εῖσθε	οῦνται
ούμεθον	εῖσθον	εῖσθον

277. VOCABULARY 29.

(Learn ἐλυόμην. λύσομαι. ἐλυσάμην. Paradigm 58.)

Provide myself with, παρασκευάζ-ομαι (παρασκευάζ-ω, *to prepare, provide*).

Enslave to myself, subjugate, δουλοῦμαι (= δουλό-ομαι) : δουλῶ τινὰ τῷ βασιλεῖ.

To wage war (from *one's own* resources, &c.), πόλεμον ποι-εῖσθαι : πόλεμον ποιεῖν = *to cause a war.*

ποιεῖσθαι, 1) sibi facere ; 2) sibi faciendum curare ; 3) putare, credere ; e. g. in δεινὸν ποιεῖ-σθαι, *to think it a terrible thing.*

To make it for oneself (i. e. in one's judgment) of less value than = *to think* any thing of less importance than, περὶ ἐλάττο-νος ποιεῖσθαί τι.

. (*I give myself to taste* =) *I taste* (*of*), gen. γεύομαι. Γεύειν = to give another *to taste.*

I wash (myself), λού-ομαι.

To anoint myself, ἀλείφ-εσθαι.

To brighten, to polish, λαμπρύν-ειν : λαμπρύν-εσθαι, *to polish* (any thing of one's own).

To cease, leave off, παύ-εσθαι (παύ-ω, *stop* another, *make to cease*).

To begin (to do any thing, i. e. by applying *my own* strength, &c.), ἄρχ-εσθαι.

I advise a person, συμβουλεύω τινί : *I consult with him,* συμ-βουλεύομαί τινι.

(*Give counsel to* myself =) *de-termine, resolve,* βουλεύ-ομαι.

(*I make trial of* myself =) *try, endeavor,* πειρά-ομαι.

I hide, conceal myself, ἀποκρύπτ-ομαι (ἐμαυτόν, Plat.) : also, (nearly as in the Act.) *to hide, conceal.*

To go through, relate, διηγέ-ομαι.

To revenge myself on, to punish, τιμωρέ-ομαι.

To serve in the field, to serve, to march, στρατεύ-ομαι.

To strike, παί-ειν : Mid. if to strike part *of oneself.*

Thigh, μηρός, οῦ, ὁ.

Shield, ἀσπίς, ἀσπίδ-ος, ἡ.

Companion, ἑταῖρος, ου, ὁ.

To transgress, παραβαίν-ειν.

Jail, ἱστίον, ου, τό.

Rudder, πηδάλιον, ου, τό.

Pilot, κυβερνήτης, ου, ὁ.

To ward off, ἀμύν-ειν : Mid. *to ward off from one's self;* also *to revenge oneself* upon any bo-dy (acc. of person : *on account* of or *for* any thing, ὑπέρ τινος).

To enjoin, to command, ἐντέλλ-εσθαι.

To rush, ὁρμᾶν (= -άειν.)

(*To show forth from oneself* =) *to declare,* ἀποφαίν-εσθαι.

I prepare, κατασκευάζ-ω : *I pre-pare for myself* = *I build, I equip* (vessels), κατασκευάζ-ομαι.

5*

☞ (1) A middle verb may take a reflexive pronoun, ἐμαυτῷ, -όν, ἑαυτῷ, -όν, &c. (2) The *Active* may be used with the reflexive pron.: σφάττειν ἑαυτόν.

Exercise 34.

278. a) Translate into English.

1. Τελαμὼν ὁ Αἰακοῦ μεθ' Ἡρακλέους ἐπὶ Λαομέδοντα ἐστρατεύσατο. 2. Ὀλίγον[a] πρὸ τῶν Μηδικῶν[b] καὶ τοῦ Δαρείου θανάτου, ὃς μετὰ Καμβύσην Περσῶν ἐβασίλευσεν, οἱ περὶ τὴν Σικελίαν τύραννοι τριήρεις κατεσκευάσαντο. 3. Πρῶτον διηγήσασθαι βούλομαι τὰ πραχθέντα τῇ τελευταίᾳ ἡμέρᾳ.[c] 4. Οὐκ ἐγώ σε ἀποκτενῶ, ἀλλ' ὁ τῆς πόλεως νόμος, ὃν σὺ παραβαίνων περὶ ἐλάττονος τῶν ἡδονῶν ἐποιήσω. 5. Οὐδὲν ἀποκρυψάμενος ἅπαντα διηγήσομαι ὑμῖν τὰ πεπραγμένα. 6. Πειράσομαι μεθ' ὑμῶν[d] τὸν ἄνδρα τιμωρήσασθαι. 7. Πάντες ἐλούσαντο. 8. Εἰς βαλανεῖον ἥκω λουσόμενος.[e] 9. Ταῦτ' ἀκούσας ὁ Κῦρος ἐπαίσατο τὸν μηρόν. 10. Ὁ Κῦρος πᾶσαν τὴν Ἀσίαν κατ-ε-στρέψατο. 11. Ἆγις οὐκ ἐκ παρέργου[e] τὸν πόλεμον ἐποιήσατο. 12. Οἱ στρατιῶται ἐλαμπρύνοντο τὰς ἀσπίδας. 13. Ἐν τῷ ἔξω[f] δρόμῳ ἠλείφοντο ἑταῖροί τέ τινες αὐτοῦ καὶ αὐτός. 14. Οἱ πολῖται τοὺς πολεμίους ὑπὲρ πολλῶν ἀδικημάτων ἀμυνοῦνται. 15. Ὁ στρατηγὸς τοῖς στρατιώταις ἐνετείλατο ἐπὶ τοὺς πολεμίους ὁρμῆσαι. 16. Ὁ κριτὴς τὴν γνώμην ἀπεφήνατο.

[a] *a little.*   [b] τὰ Μηδικά (*the Median* affairs =) the Persian invasion.   [c] Dat. of time : ἐν is expressed when there is no *adjective* or other attributive.   [d] *with you* = with your assistance.
[e] ἐκ παρέργου ποιεῖσθαι, *to make it a bye-business; to treat it as a thing of little* (or *secondary*) *importance.*   [f] ὁ ἔξω (= exterior), *the outer.*

b) Translate into Greek.

1. The enemy will march against our city. 2. We will deliberate about the safety of the citizens. 3. The

Greeks marched against the Persians. 4. All men wish to taste of honor. 5. The pilot provided himself with sails and rudders for his ship ᵉ •t h a t w e r e good for nothing. 6. His companions having anointed-themselves are coming hither. 7. The Mede will not enslave Europe. 8. After he had washed,⁵⁸ the children were brought ʰ toˢ⁹ him. 9. We will declare our opinions. 10. We revenged ourselves on the Lacedæmonians for their invasion of Attica.

ᵉ *ship, ναῦς:* see Irregular Substantives, Note 9.   ʰ *φέρειν* (ferre), *to bring* (= *carry*), has irreg. aor. pass. *ἠνέχϑην.* See List VII., Pdm. 74.

LESSON XXXVII.

Ἄν with Imperfect and Aorist of the Indicative.

279. The particle *ἄν* has a *conditional* force (= *si forte*). With the *Imperfect Indicative* this particle is usually translated by '*would* ——;' the *Aorist Indic.* by '*would have* ——.'

280. But sometimes the *Imperfect* with *ἄν* is translated by '*would have* ——.' This is when *continuance* or *repeated occurrence* at a past time is to be intimated.

     ἔ-λῡ-ον ἄν, solverem (*I would loosen*).
     ἔ-λῡσ-α ἄν, solvissem (*I would have loosened*).

     1. *εἰ ἐκέλευες, ἐποίουν ἄν* (si juberes, facerem), *if you ordered me, I would do it.*

     2. *εἰ ἐκέλευσας, ἐποίησα ἄν* (si jussisses, fecissem) *if you had ordered me, I would have done it.*

3. εἰ μὴ ἐκέλευσας, οὐκ ἂν ἐποίησα (nisi jussisses, non fecissem), *if you had not ordered me, I would not have done it.*

Obs. (a) that the *Aor.* with *εἰ* is rendered by the *English* Pluperfect: (b) that '*not*' with *εἰ* is μή.

On the place of ἄν, see Note 10.

281. Vocabulary 30.

To care for, κήδ-εσθαι.

To be on one's *guard*, φυλάττ-εσθαι (cavēre) : ποιεῖν τι, *I am on my guard against doing any thing ; I am careful not to do it.*

To deprive (acc. of person, gen. of thing), ἀποστερ-εῖν (= -έειν).

To hinder, κωλύ-ειν.

Consideration, reputation, dignity, ἀξίωμα, -ατος, τό.

To differ, διαφέρ-ειν: hence (*to be distinguished* favorably *from*=) *to excel, to surpass* (gen. of person, acc. of thing, or ἔν τινι).

Dreadful, terrible, δεινός, ή, όν.

To value, τιμᾶσθαι (= -άεσθαι) : ἐτιμησάμην ἂν πρὸ πολλῶν χρημάτων, answers to our ' *I would have given a great deal*' (lit. ' would have valued beyond much money ').

So large, τηλικοῦτος (tantus), Pdm. 52.

To be able, δύνασθαι (irreg. inf.) = *posse*, with adjectives of *quantity* (like *multum, plus, minus*, tantum valere, &c.), = ' to have much (more, so much) power.'

Sophist, σοφιστής, οῦ, ὁ.

To conquer, κρατ-εῖν (= -έειν), with gen.

To wall in, to wall round, τεχίζ-εσθαι:——ἔρυμα (lit. to wall round a stronghold =), *to construct a fortified camp.*

Brazier, coppersmith, χαλκοτύπος, ου, ὁ.

Worker in iron, blacksmith, σιδηρεύς, έως, ὁ.

Worker in leather, shoemaker, saddler, σκυτεύς, έως, ὁ.

To work, perform, ἐργάζ-εσθαι (= operari) : it changes ε into ει in the augmented tenses.

Workshop, ἐργαστήριον, ου, τό.

Carpenter, τέκτων, -ονος, ὁ.

Exercise 35.

282. *a) Translate into English.*

1. Εἴ τι ἐμοῦ ἐκήδου, οὐδενὸς ἂν οὕτως μ' ἀποστερεῖν ἐφυλάττου, ὡς ἀξιώματος καὶ τιμῆς. 2. Εἰ μὴ ὑμεῖς ἐκωλύετε, ἐπορευόμεθα ἂν ἐπὶ βασιλέα. 3. Εἰ

τὸ ἔχειν οὕτως, ὥσπερ τὸ λαμβάνειν, ἡδὺ ἦν, πολὺ ἂν διέφερον εὐδαιμονίᾳ οἱ πλούσιοι τῶν πενήτων. 4. Ὁ θάνατος οὐδὲν δεινόν, ἐπεὶ* καὶ Σωκράτει ἂν ἐφαίνετο. 5. Ἐγὼ πρὸ πολλῶν ἂν χρημάτων ἐτιμησάμην τηλικοῦτον δύνασθαι τὴν φιλοσοφίαν, ὅσον οἱ σοφισταὶ λέγουσιν. 6. Εἰ μὴ μάχῃ ἐκράτησαν, τὸ ἔρυμα τῷ στρατοπέδῳ οὐκ ἂν ἐτειχίσαντο. 7. Οἱ χαλκοτύποι καὶ οἱ τέκτονες καὶ οἱ σιδηρεῖς καὶ σκυτεῖς καὶ γραφεῖς πάντες πολεμικὰ ὅπλα κατεσκεύαζον· ὥστε τὴν πόλιν ὄντως ἡγήσω ἂν πολέμου ἐργαστήριον εἶναι. 8. Οἱ παῖδες πρὸς φιλοσοφίαν ἄριστα[b] ἐπαιδεύθησαν. 9. Κόννος ὁ Μητροβίου ἐμοῦ κάκῖον[b] ἐπαιδεύθη. 10. Κλεόφαντος πολλὰ καὶ θαυμαστὰ εἰργάζετο, ἃ ὁ πατὴρ αὐτὸν ἐπαιδεύσατο.[c]

* ἐπεί, since; a conditional clause is implied: since if it were so; or, 'since otherwise;' 'else.' [b] Neuter adj. ἄριστος, best: κακίων, worse. Neuter Adjectives are often used adverbially: the plural of the superlative is the more common; the singular of the comparative. [c] The Middle Voice sometimes means to get a thing done (269, 8). Hence παιδεύεσθαι = to have a person taught (erudiendum curare). The Aor. has here the force of Pluperf.

b) Translate into Greek.

1. In this way (οὕτως) you would have been well trained to virtue. 2. Let them rejoice * in being trained to virtue. 3. Let no one suppose you to say, that we ought to look to advantage, and not to what is just.[d] 4. If we had not been excellently trained up to virtue, we should not ever have conquered our desires. 5. If these things were true, I should not hinder you.

d τὸ δίκαιον.

LESSON XXXVIII.

283. *Moods of Present Pass. and Mid. · First Aorist Middle.*

Indicative.	Imper.	Subjunc.	Optative.	Infinitive.	Participle.
Pres. λύ-ομαι	λύ-ου	λύ-ωμαι	λυ-οίμην	λύ-εσθαι	λυ-όμενος
Aor. ἐ-λυσ-άμην	λῦσ-αι	λύσ-ωμαι	λυσ-αίμην	λύσ-ασθαι	λυσ-άμενος

	PRESENT.			
	Indicative.	Imperative.	Subjunctive.	Optative.
S.	λύ-ομαι		λύ-ωμαι	λυ-οίμην
	λύ-ῃ	λύ-ου	λύ-ῃ	λύ-οιο
	λύ-εται	λυ-έσθω	λύ-ηται	λύ-οιτο
P.	λυ-όμεθα		λυ-ώμεθα	λυ-οίμεθα
	λύ-εσθε	λύ-εσθε	λύ-ησθε	λύ-οισθε
	λύ-ονται	λυ-έσθωσαν	λύ-ωνται	λύ-οιντο
		or λυ-έσθων		
D.	λυ-όμεθον		λυ-ώμεθον	λυ-οίμεθον
	λύ-εσθον	λύ-εσθον	λύ-ησθον	λύ-οισθον
	λύ-εσθον	λυ-έσθων	λύ-ησθον	λυ-οίσθην

284. (*First*) *Aorist Middle* (in *liquid verbs* without ς).

	Indicative.	Imperative.	Subjunctive.	Optative.
S.	ἐ-λυ-σάμην		λύ-σωμαι	λυ-σαίμην
	ἐ-λύ-σω	λῦ-σαι	λύ-σῃ	λύ-σαιο
	ἐ-λύ-σατο	λυ-σάσθω	λύ-σηται	λύ-σαιτο
P.	ἐ-λυ-σάμεθα		λυ-σώμεθα	λυ-σαίμεθα
	ἐ-λύ-σασθε	λύ-σασθε	λύ-σησθε	λύ-σαισθε
	ἐ-λύ-σαντο	λυ-σάσθωσαν	λύ-σωνται	λύ-σαιντο
		or λυ-σάσθων		
D.	ἐ-λυ-σάμεθον		λυ-σώμεθον	λυ-σαίμεθον
	ἐ-λύ-σασθον	λύ-σασθον	λύ-σησθον	λυ-σαισθον
	ἐ-λυ-σάσθην	λυ-σάσθων	λύ-σησθον	λυ-σαίσθην

285. ☞ Βούλομαι (*velle*) and οἴομαι (*putare*) take ει (not ῃ) in the second singular of the Present Indicative.

286. The *Optative*, in principal sentences, stands in *wishes* (whence the name *Optative*): λύ-οιμι, *may I loosen* (habitually): λύσ-αιμι, *may I loosen* (once).

287. With εἴθε (= *utinam*) the *Optative* refers to

the *present* or *future*, the *Aorist Indicative* to the *past*, which, being *past*, is *unalterable*.

εἶϑε λύ-οιεν, λύσ-αιεν (utinam solverent), *would that they would loosen.*

εἶϑε ἔλῦσαν (utinam solvissent), *would that they had loosened.*

288. Vocabulary 31.

To be benefited, to derive advantage, ὠφελεῖσϑαι (= ἐ-εσϑαι).

A fed animal, βόσκημα, -ατος, τό. Plur. *cattle* (as fed for the butcher).

To make rich, πλουτίζ-ειν : pass. *to grow rich or be enriched.*

Ungrateful, ἀχάριστος, ον.

Elder (= senior), *an aged person,* πρεσβύτερος, ου, ὁ. (A compar. adj.)

Brother, ἀδελφός, οῦ, ὁ.

To receive, ἀποδέχ-εσϑαι.

Flute, αὐλός, οῦ, ὁ.

If (with subj.), ἐάν (= εἰ ἄν).

Native, national, ἐγχώριος, ον.

To work, ἐργάζ-εσϑαι.

To go, ἔρχ-εσϑαι.

Quiet, ἥσυχος, ον.

To be concealed from, escape the notice of, λανϑάν-ειν (latere), with acc.

To rail at, λοιδορεῖσϑαι (= ἐ-εσϑαι), with dat.

Middle, in the middle, μέσος, η, ον (medius).

To be poor, πέν-εσϑαι.

To do, fare, πράττ-ειν (with adv.): εὖ πράττειν, *to fare well,* to be prosperous.

To delight, ἥδ-εσϑαι (delectare).

To think, οἴ-εσϑαι.

Exercise 36.

289. a) *Translate into English.*

1. Ἡδέσϑω ὑπὸ λόγων ὠφελούμενος ὁ νέος. 2. Μηδεὶς οἰέσϑω με λέγειν, ὡς ἔστι δικαιοσύνη διδακτόν. 3. Εἰ ἀπὸ βοσκημάτων οἴει δεῖν πλουτίζεσϑαι, τῶν βοσκημάτων ἐπιμέλου. 4. Δεινὸν τοῖς πρεσβυτέροις λοιδορήσασϑαι. 5. Ὁ βασιλεὺς ἐνίκησε τοὺς Γελωνοὺς αὐτὸς ἐπ' αὐτοὺς στρατευσάμενος. 6. Γενναίως μαχώμεϑα περὶ τῆς πατρίδος. 7. Ἀναγκαῖόν ἐστι τὸν υἱὸν πείϑεσϑαι τῷ πατρί. 8. Πολλοὶ ἀγαϑοὶ πένονται. 9. Νόμοις τοῖς

ἐγχωρίοις ἕπεσθαι καλόν ἐστιν.   10. Μὴ ἀποδέχου τῶν φίλων τοὺς πρὸς τὰ φαῦλά σοι χαριζομένους.   11. "Εκαστος ἥσυχος μέσην τὴν ὁδὸν ἐρχέσθω.   12. Οἱ πολῖται τοῖς νόμοις πειθέσθων.   13. Τὼ ἀδελφώ μοι ἕπεσθον.   14. Εἰ βούλει καλῶς πράττειν, ἐργάζου.   15. ʼΕὰν βούλῃ καλῶς πράττειν, ἐργάζου.   16. Ψευδόμενος οὐδεὶς λανθάνει πολὺν χρόνον.   17. Οἱ Λακεδαιμόνιοι μετʼ αὐλῶν ἐστρατεύοντο.   18. Εἴθε πάντες ἄνευ ὀργῆς βουλεύοιντο.   19. Δύο καλὼ ἵππω εἰς τὴν πόλιν ἠλαυνέσθην.   20. ʼΕὰν πένῃ, ὀλίγοι φίλοι.   21. Εἴθε τὴν γνώμην καὶ σὺ ἀποφήναιο.

b) Translate into Greek.

1. If (ἐὰν) the soldiers fight courageously, they will be admired.   2. Sons should obey their fathers.   3. Let not an ungrateful man be deemed a friend.   4. Would that you would go-on-the-expedition yourself!   5. Would that the king had himself marched against the Geloni!   6. Let us obey (say : 'follow') the laws of the state.   7. Let nobody rail-at an aged •man.   8. Let nobody rail-at this old man.

LESSON XXXIX.

Moods of Aorist Passive, and Fut. Pass.

290. *Indic.*   *Imp.*   *Subj.*   *Opt.*   *Inf.*   *Particip*

Indic.	Imp.	Subj.	Opt.	Inf.	Particip
ην	ηθι	ῶ	εἴην	ῆναι	εἴς

291. EXAMPLES.

Indicative.	Imperative.	Subjunctive.	Optative.
		FUTURE.	
λυ-θήσομαι	(none.)	(none.)	λυ-θησοίμην
		FIRST AOR.	
S. ἐ-λύ-θην		λυ-θῶ	λυ-θείην
ἐ-λύ-θης	λύ-θητι	λυ-θῆς	λυ-θείης
ἐ-λύ-θη	λυ-θήτω	λυ-θῇ	λυ-θείη
P. ἐ-λύ-θημεν		λυ-θῶμεν	λυ-θείημεν, -θεῖμεν
ἐ-λύ-θητε	λύ-θητε	λυ-θῆτε	λυ-θείητε, -θεῖτε
ἐ-λύ-θησαν	λυ-θήτωσαν or -θέντων	λυ-θῶσι(ν)	λυ-θείησαν, -θεῖεν
D. ἐ-λύ-θητον	λύ-θητον	λυ-θῆτον	λυ-θείητον, -θεῖτον
ἐ-λύ-θητην	λυ-θήτων	λυ-θῆτον	λυ-θειήτην, -θείτην

292. Λύοιμι ἄν, solvam. λύσαιμι ἄν, solvam, solve-
rim : both in English, *I would*, *should*, or (sometimes)
may, *might loosen*. This Optative with ἄν is often
used (as *credam*, *crediderim*, &c. in Latin) to give a
courteous tone of *doubt* and *diffidence* to an opinion
positively entertained. It is often translated by the .
future : λύοιμι ἄν, *I will loosen*.

293. The *Present* Optative with ἄν denotes a *continued* or *repeated* action ; the *Aorist* Optative a *single*, *definite* one, considered
by itself, and without any intimation of its *duration*.

294. In dependent sentences, the *Present* and *Future* are regularly followed by the Subjunctive ; the
Historical tenses *usually* by the Optative (but with
many exceptions). Μανθάνομεν (μαθησόμεθα) ἵνα (ὡς,
ὅπως) παιδευώμεθα (παιδευθῶμεν), *discimus* (*discemus*)
ut erudiamur (*eruditi simus*) ; ἐμανθάνομεν (Αοr. ἐμά-
θομεν*) ἵνα (ὡς, ὅπως) παιδευοίμεθα (παιδευθείημεν),
discebamus (*didicimus*), *ut erudiremur* (*eruditi esse-
mus*). Just so : ἐὰν (ὅταν) μανθάνητε, παιδεύεσθε (παι-

---

* ἔμαθον is what is called a *Second Aorist* from μανθάνω. (List IV.
Pdm. 74): its fut. is of *Mid.* form, μαθήσομαι.

δευθήσεσθε), si (quum) discatis (discitis), erudimini
(erudiemini) ; but εἰ (ὅτε) μανθάνοιεν, ἐπαιδεύοντο, si
(quum) discerent (discebant), erudiebantur.

295. The *Subjunctive* and *Optative* of the *Aorist*,
when connected with particles of *time* and *condition*,
and with the *relative* used *indefinitely* or *hypothetically*
(when, that is, *who* = *whoever, whosoever*, or *if any
one*), answer to the Latin *futurum exactum :* ἐὰν, ὅταν,
ὃς ἂν μάθῃ, εἴσεται, si, quum, qui (= quicunque) *didi-
cerit, intelliget ;* εἶπεν ὅτι, εἰ, ὅτε, ὃς μάθοι, ἐπιστήσεται
(or ἐπιστήσοιτο), *dixit, si, quum, qui* (= quicunque)
didicisset, intellecturum esse.

296. The pupil should observe that, in the examples just given (which are intended for his imitation),
the relative ὅς, and the adverbs of *time* (ὅτε) and *condition* (εἰ), take ἄν when they are connected with the
Subjunctive ; and that the εἰ and ὅτε are *combined*
with this ἄν, and thus assume the forms ἐάν, ὅταν.　So
ἐπεί, ἐπειδή (*quum, postquam*), coalesce with ἄν into
the forms ἐπάν or ἐπήν, and ἐπειδάν.　The ἄν does not
coalesce with ὅπου, *where ;* ὅποι, *whither*, &c.

297. The force added by ἄν to relative pronouns
and particles (see Note 10), is that of the Latin *cunque*,
the English *-ever, -soever*.　Thus ὅπου ἂν στρατοπεδεύωνται (= *where they encamped, if haply* they did encamp =) *wherever they encamped.*—With the *Optative*
without ἄν they have this force in such sentences as
those in 295.

298. Vocabulary 32.

*To throw around themselves, to
surround themselves with,* περι-
βάλλ-εσθαι.　*To entrench themselves,* περιβάλλεσθαι τάφρον.

To encamp, στρατοπεδεύ-εσθαι.
Trench, τάφρος, ου, ἡ.
Multitude of hands or *of work-
men,* πολυχειρία, ας, ἡ.

Easily, εὐπετῶς.

Naturally, reasonably, εἰκότως.

Cowardly, δειλός, ή, όν.

Absurdity, ἀλογία, as, ή. ٭

I asked, ἠρόμην. See ἔρομαι, List I.

Exemption (from taxes, &c.), ἀτέλεια, as, ή.

To compel, ἀναγκάζ-ειν.

Quiet, ἡσυχία, as, ή. To keep quiet, ἡσυχίαν ἔχειν.

To converse, διαλέγ-εσ3αι (with dat.).

Younger, νεώτερος, a, ον.

I sail, take a voyage, πλέ-ω (Aor. ἔ-πλευ-σα).

A seed (of a pomegranate, &c.), κόκκος, ου, ὁ.

Pomegranate, ῥοιά, ᾶς, ή.

To open, ἀνοίγ-ειν.

I said, εἶπον (-ες, -ε).

To judge, pronounce a judicial sentence, κρίν-ειν.

To be worsted, ἡττ-ᾶσ3αι (= ἀ-εσ3αι).

To leave, λείπ-ειν.　・

Supreme, valid, κύριος, a, ον.

To hold an (ἀρχή) office or magistracy, ἄρχ-ειν.

Wealth, πλοῦτος, ου, ὁ.

Receptacle, grave, 3ήκη, ης, ή.

To move, to disturb, κιν-εῖν (= -έειν).

Insatiably desirous (not to be filled), ἄπληστος, ον (with gen.).

Exercise 37.

Obs. In Example 4, ταῦ3', οὔ3', are for ταῦτα, οὔτε. The short final vowel being elided by *apostrophe*, the *smooth* mute (τ) is changed into the *aspirate* (3), because the next word begins with an *aspirated* vowel.

299. a) Translate into English.

.1. Οἱ βάρβαροι, ὅπου ἂν στρατοπεδεύωνται, τάφρον περιβάλλονται εὐπετῶς διὰ τὴν πολυχειρίαν. 2. Οὐκ ἂν εἰκότως δειλὸς νομίζοιτο ὁ τοιοῦτος ; 3. Πολλὴ ἂν ἀλογία εἴη, εἰ φοβοῖτο٭ τὸν 3άνατον ὁ τοιοῦτος. 4. Ταῦ3' ὡς οὐ παρὰ τὸν νόμον ἐστίν, οὔτ' ἂν 'Ανδροτίων ἔχοι٭ λέγειν, οὔ3' ὑμεῖς πεισ3είητε. 5. Ἡδέως ἂν ἔγωγε ἐροίμην⁵⁴ Λεπτίνην, τίς αὐτὴ ἡ ἀτέλειά ἐστιν. 6. 'Ε-σκόπουν [= ἐ-σκόπε-ον] τίν' ἂν τρόπον¹⁹ ἡσυχίαν ἔχειν 'Α3ηνόδωρος ἀναγκασ3είη. 7. Οἱ ἄν3ρωποι τούτοις μάλιστα ἐ3έλουσι πεί3εσ3αι, οὓς ἂν° ἡγῶνται βελτίστους εἶναι. 8. Εἰ νεώτερος ἦν, οὐκ ἂν ἐπιστολὴν ἔπεμ-πον, ἀλλ' αὐτὸς ἄν σοι πλεύσας ᵈ ἐνταῦ3α διελέχ3ην. 9.

Δαρεῖος ῥοιὰν μεγάλην ἀνοίξας,ᵃ πυθομένου ᶠ τινὸς τί ἂ▸
ἔχειν βούλοιτο τοσοῦτον· ὅσον ἐστὶ τῶν κόκκων τὸ πλῆθος, εἶπε· Ζωπύρους· ἦν δὲ ᵍ ἀνὴρ ἀγαθὸς καὶ φίλος ὁ
Ζώπυρος. 10. Κἂν βασιλεύς τι προστάξῃ κρῖναι τῶν
μὴ δικαίων, οὐ κρινοῦμεν.

ᵃ = φοβέ-οιτο. ᵇ ἔχειν sometimes = *to have in one's power,
to be able.* ᶜ *We* should render τούτοις ... οὓς ἂν ... by '*those
whom;*' but the meaning is, *those,* whoever they may be, *whom:* in
Latin, *parēre iis, quos putent* (not *quos putant*). ᵈ πλέ-ειν
(*navigare*) makes Aor. ἔπλευσα. ᵉ *having opened* ... ἤνοιξα, Aor.
of ἀνοίγω (in the more classic Greek Aor. ἀνέῳξα). ᶠ πυθόμενος,
having asked. 'Επυθόμην is a *Second Aorist* from πυνθάνομαι. List IV.

ᵍ In Latin, *erat* autem *Zopyrus,* &c. *we* should use '*now* (*Zopyrus*
was ...).'—See δειλός. τοιοῦτος, Pdm. 52. Give *Fut.* and *Aor.* (*Act.*)
of νομίζω, and go through them.

b) Translate into Greek.

1. We will do this, that all the citizens may obey
the laws. 2. We did this, that all the citizens might
obey the laws. 3. If the Greeks are worsted
(*p*),* none will be left (*Opt. with ἄν*). 4. If you punish
those who commit-injustice (*p*), your laws will
be good and supreme. 5. If you do not punish the
boy, he will be wicked. 6. How would the soldiers
march ? 7. It is necessary, wherever··men hold-office
from •their wealth, that this should be an oligarchy.
8. If you were not a bad man, and insatiably-desirous
of wealth, you would not disturb the graves of the dead.
9. Heʰ said that the barbarians, wherever they encamped, easily entrenched their camp by reason
of (διά, *c. acc.*) their multitude-of-hands. 10. Would
you wish to injure rather than to be injured ?

ʰ See Example 1 in *a;* but make the change as in 295 : *entrenched*
may be either *Present Optat.* or *Present Indicative.*

* (*p*) means that the *preceding* clause is to be translated by a par-
ticiple.

LESSON XL..

Perfect Active.

300. *Reduplication.*] The Perfect takes a *reduplication*, when the verb can receive one.

301. The reduplication is *a syllable prefixed, made up of the initial consonant of the verb and* ε (τυπ, τε-τυπ). But if the verb begins with an aspirate mute, the smooth mute of the same organ is used for the reduplication : φευγ, πεφευγ.

302. The Perfect does not take the reduplication, but the simple augment instead of it, when the verb begins with ῥ; with a *double consonant* (32); with *two consonants* not being a *mute* and *liquid;* or with γν, γλ, βλ.

ψαλλ-, ἐ-ψαλλ-.   γνω-, ἐ-γνω-.   μνημ-, ἐ-μνημ-.

a) Of those in βλ, βλάπτω, βλασφημέω, and sometimes βλαστά-νω take the reduplication.

b) Those beginning with γλ now and then take the reduplication. γλύφω, γέγλυμμαι.—ἔγλυμμαι is more classical.

303. When the Perfect does not take a reduplication, it takes an *augment :* ζητέ-ω, ἐ-ζήτη-κα.

☞ *The reduplication or augment of the Perfect remains through the moods and in the participle.*

304. When the Perfect takes a reduplication, the *Pluperfect* prefixes the augment to it. But when the Perfect takes an augment, the Pluperfect makes no further change :

τέ-τυφα,   ἐ-τετύφειν.
ἐ-ζήτηκα,   ἐ-ζητήκειν.

305. Verbs that begin with ῥ, double ρ after the augment ; and the Perfect and Pluperfect take the syl-

labic augment (123), not the reduplication : ῥάπτω,
ἔρραφα, ἐρράφειν.

306. The termination of the *Perfect Active* is κα or
ά ; that of the Pluperfect κειν or εἰν : the rough breathing over the *a* and *ει* being used to indicate, that the
final consonant of the root is to be changed into *its*
aspirate* if it is a *smooth* or *middle* mute.

307. I. Mute Verbs :]†

	Term.	Pres.	Perf.	Pluperf.
a) P-roots + those in ππ	ά	τύπτ-ω	τέ-τυφ-α	ἐ-τε-τύφ-ειν
b) K-roots + those in κτ .	ά	πλέκ-ω	πέ-πλεχ-α	ἐ-πε-πλέχ-ειν
c) T-roots (*t*-mute thrown away)	κα	πεί϶-ω	πέ-πει-κα	ἐ-πε-πεί-κειν
d) ζ-roots: mostly as *c*, 258	κα ‡	κομίζ-ω	κε-κόμι-κα	ἐ-κε-κομί-κειν
e) σσ- (ττ-) roots : mostly as *b*, 258	ά ◊	τάσσ-ω	τέ-ταχ-α	ἐ-τε-τάχ-ειν

308. II. Liquid Verbs : characteristic λ, μ, ν, ρ ;
or λλ.] Termination κα, the vowel of the root being
shortened as in Future. (Hence φαιν-, φαν-.) But

    a) Monosyllable roots with ε or ει change their
       vowel-sound into *a*.

    b) Roots in ν change ν into γ before κα.

---

   * By '*its* aspirate' is meant the aspirate of the *same* organ. See
30, 31.

   † Roots are called *pure* or *impure*, according as they end in a *vowel*
or in a *consonant*.—*Impure* roots are divided into *mute* or *liquid roots*,
according as the *characteristic* (that is, *the last letter of the root*) is a
mute or a *liquid*.

   Mute roots are divided into *roots ending in a P-sound; roots ending
in a K-sound; roots ending in a T-sound* (30); which may be called,
for the sake of shortness, *P-roots, K-roots, T-roots.*

   ‡ The ζ-roots that are *softened* from an original K-root (see 257),
form their Perfect like the K-roots.—Of these however (which are
principally verbs expressing some *sound*), the *Perf. Act.* is hardly ever
found.

   § The σσ- (ττ-) roots that are strengthened from an original T-
root (257), form their Perfect like the T-roots.

c) But some in *ν* throw away the *ν* : especially, κρίνω (*judge*), κλίνω (*bend*), τείν-ω (*stretch*), reject the *ν* (the vowel being *shortened*, and, in the case of τείν-ω, changed into ă by rule *a*).*

Pres.	Fut.	Perf.	Pluperf.
στέλλ-ω	στελ-ῶ	ἔ-σταλ-κα	ἐ-στάλ-κειν
φαίν-ω	φᾰν-ῶ	πέ-φαγ-κα (rare)	ἐ-πε-φάγ-κειν
βραδύν-ω	βραδῠν-ῶ	βε-βράδυ-κα	ἐ-βε-βράδυ-κειν
κρίν-ω	κρῐν-ῶ	κέ-κρῐ-κα	ἐ-κε-κρί-κειν
κλίν-ω	κλῐν-ῶ	κέ-κλι-κα†	ἐ-κε-κλί-κειν
τείν-ω	τεν-ῶ	τέ-τα-κα	ἐ-τε-τά-κειν

(With the exceptions of κέκρικα, τέτικα, τέτακα, the Perfect Active from verbs in νω is hardly found in good Attic writers. *Kr.*)

Μέν-ω, νέμ-ω, form their Perfects as if from μενέω, νεμέω : μεμένηκα, νενέμηκα.

309. III. PURE VERBS : termination κα with vowel (if short) lengthened.

Pres.	Fut.	Perf.	Pluperf.
τιμά-ω	τιμήσ-ω	τε-τίμη-κα	ἐ-τε-τιμή-κειν
φιλέ-ω	φιλήσ-ω	πε-φίλη-κα	ἐ-πε-φιλή-κειν
δουλό-ω	δουλώ-σω	δε-δούλω-κα	ἐ-δε-δουλώ-κειν
δακρῡ-ω	δακρῠ-σω	δε-δάκρῡ-κα	ἐ-δε-δακρύ-κειν

310. Terminations of the Perf. and Pluperf. Indic.

Perf. a, as, ε | ᾰμεν, ᾰτε, ᾱσι(ν) | ᾰτον, ᾰτον
Pluperf. ειν, εις, ει | ειμεν, ειτε, εσαν (less commonly | ειτον, είτην
εισαν).

311. Moods.

Indic.	Imper.	Subj.	Opt.	Infin.	Partcp.
λέλυκ-α	ε	ω	οιμι	έναι	ώς
				(paroxytone)	(oxytone)

ε, έτω, &c. ⎫
ω, ῃς, ῃ, &c. ⎬ as in *Present*.
οιμι, οις, οι, &c. ⎭

ώς, υῖα, ός ⎫ See Paradigm 35, *b*.
ότος, υίας, ότος ⎭

βο πλύνω, κτείνω.　　　† In Polybius, &c.

312. VOCABULARY 33.

Belonging to women, γυναικεῖος, α, ον.

To go into, put on, ἐνδύ-ειν.

To pursue, ἐπιδιώκ-ειν.

To go under, to set (of the sun, &c.), καταδύ-ειν.

To loosen, destroy, καταλύ-ειν.

To be about or *going to do* any thing, μέλλ-ειν : τὸ μέλλον, *the future.*

To prophesy, προφητεύ-ειν.

To bring forth, φύ-ειν : πέφυκα = naturâ comparatus sum.

Concord, unity, ὁμόνοια, ας, ἡ.

Attire, dress, στολή, ῆς, ἡ.

To govern (a state), πολιτεύ-ειν.

Word, ἔπος, ους, τό : pl. *epic poetry.*

To be in earnest, σπουδάζ-ειν : perf. ἐσπούδακα = *I am in earnest,* as a fixed, permanent state ; *I am eager* or *in a hurry.*

Tragedy, τραγῳδία, ας, ἡ.

Making, composition, ποίησις, εως, ἡ.

To pollute, μιαίν-ειν.

To deny, ἀρνεῖσθαι (= -έεσθαι), Dep. pass. (i. e. with aor. of pass. form in θην).

To practise, to premeditate (a speech), μελετᾶν (= -άειν).

Exercise 38.

313. *a*) *Translate into English.*

1. Οἱ πολέμιοι ἑκατὸν πολίτας πεφονεύκᾱσιν.   2. Φερεκύδης ἔλεγε, μηδενὶ θεῷ τεθυκέναι.   3. Νέος πεφῡκὼς πολλὰ χρηστὰ μάνθανε.   4. Ὁ μάντις τὰ μέλλοντα καλῶς πεπροφήτευκεν.   5. Τὰ τέκνα εὖ πεπαίδευκας.   6. Μήδεια τὰ τέκνα πεφονευκυῖα ἔχαιρεν.   7. Οἱ Λακεδαιμόνιοι Πλαταιὰς κατελελύκεσαν.   8. Σαρδανάπᾱλος στολὴν γυναικείαν ἐνεδεδύκει.   9. Ὅτε ἥλιος κατεδεδύκει, οἱ πολέμιοι ἐπλησίαζον.   10. Πεφύκᾱσιν ἅπαντες καὶ ἰδίᾳ καὶ δημοσίᾳ ἁμαρτάνειν.   11. Ἀνεὺ ὁμονοίας οὐκ ἂν εὖ πολιτευθείη πόλις.   12. Ἐπὶ μὲν ἐπῶν ποιήσει Ὅμηρον ἔγωγε μάλιστα τεθαύμακα, ἐπὶ δὲ τραγῳδίᾳ Σοφοκλέα. 13. Τὸν σώφρονα βίον τοῦ ἀκολάστου ἡδίω κεκρίκαμεν. 14. Ἐγὼ τὸν λόγον μεμελετηκέναι φημὶ καὶ οὐκ ἂν ἀρνηθείην.

QUES. What is the English of ποιήσαιμι ἄν ?   Decline ἔπος, ποίησις. Give the Tenses of θαυμάζω, μελετάω.

b) Translate into Greek.

1. Have we not judged the temperate • *to be* happier than the intemperate ?   2. I have often wondered-at the geometer's wisdom. `3. I have sent you the notes• •that I have by (παρὰ) me.   4. This •man has polluted the temple of Hermes (= *Mercury*).   5. The sycophant has not kept his oaths.   6. If we had done this, Philip would not have been behaving insolently •for so long a time (*acc.*).

• ὑπόμνημα, τό.

LESSON XLI.

Perfect and Pluperfect Active, continued.   Sentences introduced by ὅτι, ὡς.

314. Κλέπτω, πέμπω, τρέπω (*steal, send, turn*), take *o* in the penult of Perfect and Pluperf. Act.   So λέγω (*gather*) in its *compounds*, with irregular augment εἰ.

Hence κέκλοφα, πέπομφα, τέτροφα, ξυν-είλοχα, ἐξ-είλοχα.

315. The Perfect Participle with ὦ, εἴην (*Subj.* and *Opt.* respectively, of εἰμί, *sum*) is often used as the *Subjunctive* and *Optative* of the *Perfect* and *Pluperfect.*   They denote a *still continuing* state more strongly than the regular forms.

316. The *Perfect Participle* is also used with ἔσο-μαι (*ero*) to form a *Future Perfect :* πεποιηκὼς ἔσομαι, *fecero.*

317. Liquid verbs whose characteristic is μ, and a few whose characteristic is ν or λ, undergo *metathesis* (that is, a *transposition of letters*) before the κα, κειν, are added ; the short vowel of the root is then length

6

ened as for *pure* verbs.—Several such verbs must be considered *irregular*, because either the *Present* has been irregularly strengthened, or they form their *Future* or *Aorist* irregularly.   Such verbs are :

Present in use.	Short Root.	By *metathesis*.	Perfect.
κάμν-ω (*laboro*)	καμ-	κμα-	κέ-κμη-κα
τέμν-ω (*cut*)	τεμ-	τμε-	τέ-τμη-κα
Sνήσκ-ω (*die*)	Sαν-	Sνα-	τέ-Sνη-κα
βάλλ-ω (*cast*)	βαλ-	βλα-	βέ-βλη-κα ·
καλέ-ω (*call*)	καλ-	κλα-	κέ-κλη-κα

Γιγνώσκω forms its Fut. and Perf. as if from γνο- ; its Future is of Middle form. Γιγνώσκ-ω, γνώσομαι, ἔγνωκα.

318. The Optative of the Aorist has the meaning of a *præteritum* in dependent sentences introduced by ὅτι, ὡς ('*that*'), and in *dependent interrogative sentences*, e. g. those with εἰ (*if* =) '*whether.*'

319. In these sentences the *Indicative* is used after a *principal tense*. After an *historical* tense this Indicative becomes *regularly* the *Optative ;* but very frequently this change does not take place, the *Indicative* being retained after a past tense just as after a present one.*

320. The *Future* of the *Optative* is strictly confined to the office of taking the place of the Future of the *Indicative* in *oblique narration* (that is, when a person's sentiments, words, &c. are *related* by another using a past tense). Hence it may be used in the sentences we are now speaking of, when they are dependent on a *verbum declarandi* in a past tense.

He says that h e w i l l come,	*He said that* h e w o u l d come,
λέγει ὅτι ἥξει	εἶπεν { ὅτι ἥξοι or ἔλεξεν } ὅτι ἥξει.

---

* The Present tense is usually retained where we should rather

321. ☞ From many verbs, and especially from many *mute* verbs of the *P-* and *K-* sounds, which have a *monosyllabic root*, no *Perfect* and *Pluperfect Active* can be produced. (*Kr.*)

322. VOCABULARY 34.

To steal, κλέπτ-ειν.

To throw away, ἀποβάλλ-ειν.

To call, καλεῖν (= -έειν).

Intemperate, ἀκρατής, ές (with gen.).

Wailing, crying, κλαῦμα, -ατος, τό. Κλαῦμα γίγνεταί τινι = he, any body, *will cry, or have reason to cry*.

To consider, σκοπεῖσθαι (= -έε σθαι).

Madness, λύσσα, ης, ἡ (rabies).

To fall upon, ἐμπιπτ-ειν, with dat. : perf. πέπτωκα (as if from πτό-ω), verb. irreg. List VII.

Violence, impetuosity, σφοδρότης, ητος, ἡ.

Hope, expectation, ἐλπίς, ίδος, ἡ.

(For the Opt. of εἰμί see Pdm. 68.)

Exercise 39.

323. a) Translate into English.

1. Μῶν οὐ κέκλοφας τὴν νίκην ; 2. Εἶπεν ὅτ‿ οἱ στρατιῶται ἀποβεβληκότες εἶεν τὰ ὅπλα. 3. Οὐδὲ τοὺς παῖδας ὀργῇ χρὴ κολάζειν τοὺς τὸν τῆς ἀλώπεκος σκύμνον κεκλοφότας. 4. Γαστρὸς ἀκρατῆ κεκλήκαμεν τὸν ἄνδρα διὰ τὴν σφοδρότητα τῶν περὶ ἐδωδὴν ἐπιθυμιῶν καὶ πό-σιν. 5. Ὅταν οἱ δεσπόται ἐσπουδάκωσι, κλαύματα τοῖς δούλοις γίγνεται. 6. Εἰ, ῥᾳθυμούντων ἡμῶν, ὁ βασιλεὺς ὡς ἀεί τι μεῖζον τῶν ὑπαρχόντων δεῖ πράττειν ἐγνωκὼς ἔσται, σκοπεῖσθε εἰς τί ποτ᾽ ἐλπὶς ταῦτα τελευτῆσαι. 7. Ἔδεισαν οἱ Κερασούντιοι μὴ λύσσα τις ὥσπερ κυσὶν ἡμῖν ἐμπεπτώκοι. 8. Τῇ ὑστεραίᾳ* ἧκεν ἄγγελος λέγων, ὡς ὁ πατὴρ τέθνηκεν. 9. Λέγει (*præs. histor.*) ὅτι πέντε ἡμερῶν ἄξει (or ἄξοι) αὐτοὺς ὅθεν ὄψονται τὴν θάλατταν. 10. Ἠρόμην αὐτοὺς εἰ μέλλουσιν (or μέλλοιεν) τοὺς παῖ-δας κολάσαι.

* *The next day ;* ἡμέρᾳ understood.

expect it to be changed into the Imperfect : ἠρόμην τίνες εἰσίν, **more frequently** than τίνες ἦσαν, *rogabam quinam essent.*

b) Translate into Greek.

1. Has he not invited you to dinner ?   2. Are you
not angry with those who have stolen the game ?   3.
He said that the king had cut off the prisoner's head.
4. He said that Aristodemus was dead.   5. He told me
that the soldier had thrown away his arms.

LESSON XLII.

Perfect Passive.

324. There is only one and the same *form* for the
Perfect Passive and the *Perfect Middle :* their *redu-
plication* and *augment* follow the same rules as the
Perf. Active (301, sqq.).

325. (The pupil must *by no means* suppose that a
Perfect in μαι is *both Passive* and *Middle.*   It is only
some verbs that are used in a Middle sense.)

326. The terminations of the Perf. and Pluperf. of
the Passive and Middle are respectively μαι, μην : but
the initial μ causes certain *euphonic* changes of the
characteristics, according to the following laws :

a) Any *p*-sound (or ππ) with μ = μμ $\begin{cases} \text{τέ-τριβ-μαι} \\ = \text{τέ-τριμ-μαι} \end{cases}$

b) Any *k*-sound (or κτ) with μ = γμ $\begin{cases} \text{πέ-πλεκ-μαι} \\ = \text{πέ-πλεγ-μαι} \end{cases}$

c) Any *t*-sound with μ = σμ $\begin{cases} \text{πέ-πειθ-μαι} \\ = \text{πέ-πεισ-μαι} \end{cases}$

d) (1) The ζ roots usually follow the *t*-sounds, and
take σμαι, σμην ; but (2) the few whose roots originally
ended in a *k*-sound take γμαι, γμην.

e) The σσ- (ττ-) roots usually follow the *k*-sounds,
and take γμαι, γμην ; but the few whose roots originally ended in a *t*-sound take σμαι, σμην.

f) The *liquid* roots require no change except in those in *νω*.   Of these (1) verbs in *αινω, υνω*, generally reject the *ν*, and make compensation for its loss by *ς* : but (2) a few *assimilate* the *ν* to the *μ* (that is, take *μμ* for *νμ*), (3) a *very* few reject the *ν*, and make compensation for it by *lengthening* the vowel of the penult: (4) Κρίνω, κλίνω, τείνω, reject the *ν* (as in *Perf. Act.*, 308, *c* : the last with the same change of *ει* into *α*) ; and retain the short vowel of the Future.

327. Pure verbs usually lengthen a short or doubtful vowel.

		Present.	Perfect.	Pluperfect.
	a)	τρΐβ-ω	τέ-τριμ-μαι	ἐ-τε-τρίμ-μην (*rub*)
	b)	δέχ-ομαι	δέ-δεγ-μαι	ἐ-δε-δέγ-μην (*receive*)
	c)	ψεύδ-ω	ἔ-ψευσ-μαι	ἐ-ψεύσ-μην (*deceive*)
		πείϑ-ω	πέ-πεισ-μαι	ἐ-πε-πείσ-μην (*persuade*)
d) {	1.	ϑαυμάζ-ω	τε-ϑαύμασ-μαι	ἐ-τε-ϑαυμάσ-μην (*wonder-at*)
	2.	στηρίζ-ω	ἐ-στήριγ-μαι	ἐ-στηρίγ-μην
e)	1.	μιαίν-ω	με-μίασ-μαι	ἐ-με-μιάσ-μην (*pollute*)
	2.	αἰσχύν-ω	ᾔσκυμ-μαι	ᾐσκύμ-μην (*shame*; -ομαι, *am*
	3.	τραχύ-νω	τε-τράχῡ-μαι*	ἐ-τε-τραχύ-μην [*ashamed*)
	4. {	κρίν-ω	κέ-κρῐ μαι	ἐ-κε-κρί-μην† (*judge*)
		τείν-ω	τέ-τᾰ-μαι	ἐ-τε-τά-μην (*stretch*)
	5.	στέλλ-ω	ἔ-σταλ-μαι	ἐ-στάλ-μην (*send*)
f)		ποιέ-ω	πε-ποίη-μαι	ἐ-πε-ποίη-μην (*make*)
		τιμά-ω	τε-τίμη-μαι	ἐ-τε-τιμή-μην

(Observe that *αι* of *Perf. Pass.* is considered short *in accentuation*.)

328. The terminations are :

Perfect.			Pluperfect.		
μαι,	σαι,	ται,	μην,	σο,	το,
μεϑα,	σϑε,	νται,	μεϑα,	σϑε,	ντο,
μεϑον,	σϑον,	σϑον.	μεϑον,	σϑον,	σϑην.

λέ λῠ-μαι	λε-λύ-μεϑα	λε-λύ-μεϑον
λέ-λυ-σαι	λέ-λυ-σϑε	λέ-λυ-σϑον
λέ-λυ-ται	λέ-λυ-νται	λέ-λυ-σϑον
ἐλε-λῠ-μην	ἐλε-λύ-μεϑα	ἐλε-λύ-μεϑον
ἐλέ-λυ-σω	ἐλέ-λυ-σϑε	ἐλέ-λυ-σϑον
ἐλέ-λυ-το	ἐλέ-λυ-ντο	ἐλε-λύ-σϑην

* Also τε-τράχυσ-μαι.   † So κλίνω.

The terminations that begin with μ will of course all cause the same euphonic changes : τέ-τυμ-μαι, τε-τίμ-μεϑα, &c. ; but those that begin with σ, τ, will cause *other* changes (which will be given in the next Lesson). The pupil can, at present, only be expected to form *all the persons* of *pure* verbs and of some *liquid* verbs.

329. The participle is -μένος (*paroxytone*), -μένη, -μένον.

330. Τρέπ-ω (*turn*), στρέφ-ω (*twist*), change ε of the root into *a* in the Perf. and Pluperf. Passive (τέτραμμαι, ἔστραμμαι). Τρέφ-ω, *to bring up* (nutrio), also undergoes this change : its root is ϑρεφ : the ϑ is changed into τ, to avoid the proximity of the *two* aspirates (ϑ and φ) : but when the φ disappears, *the ϑ returns :* hence Perfect Pass. τέ-ϑραμ-μαι.

331. VOCABULARY 35.

Lawgiver, νομοϑέτης, ου, ὁ. (νόμος, τιϑέναι, ponere).

To adorn, to arrange or order, κοσμεῖν (= -έειν).

Perfectly, παντελῶς.

Thing learnt, lesson (learnt), μάϑημα, ατος, τό. (μαϑ-, short root of μάνϑανειν.)

To pollute, μιαίν-ειν.

To juggle, γοητεύ-ειν.

To pay court to, ϑεραπεύ-ειν.

To set free, ἀπαλλάττ-ειν. Pass. or Mid. *to be released from* or *to set oneself free from* = *to remove* or *depart from* (with gen.).

Unclean, impure, ἀκάϑαρτος, ον.

Brutish, ϑηριώδης, ες.

I sit still, κάϑημαι (sedeo), a perf. form. Pdm. 71.

Irrational, senseless, ἄλογος, ον.

Music, μουσική (τέχνη, *art,* understood).

Gymnastics, γυμναστική (τέχνη, understood).

To be divided into factions, to be distracted by factions, στασιάζ-ειν.

To disturb, ταράσσ-ειν, or ταράττ-ειν. Pass. *to be in a state of disorder* or *anarchy.*

House, family, οἰκία, ας, ἡ.

Of or belonging to a τύραννος ; *royal ; of their tyrant,* τυραννικός, ή, όν.

Panthĕa, Πάνϑεια, ας, ἡ.

To order, arrange, appoint, τάσσ-ειν or τάττ-ειν (fut. -ξω).

To move, κινεῖν (= -έειν).

Exercise 40.

332. *a) Translate into English.*

1. Ἡ πόλις ὑπὸ τοῦ νομοθέτου εὖ τε καὶ παντελῶς κεκόσμηται. 2. Ἀνάγκη* τὸ μάθημα ἐν αὐτῇ τῇ ψυχῇ λαβόντα[b] ἀπιέναι[c] ἢ βεβλαμμένον ἢ ὠφελημένον. 3. Τῶν πονηρῶν μεμιασμένη ἡ ψυχὴ καὶ ἀκάθαρτος τοῦ σώματος ἀπαλλάττεται, ἅτε θεραπεύουσα[d] τοῦτο καὶ γεγοητευμένη ὑπ᾽ αὐτοῦ ὑπό τε τῶν ἐπιθυμιῶν καὶ ἡδονῶν. 4. Περὶ τὰ κεκρυμμένα τῶν πραγμάτων ἀνάγκη* πολλοὺς φόβους γίγνεσθαι. 5. Ἡ Πάνθεια ταχὺ πάνυ καὶ πασῶν ἐφαίνετο διαφέρουσα* τῶν ἄλλων καίπερ[f] καθημένη κεκαλυμμένη τε καὶ εἰς²⁵ γῆν ὁρῶσα.[g] 6. Ἡ οὐ καλῶς προσέταττον οἱ ἐπὶ τούτοις¹⁷ τεταγμένοι νόμοι, παραγγέλλοντες τῷ πατρὶ τῷ σῷ σε ἐν μουσικῇ καὶ γυμναστικῇ παιδεύειν; 7. Φίλιππος Θετταλοῖς στασιάζουσι καὶ τεταραγμένοις ἐπὶ[e] τὴν τυραννικὴν οἰκίαν ἐβοήθησεν· 8. Πολλή που[h] κακία πολιτείας οὕτως αἰσχρῶς τὰς γυναῖκας εἶναι τεθραμμένας. 9. Ὁ ἀκρατὴς τὸ σῶμα τῇ θηριώδει καὶ ἀλόγῳ ἡδονῇ ἐπιτρέψας ἐνταῦθα τετραμμένος[i] ζήσει.

* sc. ἐστί. [b] *having received*: acc. partcp. from λάβων, λαμβάνειν, List IV. [c] *to go away* (ἄπ-ειμι: ἀπό, εἶμι, *ibo*, Pdm. 68). Supply as acc. to the Infin. '*a man.*' [d] ἅτε θεραπεύουσα = *quippe quæ colat.* [e] διαφ. governs *gen.* [f] καίπερ = *quamvis* with *participles*: very seldom with finite verbs. [g] = ὁρά-ουσα. [h] πού (enclit.) = *opinor.* [i] lit.: '*will live turned* (here =) *hither,*' i. e. *will live with reference to this.*

QUES. What is the difference between αὐτὸς ὁ βασιλεύς and ὁ αὐτὸς βασιλεύς? 8. Why is πολλή printed with the *acute?*

b) Translate into Greek.

1. We have the times of our life appointed by the gods. 2. Thus the whole would be both a well-ordered and well-appointed thing. 3. These things have not

yet been moved. 4. The damsel has her face covered.
5. The city had been adorned with very excellent laws.
6. The souls of the wicked have been juggled by sensual pleasures. 7. Alas! I have been deceived of my
hopes. 8. Some go-away injured, and others even
benefited.

LESSON XLII.*

Persons and Moods of Perfect Passive.

333. The same changes that take place before μαι,
will of course take place before μεθον, μεθα : -

τέ-τυμ-μαι,	βέ-βρεγ-μαι,	πέ-πεισ-μαι,
τε-τύμμεθα,	βε-βρέγμεθα,	πε-πείσμεθα.

334. From the terminations beginning with σθ, the
σ is *thrown away*, when the root ends in a consonant.
Hence the *p* and *k* mutes, being conformed to θ, will
be the *aspirates :*

τέ-τριφ-θον,	λέ-λεχ-θον,	βέ-βρεχ-θον, &c.

for τέ-τριβ-σθον, λέ-λεγ-σθον, βέ-βρεχ-σθον, &c.
A *t*-mute will become σ, or, which is the same thing,
the *t*-mute is thrown away before σθον (πέ-πει-σθοι
for πέ-πειθ-σθον).

335. The changes for ν before μ have been already
given. The ν can be retained before both σ, τ, and θ.
Hence πέφαν-σαι, πέφαν-ται, πέ φαν-θον, &c.

336. By applying, in this way, the rules for the
euphonic changes [Note 8], we shall find that, when
the root ends in a *mute* or ν, these letters assume the
following forms when combined with the initial consonant of the termination.

	p-sounds.	k-sounds.	t-sounds.	ν.
S.	μμ, ψ, πτ,	γμ, ξ, κτ,	σμ, σ, στ,	μμ or σμ, νσ, ντ,
P.	μμ, φϑ, —	γμ, χϑ, —	σμ, σϑ, —	μμ or σμ, νϑ, —
D.	μμ, φϑ, φϑ.	γμ, χϑ, χϑ.	σμ, σϑ, σϑ.	μμ or σμ, νϑ, νϑ.

Of course the 2nd *pers. singular* (being a σ termination) will have the same consonant as the *Fut.*; the 2nd and 3rd dual, and 2nd plur. (ϑ terminations) the same as the *Aor.* 1. *Pass.*

337. The termination of the third person plural, νται, cannot be attached to mute roots. A circumlocution is used instead of it: the Perfect Participle with εἰσί(ν), *are*. So the Perf. Partcp. with ἦσαν for third plural of the *Pluperfect.*

338.   SINGULAR.

λείπω, *leave*. βρέχω, *wet*. ψεύδω, *cheat*. αἴρω, *lift up*. φαίνω, *show*.

λέλειμμαι   βέβρεγμαι   ἔψευσμαι   ἦρμαι   πέφασμαι
λέλειψαι   βέβρεξαι   ἔψευσαι   ἦρσαι   πέφανσαι
λέλειπται   βέβρεκται   ἔψευσται   ἦρται   πέφανται

                                 PLURAL.

λελείμμεϑα   βεβρέγμεϑα   ἐψεύσμεϑα   ἦρμεϑα   πεφάσμεϑα
λέλειφϑε   βέβρεχϑε   ἔψευσϑε   ἦρϑε   πέφανϑε
λελειμμένοι } βεβρεγμένοι } ἐψευσμένοι } ἠρμένοι } πεφασμένοι
  εἰσίν   }   εἰσίν   }   εἰσίν   }   εἰσίν   }   εἰσίν

                                 DUAL.

λελείμμεϑον βεβρέγμεϑον ἐψεύσμεϑον ἦρμεϑον πεφάσμεϑον
λέλειφϑον   βέβρεχϑον   ἔψευσϑον   ἦρϑον   πέφανϑον
λέλειφϑον   βέβρεχϑον   ἔψευσϑον   ἦρϑον   πέφανϑον

So Pluperfect : ἐλελείμμην, ἐλέλειψο, ἐλέλειπτο, &c.

339. MOODS.

Indic.	Imper.	Subj.	Opt.	Infin.	Partcp.
μαι	σο	partcp. with ὦ *	partcp. with εἴην	σϑαι	μένος.

340. In the Imperative, Infinitive, and Participle, the forms are produced, as in the Indicative, by the ejection or change of conso-

---

* There occur, however, a few *Subjunctives* and *Optatives* of the *Perf. Pass.* from verbs whose characteristic is adapted for receiving the termination of the Subjunctive, and the ι of the Optative. It is only, however, from κτάομαι, μιμνήσκω, and καλέω, that such forms are at all common.

6*

nants. The Participles (as μ terminatiqns) follow the Indic. : τέτριμ-μαι, τετριμ-μένος, τέταγ-μαι, τεταγ-μένος. They are *Paroxytone* (341)

Imperative.—Singular.

πεπαίδευσο	τέτριψο	τέταξο	πέπεισο	ἤγγελσο
πεπαιδεύσϑω	τετρίφϑω	τετάχϑω	πεπείσϑω	ἠγγέλϑω
&c.	&c.	&c.	&c.	&c.

Infinitive.

πεπαιδεῦσϑαι	τετρίφϑαι	τετάχϑαι	πεπεῖσϑαι ἠγγέλϑαι πεφάνϑαι.

Participle.

πεπαιδευμένος	τετριμμένος	τεταγμένος	πεπεισμένος ἠγγελμένος πεφασμένος.

341. The Infin. and Participle of the Perf. Pass. have the *accent* on the penult. Hence the Participle is *paroxytone;* the Infin. *properispomenon,* if the penult is a *diphthong* or *long vowel* (the αι being considered short in accentuation); if not, *paroxytone:* πεπαιδεῦσϑαι, γεγενῆσϑαι. τετύφϑαι, ἠφανίσϑαι.—τετυμμένος.

342. Vocabulary 36.

Trace, ἴχνος, εος, τό.   *To track,* ἰχνεύ-ειν.

To leave, καταλείπ-ειν.

Œnoe, Οἰνόη, ης, ἡ.

Borders, μεϑόρια, τά (prop. neut. adj.).

To surround with a wall, to fortify, τειχίζ-ειν.

Neck, throat, τράχηλος, ου, ὁ.

Temple (of the head), κρόταφος, ου, ὁ.

To stretch tight, κατατείν-ειν. Pass. *to be stretched;* hence, of veins, *to be swelled.*

Passionate, δυσόργητος, ον.

Olive, olive-complexioned, μελί-χλωρος, ον.

To dry up, ἀποψύχ-ειν. Part. of perf. pass. ἀπεψυγμένος = cold (indifferent).

To snow, νίφ-ειν.

To cause to disappear, ἀφανίζ-ειν. —τὴν γῆν = to cover the earth.

Embassy, πρεσβεία, ας, ἡ.

I fear, δέδοικα = vereor (Perf. of δείδω, with meaning of Pres.).

Forgetfulness, λήϑη, ης, ἡ.

To cause in —— *, to cause,* ἐμποιεῖν (acc. of *nearer,* dat. of *remoter* object).

Pledges, security, πιστά, τά, ('faithful things.') πιστὰ ϑεῶν ποιεῖσϑαί τινι = to swear to any one by the gods).

To shut,* κλεί-ειν.	To shut, lock-up, κατακλεί-ειν.
A summit, a castle, ἄκρα, ας, ἡ.	To be said, λέγ-εσθαι (dici).
Freedom, self-government, αὐτο-νομία, ας, ἡ.	A robber, λῃστής, οῦ, ὁ.
To implant, ἐμφυτεύ-ειν.	A treaty, συνθήκη, ης, ἡ.
To build, found, ἱδρύ-ειν.	Cube,—die, κύβος, ου, ὁ.

Exercise 41.

343. a) *Translate into English.*

1. Σὺ ταῦτα πάντα ἔχεις, ἃ οἱ ἄλλοι οὐκ ἔχουσι· πεπαίδευσαι γὰρ ἱκανῶς. 2. Ἔτι καὶ νῦν[a] ἴχνος τῆς τοῦ Θησέως πραότητος ἐν τοῖς ἤθεσιν Ἀθηναίων κατα-λέλειπται. 3. Οἰνόη οὖσα ἐν μεθορίοις τῆς Ἀττικῆς καὶ Βοιωτίας ἐτετείχιστο. 4. Τέτριπται τὸ φάρμακον. 5. Οἷς[b] τὰ περὶ τὸν τράχηλον καὶ τοὺς κροτάφους αἱ φλέβες κατατεταμέναι εἰσί, δυσόργητοι. 6. Οἱ μελί-χλωροι ἀπεψυγμένοι εἰσίν. 7. Ἰχνεύομεν τοὺς λαγώς, ὅταν νίφῃ ὁ θεός· ὥστε ἠφανίσθαι τὴν γῆν. 8. Τὸ χρό-νον γεγενῆσθαι μετὰ τὴν πρεσβείαν πολύν,[d] δέδοικα μή τινα λήθην ὑμῖν ἐμπεποιήκῃ. 9. Πέπαυσο.[e] 10. Μό-νον σὺ ἡμῖν πιστὰ θεῶν πεποίησο.[e] 11. Αἱ πύλαι ἐκέκλειντο καὶ ἐπὶ τῶν τειχῶν ὅπλα ἐφαίνετο.

[a] *Even now; even at the present day* (lit. *still even now*).   [b] *qui-bus.* τὰ περὶ τὸν τράχ. = *in the parts about the neck;* a local accusative.

[c] lit. *when the god snows* = *when it snows,* since the Greeks re-ferred *atmospheric* phenomena to Ζεύς, as the god of the air. ὥστε = *so that,* c. infin.   [d] τὸ χρ. γεγενῆσθαι πολύν (= *the circumstance that the time has become long* =) *the circumstance that much time has elapsed:* this clause is the *subject* of the verb ἐμπεποιήκῃ. On δέδοικα μὴ —— cf. K. 318. 8.   [e] Here the *Imperative* of the Perfect commands the *immediate performance* of the things commanded.

☞ Remember that in '*the house* is built' (*domus ædificata est*), 'is built' is the *Perfect;* so whenever '*am*' with the past *participle* denotes a *permanent state* as the result of a past action.

---

* Perf. Pass. κέκλεισμαι and κέκλειμαι.

b) Translate into Greek.

1. The earth is covered. 2. A cloud veiled and hid (*say:* having veiled[f] hid) the sun. 3. The soldiers have been slaughtered. 4. Two brothers have been educated by the same master. 5. The monarchy has been destroyed by the people. 6. Many temples have been built for the gods by the Athenians. 7. Let the door be shut •immediately. 8. Before action deliberate well. 9. • There is implanted in all men ‖ a desire of self-government. 10. Let the prisoners-of-war be slain. 11. The enemy are said to be shut-up in [10] the castle. 12. The •two sons of Zenophon, Gryllus and Diodōrus, had been educated in Sparta. 13. Let the die be cast.

f προ-καλύπτ-ειν.

LESSON XLIII.

Contracted Verbs in άω. Pres. and Imperf. Act.

(Learn τιμάω, Pdm. 59.)

344. Contract Pure verbs are such as have for their characteristic *a, e,* or *o,* which are contracted with the following vowel or diphthong. Contraction takes, place only in the *Present* and *Imperfect* of both Voices, because it is only in these two tenses that the characteristic vowel is followed by another vowel.

345. The contractions for verbs in άω are these:

a before an *e*-sound becomes *ā*	ι being *subscript* if the *e*-sound is ει, η; or the *o*-sound, οι.
a before an *o*-sound becomes ω	

Thus, $ae = \bar{a}$ $\quad$ $ao = \omega$
$a\eta = \bar{a}$ $\quad$ $a\omega = \omega$
$\alpha\epsilon\iota = \alpha$ $\quad$ $aoι = \omega$
$a\eta = \alpha$ $\quad$ $aou = \omega.$

346. *Ae* and *aei* are contracted into η and η (instead of into *a* and ą), from (ζάειν) ζῆν, *to. live ;* (πεινάειν) πεινῆν, *to be hungry ;* (διψάειν) διψῆν, *to be thirsty;* (χράεσθαι) χρῆσθαι, *to use.* These are also the *regular* contractions from κνάω, *scrape ;* σμάω, *smear ;* ψάω, *rub.*

347. *Contracted Verbs* have very frequently (instead of οιμι, οις, &c.) the Optative

οίην, οίης, οίη | οίημεν, οίητε, οίησαν | οίητον, οιήτην
$\quad$ | οἶμεν, οἶτε, οἶεν | or οἶτον, οίτην

For verbs in *aω,* the *a-oι = ῳ* : so that the form becomes ῴην, ῴης, ῴη, &c.

348. The *Present Optative* in οίην (for ε-οίην, ο-οίην), and ῴην (for a-οίην), is the prevailing form in the *Singular,* at least for the *first* (and *second*) Persons : in the *Plural* it is *rare ;* ῴησαν is nowhere found, οίησαν *hardly* ever. (Krüger.)

349. Vocabulary 37.

To love ; also, to be contented, ἀγαπᾷν (=άειν), *with acc. or dat.*

Immortal, ἀθάνατος, ον.

Miserably, unfortunately, ἀθλίως.

To deceive, ἐξαπατᾷν (= άειν).

To love, ἐρᾷν (with gen.).

Age ; especially youth or manhood, ἡλικία, ας, ἡ.

Boldly, θαῤῥαλέως.

Appearance, outward figure, ἰδέα, ας, ἡ.

To sound, φθέγγεσθαι.

To conquer, νικᾷν (=άειν).

To pity, ὀλοφύρεσθαι (with acc.).

To see, ὁρᾷν (see List VII).

Point, height, full power, vigor, ἀκμή, ῆς, ἡ.

To lighten, ἀστράπτ-ειν.

To thunder, βροντᾷν (=άειν).

To do, act, δρᾷν.

To rush, ὁρμᾷν.

Before, πρίν (with infin. K. 337).

How ? πῶς ;

To stir up together, throw into confusion, συγκυκᾶν.	To end, die, τελευτᾶν (=άειν).
	Dare, venture, τολμᾶν.
Fighting with, fellow-combatant, ally, σύμμαχος, ον.	To be silent, σιωπᾶν.

Exercise 42.

350. a) Translate into English.

1. Πολλάκις γνώμην ἐξαπατῶσιν ἰδέαι. 2. Μή σε νικάτω κέρδος. 3. Πολλάκις νικᾷ καὶ κακὸς ἄνδρα ἀγαθόν. 4. Οἱ ἀγαθοὶ ἐρῶσι τῶν καλῶν. 5. Πολλοὶ[a] ἄνθρωποι ἐν τῇ τῆς ἡλικίας ἀκμῇ τελευτῶσιν. 6. Ἢ σιώπα, ἢ λέγε ἀμείνονα.[b] 7. Ἀνάγκη ἐστὶ πάντας ἀνθρώπους τελευτᾶν. 8. Νοῦς ὁρᾷ καὶ νοῦς ἀκούει. 9. Θαρραλέως, ὦ στρατιῶται, ὁρμῶμεν ἐπὶ τοὺς πολεμίους. 10. Πρὶν μὲν πεινῆν, πολλοὶ ἐσθίουσι, πρὶν δὲ διψῆν, πίνουσιν. 11. Οὐκ ἔστι τοῖς μὴ δρῶσι σύμμαχος τύχη. 12. Περικλῆς ἤστραπτεν, ἐβρόντα, συνεκύκα τὴν Ἑλλάδα. 13. Εἴθε πάντες τοὺς γονέας ἀγαπῷεν. 14. Εἴθε ἠγαπήσαμεν τοῖς παροῦσιν. 15. Πῶς ἂν τολμῴην τὸν φίλον βλάπτειν; 16. Τὸ μὲν σῶμα πολλάκις καὶ πεινῇ καὶ διψῇ· ἡ δὲ ψυχὴ πῶς ἂν ἢ διψῴη ἢ πεινῴη; 17. Ψυχὴ ἀθάνατος καὶ ἄγηρως ζῇ διὰ παντός (sc. χρόνου). 18. Κρεῖττον[b] τὸ μὴ ζῆν ἐστιν, ἢ ζῆν ἀθλίως. 19. Ὀλοφυρόμεθα τὸν ἐν τῇ τῆς ἡλικίας ἀκμῇ τελευτῶντα. 20. Ὅταν ὁ αὐλὸς φθέγγηται, παντάπασι σιωπῶμεν.

[a] πολύς.   [b] Note 13.

QUES.—7. Why does the enclitic ἐστί *retain* its accent here? 10. Give the tenses of πίνειν, List VII. 11. Account for the accent of ἐστι. 18. Is οὐ or μή the usual word for 'not' with an Infin.?

b) Translate into Greek.

1. Time conquers and changes all things. 2. Anger compels many men to do evil. 3. Do not keep silence, if you see any persons ill-affected towards the

government. 4. Neither hear nor see what you ought not. 5. We honor those who brave-dangers for their country. 6. I trusted: I was utterly-deceived. 7. You (*pl.*) were deceiving the stranger. 9. Deceive no body.

LESSON XLIV.

Contracted Verbs in εω. *Present and Imperf. Act.*

351. *E*ε becomes ει. ·

εο becomes ου.

ε is thrown away before long vowels and diphthongs.

Thus,

εη = η		εεί = ει
εῃ = ῃ		εοι = οι
εω = ω		εου = ου

352. Before the Opt. in οίην (347), the ε will disappear throughout; ποι-ε-οίην = ποι-οίην.

353. VOCABULARY 38.

To be dispirited, despair, ἀϑυμεῖν.

To neglect, ἀμελεῖν (with gen.).

To flow away, ἀπορρεῖν.

To practise, ἀσκεῖν.

To want, δεῖν (=ἔειν, gen.); δεῖ, there is need, it is necessary, one must (with acc. and infin.).

To be unfortunate, δυστυχεῖν.

To sell, πωλεῖν.

To be fortunate, happy, εὐτυχεῖν.

To approve, praise, ἐπαινεῖν.

To will, be willing, ϑέλειν, ἐϑέλειν (velle).

Request, prayer, εὐχή, ης, ἡ.

To take trouble, to work, πονεῖν (laborare).

To expect, presume, προσδοκᾶν.

To accomplish, τελεῖν.

Bundle or mats of reeds, rushes, &c. ῥίψ, ῥιπ-ός, ἡ.

To do in common with any one, help, assist, συλλαμβάνειν (with dat.).

To work with any one, help, assist, συμπονεῖν (with dat.).

To think, be sensible, φρονεῖν.

To confess, to profess, ὁμολογεῖν.

To be a retail trader, καπηλεύειν.

Even if, even though, κἄν (=καὶ ἐάν).	φρονεῖν.
To be high-minded, proud, μέγα	*To demand* (money, &c.) πράττ εσθαι.

Exercise 43.

354. a) *Translate into English.*

1. Τιμῶμεν τοὺς ἀγαθούς, ἵνα ἅμα τῷ τιμᾷν ἀσκῶμεν. 2. Ὁ πεισθεὶς ἡμῶν τῷ λόγῳ εὐτυχεῖ τε καὶ εἰς χρόνον ἅπαντα εὐτυχοῖ. 3. Ἀνὴρ πονηρὸς δυστυχεῖ, κἄν εὐτυχῇ. 4. Σιγᾷν μᾶλλον, ἢ λαλεῖν πρέπει. 5. Ὅ τι* ἂν ποιῆτε, νομίζετε ὁρᾷν θεόν. 6. Φίλος φίλῳ συμπονῶν αὐτῷ πονεῖ. 7. Οἱ ἄνθρωποι θνητοὶ μὴ φρονούντων [Note 7] ὑπὲρ θεούς. 8. Ὁ μάλιστα εὐτυχῶν μὴ μέγα φρονείτω. 9. Οὐδέποτ' ἀθῡμεῖν τὸν κακῶς πράττοντα[b] δεῖ, τὰ βελτίω [Note 13] δὲ προσδοκᾷν ἀεί. 10. Τῷ πονοῦντι θεὸς συλλαμβάνει. 11. Δικαιοσύνην ἀσκεῖτε καὶ ἔργῳ καὶ λόγῳ. 12. Ἀπὸ τῆς Νέστορος γλώττης, ὥσπερ μέλι, ὁ λόγος ἀπέρρει. 13. Σωκράτης τοῦ σώματος οὐκ ἠμέλει, τοὺς δὲ ἀμελοῦντας οὐκ ἐπῄνει. 14. Εἴθε, ὦ θεός, τελοίης μοι τὴν εὐχήν. 15. Εἴθε εὐτυχοῖτε, ὦ φίλοι. 16. Θεοῦ θέλοντος, κἄν ἐπὶ ῥιπὸς πλέοις. 17. Οὐκ ἀθῡμοῦμεν τοῖς παροῦσι πράγμασιν. 18. Φύσει ὑπάρχει τοῖς ἐθέλουσι πονεῖν καὶ κινδυνεύειν τὰ τῶν ἀμελούντων. 19. Ἔστιν οἳ[c] ἀμελοῦντες τῶν οἰκείων τῶν ἀλλοτρίων ἐπιμελοῦνται. 20. Τὴν δικαιοσύνην καὶ τὴν ἄλλην ἀρετὴν ἀσκεῖτε. 21. Τὰ αὐτὰ ἐποίουν, ὅτε φεύγοντες ἐδυστύχουν αὐτοί.

* Neut. of ὅστις (Pdm. 50): printed ὅ τι or ὅ,τι, to distinguish it from ὅτι, *that.*　　[b] κακῶς πράττειν = *to be doing ill; to be unfortunate.*　　ὁ αὐτός (give the English of it).　　[c] K. 831. Rem. 4.

b) *Translate into Greek.*

1. Are we not with-reason most angry with [32] those who are most able[d] (*p*) not to act-unjustly.[e] 2. In [16]

such things they are poor, but you are rich.   3. **Those
who bring** (*p*) to you kings' garments, or wrought
copper _or gold, sell them more artfully than **those
who profess** (*p*) to be-retail-traders.   4. I would not'
praise such persons.   5. Did you not sell (*imperf.*)
vegetables?   6. Reason is the remedy for the soul
when it is sick (*p*).   7. We think that •**the man
who is fortunate** (*p*) is also wise.   8. Honor youɪ
parents, love your friends, obey rulers.

ᵈ δυνάμενος.   • μή is more usual than οὐ with the *infin.*

LESSON XLV.

Contracted Verbs in όω.   Present and Imperf. Act.

355. *O*ε, *oo*, *oov*, become ου.

oη, *oω*, become ω.

oη (subscript), *oει*, *ooι*, become *oι* (but *oει* **=** *ου*
in Infin.).

356. *Oo* and *oε* are contracted into ω (instead of
into ου), and *όη* into ῷ (instead of into οῖ), in ῥιγόω, ῥιγῶ, *to freeze*, Inf. ῥιγῶν and ῥιγοῦν, Part. Gen. ῥιγῶντος
and ῥιγοῦντος, Subj. ῥιγῶ, Opt. ῥιγῴην, &c.

357. *On the Imperfect and the Aorist of the Indic.*]
The *Imperfect Indicative* answers, not only to *our*
Imperf. (with *was* —), but also to *our* (and the *Lat.*)
Perfect.   It then denotes a *continued* or *repeated*
action; the *Aorist*, a *single, definite one*, stated without any *intimation* of its lasting.—It may necessarily
have a duration even of indefinite length, but the tense
does not intimate it.

358. *Infin. of the Aorist.*]   The Infinitive of the
Aorist is usually not a *præteritum*, except after *verba*

declarandi et putandi, and in the construction of *acc.
c. Infin. with the article :* with these exceptions it is
usually construed by the English *Present,* but denotes
single, definite actions : the *Infin.* of the *Present* being
used of *continued* or *repeated* ones.

a) Λέγομαι (νομίζομαι) ποιῆσαι $\Big\{$ = *dicor (credor)
fecisse.*

Βούλομαι (δύναμαι) ποιῆσαι $\Big\{$ = *volo (possum)
facere.*

b) Τό. σε ποιῆσαι τοῦτο, *tene hoc fecisse !*

359. Vocabulary 39.

To darken, destroy, weaken, blunt, ἀμαυροῦν (=όειν).
Carelessness, ἀμέλεια, ας, ἡ.
To live in, reside in, ἐμβιοῦν (=όειν).
To trick, entrap, δολοῦν (=όειν).
To enslave, subjugate, δουλοῦν (=όειν).
To set free, ἐλευθεροῦν (=όειν).
(*To raise up again=*) *to amend, to correct,* ἐπανορθοῦν (=όειν).
To think right or *fair, to claim, to expect,* ἀξιοῦν (=όειν).
To make equal, ἐξισοῦν (=όειν).
To emulate, ζηλοῦν (=όειν).
To seek, strive, ζητεῖν (=έειν).
Life, ζωή, ῆς, ἡ.
Divine, godlike, θεῖος, a, ον.
Hunger, λιμός, οῦ, ὁ.

Pit, ὄρυγμα, ατος, τό (ὀρύττειν, fodere).
Thing woven=snare, πλέγμα, ατος, τό.
Communion, intercourse, κοινωνία, ας, ἡ. θεία κοινωνία= *communion with the Deity.*
Desire, striving, ὄρεξις, εως, ἡ.
Intimate, οἰκεῖος, a, ον ; also, ος, ον.
To make straight, erect, ὀρθοῦν (=όειν).
Neither—nor, οὔτε—οὔτε.
To make equal, συνεξομοιοῦν (=όειν).
Violent, σφοδρός, ά, όν.
To make blind, τυφλοῦν (=όειν).
With difficulty, χαλεπῶς.

Exercise 44.

360. a) *Translate into English.*

1. Δολοῦσιν ὗς ἀγρίους πλέγμασι καὶ ὀρύγμασι.
2. Λέγεται οὗτος ὁ βασιλεὺς τὴν Αἴγυπτον ἐλευθερῶσαι. 3. Καί σε βουλοίμην ἂν ἀποφήνασθαι τὴν

γνώμην. 4. Οἱ Λακεδαιμόνιοι ἠλευθέρουν τοὺς Ἕλληνας. 5. Ἐπεὶ ἡ σάλπιγξ ἐφθέγξατο καὶ ἐπαιάνιζον οἱ Ἕλληνες, ἐνταῦθα οὐκέτι ἐδέξαντο οἱ πολέμιοι ἀλλ᾽ ἔφευγον. 6. Αἱ φιλίαι τὰ ἔθη ζητοῦσι συνεξομοιοῦν. 7. Χαλεπῶς ἂν ταῖς τῶν ἀγαθῶν ἀρεταῖς ἐξισοίης τοὺς ἐπαίνους. 8. Ζήλου, ὦ παῖ, τοὺς ἐσθλοὺς καὶ σώφρονας ἄνδρας. 9. Ἡ τύχη πολλοὺς κακῶς πράττοντας ὀρθοῖ. 10. Πλῆθος κακῶν τὴν ἀνθρωπίνην ζωὴν ἀμαυροῖ. 11. Αἱ περί τι σφοδραὶ ὀρέξεις τυφλοῦσιν εἰς τὰ ἄλλα τὴν ψυχήν. 12. Τὴν ἀρετὴν καὶ τὴν σοφίαν ζηλῶμεν. 13. Χρυσός ἐστιν ὁ δουλῶν θνητῶν φρένας. 14. Οἱ πολέμιοι τὸ στράτευμα ἡμῶν ἐδόλουν. 15. Οἱ νεανίαι τὴν σοφίαν ζηλοῖεν. 16. Οἱ πολέμιοι ἐπλησίαζον, ἵνα τοὺς αἰχμαλώτους ἐλευθεροῖεν.

b) Translate into Greek.

1. Strangers were not allowed to live-in Sparta. 2. The Ephori are empowered to punish whomsoever they please (297). 3. The Ephori were empowered to punish whomsoever they pleased. 4. Idleness destroys the excellence of natural-disposition, but instruction corrects its badness. 5. Emulate the good man and the sober-minded • one. 6. Do not tell• e v e n ᵇ to your most intimate • frieńd what you wish to be concealed. 7. It is right to give (παρέχειν) to others whatever (say: as many things as ᶜᶜ) you expect to receive• from them. 8. What is sudden and unexpected (say: the sudden and unexpected) enslaves the spirit.

ᵃ δηλοῦν = ostendere.   ᵇ K. 818. 6.   ᶜ λαβεῖν, Inf.
\or. 2. from λαμβάνω. See Irr. Verbs, List IV.

LESSON XLVI.

Verbs in aω. Pass. and Mid. Aorist Infin.

361. Vocabulary 40.

To accuse of, charge with, αἰτιᾶ-σθαι (=άεσθαι); τινά τι (as here) is *rare*, except in case of neut. pron. Also with ὅτι =to blame—because.

Introduction, commencement, ἐσή-γησις, εως, ἡ.

At once, ἤδη.

Better, λῴων (=λωΐων). Note 13.

To proclaim, κηρύττ-ειν.

To hear, listen to, ἀκροᾶσθαι (=άεσθαι,) with *gen.*

To devise, contrive, μηχανᾶσθαι (=άεσθαι).

Not befitting, disgraceful, ἀει-κής, ές.

One running through the whole day, a courier, ἡμεροδρόμος, ου, ὁ (ἡμέρα, δραμεῖν, to run).

To endeavor, to try, πειρᾶσθαι (=άεσθαι).

The buying of a horse, ἱππωνεία, ας, ἡ (ἵππος, ὠνεῖσθαι, to buy).

To be raised-in-price (of corn), to be rising, ἐπιτιμᾶσθαι.

To give over, λήγ-ειν (used with the participle).

To acquire, κτᾶσθαι (=άεσθαι). Perf. κέκτημαι (*I have acquired*=) I possess.

Sandal, shoe, ὑπόδημα, ατος, τό.

To use, employ, χρῆσθαι (=άεσθαι).

362. For the meaning of the *Aor. Infin.* cf. 358: and for that of the *Aor. Opt.* and the construction of clauses introduced by ὅτι, ὡς, cf. 318, 319.

1. *He says, that he* has done *it,*
λέγει, ὅτι ἐποίησε (or φησὶ ποιῆσαι)

He' said, that he had done *it,*
εἶπεν ⎰ ὅτι ποιήσειεν
(ἔλεξεν) ⎰ ὅτι ἐποίησεν.
ἔφη ποιῆσαι.

2. ⎰ βούλεται κλέψαι (τι) = *vult* furari (aliquid).
  ⎰ φησὶ κλέψαι (τι) = *dicit* se (aliquid) furatum esse.

3. θαυμαστὸν τὸ πεισθῆναί τινας, ὡς —, *it is strange that some persons* should have been persuaded *that —,* &c.

An infinitive or participle dependent on a *præteritum*, is considered as a præteritum.

Exercise 45.

363. a) *Translate into English.*

1. Οἱ Λακεδαιμόνιοι ἠτιῶντο αὐτοὺς τήν τε ἐσήγησιν τοῦ παντός, καὶ ἔφασαν˙[a] αὐτοὺς ἤδη ἀδικεῖν, ὅτι οἱ δέ- χονται[b] τὰς Ἀθηναίων σπονδάς. 2. Σωκράτης ἀκού- σας ἠτιᾶτο αὐτόν, ὅτι οὐ τοῦτο πρῶτον ἠρώτα,[c] πότερον λῷον εἴη αὐτῷ πορεύεσθαι ἢ μένειν. 3. Ἐπεὶ ταῦτα ἐκηρύχθη, ἔγνωσαν[d] οἱ στρατιῶται ὅτι κενὸς ὁ φόβος εἴη.[e] 4. Κῦρος μεταπεμψάμενος τοὺς στρατηγοὺς τῶν Ἑλλήνων, ἔλεγεν ὅτι ἡ ὁδὸς ἔσοιτο πρὸς βασιλέα μέγανεἰς Βαβυλῶνα. 5. Ὁμοίως̓ ἀμφοῖν ἀκροάσασθαι δεῖ. 6. Ἔλεγεν ὅτι ὁμοίως ἀμφοῖν ἀκροάσασθαι δέοι (or δεῖ). 7. Εὔνους[f] λόγος λύπην ἰᾶται. 8. Περικλῆς ὑπὸ τῶν Ἀθηναίων ἠγαπᾶτο καὶ ἐτιμᾶτο. 9. Οἱ ἡμερο- δρόμοι οὐκ ἐχρῶντο ὑποδήμασιν ἐν ταῖς ὁδοῖς. 10. Οὐκ ἀεικές, ἐάν τις ὑπ᾽ ἐχθρῶν ἐξαπατᾶται [Note 7]. 11. Εἴτε ὑπὸ φίλων ἐθέλεις ἀγαπᾶσθαι, τοὺς φίλους εὐεργέτει˙ εἴτε ὑπό τινος πόλεως ἐπιθυμεῖς τιμᾶσθαι, τὴν πόλιν ὠφέλει˙ εἴτε ὑπὸ τῆς Ἑλλάδος˙πάσης ἀξιοῖς ἐπ᾽ ἀρετῇ θαυμάζεσθαι, τὴν Ἑλλάδα πειρῶ εὖ ποιεῖν.

b) *Translate into Greek.*

1. Those who ·confer-benefits (*p*) n e v e r c e a s e to be l o v e d (*say:* continue᷎ being loved). 2. We do not obtain our friends by b e i n g t r e a t e d ʰ well, but by treating ¹ ·them w e l l. 3. We will first write how ᵏ a man may be least deceived in buying-a-horse. 4. We see the corn raised-in-price in the Piræus. 5. (W h y

have not you declared =) declare at once your opinion about what is now asked (*p*). 6. They will not give-over devising and preparing all •manner of contrivances, until¹ you are willingly deceived. 7. You the injured ‖ •party do not at all accuse him, but are blaming some of yourselves. 8. These persons are devising and preparing the death of their neighbors (*say:* death to their neighbors).

g διατελεῖν.   h Say *suffering* (πάσχοντες), i. e. being the recipients.   i εὖ δρᾷν, c. acc.   k ὡς ἀν (= quomodo si ita forte sit, c. subj.).   l ἕως ἀν (c. subj.).

LESSON XLVII.

Verbs in εω.   *Pass. and Mid.*

364. VOCABULARY 41.

To be ashamed before any one, *reverence, esteem,* αἰδεῖσθαι (=έεσθαι), with *acc.*

To distrust, ἀπιστεῖν (=έειν), with *dat.* ἀπιστεῖσθαι, *to be disbelieved.*

To want, δεῖσθαι (with *gen.*).

The year, ἔτος, εος, τό.

Strong, powerful, ἰσχυρός, ά, όν.

To break into (lit. *to dig through*), διορύττ-ειν.

To despise, καταφρονεῖν (with *gen.*). καταφρονεῖσθαι, *to be despised.*

Talkative, λάλος, ον.

To hate, μισεῖν (=έειν).

To move, κινεῖν.   Mid. *to move oneself, to move* (intrans.).

To hum, βομβεῖν (=έειν).

As, in order that, ὅπως (subj. after a principal tense; opt. after a historical tense; after verbs of care, endeavor, &c., indic. fut.

Near, πλήσιος, a, ον.   Οἱ πλήσιον (adv.), *those near, our fellow-men.*

To besiege, πολιορκεῖν.

Having undivided wings, ὁλόπτερος, ον: τὰ ὁλόπτ. = *insects whose wings are undivided.*

To frighten, φοβεῖν (=έειν). Mid. *to be frightened, to fear.*

Exercise 46.

365. *a) Translate into English.*

1. Ὅτε πλούσιος ἦν, ἐφοβούμην μή τίς μου τὴν οἰκίαν διορύξας καὶ τὰ χρήματα λάβοι καὶ αὐτόν τί με κακὸν ἐργάσαιτο. 2. Οἷς αἴσθησις ὑπάρχει, καὶ τὸ λυπεῖσθαι καὶ χαίρειν. 3. Παντὶ τῷ πεφυκότι κινεῖσθαι μὴ δυναμένῳ δ᾽ ἀεὶ καὶ συνεχῶς κινεῖσθαι μεθ᾽ ἡδονῆς ἀναγκαῖον εἶναι καὶ ὠφέλιμον τὴν ἀνάπαυσιν. 4. Βομβοῦντα φαίνεται τὰ ὀλόπτερα, ὅταν κινῆται. 5. Αἰδοῦ τοὺς θεούς. 6. Τὸν ἀγαθὸν ἄνδρα ποιοῦ ἑταῖρον. 7. Φιλοῦντες φιλοῦνται, μισοῦντες μισοῦνται. 8. Τὸν ἰσχῡρὸν δεῖ πρᾶον εἶναι, ὅπως οἱ πλησίον αἰδῶνται μᾶλλον, ἤ, φοβῶνται. 9. Αἰδεῖσθαι δεῖ φίλους. 10. Ἀπιστοῦνται οἱ λάλοι, κἂν ἀληθεύωσιν. 11. Οἱ Πέρσαι ὑπὸ τῶν Ἑλλήνων ἐμισοῦντο καὶ κατεφρονοῦντο. 12. Ὁ μηδὲν ἀδικῶν οὐδενὸς δεῖται νόμου.

b) Translate into Greek.

1. Do not only praise the good, but also imitate them. 2. In Thymbrium there was a fountain called that* of Midas. 3. Cyrus did not suffer[b] the evil-doers and unjust to laugh-at °him, but punished them (≟ used to punish: *imperf.*) all most-unsparingly. 4. That which is held-in-estimation at any time° is practised. 5. Some °persons move whilst they are asleep (*p*), and do many waking °actions. 6. We who were then delighted (*p*) are now grieved. 7. Troy was besieged ten years (*acc.*) by the Greeks. 8. The citizens feared lest the city should be besieged. 9. Let nobody fear death.

* Say: '*the.*'   b ἐᾶν = ἐά-ειν, sinere, takes for its augment
ι after the ε: imperf. εἴων, &c.   ° ἀεί (= *semper*).

LESSON XLVIII.

Contracted Verbs in όω. ‾ *Pass. and Mid.*

366. Vocabulary 42.

Strength, ἀλκή, ῆς, ἡ.

To make proud, γαυροῦν (=όειν).
Mid. *to be proud of, exult in*
(*acc.* or with ἐπί and *dat.*).

To oppose, resist, thwart, ἐναν-
τιοῦσθαι (with *dat.*).

To obscure utterly, to blot out,
annihilate, ἐξαμαυροῦν.

Custom, manner, character, ἦθος,
εος (ους) τό.

To part, divide, μερίζ-ειν.

Flesh, σάρξ, σαρκός, ἡ.

Haughty, proud, ὑπερήφανος, ον.

To bring low, to humble, ταπεινοῦν.

To worst, subdue, subjugate, χειροῦσθαι.

To convert into blood, ἐξαιμα-
τοῦν.

To punish, ζημιοῦν.

Exercise 47.

367. *a) Translate into English.*

1. Οὐκ ἀναμένομεν ἕως ἂν ἡ ἡμετέρα χώρα κακῶ-
ται. 2. Δουλούμεθα τῇ σαρκὶ καὶ τοῖς πάθεσιν. 3.
Ὑπὸ τῆς ἀνάγκης πάντα δουλοῦται ταχύ. 4. Ἡ φιλία
εἰς πολλοὺς μεριζομένη ἐξαμαυροῦται. 5. Τοὺς φίλους
ἐλευθερῶμεν, τοὺς δὲ ἐχθροὺς χειρώμεθα. 6. Μὴ γαυροῦ
σοφίᾳ, μήτ᾽ ἀλκῇ, μήτε πλούτῳ. 7. Τὸ ἦθος μάλιστα ἐκ
τῶν ἔργων δηλοῦται. 8. Ὁ ὑπερήφανος ταπεινοῖτο.
9. Οὐ καλόν ἐστι, ἐπὶ τῇ σοφίᾳ γαυροῦσθαι. 10. Οἱ
τοῖς ἀγαθοῖς ἐναντιούμενοι ἄξιοί εἰσι ζημιοῦσθαι. 11. Οἱ
στρατιῶται ὑπὸ τῶν βαρβάρων ἐδολοῦντο. 12. Πάντες
κακοὶ ζημιοῖντο.

b) Translate into Greek.

1. The Greeks are enslaving themselves.* 2. How
would a man be less punished by the state, or how
would •h e be more honored than if he w e r e to o b e y
(εἰ with Opt. Pres.) the laws? 3. This •man is doing
what he pleases, and enslaving the cities of the Greeks.

4. The secreted-essence [b] of the food is c h a n g e d (p) and converted-into-blood.   5. Alas! we are ·enslaving ourselves.   6. They said,[c] that the citizens had enslaved themselves.

[a] *Oneself, themselves.* As *ipse* in Latin is often prefixed to *sibi, se,* so αὐτός, in Greek, to ἑαυτ-ῷ, -όν, -ούς : αὐτ-ῷ, -όν, -ούς.   [b] ἀνα-θυμίασις, ἡ, properly, *a vapor rising, an exhalation :* probably considered here as a *subtle essence* extracted from the solid food.   [c] ἐλέγον. λέγω takes mostly ὅτι : φημί mostly *acc. c. infin.*

LESSON XLIX.

Tempora Secunda.   Second Aorist.

368. The *Second Aorist* is an Aorist formed from the *short root* (235) by augmenting it, and adding the following terminations :

Act.	Mid.	Pass.
ον	όμην	ην

(ον, όμην being conjugated like the *Imperfects* with those terminations ; ην like the *First Aor. Pass.*).

369. Comparatively few, and those mostly *primitive* (many of them *irregular*) verbs, form the *Second Aorist.* It is not formed from any with the derivative endings άω, έω, όω, εύω, αίνω, ύνω, άζω : hardly from verbs whose true characteristic is a *t-sound;* nor when such an Aorist would be *identical in form* with the Imperfect (whether distinguished from it by quantity ʼor not). · Thus not ἔγραφον ; but the pass. ἐγράφην is formed.

370. Very few verbs have both a *First Aorist* (as we must henceforth call it) and a *Second Aorist* in the *Active* and *Middle.* The co-existence of the two forms is less uncommon in the *Passive.* Τρέπω is the only verb that has *all* the possible Aorists.

371. Besides the changes given (in 235) as the necessary steps for obtaining the short root (η and αι into a ; ει, ῑ into ῐ : ευ into υ), the ε of *monosyllable*

7

roots is always changed into *a* for *liquid* verbs, and sometimes for *mute* verbs.

EXAMPLES.

	ACT.	MID.	PASS.
βάλλω (*cast*)	ἔβαλον	ἐβαλόμην	
τρέπω (*turn*)		ἐτραπόμην	ἐτράπην
φεύγω (*fly*)	ἔφυγον		
τρίβω (*rub*)			ἐτρίβην
κλέπτω (*steal*)			ἐκλάπην
τέμνω (*cut*)	ἔτεμον*		
χαίρω (*rejoice*)			ἐχάρην
πλέκω (*weave*)			ἐπλάκην
λείπω (*leave*)	ἔλιπον	[ἐλιπόμην]	[ἐλίπην]

372. The following are very common Second Aorists from *irregular* verbs.

EXAMPLES.

	ACT.	MID.
λαμβάνω (ληβ-) (capio)	ἔλαβον	ἐλαβόμην
λανθάνω (ληθ-) (lateo)	ἔλαθον	ἐλαθόμην
μανθάνω (μηθ-) (disco)	ἔμαθον	
τυγχάνω, (*chance ; hit*)	ἔτυχον	
πυνθάνομαι (πευθ-) (*inquire, learn by inquiry*)		ἐπυθόμην
δάκνω (*bite*)	ἔδακον	
κάμνω (laboro)	ἔκαμον	

Λανθάνω ποιῶν τι = *I do it unconsciously* (to myself) or *with not being observed* (by others).

373. Some Second Aorists have *not* the short penult. Two such, of very frequent use, are ἦλθον, *veni*, and εὗρον, *inveni* (see ἔρχομαι, List VII : εὑρίσκω, List V). Εἷλον (ἕλε, &c.) is Aor. 2. from obsolete root ἑλ-, used to supply the wanting tense of αἱρέω (List VII). ἁμαρτάνω, ἥμαρτον (List III).

---

* Observe the ε: it has ἔταμον once in Thuc. ; the only instance in Attic prose before Aristot. (*Kr.*)

374. ☞ Τρέψασθαι = *in fugam convertere* (e. g. hostes) : τραπέσθαι = *se convertere* (*to turn oneself; to go*).

375. The Moods of Aor. 2. for the *Active* and *Mid.*
have the same terminations as the Present Act. and
Mid.; those for Aor. 2. *Pass.* the same as for Aor. 1.
Pass.

But

    a) Infin. Aor. 2. Act. is *perispomenon:* εῖν.

    b) Partcp. Aor. 2. Act. is *oxytone:* ών, οὖσα, όν (όντος, &c.).

    c) Imperat. Aor. 2. Mid. is *perispomenon:* οῦ.

    d) Infin. Aor. 2. Mid. is *paroxytone:* έσθαι.

376. Remember that when you find a participle in ών, όν, *oxytone*
(or in όντος, όντι, όντα, &c. *paroxytone*), you may conclude it is the
participle of a Second Aor.

377. The Subj., Infin., and Partcp. of Aor. 2. Pass.
are (as in Aor. 1. Pass.) ῶ (*perispomenon*), ῆναι (*properispomenon*), είς (cùm acuto).

ἔλαβον	λαβέ*	λάβω	λάβοιμι	λαβεῖν	λαβών
ἐλαβόμην	λαβοῦ	λάβωμαι	λαβοίμην	λαβέσθαι	λαβόμενος
ἐγράφην	γράφητι	γραφῶ	γραφείην	γραφῆναι	γραφείς.

378. Vocabulary 43.

To aim at, στοχάζ-εσθαι (with gen.).

To chance, to hit (gen.) τυγχάν-ειν : hence, *to obtain, attain to.* τυγχάνω ποιῶν τι = *I happen* or *chance to be doing it:* often but little stronger than *I am doing it*, especially τυγχάνω ὤν.

To miss (a mark, gen.), *to err, sin,* ἁμαρτάν-ειν : aor. 2. ἥμαρτον.

To light upon, meet (with), ἐν-τυγχάν-ειν (with *dat.*).

Defiled, impure, vile (of persons), μιαρός, ά, όν.

To make drunk, καταμεθύσκ-ειν. Fut. καταμεθύσω.

To take up, ἀναιρεῖν (aor. 2. ἀνεῖλον, List VII).

To grow weary, ἀποκάμν-ειν (aor. 2. ἀπέκαμον) : aor. (in moods) *to be wearied, tired,* &c. (used with partic.).

---

* εἰπέ, εὐρέ, ἐλθέ, and in Attic λαβέ, ἰδέ, are *oxytone:* but in their compound forms the accent is thrown back : ἔξελθε · ἀπόλαβε.

To fling into, ἐμβάλλ-ειν.
By night, νύκτωρ (noctu).
To cut the throat (of any body),
ἀποσφάττ-ειν.

Book, βιβλίον, ου, τό.
A windfall, lucky discovery, ἔρμαιον, ου, τό (supposed to be
· sent by Hermes).

ἁμαρτάνω, ἁμαρτήσομαι, &c. Aor. 2. ἥμαρτον, List III

Exercise 48.

379. a) Translate into English.

1. Νῦν δὴ ἄμεινον ἂν μάθοις ὃ ἀρτὶ ἠρώτων. 2. Ὅταν ὅπλοις δέῃ ᵃ πρὸς ὅπλα χρῆσθαι, διαφέρει πάμπολυ ὁ μαθὼν τοῦ μὴ μαθόντος. 3. Ἄλλου στο- χαζόμενος ἔτυχε τούτου. 4. Ἡσίοδος ὁ ποιητὴς λέ- γεται ὑπὸ τῶν ταύτῃ ᵇ ἀποθανεῖν. 5. Τῶν ἀποθα- νόντων τὰ ὀστᾶ ἀνελόντες ἐξέβαλον. 6. Πόθεν τοῦτο τὸ ἔρμαιον εὑρέτην ; 7. Σύ μοι, ὦ ξένε, μηδαμῶς ἀποκάμῃς χαριζόμενος. ᶜ 8. Ταῦτα ἀκούων σφόδρα ἐχάρην. 9. Ὁ μιαρὸς οὗτος καταμεθύσας τὸν ξένον, ἐμβαλὼν εἰς ἅμαξαν, νύκτωρ ἐξαγαγὼν ᵈ ἀπέσφαξε, καὶ ταῦτα ἀδικήσας ἔλαθεν ἑαυτὸν ἀθλιώτατος γενόμε- νος. 10. Σχεδόν τί μοι ὥρα τραπέσθαι πρὸς τὸ λου- τρόν. 11. Τίς γὰρ ἄν ποτε ῥήτωρ ἐνεθυμήθη ἢ νομο- θέτης ἤλπισεν ἁμαρτήσεσθαί τινα τῶν πολιτῶν τοσαύ- την ἁμαρτίαν; ᵉ 12. Ὦ Εὐκλείδη, εἰ μειρακίῳ τινὶ ἐνέτυχες ἀξίῳ λόγου, ἡδέως ἂν πυθοίμην. 13. Παῖ, λαβὲ τὸ βιβλίον καὶ λέγε. ᶠ 14. Οὐκ ἔχω ὅποι τράπω- μαι. ᵍ

ᵃ δεῖ, oportet : Subj. δέῃ, δέοι, δεῖν, δέον : Fut. δεήσει—δεῆσαι.
ᵇ οἱ ταύτῃ = the men here, the people of this neighborhood. ᶜ How
are μή and its compounds used in prohibitions ? (K. 318. 3.) ἀπέκαμον ποιῶν τι = I am wearied (or tired) of doing it. (K. 310. 4.)
ᵈ A Second Aorist Participle (with what is called the Attic reduplication) from ἐξ-άγω. Aor. 2. ἐξ-ήγαγον. ᵉ ἁμαρτάνειν ἁμαρτίαν
(to sin a sin =) to commit a sin, K. 278. ᶠ Observe λαβέ.
single completed action (Aor.); λέγε, continued one (Pres.).
ᵍ = non habeo quo me vertam.

b) Translate into Greek.

1. The ambassadors of the Thebans did not receive these things. 2. The money slipt-away without his knowing it.[h] 3. It is a very great thing, to attain-to preservation. 4. If you (*pl.*) had done this, not one of you all would have attained-to safety.[i] 5. Let him pay what he has stolen (*p*) twice over.[k] 6. Did you not fling the corpse into a cart? 7. This •at least is not an easy thing, to hit that mark. 8. The boy, like some mad dog, bit his companions. 9. Whence did you learn so accurately what was done (*p*) by them? 10. I should like to learn Geometry. 11. He is said to have missed the mark.

[h] *Any thing slips away from any body without his knowing it,* λαν-θάνει τινά τι διαρρυέν (*neut. partcp.*), from Aor. 2. δι-ερρύην (from δια-ρρεῖν). Pdm. 63. ᵢ K. 260. 2. [k] *To pay any thing twice over,* or *restore it twofold,* ἐκτίνειν τι διπλάσιον.

LESSON L.

Second Perfect.

380. The *Second Perfect* and *Pluperfect* are formed from the *short root;* their terminations are *a,* ειν (the change for the other persons, and the rules for *augment* and *reduplication,* being the same as for the First Perf. and Pluperf.).—πέ-φευγ-α (φεύγω).

381. These tenses change the short *a, ε, ι* of the root into *η, o, οι* respectively: θάλλ-ω (θαλ-), τέθηλα: φαίνω (φαν-), πέφηνα: φθείρ-ω (φθερ-), ἔφθορα: λείπ-ω (λιπ-), λέλοιπα.

382. For roots which have ει in the Present, *liquid* roots have *o* in Perf. 2 (because their short root has ε);

mute-roots οι (because *their* short root has ι) : φθείρω, κτείνω, ἔφθορα, ἔκτονα ; λείπω, πείθω, λέλοιπα, πέποιθα.

383. Long *a* remains unchanged in πέπρᾱγα (πράσσω) and κέκρᾱγα (κράζω).

384. The partiality of the Perf. 2. for the *o*-sounds is shown in the irregular Perfects οἶδα (novi), *I know* (Pdm. 70) ; ἔοικα, *I resemble, or am like* (εἴκω) ; ἔῤῥωγα, *I am torn* (ῥήγνυμι, List IX) ; εἴωθα (solitus sum), *I am accustomed or wont* (ἔθω).

385. From verbs that have a *causative* meaning (i. e. that signify to *cause* to do any thing), the Perf. 2. has usually the *immediative* meaning (i. e. the meaning of *being caused to do*), which is an *intransitive* meaning : hence many of them have the meaning of a *new Present* (e. g. those in the last rule) with an (*immediative*) intransitive meaning.   Thus πήγνυμι, *I fix* (i. e. *cause* a thing to remain unmoved): πέπηγα, *I am fixed* (i. e. *am caused* to remain unmoved).—It is in this way that some Second Perfects *appear* to belong to the Middle Voice, since the (*causative*) Perf. Act. is not in use, but the Middle (in an *immediate* sense) is : thus γίγνομαι = fio ; Perf. 2. γέγονα (= I have been caused to exist), *I do exist, I am* (also as Perf. to εἰμί : κακὰ γέγονε, καὶ ἔστι, καὶ ἔσται) : μαίνομαι, *I am becoming mad ;* μέμηνα (I have been rendered mad =) *I am mad* (the verb μαίνω, insanum facio, being obsolete).

386. *Futurum Atticum.*] When σω is preceded by a short vowel, the σ of *Fut. Act.* and *Mid.* is sometimes left out in the Attic .dialect, and the two vowels contracted, so that the terminations become ῶ, οῦμαι : τελέω, *Attic Future* τελῶ ; *Mid.* τελοῦμαι.

From verbs in ἐω, άζω (Fut. ἐσω, άσω) this Fut. occurs *often* (not *always*) only in καλέω, τελέω, βιβάζω. In Mid. μαχοῦμαι (from μάχομαι). ᾿Ελῶ, ᾷς, ᾷ (= ἐλάσω, from ἐλαύνω) is also the usual form : and σκεδῶ, ᾷς, ᾷ, &c. (= σκεδάσω, from σκεδάννυμι, List X), probably the *only* Attic form.

387. When the short vowel is ι, the two vowels are not capable of contraction ; but the ω is circumflexed, and conjugated *as if* a contraction had taken place. Thus (νομίσω), νομιῶ, εῖς, &c.

τελέσω—τελῶ, τελεῖς,　⎫
νομίσω—νομιῶ, νομιεῖς,　⎬　εῖ | οὖμεν, εῖτε, οὖσι(ν). | εῖτον, εῖτον
βιβάσω—βιβῶ, βιβᾷς, βιβᾷ　⎭　　| ῶμεν, ᾶτε, ῶσι(ν). | ᾶτον, ᾶτον

So in the Mid. κομίζω, κομίσομαι, Att. Fut. κομιοῦμαι, εῖ, εῖται, &c.

This form of the Fut. never occurs in the *Optative :* e. g. τελῶ, τελεῖν, τελῶν : but Opt. τελέσοιμι (*K*.).

388. Vocabulary 44.

To speak with frankness, παρρη-σιάζ-εσθαι.　καλῶς παρρ. *to speak with an honorable frankness.*

To spoil, to corrupt, to destroy, διαφθείρ-ειν.

To contend for a prize, ἀγωνίζ-εσθαι.

To burn (up), καταφλέγ-ειν.

To trade for profit, to make money by trade, χρηματίζ-εσθαι.

(*To write upon* =) *to inscribe, to entitle,* ἐπιγράφ-ειν.

To throw beyond = *to exceed, surpass,* ὑπερβάλλ-εσθαι.

Renown, reputation, εὔκλεια, as, ἡ.

Pugilist, boxer, πύκτης, ου, ὁ.

To knock to pieces, to batter, συγ-κόπτ-ειν.

To awaken, i. e. *cause to wake,* ἐγείρ-ειν : ἐγρήγορα = *I am awake* (an irreg. Perf. 2).

To quit, to desert, ἀπολείπ-ειν.

To leave behind, καταλείπ-ειν.

Suggestion, ὑποθήκη, ης, ἡ.

To break, ἄγνυμι (List IX).

To break (of bones, &c.), κατάγ-νυμι.

Wrist, καρπός, οῦ, ὁ.

Exercise 49.

389. *a) Translate into English.*

1. Καλῶς ἐπαρρησιάσατο ὁ Σόλων πρὸς Κροῖσον ὑπ' εὐτυχίας διεφθορότα, τὸ τέλος ὁρᾶν κελεύων. 2. Ὀνήτωρ βιβλίον ἐξέδωκεν[a] ἐπιγραφόμενον· 'Εἰ χρηματιεῖται ὁ σοφός.' 3. Οἱ πύκται τὰ ὦτα συγκεκομμένα εἶχον καὶ ἐαγότα.[b] 4. Ἀριστοτέλης τὴν ἐλπίδα ἐγρηγορότος εἶπεν ἐνύπνιον. 5. Αἰδὼς καὶ Νέμεσις τὸν ἀνθρώπινον βίον ἀπολελοίπασιν. . 6. Ξένῳ σιγᾶν κρεῖττον· ἢ κεκραγέναι. 7. Νομιοῦμεν ὁμοίως ἀσεβεῖν τούς τε τὰ ψευδῆ λέγοντας περὶ τῶν θεῶν καὶ τοὺς πιστεύοντας αὐτοῖς. 8. Τῶν ποιητῶν τινες ὑποθήκας ὡς χρὴ ζῆν ἡμῶ καταλελοίπασιν. 9. Λέγεται πεπομφέναι Κροῖσον εἰς Λακεδαίμονα περὶ συμμαχίας. 10. Μὴ νομίζετε τῷ Φιλίππῳ τὰ πράγματα πεπηγέναι ἀθάνατα. 11. Σωκράτης, στρέψαντος Ἀντισθένους τὸ διερρωγὸς[d] τοῦ τρίβωνος εἰς τοὐμφανές,[e] 'Ὁρῶ σου, ἔφη, διὰ τοῦ τρίβωνος τὴν κενοδοξίαν.

[a] Aor. 1. of ἐκ-δίδωμι, *to put forth ; to publish.*   [b] Perf. 2. of ἄγνυμι, List IX.   [c] Note 13.   [d] δι-έρρωγα, Perf. 2. of διαῤ-ῥήγνυμι. τὸ διερρωγὸς = *the torn part.* ῥήγνυμι, List IX.
[e] = εἰς τὸ ἐμφανές (lit. *to the visible* =) *so as to let it be seen.*

b) Translate into Greek.

1. It is a benefit from the gods, that some alliance has appeared for us. ‖ 2. They say[f] that the general himself fled. 3. They said[f] that the general himself had fled. 4. The boxer has his wrist broken. 5. Is the boy asleep or awake? 6. You are more like °a man asleep than °one awake. 7. You will not rightly deem that your °prosperous affairs are fixed for you immutably (*say:* ''°as immortal').

[f] Use λέγω (ὡς or ὅτι).

LESSON LI.

Comparative and Superlative.

390. The *comparative* and *superlative* (1) from ος are ότερος, ότατος, or, if the preceding syllable is *short*, ώτερος, ώτατος [but here a *muta cum liquidâ* is considered to lengthen the syllable: σφοδρός, σφοδρότερος, σφοδρότατος].—(2) from ης, έστερος, έστατος [σαφ|ής, σαφέστερος, &c.]—(3) from υς, ύτερος, ύτατος [γλυκ-ύς, γλυκ-ύτερος, &c.—(4) from ων, ον-έστερος, ον-έστατος (εὐδαίμων, Gen. εὐδαίμον-ος, εὐδαιμ-ον-έστερος, &c.).

391. A few in ύς, ρός, have ίων, ιστος. The ιων has neut. ιον (G. ιονος, &c.), and the ι is long in Attic Greek. —The only *regular* adjectives that take this form in Attic prose are ἡδύς, ταχύς, αἰσχρός, ἐχθρός (those in ρος lose the ρ, αἰσχίων, &c.).

For ταχίων, τάχιον, the Attics said θάσσων, θᾶσσον, later θάττων, θᾶττον.

(*Eng.*)   Too wise to be deceived.
(*Greek.*)   Wiser *than so-as* (ἢ ὥστε) to be deceived.

392. VOCABULARY 45.

Spiritless, faint-hearted, ἄθυμος, ον.

Soft, μαλακός, ή, όν.

Mischievous, κακοῦργος, ον.

Impetuous, προπετής, ές (πρόπετ-, short root of πίπτω = πιπέτ-ω, cado).

Thoughtful, φροντιστικός, ή, όν.

Spirited, courageous, θυμώδης, ες.

Savage, ἄγριος, α, ον.

Plotting, treacherous, ἐπίβουλος, ον.

Compassionate, ἐλεήμων, -ονος.

Tearful, ἀρίδακρυς, υ.

Envious, φθονερός, ά, όν.

Dissatisfied, repining, μεμψίμοιρος, ον.

Bitter, πικρός, ά, όν.

Abusive, φιλολοίδορος, ον.

Disposed to strike, quarrelsome, πληκτικός, ή, όν.

Desponding, δύσελπις, ιδος.

Shameless, ἀναιδής, ές.

Easily deceived, εὐαπάτητος. ον.

Having a retentive memory, μνημονικός, ή, όν.

Sleepless, ἄγρυπνος, ον.

Timid, ὀκνηρός, ά, όν.

7*

Immovable, not easily moved, ἀκίνητος, ον.	Panther, πάρδαλις, εως, ἡ.
	Male, ἄῤῥην, ἄῤῥεν.
Ready or able to help, βοηθητικός, ἡ, όν.	Female, θῆλυς, εια, υ.
	Desponding, down-hearted, δύσ-
Bear, ἄρκτος, ου, ἡ.	θῦμος, ον.

Exercise 50.

393. a) Translate into English.

1. Ἀθυμότερα τὰ θήλεα πάντα τῶν ἀῤῥένων πλὴν ἄρκτου καὶ παρδάλεως· τούτων δὲ ἡ θήλεια δοκεῖ εἶναι ἀνδρειότερα· ἐν δὲ τοῖς ἄλλοις γένεσι τὰ θήλεα μαλακώτερα καὶ κακουργότερα καὶ ἧττον ἁπλᾶ καὶ προπετέστερα καὶ περὶ τὴν τῶν τέκνων τροφὴν φροντιστικώτερα, τὰ δ' ἄρρενα τἀναντία·[*] θυμωδέστερα γὰρ καὶ ἀγριώτερα καὶ ἁπλούστερα καὶ ἧττον[b] ἐπίβουλα. 2. Γυνὴ ἀνδρὸς ἐλεημονέστερον καὶ ἀρίδακρυ μᾶλλον, ἔτι δὲ φθονερώτερόν τε καὶ μεμψιμοιρότερον καὶ φιλολοίδορον μᾶλλον καὶ πληκτικώτερον, ἔτι δὲ καὶ δύσθυμον μᾶλλον τὸ θῆλυ τοῦ ἄρρενος καὶ δύσελπι καὶ ἀναιδέστερον καὶ ψευδέστερον· εὐαπατητότερον δὲ καὶ μνημονικώτερον· ἔτι δὲ ἀγρυπνότερον καὶ ὀκνηρότερον καὶ ὅλως ἀκινητότερον τὸ θῆλυ τοῦ ἄρρενος, καὶ τροφῆς ἐλάττονός[b] ἐστιν· βοηθητικώτερον δὲ ὥσπερ ἐλέχθη, καὶ ἀνδρειότερον τὸ ἄῤῥεν τοῦ θήλεός ἐστιν (Aristot.). 3. Ὁ βαθύτατος ὕπνος ἥδιστός ἐστιν. 4. Οὐδὲν θᾶττόν ἐστι τῆς ἥβης.

[*] = τὰ ἐναντία, sc. ἐστί, are the opposite [o]of all this.
b Note 13.

b) Translate into Greek.

1. Nothing is more bitter than compulsion. 2. He asked if the son were braver than his father. 3. Is the son wiser than his father?—[No. K. 344. 5.] 4. The man is more shameless than brave. 5. This woman is very envious and dissatisfied. 6. I hate abusive [o]persons. 7. The soldier is too brave to

fear death. 8. The man has a most immovable nature. 9. Friendship is the most delightful of all things. 10. Nothing is more disgraceful than to have one thing in one's mind and to utter another.*

*Say: *other things—but others; ἄλλα μὲν—ἄλλα δέ.*

LESSON LII.

Verbs in μι. Τίθημι.

394. VOCABULARY 46.

I place, I appoint, I hold or set down (as); I make, render; I enact, appoint, &c. (laws), τίθημι.

I put up, offer, ἀνατίθημι.

I dispose (a person), διατίθημι.

I put in, instil, ἐντίθημι.

I put down, I lay (down) upon, κατατίθημι.

I change, alter, μετατίθημι.

I put or set round, περιτίθημι.

I add, προστίθημι.

I put before, lay out (for view), set out for display, προτίθημι.

Citadel, ἀκρόπολις, εως, ἡ.

Lioness, λέαινα, ης, ἡ.

Another's, of others, ἀλλότριος, α, ον (alienus).

Heavy, troublesome, ἀργαλέος, έα, έον.

One who rules, ruler, Archon (at Athens), ἄρχων, οντος, (properly, partcp. of ἄρχειν).

Head-band, diadem, διάδημα, α-τος, τό.

Sweat, toil, ἱδρώς, ῶτος, ὁ.

Thyrsus (i. e. the staff of the Bacchantes, wound round with ivy and vine leaves), θύρσος, ου, ὁ.

Ivy, κισσός or κιττός, ου, ὁ.

Exercise 51.

[*The Act. Voice of* τίθημι *is to be learnt by heart.*]

395. a) Translate into English.

1. Τόδε θαυμάζω εἰ· ἐν ἀρετῆς καὶ σοφίας τίθης μέρει· τὴν ἀδικίαν. 2. Ὁ πλοῦτος πολλάκις μετατίθησι τὸν τῶν ἀνθρώπων τρόπον. 3. Πολλάκις οἱ ἄνθρωποι τοῖς ἰδίοις κακοῖς ἀλλότρια προστιθέασιν. 4.

Εἰς τὸ βέλτιον τίθει τὸ μέλλον. 5. Ἀντίγονος Διόνυσοι πάντα· ἐμιμεῖτο, καὶ κιττὸν μὲν περιτιθεὶς τῇ κεφαλῇ ἀντὶ διαδήματος Μακεδονικοῦ, θύρσον δὲ ἀντὶ σκήπτρου φέρων. 6. Οἱ σοφισταὶ τὴν ἀρετὴν προετίθεσαν. 7. Ἐντιθῶμεν τοῖς νέοις τῆς σοφίας ἔρωτα. 8. Ἡ τύχη πάντα ἂν μετατιθείη. 9. Οὐ ῥᾴδιον τὴν φύσιν μετατι θέναι. 10. Ἀθηναῖοι χαλκῆν ποιησάμενοι λέαιναν ἐν πύλαις τῆς ἀκροπόλεως ἀνέθεσαν. 11. Ῥᾷον [Note 13] ἐξ ἀγαθοῦ θεῖναι κακόν, ἢ ἐκ κακοῦ ἀγαθόν. 12. Τὸ κακὸν οὐδεὶς χρηστὸν ἂν θείη. 13. Μετάθετε τὰς δια- φοράς. 14. Ὁ πόλεμος πάντα μετατέθεικεν. 15. Πρὸ τῆς ἀρετῆς θεοὶ ἱδρῶτα ἔθηκαν. 16. Οἱ παλαιοὶ τοῖς ἀποθανοῦσιν ὀβολὸν εἰς τὸ στόμα κατέθηκαν. 17. Ὅπως ἂν τοὺς ἄλλους πρὸς σαυτὸν διαθῇς, οὕτω καὶ σὺ πρὸς ἐκείνους ἕξεις. d

ᵃ θαυμάζω εἰ — = I am surprised that —: literally, I am surprised if you do it; courteously implying a doubt whether you really do it.

ᵇ τιθέναι τι ἐν μέρει τινός = to set it down in the class or sphere of = to reckon or look upon it as —. ᶜ in all things or respects (neut. adj. used adverbially). ᵈ See ἔχω in Index.

b) Translate into Greek.

1. Zeus (Jupiter) places all things as* he chooses. 2. Rulers who attempt (p) to enact laws, enact some *laws properly, and some few ᶠ not properly. 3. Let us set-down geometry as a study for the young. 4. I admire Lycurgus, him who enacted (p) their laws for the Lacedæmonians, and think him wise in an extreme degree.ᵍ 5. You propose an embarrassingʰ choice. 6. Shall we not place sweetmeats before the boys? 7. Who would not place meat and bread, not sweetmeats, before one who is excessively hungry (p)? 8. Do you wish me to set-down ᶦ that you are afraid?

* ὅπη (ubi quo), where; how. ᶠ τοὺς δέ τινας —. ᵍ εἰς
τὰ ἔσχατα = to the last (degree). ʰ ἄπορος (ἀ, non. πόρος, trans-

itus), prop. *from which there is no outlet, no means of extricating oneself,*
ὁ, ἡ.   ι βούλει σε θῶ (deliberative subj. [238] after βούλει, 2nd
sing. 285); = *visne?*

LESSON LIII.

Verbs in μι. Ἵστημι.

396. On the meaning of the verb ἵστημι, the following things are to be noted: the Pres., Impf., Fut.
and first Aor. Act. have a transitive meaning, *to place;*
but the second Aor., Perf. and Pluperf. Act. (with the
Fut. ἑστήξω, later -ομαι) have a reflexive or intransitive
meaning, *to place oneself = to stand:* ἔστην, *I stood,*
ἕστηκα, *I have placed myself = I stand,* sto, ἑστήκειν
(or εἱστήκειν), stabam, ἑστήξω, stabo (ἀφεστήξω, *I shall
withdraw*). The Fut. Mid. στήσομαι = *I will stand;*
or *I will place for myself* (i. e. corresponds both to
ἔστην and ἔστησα).

The forms ἕστηκα, (ἑστήκειν) εἱστήκειν, ἔστην, are
used for the corresponding forms of the *Pass.* or *Mid.;*
but the Aor. Pass. ἐστάθην is in general use, often bor-
dering on the meaning of ἔστην: ἔσταμαι, ἐστάμην are
very seldom found; the Aor. 2. ἐστάμην never.—Whether ἔστησαν belongs to ἔστησα or ἔστην can only be
known from the context. (*Kr.*)

397: VOCABULARY 47.

I place, I raise, ἵστημι.

I set, raise up, ἀνίστημι. Mid.
raise myself up, stand up.

*I put away, turn aside from,
cause to revolt,* ἀφίστημι: Aor.
2. *fell away:* Mid. *I go, stand
apart.*

I place apart, separate, διΐστημι.

I put into, ἐνίστημι: perf. *I am
present.*

I lay down, establish, καθίστημι:
καταστῆναι = *to be reduced to,
to be placed in:* καθεστηκέναι
= *to be established, to be.*

I place beside, παρίστημι.	Marsh, pond, lake, λίμνη, ης, ἡ.
Cretan, Κρητικός, ή, όν.	Where, πῆ.
To draw away, ἀποσπᾶν (= ά-εἰν).	Constitution, πολιτεία, as, ἡ.
	Difficulty, perplexity, embarrass-
To turn away, to alienate, ἀπ-οστρέφ-ειν.	ment, ἀπορία, as, ἡ.
Dry, thirsty, αὗος, η, ον.	Multitude of friends, πολυφιλία, as, ἡ.
Sacrifice, ϑυσία, as, ἡ.	That, ὡς.

Exercise 52.

[Go through the Act. Voice of ἵστημι.]

398. a) Translate into English.

1. Ἀθυμοῦντες ἄνδρες οὔπω τροπαιον ἔστησαν.   2. Καθέστηκέ τι ἔϑος δίκαιον πᾶσιν ἀνθρώποις, τῶν αὐτῶν ἀδικημάτων· a μάλιστα ὀργίζεσϑαι b τοῖς μάλιστα δυναμένοις μὴ ἀδικεῖν. 3. Τὴν Κρητικὴν πολιτείαν λέγεται πρῶτος καταστῆσαι· Μίνως. 4. Ἡ πολυφιλία διίστησι καὶ ἀποσπᾶ καὶ ἀποστρέφει.   5. Εἴ τις ϑυσίαν προσφέρων εὔνουν νομίζει τὸν ϑεὸν καθιστάναι, φρένας κούφας ἔχει.   6. Φυλάττου, μὴ τὸ κέρδος σε τῆς δικαιοσύνης ἀφιστῇ.   7. Μὴ ἀφίστη τοὺς νέους τῆς ἐπὶ τὴν ἀρετὴν ὁδοῦ.   8. Ὁ Τάνταλος ἐν τῇ λίμνῃ αὗος εἱστήκει.   9. Τὸ μὲν τοῦ χρόνου d γεγονός, τὸ δὲ ἐνεστώς· ἐστι, τὸ δὲ μέλλον.   10. Οἱ Κορίνθιοι πολλοὺς συμμάχους ἀπέστησαν ἀπὸ τῶν Ἀθηναίων.   11. Οἱ Νάξιοι ἀπὸ τῶν Ἀθηναίων ἀπέστησαν.   12. Παράστᾱ τοῖς ἀτυχέσιν. 13. Πῆ στῶ ;f πῆ βῶ ;   14. Οἱ Ἀθηναῖοι τοῖς Ναξίοις ἀποστᾶσιν ἀπ' αὐτῶν ἐπολέμησαν.

a for the same faults.   b -K. 284. 8. 6.   c What force has the Aor. Infin. after a verbum dicendi?   d τὸ μὲν... τὸ δὲ, one part ... another, &c.   e ἐνεστώς = praesens, Perf. partcp. syncopated, Pdm. 63. γεγονός (= quod fuit, praeteritum), Perf. partcp. neut. from γέγονα, Perf. of γίγνομαι.   f The deliberative subjunctive, 238. βῶ is subj. of βαίνω, Pdm. 66.

b) Translate into Greek.

1. The bad reduce you to a total-want ᵉ of friends.
2. Lycurgus established the •national truces •as a
common benefit.   3. Lycurgus did not attempt to
establish his laws before he had made the most
powerful •men in the state ʰ •to be of-one-mind.   4.
After this man Alcamĕnes received the supreme
power,ⁱ after whom Alcander, a moderate man, was
at the head of affairs.ᵏ   5. The cities place the
images of their benefactors in the temples.   6. Makeⁱ
your own temperance an example to others.   7.
Change what is not rightly established.ᵐ   8.
Conon raised the walls of Athens (*say :* of the Athenians).

ᵉ ἐρημία.   ʰ *Say :* the most powerful of those in the state.
    ⁱ τὰ πράγματα, *affairs = the management* of (state) affairs.
ᵏ *To be at the head of affairs,* προστῆναι.   ⁱ καθίστημι.
ᵐ *Say :* the things not rightly established ; and use *perf. partcp.* of
the syncopated form from καθίστημι, Pdm. 65.

LESSON LIV.

Δίδωμι. Act.   Acc. from impure Nouns in ις.

399. *Acc. of Third Decl. in ν.*]   This Acc. belongs
to the terminations ις, υς, αυς, ους.   We have seen that
pure nouns (i. e. those with a *vowel* before the termination of the cases) all take this Acc.—For *impure* nouns
(those whose root ends in a *consonant*) the following
rule *generally* holds good for *Attic* prose.

a) Acc. is *never* ν if the final syllable of the (impure) root is accented : ἀσπίς, ἀσπίδ·ος, *shield ;*
acc. ἀσπίδα.

b) Acc. is *never* ν for a *monosyllable* root : πούς,
ποδ-ός, *foot ;* acc. πόδα.

c) If a *hypermonosyllable impure* root is *not accented on the final syllable*, the acc. is usually ν.—
This applies principally to ἔρις, ἐριδ-ος, *strife ;* acc.
ἔριν : χάρις, χάριτ-ος, *gratia ;* acc. χάριν (but Χάριτα
= one of the *Graces*).

400. VOCABULARY 48.

I give, grant, δίδωμι.	*Immediately,* εὐθύς.
I give back, repay, ἀποδίδωμι : Mid. *I sell.*	*Happy, blessed,* μάκαρ, αρος.
I give any one a share of any thing, μεταδίδωμι τινί τινος.	*Thoroughly bad,* πάγκακος, ον.
I betray, προδίδωμι (prodo).	*Again, on the contrary,* παλιν.
Salt, ἅλς, ἁλός, ὁ. (Note 9.)	*I am in want,* χρῄζω (with gen.).
Firm, sure, lasting, ἔμπεδος, ον.	*To fatten,* πιαίν-ειν.
I forget, ἐπιλανθάνομαι.	*Favor, grace,* χάρις, χάριτ-ος, ἡ. χάριν ἀποδιδόναι ·(= gratiam reddere), *to make a return.*

Exercise 53.

[*Go through the Act. Voice of* δίδωμι.]

401. *a) Translate into English.*

1. Πιαίνει μάλιστα τὸ πρόβατον τὸ πότον· διὸ καὶ
τοῦ θέρους.διδόασιν ἅλας ͣ διὰ ⁷ πέντε ἡμερῶν. 2.
Γυναικὶ ἄρχειν οὐ δίδωσιν ἡ φύσις. 3. Χάριν λαβὼν ᵇ
μέμνησο,ᶜ καὶ δοὺς ἐπιλαθοῦ. 4. Λαβὼν ἀπόδος, καὶ
λήψῃ ᵈ πάλιν. 5. Ὦ μάκαρες θεοί, δότε μοι ὄλβον καὶ
δόξαν ἀγαθὴν ἔχειν. 6. Ὁ πλοῦτος, ὃν ἂν δῶσι θεοί,
ἔμπεδός ἐστιν. 7. Ἃ ἡ φύσις δέδωκε, ταῦτ' ἔχει μόνα ὁ
ἄνθρωπος. 8. Ὧν ͤ σοι θεὸς ἔδωκε, τούτων χρῄζουσι
δίδου. 9. Θεός μοι δοίη φίλους πιστούς· 10. Τοῖς πλου-
σίοις πρέπει ͥ τοῖς πτωχοῖς δοῦναι. 11. Οἱ στρατιῶται
τὴν πόλιν τοῖς πολεμίοις προὐδίδοσαν. 12. Ὁ ἀγαθὸς
χαίρει τοῖς πένησι χρημάτων μεταδιδούς. 13. Δεῖ τοὺς
ἀγαθοὺς ἄνδρας γενναίως φέρειν, ὅ τι ἂν ὁ θεὸς διδῷ.

14. Ὅς ἂν μέλλῃ τὴν πατρίδα προδιδόναι, μεγίστης·
ζημίας ἄξιός ἐστιν. 15. Οἱ θεοί μοι ἀντὶ κακῶν ἀγαθὰ
διδοῖεν. 16. Φίλος φίλον οὐ προδώσει. 17. Εὖ παθόν·
τες ʰ ὑπ' ἐμοῦ τοιαύτην χάριν ἀπέδοσαν.

* Note 9.　　　ᵇ Aor. 2. partcp. fr. ϰαμβάνω, List IV.
* μέμνημαι (I have recollected =) I remember.　　ᵈ Aor. 2. Imper
fr. ἐπι-λανθάν-ομαι, List IV.　　* Attraction.　　ᶠ τρέπειν, ᾳ
dat.　　ᵍ Note 13.　　ʰ Aor. 2. partcp. fr. πάσχω, List VII.

b) Translate into Greek.

1. The gods give all things. 2. Give immediately
to a poor man. 3. Endeavor (*pl.*) to give each manᶦ
his dueᵏ accurately. 4. He repaid the money. 5. If
you give him money, he will make you also wise.
6. If any one were to giveᶦ him money, he would make
him also wise. 7. If you had given him money, he
would have made you also wise. 8. The earth, giving
us food, is seen to be a kind of mother. 9. Give me
my shield. 10. Give (*pl.*) me an example of this kind
•of thing. 11. The gods have·given (*Aor.*) this •as
a privilegeᵐ to •but a few that are easily-counted.ⁿ

ᶦ εἷς ἕκαστος, *lit.* 'each one man.'　　ᵏ τὸ προσῆκον (partcp. of
προσήκειν, *to come to him* =) to belong to him.　　ᶦ K. 260. 2.
　　ᵐ Use οὗτος, *without* prefixing the article to γέρας.
ⁿ εὐαριθμήτοις δή τισιν (δή adds *emphasis* to the superlative).

LESSON LV.
Verbs in ῡμι. Δείκνῡμι.

402. VOCABULARY 49.

I show, δείκνῡμι.

I show, represent, explain, declare
any one as any thing ; hence;

I appoint, ἀποδείκνῡμι (with

two accus.) : Mid. show of myself, express, declare, display,
render.

Not to be seen, ἀθέατος, ον.

Justly, fairly, δικαίως.

Inconsiderately, unadvisedly, εἰκῆ.

To remain with, abide by, ἐμμέν-
εἰν (with dat.).

Within, ἐντός (with gen.).

To cause to swear, administer an
oath to, ἐξορκοῦν (=όειν).

Forsworn, perjured, false, ἐπίορ-
κος, ον.

I swear by, ἐπόμνυμι (with acc.).

Moderate, μέτριος, α, ον. (Attic,
-ος, -ον.)

Never, μήποτε.

An imitator, μιμητής, οῦ, ὁ.

I swear, ὄμνυμι.

An oath, ὅρκος, ου, ὁ.

In every way, throughout, wholly,
πάντως.

To order, παραγγέλλ-ειν.

Modelling (art), sculpture, πλα-
στική (τέχνη, underst.).

I strengthen, ῥώννυμι.

Rarely, seldom, σπανίως.

A decree, a resolution, ψήφισμα,
ατος, τό.

I lie (jaceo), I am enacted (ol
laws), κεῖμαι.

Exercise 54.

[Go through the Act. Voice of δείκνυμι.]

403. a) *Translate into English.*

1. Νόμος δὴ κείσθω δικαστὴν ὀμνύναι δικάζειν μέλλοντα. 2. Ὅρκον φεῦγε, κἂν δικαίως ὀμνύῃς. 3. Μή τι.
θεοὺς ἐπίορκον ἐπόμνυ. 4. Ὁ οἶνος μέτριος ληφθεὶς
ῥώννυσιν. 5. Οἱ διδάσκαλοι τοὺς μαθητὰς μιμητὰς ἑαυ-
τῶν ἀποδεικνύᾶσιν. 6. Πυθαγόρας παρήγγειλε τοῖς
μανθάνουσι, σπανίως μὲν ὀμνύναι, χρησαμένους δὲ τοῖς.
ὅρκοις πάντως ἐμμένειν. 7. Ἡ πλαστικὴ δείκνῦσι τὰ
εἴδη τῶν θεῶν, τῶν ἀνθρώπων, καὶ ἐνίοτε καὶ τῶν θηρῶν.
8. Ἀνδρὸς νοῦν οἶνος ἔδειξεν.ᵃ 9. Φρύγες ὅρκοις οὐ χρῶ-
νται οὔτ᾽ ὀμνύντες, οὔτ᾽ ἄλλους ἐξορκοῦντες. 10. Ὀλί-
γοις δείκνῦ τὰ ἐντὸς φρενῶν. 11. Οἱ κριταὶ τὰ ψηφί-
σματα ἀπεδείκνυσαν. 12. Μήποτε εἰκῆ ὀμνύοιτε. 13. Ὁ
βασιλεὺς τὸν αὑτοῦ υἱὸν στρατηγὸν ἀποδέδειχεν.

ᵃ The Aor. is often used in making *general assertions* founded on
experience. *We* should use the *Present*.

b) *Translate into Greek.*

1. If you fear (pl.) the gods, you will not ever
swear a false oath. 2. He is said to have sworn a

false oath. 3. We are swearing false oaths. 4. Let us endeavor both to investigate and to prove why in the world▸ such persons are unfortunate. 5. They appointed Alcibiades general, with four others. 6. Even though⁞ you should not swear, all will trust you. 7. Such a man will swear false oaths. 8. My (*say:* the) tongue·hath sworn, but my mind·is unsworn.

▸ τί ποτε (= quid tandem).   ⁞ κἂν = καὶ ἐάν (c. subj.).

LESSON LVI.

Τίθημι. *Pass. and Mid.*

404. VOCABULARY 50.

I put away, ἀποτίθημι: Mid. *lay aside, take off* (from myself).

I put in order, manage; with an adv. *put into a disposition,* διατίθημι. Pass. *to be affected by.* κακῶς (ἀθλίως, &c.), *to be miserably indisposed, distressed,* &c.

I add, put upon, ἐπιτίθημι. Mid. *put on* (oneself); with *dat., attack, set upon.*

I lay down, κατατίθημι. Mid. *lay down for oneself, to deposit* (money in any body's hands), *to lay by* or *up.*

I place by or *near,* παρατίθημι; τὰ παρατιθέμενα (ea quæ apponuntur), *the dishes placed on the table.*

Celtiberian, Κελτίβηρ, -ηρος, ὁ.

Self-control, continence, ἐγκράτεια, ας, ἡ.

Travelling-money, provisions (for the way), ἐφόδιον, ου, τό (viaticum).

Foundation, θεμέλιον, ου, τό.

Helmet, κράνος, εος, τό.

Cretan, Κρής, Κρητός.

Crest, λόφος, ου, ὁ.

To legislate, to make laws, νομοθετεῖν.

Purple, φοινίκεος, έα, εον (contract. οῦς, ῆ, οῦν).

Exercise 55.

[*Go through Pass. and Mid. of* τίθημι]

405. *a*) **Translate into English.**

1. Προσήκειν ἔγωγε νομίζω, ὅταν μὲν νομοθετῶμεν, τοῦθ᾽ ἡμᾶς σκοπεῖν, ὅπως καλῶς ἔχοντας καὶ συμφέροντας νόμους τῇ πόλει θησόμεθα, ἐπειδὰν δὲ νομοθετήσωμεν, τοῖς νόμοις τοῖς κειμένοις πείθεσθαι. 2. Οἱ Κρῆτες ἄρχονται τῶν παρατιθεμένων ἀπὸ τῶν ξένων· μετὰ δὲ τοὺς ξένους τῷ ἄρχοντι διδόασι τέσσαρας μοίρας. 3. Οἱ Κελτίβηρες περὶ τὰς κεφαλὰς κράνη χαλκᾶ περιτίθενται φοινικοῖς ἠσκημένα* λόφοις. 4. Οὐδένα θησαυρὸν παισὶ καταθήσῃ ἀμείνω[b] αἰδοῦς. 5. Τίς ἂν ἑκὼν φίλον ἄφρονα θοῖτο; 6. Ξενοφῶντι θύοντι ἧκέ τις ἐκ Μαντινείας ἄγγελος λέγων, τὸν υἱὸν αὐτοῦ τὸν Γρύλλον τεθνάναι·[c] κἀκεῖνος ἀπέθετο μὲν τὸν στέφανον, διετέλει δὲ θύων· ἐπεὶ δὲ ὁ ἄγγελος προσέθηκε καὶ ἐκεῖνο, ὅτι νικῶν[d] τέθνηκε, πάλιν ὁ Ξενοφῶν ἐπέθετο τὸν στέφανον. 7. Ἀλκιβιάδης ἔφυγεν εἰς Σπάρτην καὶ τοὺς Λακεδαιμονίους παρώξυνεν ἐπιθέσθαι τοῖς Ἀθηναίοις. 8. Οἱ πολῖται φοβοῦνται, μὴ οἱ πολέμιοι τῇ πόλει ἐπιτιθῶνται.

---

* ἀσκεῖν (= έ-ειν), *to work curiously; adorn ; ornament.* [b] **Note**
13. [c] Pdm. 65. [d] νικᾶν = *victor sum.*

b) **Translate into Greek.**

1. The citizens attack the enemy. 2. They had feared that the enemy would attack the city. 3. The boys put-on their garlands. 4. Do you wish that I[i] should set-upon[e] the man? 5. They are afraid that the Lacedæmonians will attack them if they divide their forces.[f] 6. We call the sign of a sound that is affixed[g] *to it its name. 7. Place very great gates to your ears. 8. Then at once (τότε ἤδη) we will attack the enemy. 9. The judge was reduced to a sad

condition ᵇ by the disease.   10. They had been grievously indisposed both in body and soul.

ᵉ K. 259. 1.   ᶠ *To divide their forces, γίγνεσθαι δίχα.*
ᵍ *To be affixed to —, ἐπιτεθῆναι.*   ʰ *To be reduced to a sad condition, ἀθλιώτατα διατεθῆναι.*

LESSON LVII.

Ἵστημι, &c.   Passive and Mid. Voices.

406. VOCABULARY 51.

I know, I understand, ἐπίσταμαι (with pass. aor.).

I put together, συνίστημι: Mid. assemble, unite, bring together.

To keep awake, to spend a sleepless night, to forego sleep, ἀγρυπνεῖν (=έειν).

Worth mentioning, noticeable, memorable, ἀξιόλογος, ον.

Second, δεύτερος, a, ον.

To be able, can, δύναμαι (with pass. aor.); with πολλά, οὐδέν,

&c. = I have power (like multum, nihil, &c., valère).

Foolish, μωρός, ά. όν: ὁ μωρός, the fool.

Drunkenness, μέθη, ης, ἡ.

Belonging to ships, nautical, ναυτικός, ή, όν: ναυτικὴ δύναμις, naval power.

The rule of a few, oligarchy, ὀλιγαρχία, ας, ἡ.

First, πρῶτος, η, ον.

To fill, πληροῦν (= όειν).

Exercise 56.

[*Go through Pass. and Mid. of ἵστημι.*]

407. a) Translate into English.

1. Αἱ ἐν Λακεδαίμονι γυναῖκες ᵃ τρέφουσὶ τὰ τέκνα ὥστε μηδέποτε πληροῦν, ἵνα ἐθίζωνται δύνασθαι πεινῆν. ᵇ 2. Οἱ Λακεδαιμόνιοι ἐθίζουσι τοὺς παῖδας κλέπτειν καὶ τὸν ἁλόντα ᶜ κολάζουσι πληγαῖς, ἵν' ἐκ τούτου πονεῖν καὶ ἀγρυπνεῖν δύνωνται ἐν τοῖς πολέμοις.   3. Ὁ πλοῦτος πολλὰ δύναται.   4. Τίς ἂν μωρὸς δύναιτο ἐν οἴνῳ σιωπᾶν;   5. Ἀνὴρ δίκαιός ἐστιν, ὅστις ἀδικεῖν δυνάμενος

μὴ βούλεται.　6. Πρᾶττε μηδὲν ὧν μὴ ἐπίστασαι.
7. ῎Αριστόν ἐστι πάντ' ἐπίστασθαι καλά.　8. Ζῶμεν ᵇ
οὐχ ὡς ἐθέλομεν, ἀλλ' ὡς δυνάμεθα.　9. Πρὸ μέθης
ἀνίστασο.　10. Τί συμφέρει ἐνίοις πλουτεῖν, ὅταν μὴ
ἐπίστωνται τῷ πλούτῳ χρῆσθαι;ᵇ　11. Καταλυθέντος
τοῦ Πελοποννησιακοῦ πολέμου, ὀλιγαρχίαν ἐν ταῖς πλεί-
σταις πόλεσι καθίσταντο.　12. Οἱ πολέμιοι οὐκ ἀποστή-
σονται, πρὶν ἂν ἕλωσιᵈ τὴν πόλιν

ᵃ See 346.　　　ᵇ How is πεινάω contracted? how ζάω? how
χρά-εσθαι? 346.　　ᶜ ἁλούς, -όντος, Aor. 2. partcp. from ἁλίσκεσθαι. Pdm. 64.　　ᵈ αἱρέω, List VII.

b) Translate into Greek.

1. Men have much power through wealth.　2. Rise-
up (*pl.*) before intoxication.　3. The enemy were not
able to take the city.　4. Of what use is it to you to
be rich, if you do not know-how to employ riches?
5. Did the good men understand this virtue?　6. About
such •matters you know better than they.　7. Who
could better know-how to count?　8. Thus you also
would understand music.•　9. No man is able to know
all things.　10. I should′not be able to contradict you.
11. I shall ̓not be able to learn such •subjects.

• ἐπίστασθαι περὶ μουσικῆς.

LESSON LVIII.
Δίδωμι.　Pass. and Mid.

408. VOCABULARY 52.

I give at the same time, συνεπι-	*An army*, στρατός, οῦ, ὁ.
δίδωμι: Mid. *I give myself up*	*Option, choice*, αἵρεσις, εως, ἡ.
with others to a thing.	*Gladly, readily*, ἄσμενος, η, ον
Exchange, recompense, return,	(libens = libenter).
ἀμοιβή, ῆς, ἡ.	

Exercise 57.

[*Go through Pass. and Mid. of δίδωμι.*]

409. a) Translate into English.

1. Τῷ εὖ ποιοῦντι πολλάκις κακὴ ἀποδίδοται ἀμοιβή.
2. Πατρίδες πολλάκις διὰ κέρδος προὐδόθησαν. 3. Πολλὰ δῶρα δέδοται τοῖς ἀνθρώποις παρὰ τῶν θεῶν. 4. Ὡς
μέγα τὸ μικρόν ἐστιν ἐν καιρῷ δοθέν. 5. Ὅτε εἷλε τὴν
Θηβαίων πόλιν Ἀλέξανδρος, ἀπέδοτο τοὺς ἐλευθέρους
πάντας. 6. Ὁμοίως αἰσχρόν, ἀκούσαντα χρήσιμον λόγον μὴ μανθάνειν, καὶ διδόμενόν τι ἀγαθὸν παρὰ τῶν
φίλων μὴ λαμβάνειν. 7. Οἱ πολῖται φοβοῦνται, μὴ ἡ
πόλις προδιδῶται. 8. Μήποτε ὑπὸ τῶν φίλων προδι-
δοῖο. 9. Ὁ στρατὸς ὑπ᾽ αὐτοῦ τοῦ στρατηγοῦ προὐδί-
δοτο. 10. Ἀπόδου τὸ κύπελλον.

b) Translate into Greek.

1. I gladly receive the things given • m e by (παρά,
K. 297) my friends. 2. The property was restored.
3. They sold eight-hundred of the Corcyreans, who
were slaves. 4. Pay was given to the others according
to this same proportion. 5. They learnt • • t h a t the
island • w a s given to the Corinthians. 6. If a choice
were given, which of these • t w o t h i n g s would you
choose?[b] 7. They think that if peace is offered
(*p*), the Athenians will receive • it gladly.

---

* αἰσθάνομαι, List III; with *partcp.* K. 810. 4.   [b] Use Aor.
Mid. of αἱρέω, List VII.

LESSON LIX.

Δείκνῦμαι.

410. Vocabulary 53.

I show, ἐνδείκνυμι: Mid. *I show any thing of myself.*

I show braggingly, make a boastful display of, ἐπιδείκνυμι: Mid. *I show any thing of myself boastfully, show off.*

Truly, in reality, ἀληθῶς.

I put on, dress in, ἀμφιέννυμι.

I ruin, ἀπόλλυμι: Mid. *I am ruined* or *lost, I perish.*

I mix, κεράννῦμι.

I quench, extinguish, σβέννῦμι.

Freedom in speaking, frankness, παρρησία, ας, ἡ.

I ruin at the same time, συναπόλλῦμι: Mid. *I go to ruin at the same time, I am ruined with* (some one else).

Dress, ἐσθής, ἐσθῆτ-ος, ἡ.

Garment, ἱμάτιον, ου, τό.

To dwell, οἰκεῖν (=έειν). οἰκεῖν σποράδην (*to live dispersedly*=), *to live some here and some there.*

Exercise 58.

411. a) Translate into English.

1. Οἱ τοιοῦτοι ἀρετὴν ἀντὶ ἱματίων ἀμφιέσονται. 2. Τὸ ἀπαλλάττεσθαι τῆς οὐσίας ἆρα* οὐκ ἀπόλλυσθαι καλεῖς; 3. Οὕτως ἡ ψυχὴ ἂν γίγνοιτό τε καὶ ἀπολλύοιτο. 4. Οἱ ἄνθρωποι, οἰκοῦντες σποράδην, ἀπώλλυντο ὑπὸ τῶν θηρίων, διὰ τὸ πανταχῇ ἀσθενέστεροι αὐτῶν εἶναι. 5. Ἀνδρὸς δικαίου καρπὸς οὐκ ἀπόλλυται. 6. Αἱ γυναῖκες χαίρουσιν ἀμφιεννύμεναι καλὰς ἐσθῆτας. 7. Οἱ ἀληθῶς σοφοὶ οὐ σπεύδουσιν ἐπιδείκνυσθαι τὴν αὐτῶν σοφίαν. 8. Ὁ οἶνος, ἐὰν ὕδατι κεραννύηται, τὸ σῶμα ῥώννυσιν. 9. Ἡ ὀργὴ εὐθὺς σβεννύοιτο. 10. Ἀεὶ ἐν τῷ βίῳ ἀρετὴν καὶ σωφροσύνην ἐνδείκνυσο. 11. Οἱ Πέρσαι πολυτελεῖς στολὰς ἀμφιέννυντο. 12. Ὁ ῥήτωρ τὴν γνώμην μετὰ παρρησίας ἀπεδείξατο. 13. Ἀλκιβιάδης ὑπὸ τῶν Ἀθηναίων στρατηγὸς ἀπεδείχθη.

* K. 344. 5.

b) **Translate into Greek.**

1. The soul never perishes. 2. He was in fear‣ about himself, and his children and his wife, lest they should be destroyed by their slaves. 3. The tale was lost. 4. The woman puts-on a certain expensive attire. 5. The sophist is displaying his wisdom to his admirers. 6. You have now beheld this man showing-off.

‣ *ἐν φόβῳ γενέσθαι.* See *γίγνομαι*, in Index.

LESSON LX.

The Verbs ἵημι, εἰμί, *and* εἶμι.

412. VOCABULARY 54.

I am away, absent, ἄπειμι. Pres. usually = *I will go away.*

I go away, ἄπειμι.

I satisfy myself, ἀρκέομαι (with dat.).

I let go, give up, neglect, ἀφίημι.

That which is owed, duty, δέον (δεῖ), τό.

Namely, δῆθεν (scilicet).

I go or come into, εἴσειμι.

To drive into the net or snare, ἐμβροχίζ-ειν.

I let or send out, ἐξίημι: *of rivers,* ἐξιέναι = *to discharge itself.*

I send up to, ἐφίημι: Mid. (with gen.), *I send myself or thoughts after any thing* = *I desire.*

Afterwards, then, ἔπειτα.

I let down, lay down, καθίημι.

Goat, κάπρος, ου, ὁ.

Strong, καρτερός, ά, όν.

Cry, κραυγή, ῆς, ἡ.

Stone, λίθος, ου, ὁ.

I let go, I give up, μεθίημι.

To remain, μέν-ειν.

To prepare, παρασκευάζ-ειν: Mid. *prepare oneself.*

I let pass, loose, παρίημι.

Oftener, πλεονάκις.

I go to, approach, πρόσειμι.

Mouth, στόμα, ατος, τό.

To help, τιμωρεῖν: Mid. *revenge oneself on* (with acc.).

Evident, known, φανερός, ά, όν.

Snow, χιών, χιόνος, ἡ.

8

Exercise 59.

413. a) *Translate into English.*

1. Σάμον τὸ μὲν ἐξ ἀρχῆς ᵃ ἐρήμην οὖσαν λέγεται κατέχειν πλῆθος θηρίων μεγάλην φωνὴν ἀφιέντων. 2. Οἱ ἀγαθοὶ οὐ διὰ τὸν ὕπνον μεθιᾶσι τὰ δέοντα πράττειν. 3. Ἀφεὶς τὰ φανερὰ μὴ δίωκε τὰ ἀφανῆ. 4. Πολλοὶ ἄνθρωποι ἐφίενται πλούτου. 5. Ἡρακλῆς τὸν Ἐρυμάνθιον κάπρον διώξας μετὰ κραυγῆς εἰς χιόνα πολλὴν παρειμένον ἐνεβρόχισεν. 6. Ὁ Νεῖλος ἐξίησιν εἰς τὴν θάλατταν ἑπτὰ στόμασιν. 7. Ἅττα ᵇ ἔπειτ' ἔσται, ταῦτα θεοῖς μέλει. 8. Εἰ θνητὸς εἶ, βέλτιστε ᶜ θνητὰ καὶ φρόνει. 9. Μέμνησό ᵈ νέος ὤν, ὡς γέρων ἔσῃ ποτέ. 10. Δίκαιος ἴσθ', ἵνα καὶ δικαίων τύχῃς. ᵉ 11. Βίας παρούσης, οὐδὲν ἰσχύει νόμος. 12. Εὐδαίμων εἴην καὶ θεοῖς φίλος. 13. Ἀλέξανδρος εἶπεν· ᶠ εἰ μὴ Ἀλέξανδρος ἦν, Διογένης ἂν ἦν. 14. Ἀγάπα τοῖς παροῦσι, τῶν ἀπόντων οὐκ ἐφιέμενος. 15. Καὶ νεότης καὶ γῆρας ἄμφω καλὰ ἔστον. 16. Οἱ ἄνθρωποι εὐδαιμονεῖν δύνανται, κἂν πένητες ὦσιν. 17. Ἀλήθειά σοι παρέστω. 18. Ἴωμεν, ὦ φίλοι. 19. Φεῦγε διχοστασίας καὶ ἔριν, πολέμου προσιόντος. 20. Ἐπεὶ ἡ Μανδάνη παρεσκευάζετο ὡς ἀπιοῦσα πάλιν πρὸς τὸν ἄνδρα, ὁ Ἀστυάγης ἔλεγε πρὸς τὸν Κῦρον· Ὦ παῖ, ἢν μένῃς παρ' ἐμοί, πρῶτον μέν, ὅταν βούλῃ εἰσιέναι ὡς ἐμέ, ἐπὶ σοὶ ἔσται, ᵍ καὶ χάριν σοι μᾶλλον ἕξω, ὅσῳ ἂν πλεονάκις εἰσίῃς ὡς ἐμέ. 21. Ἔπειτα δὲ ἵπποις τοῖς ἐμοῖς χρήσῃ, καί, ὅταν ἀπίῃς, ἔχων ἄπει οὓς ἂν αὐτὸς ἐθέλῃς ἵππους.

ᵃ τὸ ἐξ ἀρχῆς = *originally.*   ᵇ Pdm. 50.   ᶜ Note 18.   ᵈ Μέμνημαι (= memini), *I remember.*   ᵉ List IV. Gen. K. 278. 8. b.   ᶠ List VII.   ᵍ εἶναι ἐπί τινι, *to be in any body's power; to depend on him.*

b) Translate into Greek.

1. Men utter indeed the same voice, but not the same language.   2. We ought to be satisfied with what we have (*say:* with present •things).   3. Not every one who wishes (*p*) will enter into this abode.   4. The chorus of the Muses will most probably come-in first. 5. We went in to⁹⁹ Socrates.   6. It would not become me to come before¹⁰ you, framing studied speeches.ᵇ 7. There are two forms of government.   8. O Greeks, ye are always children.   9. You and I (*say:* I and you) are not poets.   10. Do not be harsh towards³⁰ us.   11. Know well,ⁱ that this will be so (*say:* will have •itself so).   12. They were not one •person, but two.   13. Such a person would not be able to employ his wealth.   14. Come now,ᵏ read¹ me the decree.   15. Let us go back-again to the beginning. 16. It is right (δεῖ) that this man, looking at⁷ one •object, should ever shoot all his arrows at⁷ it.

ᵇ *To frame studied speeches,* πλάττειν λόγους.   ⁱ Pdm. 70, Note 7.   ᵏ δή: for *come* use imper. of εἶμι.   ¹ Imper Aor. of ἀνα-γιγνώσκ-ω   See ἔγνων in Pdm. 63.

NOTES.

On the Division of Syllables.

1. Beside what is stated in 38, 39, it may be remarked that when *two* or *three* consonants come together, they are usually considered to belong to the following *syllable*, if they are so *easily pronounceable* that they can begin a word (e. g. ἄ-μνος, ἀ-κμή, δε-σμός, ἔ-στρο-φα).

Sometimes a *mute* before μ or ν is connected with the following syllable, even though no word begins with that combination, provided any word begins with *another mute* of the same organ and μ or ν.

Thus φά-τνη (no word begins with τν, but some do with 3ν).

So δη-γμός, δά-φνις, because words begin with κμ, πν.

Three consonants are connected with the following syllable when the *first pair* and the *second pair* can each begin a word (ἐ-σθλός, ἐ-χθρός; since words begin with χθ, 3ρ.) (So ἄ-σθμα: since words begin with τμ, though not with 3μ.) *Kr.*

According to these rules, φαιδρός is divided into the syllables φαι-δρός, not φαιδ-ρός. ψήφισμα into ψήφι-σμα.

2. *Lesson* 3.]—The accent of a verb is, as a *general* rule, as far back (i. e. as near the *root*) as possible. Hence (*a*) in verbs when a *long termination* is exchanged for a *short one*, an *acute on the penult* is thrown to the *antepenult* (if the verb is *hyperdissyllable*): τύπτω, τύπτετε.

b) If the *penult*, being the *tone-syllable*, has a *long vowel* or *diphthong*, and the verb is *dissyllable*, the *acute* will pass into *circumflex* when the final becomes short: φεύγω, φεῦγε (but κελεύω, κέλευε).

[For the general rules for the accentuation of verbs, see Pdms. 56, 57.]

3. *Lesson* 11, (95).]—*a*, G. *as*, is *always long* from an oxytone or paroxytone (if a *hyperdissyllable*).
But *a*, G. *as*, is short in

1) Polysyllable feminine names or appellatives: ψάλτρια, Ἐρέ-τρια.

2) -ρα is short if the penult has υ or any diphthong but αυ·
γέφῡρα, μοῖρα, also in Τάναγρα (by 1).

8) In polysyllables in εια, οια, it is *short*, except in (a) *abstract
substantives* from verbs in ευω, and (β) *dissyllables* in εια.
ἄνοια, ἀλήϑεια (from adj. ἀληϑής), ὠφέλεια (from ὀφε-
λεῖν) : but δουλείᾱ (from δουλεύειν).
βασίλεια = *queen* (from βασιλεύς).
βασιλείᾱ = *reign* (from βασιλεύειν, *to reign*).

4. From Adjectives in os, the α is long in Nom. Sing. So
πλέα, fem. of πλέως. From *Adjectives* and *Participles* in as, υs, εις,
ους, ως, ων, it is *short*. Hence the former are paroxytone : the latter
proparoxytone or properispomenon.

N. B. *Acc.* and *Voc.* singular follow the *Nom.*

5. A *muta cum liquidâ* does not lengthen a *short* vowel [i. e.
does not make a syllable long by *position*], unless it be a middle
mute (β, γ, δ) before λ, μ, ν.

Hence ἄτεκνος, ἄπεπλος, 'ἀκμή, βότρυς : but βίβλος, εὔοδμος,
πέπλεγμαι.

6.   *Usual Contractions.*

	A	E	H	O	Ω	I	Υ
A	αα = ᾱ ααι = ᾳ	αε = ᾱ: αει = ᾳ αη = ᾱ: αη = ᾳ		αο = ω: αοι = ῳ αου = ω: αω = ω		ᾱῐ = αι : ᾱι = ᾳ ᾱῠ = αυ: ᾱῠ = ᾱῠ	
E	εα = η; *sis.* ᾱ εαι = η, ει εας = εις	εε = ει, η: εει = ει εες = εις, ης εη = η : εη = η		εο = ου, εοι = οι εου = ου εω = ω : εῳ = ῳ		εῖ = ει εῡ = ευ	
O	οα = ω, *sis.* ᾱ οαι = αι	οε = ου οει = ου, οι οη = ω, η οη = ῳ, οι		οο = ου οοι = οι οου = ου οω = ω: οῳ = ῳ		οῖ = οι	
H	ηαι = ῃ	ηε = η ηει = η				ηῐ = η ηῠ = ηυ	
Ω	ωα = ω			ωο = ω		ωῖ = ῳ	
I	ιας = ῑς	ιες = ῑς				ιι = ῑ	
Υ	υας = ῡς	υες = ῡς					

From this table it appears generally,

a) That in the collision of A and E sounds, the vowel which precedes the other, remains predominant in the contracted syllable, although its shape may be modified : λείπεαι, λείπῃ or λείπει : τίμᾶς, τίμᾶ : πόλεας, πόλεις : except in εα, which, in the first two declensions, 's contracted into ā : ὀστέα, ὀστᾶ : βορρέας, βορρᾶς.

δ) That, where an O sound appears, it maintains itself, in contraction, against all A and E sounds, νόε, νοῦ : ὀστέον, ὀστοῦν : βόας, βοῦς : τιμάοιμι, τιμῷμι : φιλέουσι, φιλοῦσι : except that, in adjectives, *οη* becomes η : ἁπλόη, ἁπλῆ, and *οα* sometimes α : ἁπλόα, ἁπλᾶ : also ἁπλόαι, ἁπλαῖ (*Thiersch.*)

---

7. There are some *words, cases,* and *moods* that must be carefully distinguished, because they *look like* what they are not. The following are a few instances of the kind that occur in these lessons.

    a) -ους, as *nom.* or *acc.* pl. of a comparative in ὼν, e. g. μείζους = μείζ-ονες, μείζ-ονας.
        -ω, acc. sing. or nom. pl. of ditto.
    b) ὄντων, 3rd plur. of Imperative Present, which looks like gen. plur. of *Pres. Partcp. Act.*
        ὤντων = αόντων, 3rd pl. Imper. Present from verb in άω (also gen. pl. of *Pres. partcp. Act.*).
        οὔντων = ε-όντων, 3rd pl. Imperat. Pres. from verb in έω (also gen. pl. of *Pres. partcp. Act.*).
    c) ᾶται, 3rd sing. of the *Pres. Indic.* or *Subj.* (Pass. or *Mid.*) from άω.
    d) Ἴσθι (from οἶδα) '*know,*' and ἴσθι, '*be.*'

Euphonic Rules.

8. When two consonants come together in the formation of words, the former is often changed for the sake of easier pronunciation.

The principal changes of this kind are the following :*

---

* These changes may be exhibited in the following table, which is arranged as the multiplication table often is :

	τ	δ	ϑ	σ	μ
Any *p*-sound with	πτ	βδ	φϑ	ψ	μμ
Any *k*-sound with	κτ	γδ	χϑ	ξ	γμ
Any *t*-sound with	στ	—[1]	σϑ	σ	σμ

[1] This combination does not occur.

Any *p*-sound with τ becomes πτ.

Any *p*-sound with δ becomes βδ.

Any *p*-sound with 3 becomes φ3.

Any *p*-sound with *s* becomes ψ.

Any *p*-sound with μ becomes μμ.

Any *k*-sound with τ becomes κτ.

Any *k*-sound with δ becomes γδ.

Any *k*-sound with 3 becomes χ3.

Any *k*-sound with *s* becomes ξ.

Any *k*-sound with μ becomes γμ.

Any *t*-sound with τ becomes στ.

Any *t*-sound with δ (*this combination does not occur*).

Any *t*-sound with 3 becomes σ3.

Any *t*-sound with σ becomes σ (i. e. the *ι*-sound is thrown away).

Any *t*-sound with μ becomes σμ.

☞ This table shows : (1) that a *p* or *k*-sound before a *t*-sound must be of the *same order of breathing* as the *t*-sound :* (2) that a *t*-sound before *s* is thrown away.

Obs. Ἐκ, 'out of,' in compound words retains its κ : thus, ἐκ-δίδωμι, ἐκ-3έω, not ἐγ-δίδωμι, &c.

(Examples.)

τέτριβται	=	τέτριπται.	λέλεγται	=	λέλεκται.
ἔστραφται	=	ἔστραπται.	βέβρεχται	=	βέβρεκται.
ῥάπδος	=	ῥάβδος.	ὄκδοος	=	ὄγδοος.
ἐπιγράφδην	=	ἐπιγράβδην.	πλέκδην	=	πλέγδην.
ἐτύπ3ην	=	ἐτύφ3ην.	ἐπλέκ3ην	=	ἐπλέχ3ην.
τριβ3ήσομαι	=	τριφ3ήσομαι.	λεγ3ήσομαι	=	λεχ3ήσομαι.
ἐπείσ3ην	=	ἐπείσ3ην.	ἀνύτσω	=	ἀνύσω
ἠρείδ3ην	=	ἠρείσ3ην.	ἐρείδσω	=	ἐρείσω.
λείπσω	=	λείψω.	πεί3σω	=	πείσω.
τρίβσω	=	τρίψω.	τέτυπμαι	=	τέτυμμαι.
γράφσω	=	γράψω.	τέτριβμαι	=	τέτριμμαι.
πλέκσω	=	πλέξω.	γέγραφμαι	=	γέγραμμαι.

---

* That is, the first becomes a *smooth* mute, if the second is a *smooth* mute ; a *middle* or *aspirate*, respectively, if the second is a *middle* or *aspirate*.

λέγσω	= λέξω.	πέπλεκμαι	=	πέπλεγμαι.
βρέχσω	= βρέξω.	βέβρεχμαι	=	βέβρεγμαι.

N before a P-sound (or ψ) becomes μ.
N before a K-sound (or ξ) becomes γ.
N before a T-sound remains unaltered.
N before a liquid is changed into that liquid.

N is usually * dropt before ζ, before σ in inflexion,† and in those compound words in which another consonant follows σ.

(Examples.)

ἐν-πειρία	= ἐμπειρία.	συν-ξέω	=	συγξέω.
ἐν-βάλλω	= ἐμβάλλω.	συν-λογίζω	=	συλλογίζω.
ἔν-φρων	= ἔμφρων.	συν-μετρία	=	σὐμμετρία.
ἔν-ψῦχος	= ἔμψῦχος.	συν-ζυγία	=	συζυγία.
συν-καλέω	= συγκαλέω.	δαίμον-σι	=	δαίμοσί.
συν-γιγνώσκω	= συγγιγνώσκω.	σύν-στημα	=	σύστημα.
σύν-χρονος	= σύγχρονος.			

But : συντείνω, συνδέω, συνθέω.

Exceptions. The enclitics; as: ὅνπερ, τόνγε.
ἐν before ρ; as: ἐνρίπτω.

When a T-*sound* and ν together are ejected before σ, the remaining vowel, if *short*, is changed into a diphthong (ε into ει, and ο into ου) ; if *doubtful*, it is lengthened. The long vowels (η, ω) are left unchanged. Thus:

τυφθέ(ντ)σι	becomes τυφθεῖσι.	τύψα(ντ)σι	becomes τύψᾶσι.
σπέ(νδ)σω	becomes σπείσω.	γίγα(ντ)σι	becomes γίγᾶσι.
λέο(ντ)σι	becomes λέουσι.	δείκνυ(ντ)σι	becomes δείκνῦσι.
τύπτο(ντ)σι	becomes τύπτουσι.	τύπτω(ντ)σι	becomes τύπτωσι.

When the *same* aspirate would regularly be doubled, the former is changed into the kindred *smooth:* as Σαπφώ (not Σαφφώ). Βάκχος (not Βάχχος). Ἀτθίς (not Ἀθθίς).‡

---

* *Exceptions.* Ἐν, as; ἐνσπείρω, ἐνζεύγνυμι: πάλιν, as; παλίνσκιος: some forms of inflexion and derivation in σαι and σις, as; πέφανσαι, fr. φαίνω: and some few substantives in ινς and υνς. The ν in σύν becomes σ in composition before σ followed by a vowel; as: συσσόζω, instead of συνσόζω.

† That is, in the *declensions* and *conjugations.*

‡ Even the *middle* mutes (β, γ, δ) are very seldom doubled, with

Of two aspirates in two *consecutive* syllables, the former is often changed into its kindred *smooth*.

This rule applies principally to roots beginning with Ꙃ and ending with some other aspirate. The initial aspirate reappears, when, in the formation of cases or tenses, the *final aspirate* is changed.

Thus the roots Ꙃρεφ, Ꙃριχ, become τρεφ, τριχ : but when the φ, for instance, is changed into ψ or μ, the reason for getting rid of Ꙃ no longer remains, and Ꙃ will reappear : Ꙃρεψ, Ꙃρεμ. So τριχ-ός, τριχ-ί, but Ꙃρίξ, Ꙃριξίν.

In the Imperative of the 1st Aor. Pass. the *last* aspirate is changed in the 2nd pers. sing.: e. g. γράφητι (not γράφηꙂι) : κρύφ-Ꙃητι (not κρύφꙂηꙂι).

Irregular Substantives.

9. ☞ R. means root (from which the word is declined *regularly*).

ἀηδών, (ἡ), *nightingale.* G. ἀηδοῦς (*for* ἀηδόνος). V. ἀηδοῖ.

ἅλς, ἁλός (ὁ), *salt.* Pl. usually οἱ ἅλες, ῶν, &c.

ἅλως (ἡ), *threshing-floor :* mostly after Attic 2nd Decl. (with acc. ἅλω) ; ἅλωνος, &c. later.

ἄναξ, ἄνακτ-ος, *king.* V. ἄνα (*but only when a god is invoked*).

Ἀπόλλων, ωνος, *Apollo.* Acc. Ἀπόλλω. V. Ἄπολλον.

Ἄρης (*Mars*). G. Ἄρεως : in the poets (for the sake of the metre), Ἄρεος, Ἄρει, Ἄρη and Ἄρην. V. Ἄρες.

ἀστήρ, *star.* Dat. pl. ἀστράσι, but not syncopated in other cases.

γάλα (τό), *milk.* R. γάλακτ. (Dat. pl. γάλαξι, *Plat.*)

γέλ-ως, ωτος, &c. (ὁ), *laughter.* Acc. γέλωτα, and, in poets and Lucian, γέλων.

γόνυ (τό), *knee.* R. γόνατ.

γυνή, *woman, wife.* R. γυναικ.* V. γύναι.

δένδρον, *tree.* Regular : but in D. pl. (usually) δένδρεσι(ν).

δόρυ (τό), *spear.* R. δόρατ. Thuc. has old D. δορί.

ἔγχελυς (ὁ), *eel.* G. -υος, &c. ; but in dual and pl. like πῆχυς.

---

the exception of γγ (of which the first γ = ng). Of the *smooth* mutes, π and κ are but *seldom* doubled (ἵππος, λάκκος): τ *frequently ;* as are also σ and the *liquids*.

* With accent on the ult. of G. and D. γυναικός, γυναικί, γυναικῶν, γυναιξί, γυναικοῖν (*Aesch. Choeph.* 802), &c., but γύναικα, γύναικες, &c.

εἰκ-ών, όνος (ἡ), *image.* G. εἰκοῦς. Acc. εἰκώ (mostly Ion. and poet.). Acc. pl. εἰκούς (Observe the accent).

Ζεύς, *Jupiter.* Δι-ός, Διῖ, Δία. V. Ζεῦ. [Ζηνός, Ζηνί, Ζῆνα, poet.].

ἥρ-ως, ωος, *hero.* Acc. ἥρωα, and also ἥρω. In poets τῷ ἥρῳ, and οἱ, τοὺς ἥρως (the last also Luc.).

Θαλῆς, *Thales.* Θάλεω, Θαλῇ, Θαλῆν. In later writers also Θαλοῦ, and Θάλητος, -τι, &c.

θρίξ (ἡ), *hair.* G. τριχ-ός, &c. D. pl. θριξί(ν). [R. θριχ.]

κάρα (τό), *head.* G. κρατός. D. κρατί and κάρᾳ. A. τὸ κάρα, and (*Trag.*) τὸν and τὸ κρᾶτα. Acc. pl. τοὺς κρᾶτας (*Eur.*).

κλείς (ἡ), *key.* κλειδός, κλειδί, κλεῖδα and *more commonly* κλεῖν. Plur. κλεῖδες. Acc. κλεῖς, later κλεῖδας. [Eur. κλῇδα, -δας from old Att. κλῄς.]

:υκέων (ὁ), *mess; porridge.* Acc. κυκεῶ, *for* κυκεῶνα.

κύων, *dog.* R. κῠν. V. κύον.

λᾶας, λᾶς (ὁ), *stone.* λᾶος (in Soph. λάου), λᾶϊ, λᾶαν and λᾶν (λᾶα, Callim.). Pl. λᾶες, λάων, λάεσσιν and λάεσιν.

λίπᾰ, prob. *acc.* from obsol. τὸ λίπα; found with ἀλείφειν, as *acc. cognatæ significationis.*

μάρτυς, *witness.* μάρτυρ-ος, ι. Acc. α and (*less commonly*) μάρτυν. D. pl. μάρτῠσι(ν). [Μάρτυρ nom. Æol. and late.]

ναῦς (ἡ), *ship.* The Attic forms are: νεώς, νηῗ, ναῦν | (νέε?), νεοῖν | νῆες, νεῶν, ναυσί, ναῦς. [G. νηός, &c. Att. poets and later prose.]

Οἰδίπους, *Œdipus.* Οἰδίποδος and Οἰδίπου. D. Οἰδίποδι. Acc. Οἰδίποδα and Οἰδίπουν. V. Οἰδίπου.

ὄρνις (ὁ, ἡ), *bird,* ὄρνῑθος, &c. Acc. ὄρνῑθα, less commonly ὄρνῑν. Pl. reg. also (*more poetical*) ὄρνεις, ὀρνέων. D. ὄρνῑσι(ν), only Acc. ὄρνεας, or ὄρνῑς. [On the quantity of the ι see Liddell and Scott.]

οὖς (τό), *ear.* R. ὠτ. [G. plur. ὤτων.]

Πνύξ (ἡ), *the Pnyx.* G. Πυκν-ός, &c. *with transposition of the consonants.*

Ποσειδῶν, *Neptune.* Acc. Ποσειδῶ. V. Πόσειδον.

σκώρ (τό), *filth.* R. σκατ. Hence G. σκατός, &c.

ὕδωρ (τό), *water.* R. ὑδατ.

χείρ (ἡ), *hand.* χειρός, &c. *but* G. *and* D. *Dual,* χεροῖν, Dat. Pl. χερσί.

χελῑδών (ἡ), *swallow.* χελιδόνος, but D. χελιδοῖ.

υἱός, *son.* G. υἱοῦ, reg., *but also the following cases from* υἱεύς, υἱέος, υἱεῖ. Du. υἱέε, υἱέοιν. Pl. υἱεῖς, υἱέων, υἱέσι(ν), υἱεῖς. Thucydides, Plato, and the orators prefer these forms.

On the place of ἄν.

10. As ἄν represents the *predicate* as conditional, it ought properly to be joined with the predicate, e. g. λέγοιμι ἄν, ἔλεγον ἄν; yet it commonly follows that member of a sentence which is to be made emphatic, e. g. καὶ οὐκ οἴει ἄσχημον ἄν φανεῖσθαι τὸ τοῦ Σωκράτους πρᾶγμα. Hence it is regularly joined to such words as modify the whole meaning of the sentence, viz. to *negative verbs* and *interrogatives*: οὐκ ἄν, οὐδ᾽ ἄν, οὔποτ᾽ ἄν, οὐδέποτ᾽ ἄν, &c.—τίς ἄν, τί ἄν, τί δ᾽ ἄν, τί δῆτ᾽ ἄν, πῶς ἄν, πῶς γὰρ ἄν, ἆρ᾽ ἄν, &c.;—also to *adverbs of place, time, manner,* and other adverbs, which in various ways modify the expression contained in the predicate and define it more exactly: ἐνταῦθα ἄν, τότ᾽ ἄν, εἰκότως ἄν, ἴσως ἄν, τάχ᾽ ἄν, μάλιστ᾽ ἄν, ἥκιστ᾽ ἄν, ῥᾳδίως ἄν, ἡδέως ἄν, &c.; to εἰ, ἐπειδή, ὅτε, ὁπότε, ὅς with *Subj.* (hence ἐάν [ἤν, ἄν,] ἐπειδάν, ὅταν, ὁπόταν—ὅς ἄν=*quicunque; si quis*).

Crasis.*

11. Both *Crasis* and *Elision* are marked, as the soft breathing is, by a comma over the syllable.

When two words, one of which ends and the other begins with a vowel, come together, it often happens that these vowels are changed into one *long* vowel-sound. This union is called *Crasis*, and the sign of it *Corōnis*. The Corōnis is placed above the *vowel-sound formed by Crasis*; and when this is a diphthong, above the *second* vowel; but it is omitted when the word *begins* with the vowel-sound formed by *Crasis*; as: τὸ ὄνομα = τοὔνομα, τὸ ἔπος = τοὖπος, τὰ ἀγαθά = τἀγαθά, ὁ οἶνος = ᾧνος.

When the combination formed by *crasis* is a *dissyllable* or *trochaic word* (⁻⁀), some grammarians still *retain the accent* of the second word; others change the *acute* into the *circumflex*. Thus, when the second word is *paroxytone*, some write τοὔπος, τἄλλα, τἄργα (for τὸ ἔπος, τὰ ἄλλα, τὰ ἔργα): others, τοῦπος, τᾶλλα, τᾶργα. The change into the circumflex is founded on the authority of the best MSS. It is, however, against the principle, that in contractions the circumflex arises only when the first of the contracted syllables has the *acute*, the second the *grave*.

If of the *two* vowel-sounds that are blended into one sound by *Crasis*, the *latter* is *a diphthong that contains ι*, the *ι is written under*

---

* Κρᾶσις means *a mixing* or *blending*. Κορωνίς, *any thing curved*; hence, *a little curved mark* with the pen.

(*ι subscript*) : it is *not* underwritten, when only the former is such a diphthong. Thus : καὶ εἶτα = κᾆτα ; but καὶ ἔπειτα = κἄπειτα.

*Elision** consists in simply *throwing away a short vowel at the end of a word before another beginning with a vowel.* The sign of this is called *Apostrophe ;** e. g. ἀπὸ οἴκου = ἀπ' οἴκου.

If the elision causes a *smooth mute* to precede an *aspirate*, the smooth mute must be changed into the aspirate. Thus, not ἀπ' οὗ, but ἀφ' οὗ ; not ἀντ' ὧν, but ἀνθ' ὧν.—So in *Crasis* ; a smooth mute before an aspirated vowel is changed into the aspirate mute of the same organ : τὰ ἕτερα = θάτερα.

Correlative Adjectives and Adverbs.

12. *Correlative* words are those which express a *mutual relation* (*correlation*) to each other, and represent this relation by a corresponding form.

(a) Adjective Correlatives.

Interrogative.	Indefinite.	Demonstrative.	Relat. and Depend. Interrog.
πόσος, -η, -ον ; how great ? how much ? quantus ?	ποσός, -ή, -όν, of some size or number, aliquantus	τόσος, -η,† -ον, so great, so much, tantus τοσόσδε, τοσήδε, τοσόνδε τοσοῦτος, -αύτη. -οῦτο(ν)	ὅσος, -η, -ον, and ὁπόσος, -η, -ον,‡ quantus
ποῖος, -ά, -ον ; of what kind? qualis ?	ποιός, -ά, -όν, of some kind	τοῖος, -ά, -ον,† of such a kind, talis τοιόσδε, τοιάδε, τοιόνδε τοιοῦτος, -αύτη, -οῦτο(ν)	οἷος, -ά, -ον, and ὁποῖος, -ά, -ον, qualis
πηλίκος, -η, ον ; how great ? how old ?	wanting	τηλίκος, -ον, so great, so old τηλικόσδε, -ήδε, -όνδε τηλικοῦτος, -αύ-τη, -οῦτο(ν)	ἡλίκος, -η, -ον, and ὁπηλίκος, -η, -ον, how great, how old

* *Elisio* (Lat.), *a squeezing out.* Ἀποστροφή means *a turning away.*

† Except in the combinations τοῖος καὶ (ἢ) τοῖος· τόσος καὶ τόσος· ὅσῳ—τόσῳ (= *quo—eo*, rare), and ἐκ τόσου, these forms were superseded by the compound forms : τοιόσδε, &c.

‡ The forms beginning with ὁπ- are regularly the dependent inter-

(b) Adverbial Correlatives.

Interrogative.	Indefinite.	Demonstrative.	Relative.	Dependent Interrog.
ποῦ; *where?* ubi ?	πού, *some-where*, ali-cŭbi	wanting [ἐν-ταῦϑα, ἐνϑά-δε, *here:* ἐκεῖ, *there*]	οὖ, *where*, ubi	ὅπου, *where*, ubi
πόϑεν; *whence?* unde ?	ποϑέν, *from some place*, alicunde	wanting [ἐν-ϑένδε, ἐντεῦ-ϑεν, *hence:* ἐ-κεῖϑεν, *thence*]	ὅϑεν, *whence*, unde	ὁπόϑεν, *whence*, un-de
ποῖ; *whither?* quo ?	ποί, *to some place*, ali-quo	wanting [ἐ-κεῖσε, *thither:* sts. ἐνταῦϑα, ἐνϑάδε = *hither*]	οἷ, *whither*, quo	ὅποι, *whi-ther*, quo
πότε; *when?* quando ?	ποτέ, *some-time*, ali-quando	τότε, *then*, tum	ὅτε, *when*, quum	ὁπότε, *when*, quando
ἡνίκα; quo temporis pun-cto ? quotâ horâ ?	wanting	τηνι-κάδε } τηνι-καῦτα } hoc ipso tem-pore	ἡνίκα, *when*, quo ipso tempore	ὁπηνίκα, *when*, quo ipso tem-pore
πῶς; *how?*	πώς, *some how*	οὕτω(ς), ὧδε, *so*	ὡς, *how*	ὅπως, *how*
πῆ; *whither?* [also *where?*] *how?*	πή, *to some place, some how*	τῇδε } ταύτῃ } *hither or here*	ᾗ, *where, whither*	ὅπη, *where, whither.*

Irregular Comparison.

13. These comparatives and superlatives really belong to some. *obsolete* positive, but are conveniently arranged under some *extant* positive with which they agree in meaning.

Positive.	Comparative.	Superlative.
1. ἀγαϑός, *good*	ἀμείνων, neut. ἄμεινον βελτίων κρείσσων, Att. κρείτ-των* λῴων (for λωΐων)	ἄριστος. βέλτιστος. κράτιστος. λῷστος.
2. κακός, *bad*	κακίων χείρων ἥσσων, Att. ἥττων* (*inferior*).	κάκιστος. χείριστος.

* The forms in -σσων occur in the earlier Attic writers.

3. καλός, *beautiful*	καλλίων	κάλλιστος.
4. ἀλγεινός, *painful* {	ἀλγεινότερος	{ ἀλγεινότατος.
	ἀλγίων	{ ἄλγιστος.
5. μακρός, *long*	μακρότερος	μακρότατος and μήκι-
6. μικρός, *small* {	μικρότερος	μικρότατος. [στος
	μείων	
	ἐλάσσων, Att. ἐλάττων*	ἐλάχιστος.
7. ὀλίγος, *little*		ὀλίγιστος.
8. μέγας, *great*	μείζων	μέγιστος.
9. πολύς, *much*	πλείων or πλέων	πλεῖστος.
10. ῥάδιος, *easy*	ῥάων	ῥᾷστος.
11. πέπων, *ripe*	πεπαίτερος	πεπαίτατος.
12. πίων, *fat*	πιότερος	πιότατος.

* The form in -σσων occurs in the earlier Attic writers.

PARADIGMS.

☞ For the convenience of the pupil and for easy reference, the various Paradigms given at intervals (as well as the others required for use) are here collected together.

1. *The Article.*

	Singular.				Plural.				Dual.		
	m.	*f.*	*n.*		*m.*	*f.*	*n.*		*m.*	*f.*	*n.*
N.	ὁ	ἡ	τό	N.	οἱ	αἱ	τά	N. A.	τώ	[τά]	τώ
G.	τοῦ	τῆς	τοῦ	G.	τῶν	τῶν	τῶν	G. D.	τοῖν	[ταῖν]	τοῖν
D.	τῷ	τῇ	τῷ	D.	τοῖς	ταῖς	τοῖς				
A.	τόν	τήν	τό	A.	τούς	τάς	τά				

a) In the dual the feminine is more commonly τώ, τοῖν, than τά, ταῖν. Τά (as *fem. dual*) is very uncommon.

2. *Terminations of the Three Declensions.*

	I.		II.	III.
	fem.	*mas.*	*m.f.*	
Sing. Nom.	η, ᾰ, ᾱ,	ης, ᾱς,	os, neut. ον	various
Gen.	ης or ας	ου	ου	os (ως)
Dat.	η or ᾳ		ῳ	ι
Acc.	ην or αν		ον, neut. ον	α or ν { neut. as
Voc.	η or α		ε, neut. ον	— { nom.
Plur. N. V.	αι		οι, neut. ᾰ	ᾰς, neut. ᾰ
Gen.	ῶν (circumflexed)		ων	ων
Dat.	αις		οις	σιν or σι
Acc.	ᾱς		ους, neut. ᾰ	ᾱς, neut. α
Dual. N.A.V.	ᾱˑ		ω	ε
G. D.	αιν		οιν	οιν

In the *second* declension, and in masculine nouns of the *first*, the original termination of the gen. sing. was *o* (the final letter of the roots being *a*, *o*, respectively); *a-o* and *o-o* being contracted into *ov*. The termination of the *dative singular* is *ι* in all the declensions, but in the first two it is *subscript*.

In the formation of the dative plural the T-sounds and *ν* are rejected: and

	αντσι	εντσι	οντσι	υντσι
become	ᾱσι	εισι	ουσι	ῡσι.

3. *First Declension.*

		victory.	attempt.	Muse.	citizen.	young man.
Sing.	Nom.	νίκη	πεῖρα	Μοῦσᾰ	πολίτης (ῐ)	νεανίᾱς
	Gen.	νίκης	πείρας	Μούσης	πολίτου	νεανίου
	Dat.	νίκῃ	πείρᾳ	Μούσῃ	πολίτῃ	νεανίᾳ
	Acc.	νίκην	πεῖραν	Μοῦσαν	πολίτην	νεανίᾱν
	Voc.	νίκη	πεῖρα	Μοῦσα	πολῖτᾰ	νεανίᾱ
Plur.	Nom.	νῖκαι	πεῖραι	Μοῦσαι	πολῖται	νεανίαι
	Gen.	νικῶν	πειρῶν	Μουσῶν	πολιτῶν	νεανιῶν
	Dat.	νίκαις	πείραις	Μούσαις	πολίταις	νεανίαις
	Acc.	νίκας	πείρας	Μούσας	πολίτας	νεανίας
	Voc.	νῖκαι	πεῖραι	Μοῦσαι	πολῖται	νεανίαι
Dual.	N.A.V.	νίκᾱ	πείρᾱ	Μούσᾱ	πολίτᾱ	νεανίᾱ
	G. D.	νίκαιν	πείραιν	Μούσαιν	πολίταιν	νεανίαιν

4. *Second Declension.*

		word.	island.	way.	garment.
Sing.	N.	λόγος	νῆσος	ὁδός	ἱμάτιον
	G.	λόγου	νήσου	ὁδοῦ	ἱματίου
	D.	λόγῳ	νήσῳ	ὁδῷ	ἱματίῳ
	A.	λόγον	νῆσον	ὁδόν	ἱμάτιον
	V.	λόγε	νῆσε	ὁδέ	ἱμάτιον
Plur.	N.	λόγοι	νῆσοι	ὁδοί	ἱμάτια
	G.	λόγων	νήσων	ὁδῶν	ἱματίων
	D.	λόγοις	νήσοις	ὁδοῖς	ἱματίοις
	A.	λόγους	νήσους	ὁδούς	ἱμάτια
	V.	λόγοι	νῆσοι	ὁδοί	ἱμάτια.
Dual.	N.A.V.	λόγω	νήσω	ὁδώ	ἱματίω
	G. D.	λόγοιν	νήσοιν	ὁδοῖν	ἱματίοιν

The Vocative of words in ος sometimes ends in ος; as: ὦ φίλε
and ὦ φίλος; always ὦ θεός.

5. (*Adjectives in* ος.)

	(good.)			(hateful, hostile.)		
Sing.	m.	f.	n.	m.	f.	n.
Nom.	ἀγαθός	ἀγαθή	ἀγαθόν	ἐχθρός	ἐχθρά	ἐχθρόν
Gen.	ἀγαθοῦ	ἀγαθῆς	ἀγαθοῦ	ἐχθροῦ	ἐχθρᾶς	ἐχθροῦ
Dat.	ἀγαθῷ	ἀγαθῇ	ἀγαθῷ	ἐχθρῷ	ἐχθρᾷ	ἐχθρῷ
Acc.	ἀγαθόν	ἀγαθήν	ἀγαθόν	ἐχθρόν	ἐχθράν	ἐχθρόν
Voc.	ἀγαθέ	ἀγαθή	ἀγαθόν	ἐχθρέ	ἐχθρά	ἐχθρόν
Plur.						
Nom. V.	ἀγαθοί	ἀγαθαί	ἀγαθά	ἐχθροί	ἐχθραί	ἐχθρά
Gen.	ἀγαθῶν	ἀγαθῶν	ἀγαθῶν	ἐχθρῶν	ἐχθρῶν	ἐχθρῶν
Dat.	ἀγαθοῖς	ἀγαθαῖς	ἀγαθοῖς	ἐχθροῖς	ἐχθραῖς	ἐχθροῖς
Acc.	ἀγαθούς	ἀγαθάς	ἀγαθά	ἐχθρούς	ἐχθράς	ἐχθρά.
Dual.						
N. A. V.	ἀγαθώ	ἀγαθά	ἀγαθώ	ἐχθρώ	ἐχθρά	ἐχθρώ
G. D.	ἀγαθοῖν	ἀγαθαῖν	ἀγαθοῖν	ἐχθροῖν	ἐχθραῖν	ἐχθροῖν

6. Contraction of the Second Declension.

		(a) voyage.	(b) voyage round.	(c) bone.
S.	N.	πλόος = πλοῦς	περίπλοος = περίπλους	ὀστέον = ὀστοῦν
	G.	πλοῦ	περίπλου	ὀστοῦ
	D.	πλῷ	περίπλῳ	ὀστῷ
	A.	πλοῦν	περίπλουν	ὀστοῦν
	V.	πλοῦ	περίπλου	ὀστοῦν
P.	N.	πλοῖ	περίπλοι	ὀστᾶ
	G.	πλῶν	περίπλων	ὀστῶν
	D.	πλοῖς	περίπλοις	ὀστοῖς
	A.	πλόυς	περίπλους	ὀστᾶ
	V.	πλοῖ	περίπλοι	ὀστᾶ
D.	N. A. V.	πλώ	περίπλω	ὀστώ
	G. D.	πλοῖν	περίπλοιν	ὀστοῖν

7. Adjectives in (εος, οος =) ους.

	(a)			(b)		
S.	(χρύσε-ος	χρυσέ-α	χρύσε-ον)	(ἁπλό-ος	ἁπλό-η	ἁπλό-ον
	χρυσοῦς	χρυσῆ	χρυσοῦν	ἁπλοῦς	ἁπλῆ	ἁπλοῦν
	χρυσοῦ	χρυσῆς	χρυσοῦ	ἁπλοῦ	ἁπλῆς	ἁπλοῦ
	χρυσῷ	χρυσῇ	χρυσῷ	ἁπλῷ	ἁπλῇ	ἁπλῷ
	χρυσοῦν	χρυσῆν	χρυσοῦν	ἁπλοῦν	ἁπλῆν	ἁπλοῦν
P.	χρυσοῖ	χρυσαῖ	χρυσᾶ	ἁπλοῖ	ἁπλαῖ	ἁπλᾶ
	χρυσῶν (m. f. n.)			ἁπλῶν (m. f. n.)		
	χρυσοῖς	χρυσαῖς	χρυσοῖς	ἁπλοῖς	ἁπλαῖς	ἁπλοῖς
	χρυσοῦς	χρυσᾶς	χρυσᾶ	ἁπλοῦς	ἁπλᾶς	ἁπλᾶ
D.	χρυσῶ	χρυσᾶ	χρυσῶ	ἁπλῶ	ἁπλᾶ	ἁπλῶ
	χρυσοῖν	χρυσαῖν	χρυσοῖν	ἁπλοῖν	ἁπλαῖν	ἁπλοῖν

(The fem. έα = ᾶ, when a vowel or ρ precedes : (ἀργύρεος =) ἀργυροῦς, ἀργυρᾶ, ἀργυροῦν.)

8. Attic (Second) Declension.

Lesson 18.]		(a) people.	(b) rope.	(c) dining-room.
Sing.	N.	ὁ λεώς	ἡ κάλως	τὸ ἀνώγεων
	G.	λεώ	κάλω	ἀνώγεω
	D.	λεῷ	κάλῳ	ἀνώγεῳ
	A.	λεών	κάλων	ἀνώγεων
	V.	λεώς	κάλως	ἀνώγεων
Pl.	N.	λεῴ	κάλῳ	ἀνώγεω
	G.	λεών	κάλων	ἀνώγεων
	D.	λεῷs	κάλῳς	ἀνώγεῳς
	A.	λεώς	κάλως	ἀνώγεω
	V.	λεῴ	κάλῳ	ἀνώγεω
Dual.	N. A. V.	λεώ	κάλω	ἀνώγεω
	G. D.	λεῴν	κάλῳν	ἀνώγεῳν

9. *Adjective in* εως (*m. f.*), εων (*n.*).

	Sing.		Plur.
	m. f.	*n.*	
N.	ἵλεως	ἵλεων	ἵλεῳ
G.	ἵλεω	ἵλεω	ἵλεων
D.	ἵλεῳ	ἵλεῳ	ἵλεῳς
A.	ἵλεων	ἵλεων	ἵλεως
V.	ἵλεως	ἵλεων	ἵλεῳ

Dual. N. A. V. ἵλεω   G. D. ἵλεῳν

10. *Third Declension.*

Roots, κορακ, παιδ, Ͽω, πραγματ, Ͽηρ, αἰων, δαιμον, λεοντ, γιγαντ

Sing.		ὁ (*raven*)	ὁ, ἡ (*child*)	ὁ (*jackal*)	τό (*thing*)
	N.	κόραξ	παῖς	Ͽώς	πρᾶγμα
	G.	κόρακος	παιδός	Ͽωός	πράγματος
	D.	κόρακι	παιδί	Ͽωῖ	πράγματι
	A.	κόρακα	παῖδα	Ͽῶα	πρᾶγμα
	V.	κόραξ	παῖ	Ͽώς	πρᾶγμα
Plur.					
	N.	κόρακες	παῖδες	Ͽῶες	πράγματα
	G.	κοράκων	παίδων	Ͽώων	πραγμάτων
	D.	κόραξι(ν)ᵃ	παισί(ν)ᵇ	Ͽωσί(ν)	πράγμασι(ν)ᶜ
	A.	κόρακας	παῖδας	Ͽῶας	πράγματα
	V.	κόρακες	παῖδες	Ͽῶες	πράγματα
Dual.					
N. A. V.		κόρακε	παῖδε	Ͽῶε	πράγματε
G. D.		κοράκοιν	παίδοιν	Ͽώοιν	πραγμάτοιν.

ᵃ = κόρακ-σι(ν).   ᵇ = παιδ-σίν.   ᶜ = πράγματ-σιν.

Sing.		ὁ (*animal*)	ὁ (*age*)	ὁ, ἡ, (*divinity*)	ὁ (*lion*)	ὁ (*giant*)
	N.	Ͽήρ	αἰών	δαίμων	λέων	γίγᾱς
	G.	Ͽηρός	αἰῶνος	δαίμονος	λέοντος	γίγαντος
	D.	Ͽηρί	αἰῶνι	δαίμονι	λέοντι	γίγαντι
	A.	Ͽῆρα	αἰῶνα	δαίμονα	λέοντα	γίγαντα
	V.	Ͽήρ	αἰών	δαῖμον	λέον	γίγαν
Plur.						
	N.	Ͽῆρες	αἰῶνες	δαίμονες	λέοντες	γίγαντες
	G.	Ͽηρῶν	αἰώνων	δαιμόνων	λεόντων	γιγάντων
	D.	Ͽηρσί(ν)	αἰῶσι(ν)ᵈ	δαίμοσι(ν)ᵉ	λέουσι(ν)ᶠ	γίγᾱσι(ν)ᵍ
	A.	Ͽῆρας	αἰῶνας	δαίμονας	λέοντας	γίγαντας
	V.	Ͽῆρες	αἰῶνες	δαίμονες	λέοντες	γίγαντες
Dual.						
N. A. V.		Ͽῆρε	αἰῶνε	δαίμονε	λέοντε	γίγαντε
G. D.		Ͽηροῖν	αἰώνοιν	δαιμόνοιν	λεόντοιν	γιγάντοιν

ᵈ = αἰῶν-σι(ν).   ᵉ = δαίμον-σι(ν).   ᶠ = λέοντ-σι(ν).
ᵍ = γίγαντ-σι(ν).

Comparative in ων.

11.   12.

(Root εὐδαιμον.)   Singular.

	m. f.	n.	m. f.		n.
N.	εὐδαίμων	εὔδαιμον	μείζων		μεῖζον
G.	εὐδαίμονος			μείζονος	
D.	εὐδαίμονι			μείζονι	
A.	εὐδαίμονα	εὔδαιμον	μείζονα or μείζω		μεῖζον
V.	εὔδαιμον			μεῖζον	

Plural.

N.V.	εὐδαίμονες	εὐδαίμονα	{ μείζονες / μείζους		{ μείζονα / μείζω
G.	εὐδαιμόνων			μειζόνων	
D.	εὐδαίμοσι(ν)			μείζοσι(ν)	
A.	εὐδαίμονας	εὐδαίμονα	{ μείζονας / μείζους		{ μείζονα / μείζω

Dual.

N.A.V.	εὐδαίμονε		μείζονε
G.D.	εὐδαιμόνοιν		μειζόνοιν

13.   14.

(Root μελαν.)   Singular.   (Root χαριεντ.)

N.	μέλᾱς	μέλαινα	μέλᾰν	χαρίεις	χαρίεσσα	χαρίεν
G.	μέλανος	μελαίνης	μέλανος	χαρίεντος	χαριέσσης	χαρίεντος
D.	μέλανι	μελαίνῃ	μέλανι	χαρίεντι	χαριέσσῃ	χαρίεντι
A.	μέλανα	μέλαιναν	μέλαν	χαρίεντα	χαρίεσσαν	χαρίεν
V.	μέλας	μέλαινα	μέλαν	χαρίεν	χαρίεσσα	χαρίεν

Plural.

N.V.	μέλανες	μέλαιναι	μέλανα	χαρίεντες	χαρίεσσαι	χαρίεντα
G.	μελάνων	μελαινῶν	μελάνων	χαριέντων	χαριεσσῶν	χαριέντων
D.	μέλασι(ν)	μελαίναις	μέλασι(ν)	χαρίεσι(ν)*	χαριέσσαις	χαρίεσι(ν)
A.	μέλανας	μελαίνας	μέλανα	χαρίεντας	χαριέσσᾱς	χαρίεντα

Dual.

N.A.V.	μέλανε	μελαίνᾱ	μέλανε	χαρίεντε	χαριέσσᾱ	χαρίεντε
G.D.	μελάνοιν	μελαίναιν	μελάνοιν	χαριέντοιν	χαριέσσαιν	χαριέντοιν

15.

Singular.   (Root παντ.)   Plural.

N.V.	πᾶς	πᾶσα	πᾶν	πάντες	πᾶσαι	πάντα
G.	παντός	πάσης	παντός	πάντων	πασῶν	πάντων
D.	παντί	πάσῃ	παντί	πᾶσι(ν)	πάσαις	πᾶσι(ν)
A.	πάντα	πᾶσαν	πᾶν	πάντας	πάσας	πάντα

Dual. N.A.V.	πάντε	πάσα	πάντε		
G.D.	πάντοιν	πάσαιν	πάντοιν .		

* *Obs.* dat. χαρίεσι, not χαρίεσσι.

16. *Participle of Pres. Act.*   (Root λειποντ.)

Sing.	N.V.	λείπων	λείπουσα	λεῖπον
	G.	λείποντος	λειπούσης	λείποντος
	D.	λείποντι	λειπούσῃ	λείποντι
	A.	λείποντα	λείπουσαν	λεῖπον
Plural.	N.V.	λείποντες	λείπουσαι	λείποντα
	G.	λειπόντων	λειπουσῶν	λειπόντων
	D.	λείπουσι(ν)	λειπούσαις	λείπουσι(ν)
	A.	λείποντας	λειπούσας	λείποντα
Dual.	N.A.V.	λείποντε	λειπούσα	λείποντε
	G.D.	λειπόντοιν	λειπούσαιν	λειπόντοιν

17. *Participle of Aor. 1. Act.*   (Root λειψαντ.)

Sing.	N.V.	λείψᾱς	λείψᾱσα	λεῖψᾰν
	G.	λείψαντος	λειψάσης	λείψαντος
	D.	λείψαντι	λειψάσῃ	λείψαντι
	A.	λείψαντα	λείψασαν	λεῖψαν
Plural.	N.V.	λείψαντες	λείψασαι	λείψαντα
	G.	λειψάντων	λειψασῶν	λειψάντων
	D.	λείψᾱσι(ν)	λειψάσαις	λείψᾱσι(ν)
	A.	λείψαντας	λειψάσας	λείψαντα
Dual.	N.A.V.	λείψαντε	λειψάσα	λείψαντε
	G.D.	λειψάντοιν	λειψάσαιν	λειψάντοιν

18.

	(a) Sing.			(b) Sing.		
N.	πολύς	πολλή	πολύ	μέγας	μεγάλη	μέγα
G.	πολλοῦ	πολλῆς	πολλοῦ	μεγάλου	μεγάλης	μεγάλου
D.	πολλῷ	πολλῇ	πολλῷ	μεγάλῳ	μεγάλῃ	μεγάλῳ
A.	πολύν	πολλήν	πολύ	μέγαν	μεγάλην	μέγα
V.	πολύ	πολλή	πολύ	μέγα	μεγάλη	μέγα
	Plural.			Plural.		
N.	πολλοί	πολλαί	πολλά	μεγάλοι	μεγάλαι	μεγάλα
G.	πολλῶν	πολλῶν	πολλῶν	μεγάλων	μεγάλων	μεγάλων
	etc. regular.			etc. regular.		

19.

		(a) father.	(b) mother.	(c) daughter.	(d) man
Sing.	N.	ὁ πατήρ	ἡ μήτηρ	ἡ θυγάτηρ	ὁ ἀνήρ
	G.	πατρός	μητρός	θυγατρός	ἀν-δ-ρός
	D.	πατρί	μητρί	θυγατρί	ἀν-δ-ρί
	A.	πατέρα	μητέρα	θυγατέρα	ἄν-δ-ρα
	V.	πάτερ	μῆτερ	θύγατερ	ἄνερ
Plural.	N.	πατέρες	μητέρες	θυγατέρες	ἄν-δ-ρες
	G.	πατέρων	μητέρων	θυγατέρων	ἀν-δ-ρῶν
	D.	πατράσι(ν)	μητράσι(ν)	θυγατράσι(ν)	ἀν-δ-ράσι(ν)
	A.	πατέρας	μητέρας	θυγατέρας	ἄν-δ-ρας
	V.	πατέρες	μητέρες	θυγατέρες	ἄν-δ-ρες
Dual.	N.A.V.	πατέρε	μητέρε	θυγατέρε	ἄν-δ-ρε
	G.D.	πατέροιν	μητέροιν	θυγατέροιν	ἀν-δ-ροῖν

20.

Sing.	N.	τὸ κέρας	τὸ κρέας
	G.	κέρᾰτ-ος, κέρως	κρέως
	D.	κέρατ-ι, κέρᾳ	κρέᾳ
	A.	κέρας	κρέας
Plural.	N.	κέρατ-α, κέρᾱ	κρέᾱ
	G.	κεράτ-ων, κερῶν	κρεῶν
	D.	κέρα-σι(ν)	κρέα-σι(ν)
	A.	κέρατ-α, κέρᾱ	κρέᾱ
Dual.	N.A.V.	κέρατ-ε, κέρᾱ (?)	κρέᾱ
	G.D.	κεράτ-οιν, κερῷν (?)	κρεῷν

21.

Singular.

		trireme.		wall.
N.		ἡ τριήρης		τὸ τεῖχος
G.	(τριήρεος)	τριήρους	(τείχεος)	τείχους
D.	(τριήρεῖ)	τριήρει	(τείχεῖ)	τείχει
A.	(τριήρεα)	τριήρη		τεῖχος
V.		τριῆρες		τεῖχος

Plural.

N.	(τριήρεες)	τριήρεις	(τείχεα)	τείχη
G.	(τριηρέων)	τριήρων	(τειχέων)	τειχῶν
D.		τριήρεσι(ν)		τείχεσι(ν)
A.	(τριήρεας)	τριήρεις	(τείχεα)	τείχη
V.	(τριήρεες)	τριήρεις	(τείχεα)	τείχη

Dual.

N.A.V.	(τριήρεε)	τριήρη	(τείχεε)	τείχη
G.D.	(τριηρέοιν)	τριήροιν	(τειχέοιν)	τειχοῖν

22. *Adjective in* ης.

		m. f.		n.
Sing.	N.	σαφής		σαφές
	G.		(σαφέ-ος) σαφοῦς	
	D.		(σαφέ-ϊ) σαφεῖ	
	A.	(σαφέ-α) σαφῆ		σαφές
	V.		σαφές	σαφές
Plural.	N.	(σαφέ-ες) σαφεῖς		(σαφέ-α) σαφῆ
	G.		(σαφέ-ων) σαφῶν	
	D.		σαφέσι(ν)	
	A.	(σαφέ-ας) σαφεῖς		(σαφέ-α) σαφῆ
	V.	(σαφέ-ες) σαφεῖς		(σαφέ-α) σαφῆ
Dual.	N.A.V.	σαφέ-ε	σαφῆ	
	G.D.	σαφέ-οιν	σαφοῖν	

☞ *Compound paroxytones* in ης remain paroxytones in the contracted Gen. pl.; as : συνήϑων, αὐτάρκων (fr. συνήϑης, αὐτάρκης).

23.

Sing.	Plur.
	city, town.
N. πόλῐς (ἡ)	πόλεις
G. πόλεως	πόλεων
D. πόλει	πόλεσι(ν)
A. πόλῐν	πόλεις
V. πόλῐ	πόλεις

Dual. N.A.V. πόλεε (πόλη)
　　　G.D. πολέοιν

24.

Sing.	Plur.
	fore-arm; cubit.
N. πῆχῦς (ὁ)	πήχεις
G. πήχεως	πήχεων
D. πήχει	πήχεσι(ν)
A. πῆχυν	πήχεις
V. πῆχυ	πήχεις

{ Dual of πῆχυς and
{ ἄστυ not found.

25.

Sing.	Plur.
	city.
N. ἄστυ (τό)	ἄστη
G. ἄστεος	ἄστεων
D. ἄστει	ἄστεσι(ν)
A. ἄστυ	ἄστη
V. ἄστυ	ἄστη

26.

(Adjectives in υς are contracted in some forms.)

| | Singular. | | | Plural. | |
	m.	f.	n.	m.	f.	n.
N.	γλυκύς	γλυκεῖα	γλυκύ	γλυκεῖς	γλυκεῖαι	γλυκέα
G.	γλυκέος	γλυκείας	γλυκέος	γλυκέων	γλυκειῶν	γλυκέων
D.	γλυκεῖ	γλυκείᾳ	γλυκεῖ	γλυκέσι(ν)	γλυκείαις	γλυκέσι(ν)
A.	γλυκύν	γλυκεῖαν	γλυκύ	γλυκεῖς	γλυκείᾱς	γλυκέα
V.	γλυκύ	γλυκεῖα	γλυκύ	γλυκεῖς	γλυκεῖαι	γλυκέα

Dual. N.A.V.　γλυκέε　　γλυκεία　　γλυκέε
　　　G.　　　γλυκέοιν　γλυκείειν　γλυκέοιν

27.

Singular.	Plural.	Dual.
	a king.	
N. ὁ βασιλεύς	N. βασιλεῖς (old Att. βασιλῆς)	N.A.V. βασιλέε
G. βασιλέως	G. βασιλέων	G.D. βασιλέοιν
D. βασιλεῖ	D. βασιλεῦσι(ν)	
A. βασιλέᾱ	A. βασιλέας (βασιλεῖς)	
V. βασιλεῦ	V. βασιλεῖς	

28.

Singular.	Plural.	Dual.
N. ἰχθύς	N. ἰχθύες	N.A. { [ἰχθύε]
G. ἰχθύος	G. ἰχθύων	{ ἰχθῦ
D. ἰχθύῑ	D. ἰχθύσιν	G.D. ἰχθύοιν
A. ἰχθύν	A. ἰχθῦς	
V. ἰχθύ	V. ἰχθύες	

29.

Singular.		Plural.			
N. βοῦς	γραῦς	βόες	[βοῦς]	γρᾶες	[γραῦς]
G. βοός	γραός	βοῶν		γραῶν	
D. βοΐ	γραΐ	βουσίν		γραυσίν	
A. βοῦν	γραῦν	[βόας]	βοῦς	[γρᾶας]	γραῦς
V. [βοῦ]	γραῦ	βόες	[βοῦς]	γρᾶες	[γραῦς]

Dual. N.A.V. βόε.　　G.D. βοοῖν.

		30.	31.	32.
Sing.	N.	ὁ, ἡ πόρτις, calf.	ἡ ἔγχελυς, eel.	ὁ, ἡ οἶς, sheep.
	G.	πόρτι-ος	ἐγχέλυ-ος	οἰός
	D.	πόρτι-ι, πόρτῑ	ἐγχέλυ-ῐ	οἰΐ
	A.	πόρτιν	ἔγχελυν	ὄῐν
	V.	πόρτι	ἔγχελυ	οἶς
Plur.	N.	πόρτι-ες, πόρτῑς	ἐγχέλεις	οἶες
	G.	πορτί-ων	ἐγχέλε-ων	οἰῶν
	D.	πόρτι-σι(ν)	ἐγχέλε-σι(ν)	οἰσί(ν)
	A.	πόρτι-ας, πόρτῑς	ἐγχέλεις	οἶας, rarer οἶς
	V.	πόρτι-ες, πόρτῑς	ἐγχέλεις	οἶες
Dual.	N.A.V.	πόρτι-ε	ἐγχέλε-ε	οἶε
	G.D.	πορτί-οιν	ἐγχελέ-οιν	οἰοῖν

• Xenophon uses the Ionic forms of οἶς, viz. ὄϊν, ὄϊες, ὀΐων, ὄϊας and ὄϊς.—K.

33. *Participle of Aor. 1. Pass.* (Root λειφθέντ.)

		m.	f.	n.
Sing.	N.	λειφθείς (oxytone)	λειφθεῖσα	λειφθέν
	G.	λειφθέντος	λειφθείσης	λειφθέντος
	D.	λειφθέντι	λειφθείσῃ	λειφθέντι
	A.	λειφθέντα	λειφθεῖσαν	λειφθέν
	V.	λειφθείς	λειφθεῖσα	λειφθέν
Plur.	N.	λειφθέντες	λειφθεῖσαι	λειφθέντα
	G.	λειφθέντων	λειφθεισῶν	λειφθέντων
	D.	λειφθεῖσι(ν)	λειφθείσαις	λειφθεῖσι(ν)
	A.	λειφθέντας	λειφθείσᾱς	λειφθέντα
	V.	λειφθέντες	λειφθεῖσαι	λειφθέντα
Dual.	N.A.V.	λειφθέντε	λειφθείσᾱ	λειφθέντε
	G.D.	λειφθέντοιν	λειφθείσαιν	λειφθέντοιν

34. *Participle of Aor. 2. Act.* (Root λιπόντ.)

		m.	f.	n.
Sing.	N.	λιπών (oxytone)	λιποῦσα	λιπόν
	G.	λιπόντος	λιπούσης	λιπόντος
	D.	λιπόντι	λιπούσῃ	λιπόντι
	A.	λιπόντα	λιποῦσαν	λιπόν
	V.	λιπών	λιποῦσα	λιπόν
Plur.	N.	λιπόντες	λιποῦσαι	λιπόντα
	G.	λιπόντων	λιπουσῶν	λιπόντων
	D.	λιποῦσι(ν)	λιπούσαις	λιποῦσι(ν)
	A.	λιπόντας	λιπούσᾱς	λιπόντα
	V.	λιπόντες	λιποῦσαι	λιπόντα
Dual.	N.A.V.	λιπόντε	λιπούσᾱ	λιπόντε
	G.D.	λιπόντοιν		λιπόντοιν

9

35. Participle of Perf. Act.   (Root λελυκότ.)

		m.	f.	n.
Sing.	N. V.	λελυκώς	λελυκυῖα	λελυκός
	G.	λελυκότος	λελυκυίας	λελυκότος
	D.	λελυκότι	λελυκυίᾳ	λελυκότι
	A.	λελυκότα	λελυκυῖαν	λελυκός
Plural.	N. V.	λελυκότες	λελυκυῖαι	λελυκότα
	G.	λελυκότων	λελυκυιῶν	λελυκότων
	D.	λελυκόσι(ν)	λελυκυίαις	λελυκόσι(ν)
	A.	λελυκότες	λελυκυίας	λελυκότα
Dual.	N. A. V.	λελυκότε	λελυκυία	λελυκότε
	G. D.	λελυκότοιν	λελυκυίαιν	λελυκότοιν

36. Declension of the first four numerals.

N.	1 εἷς, μίᾰ, ἕν	3 τρεῖς, τρία	Τέσσαρες or τέτ-
G.	1 ἑνός, μιᾶς, ἑνός	3 τριῶν	ταρες. — Δύο may
D.	1 ἑνί, μιᾷ, ἑνί	3 τρισί(ν)	also be used as in-
A.	1 ἕνα, μίαν, ἕν	3 τρεῖς, τρία	declinable for *any*
			case.—δύω is found
N.	2 δύο	4 τέσσαρες, a	(when the verse re-
G.	2 δυοῖν (very seld. δυεῖν)	4 τεσσάρων	quires it) in *non-*
D.	2 δυοῖν (un-Att. δυσί)	4 τέσσαρσι(ν)	*Attic* poets [not
A.	2 δύο	4 τέσσαρας, a	Pindar].

37. Τίς; (interrog.)   38. Τὶς (indef.).

		m. f.	n.	m. f.	n.
Sing.	N.	τίς	τί	τὶς	τὶ
	G.	τίνος	τίνος	τινός	τινός
	D.	τίνι	τίνι	τινί	τινί
	A.	τίνα	τί	τινά	τὶ
Plur.	N.	τίνες	τίνα	τινές	τινά
	G.	τίνων	τίνων	τινῶν	τινῶν
	D.	τίσι(ν)	τίσι(ν)	τισί(ν)	τισί(ν)
	A.	τίνας	τίνα	τινάς	τινά
Dual.	N. A.	τίνε		τινέ	
	G. D.	τίνοιν		τινοῖν	

In sing. G. τοῦ, and D. τῷ are also found; *enclitic* when for τινός. For *neut. pl.* τινά (*not* for τίνα), ἅττα (*not* enclit.) is also found in Attic.

39.   40.

			Singular.		
N.	οὔτις	οὔτι	οὐδείς	οὐδεμίᾰ	οὐδέν, no one
G.	οὔτινος		οὐδενός	οὐδεμιᾶς	οὐδενός
D.	οὔτινι		οὐδενί	οὐδεμιᾷ	οὐδενί
A.	οὔτινα	οὔτι	οὐδένα	οὐδεμίαν	οὐδέν

Plural.

N.	οὕτινες	οὕτινα
G.	οὕτινων	
D.	οὕτισι	
A.	οὕτινας	οὕτινα

Dual.

N	οὕτινε
G.N.	οὕτινοιν

Though οὐδείς, μηδείς = *not even one*, yet (like our ' *none*') they are sometimes found in the *pl.*, principally in *nom.* and *acc.* (less commonly *gen.* and *dat.*) masc. οὐδ-ένες (-ένων, -έσιν), -ένας.

Just so μηδείς, μηδεμία, μηδέν.

Αμφω (*both*) is declined like a dual: N. A. V. ἄμφω, G. & D. ἀμφοῖν

		41.	42.	43.
Sing.	N.	ἐγώ	σύ	[ἵ]
	G.	ἐμοῦ, μοῦ	σοῦ	(οὗ)
	D.	ἐμοί, μοί	σοί	οἷ
	A.	ἐμέ, μέ	σέ	(ἕ)
Plural.	N.	ἡμεῖς	ὑμεῖς	σφεῖς [neut. σφέα]
	G.	ἡμῶν	ὑμῶν	σφῶν
	D.	ἡμῖν	ὑμῖν	σφίσι(ν)
	A.	ἡμᾶς	ὑμᾶς	σφᾶς [neut. σφεα]
Dual.	N. A.	[νῶι], νώ	[σφῶι], σφώ	[σφωέ]
	G. D.	[νῶιν], νῷν	[σφῶιν], σφῷν	[σφωίν]

44.

The *reflexive* pronouns are: m. ἐμαυτοῦ, f. ἐμαυτῆς, *of myself*; m. σεαυτοῦ (or σαυτοῦ), f. σεαυτῆς (or σαυτῆς), *of thyself*; m. n. ἑαυτοῦ (or αὑτοῦ), f. ἑαυτῆς (or αὑτῆς), *of himself, herself, itself.* The compound forms, ἡμεῖς (ὑμεῖς) αὑτοί, are used for pl. of ἐμαυτοῦ, σεαυτοῦ.

S.	m.	ἐμαυτ-οῦ	-ῷ	-όν	σεαυτ-(σαυτ-)οῦ	-ῷ	-όν	
	f.	ἐμαυτ-ῆς	-ῇ	-ήν	σεαυτ-(σαυτ-)ῆς	-ῇ	-ήν	
P.	m.	ἡμεῖς αὑτοί ἡμῶν αὑτῶν			ὑμεῖς αὑτοί ὑμῶν αὑτῶν &c.			
	f.	ἡμεῖς αὑταί ἡμῶν αὑτῶν			ὑμεῖς αὑταί ὑμῶν αὑτῶν &c.			
S.	m. n.	ἑαυτ-οῦ	-ῷ	-όν, n. -ό	(or) αὑτ-οῦ	-ῷ	-όν, n. -ό	
	f.	ἑαυτ-ῆς	-ῇ	-ήν	(or) αὑτ-ῆς	-ῇ	-ήν	
P.	m. n.	ἑαυτ-ῶν	-οῖς	-ούς, n. ά	(or) αὑτ-ῶν	-οῖς	-ούς, n. ά	
	f.	ἑαυτ-ῶν	-αῖς	- άς	(or) αὑτ-ῶν	-αῖς	-άς	

For *pl.* the compound forms are often used (with more emphasis).

P. m. σφῶν αὑτῶν, σφίσιν αὑτοῖς, σφᾶς αὑτούς
 f. σφῶν αὑτῶν, σφίσιν αὑταῖς, σφᾶς αὑτάς

45.

The reciprocal pronoun expresses that *each* object does the action to the *other* or *others.*

Plural. G.	ἀλλήλων, *of each other*	Dual. ἀλλήλοιν αιν οιν
D.	ἀλλήλοις αις οις	
A.	ἀλλήλους ας α	ἀλλήλω ά ω.

Demonstrative (or *Pointing-out*) *Pronouns.*

		this.		**46.**			*these.*	
Sing.	N.	ὅδε	ἥδε	τόδε	Plur. N.	οἵδε	αἵδε	τάδε
	G.	τοῦδε	τῆσδε	τοῦδε	G.	τῶνδε	τῶνδε	τῶνδε
	D.	τῷδε	τῇδε	τῷδε	D.	τοῖσδε	ταῖσδε	τοῖσδε
	A.	τόνδε	τήνδε	τόδε	A.	τούσδε	τάσδε	τάδε

Dual. N. A. τώδε   τάδε   τώδε
      G. D. τοῖνδε   ταῖνδε   τοῖνδε

47.   **48.**

ipse (in the oblique cases, *ejus, ei. eum,* &c.).

		this.			*ipse*		
Sing.	N.	οὗτος	αὕτη	τοῦτο	αὐτός	αὐτή	αὐτό
	G.	τούτου	ταύτης	τούτου	αὐτοῦ	αὐτῆς	αὐτοῦ
	D.	τούτῳ	ταύτῃ	τούτῳ	αὐτῷ	αὐτῇ	αὐτῷ
	A.	τοῦτον	ταύτην	τοῦτο	αὐτόν	αὐτήν	αὐτό
Plur.	N.	οὗτοι	αὗται	ταῦτα	αὐτοί	αὐταί	αὐτά
	G.	τούτων	τούτων	τούτων	αὐτῶν	αὐτῶν	αὐτῶν
	D.	τούτοις	ταύταις	τούτοις	αὐτοῖς	αὐταῖς	αὐτοῖς
	A.	τούτους	ταύτας	ταῦτα	αὐτούς	αὐτάς	αὐτά
Dual.	N. A.	τούτω	ταύτα	τούτω	αὐτώ	αὐτά	αὐτώ
	G. D.	τούτοιν	ταύταιν	τούτοιν	αὐτοῖν	αὐταῖν	αὐτοῖν.

49.

Relative Pronouns.

	Singular.			Plural.			Dual.		
N.	ὅς (qui)	ἥ	ὅ	οἵ	αἵ	ἅ	ὥ	ἅ	ὥ
G.	οὗ	ἧς	οὗ	ὧν	ὧν	ὧν	οἷν	αἷν	οἷν
D.	ᾧ	ᾗ	ᾧ	οἷς	αἷς	οἷς	οἷν	αἷν	οἷν
A.	ὅν	ἥν	ὅ	οὕς	ἅς	ἅ	ὥ	ἅ	ὥ.

Often with -περ added : ὅσπερ, ἥπερ, ὅπερ, &c.

50.

Sing.	N.	ὅστις, *who(ever)*	ἥτις	ὅ τι [or ὅ, τι]
	G.	οὗτινος or ὅτου	ἧστινος	(as masc.)
	D.	ᾧτινι or ὅτῳ	ᾗτινι	(as masc.)
	A.	ὅντινα	ἥντινα	ὅ τι [or ὅ, τι]
Plural.	N.	οἵτινες	αἵτινες	ἅτινα or ἅττα
	G.	ὧντινων (more rarely ὅτων)		
	D.	οἷστισι(ν) (more rarely ὅτοις)	αἷστισι(ν)	οἷστισι(ν)
	A.	οὕστινας	ἅστινας	ἅτινα or ἅττα
Dual. N. A.	ὥτινε, ἅτινε	G. D. οἷντινοιν, αἷντινοιν		

51.

(*alius*)	ἄλλος	ἄλλη	ἄλλο }	quite regular except
(*ille*)	ἐκεῖνος	ἐκείνη	ἐκεῖνο }	neut. o.

52.

τοσοῦτος (*quantus*). τοιοῦτος (*talis*).

	Sing.			Plur.	
N.	τοσοῦτος τοσαύτη τοσοῦτο(ν)		τοσοῦτοι	τοσαῦται	τοσαῦτα
G.	τοσούτου τοσαύτης τοσούτου		τοσούτων	τοσούτων	τοσούτων
D,	τοσούτῳ τοσαύτῃ τοσούτῳ		τοσούτοις	τοσαύταις	τοσούτοις
A.	τοσοῦτον τοσαύτην τοσοῦτο(ν)		τοσούτους	τοσαύτας	τοσαῦτα

Dual.

N.A. τοσούτω τοσαύτα τοσούτω
G.D. τοσούτοιν τοσαύταιν τοσούτοιν

So τοιοῦτος, τοιαύτη, τοιοῦτο(ν), τηλικοῦτος, τηλικαύτη, τηλικοῦτο(ν).

53.

Terminations of the Tenses of a Verb in the first person sin-gular of the Indicative Mood.

The names of the *principal* tenses are in capital letters.

Active. Middle. Passive.

	Active	Middle	Passive	
PRESENT,	ω	ομαι		with the *strength-ened* root (if the verb has one).
Imperfect,	ον	όμην		
PERFECT,	κα or ά*	μαι		root usually changed, by laws of euphony when termination is ap-pended.
Pluperfect,	κειν or είν	μην		
FUTURE 1.	σω	σομαι	Ͽήσομαι	
Aor. 1. for liquid verbs.	σα	σάμην		
	α	άμην	Ͽην	
FUTURE 3.	(none)	(none)	σομαι†	(with redupl. root).

Tempora Secunda.

	Active	Middle	Passive	
FUTURE 2.‡	ῶ	οῦμαι	ήσομαι	from short root: the vowel-sound being lengthened in *Perf.* 2 and *Plup.*, except in the case of *o*.
Aorist 2.	ον	όμην	ην	
PERFECT 2.	α	(none)	(none)	
Pluperfect 2.	ειν	(none)	(none)	

* ά, είν belong to Mute Verbs whose characteristic is a P or a K sound. The *rough breathing* means that the *characteristic* (i. e. the final consonant of the root) is *aspirated* when the termination is ap-pended.

† The Third Future is supplied in the Active Voice by ἔσομαι (*I shall be*) with the *Perfect Participle*, as τετυφὼς ἔσομαι.

‡ The so-called 2nd Future is the regular Future of *liquid* verbs.

54. *Terminations of the Moods and Participles.*

☞ The Greek language has five Moods : one *Objective* Mood ; the *Indicative* ; and four *Subjective* Moods : (1) the *Imperative* ; (2) the *Subjunctive* ; (3) the *Optative* ; (4) the *Infinitive* ; (Kr.)

The *Subjective* Moods and the Participles are formed only from the *Principal Tenses* and the *Aorists* (not from the *Imperfect* and *Pluperfect*) : the *Futures* have no *Imperative* or *Subjunctive.*

Terminations of the *Subjective* Moods and of the Participles for the *Active*—

Imper.	Subj.	Opt.	Infin.	Part.	Inf. Ptcp.
ε But Aor. 1. has	ω	οιμι	ειν	ων $\left\{\begin{array}{l}\text{in Aor. 2. } ε ιν, ω ν \\ \text{in Perf. } ε ν α ι, ω s\end{array}\right\}$	
ον Fut. 2.	ω ——	αιμι οιμι	αι ειν	ās ων	

Terminations of the *Subjective* Moods and of the Participles for *Passive* and *Middle*—

Imper.	Subj.	Opt.	Infin.	Part.
ου But Aor. 1. Mid.	ωμαι	οιμην	εσθαι	όμενος (Inf. of Aor. 2. Mid. [ε σ θ α ι).
αι Aor. 1. 2. Pass.	ωμαι	αιμην	αοθαι	άμενος
ηθι Perf. Pass.	ῶ	ειην	ῆναι	εις [ηθι becomes ητι in [Aor. 1].
σο Fut. 2. Mid.	—— ——	—— οιμην	σθαι εισθαι	μένος ούμενος

The Subj. and Optat. of the *Perf. Pass.* are for the most part supplied by its participle with **ὰ**, εἴην (the *Subj.* and *Opt.*, respectively, of εἶναι, *to be*).

55. CONSPECTUS OF THE MOODS OF A BARYTONE VERB.

It must not be supposed that τύπτω has all these forms: they are given as the forms that may occur in verbs of this kind.

ACTIVE.

	Indic.	Imper.	Subj.	Opt.	Infin.	Part.
Present,	τύπτω	τύπτε	τύπτω	τύπτοιμι	τύπτειν	τύπτων
Imperfect,	ἔτυπτον					
Perfect 1.	τέτυφα	τέτυφε	τετύφω	τετύφοιμι	τετυφέναι	τετυφώς
Pluperfect 1.	ἐτετύφειν					
Perfect 2.	τέτυπα	τέτυπε	τετύπω	τετύποιμι	τετυπέναι	τετυπώς
Pluperfect 2.	ἐτετύπειν					
Future 1.	τύψω	τύψον	τύψω	τύψαιμι	τύψειν	τύψων
Aorist 1.	ἔτυψα			ἀγγελοῖμι*	τύψαι	τύψας
Future 2.	ἀγγελῶ				ἀγγελεῖν	ἀγγελῶν
Aorist 2.	ἔτυπον	τύπε	τύπω	τύποιμι	τυπεῖν	τυπών

PASSIVE.

	Indic.	Imper.	Subj.	Opt.	Infin.	Part.
Present,	τύπτομαι	τύπτου	τύπτωμαι	τυπτοίμην	τύπτεσθαι	τυπτόμενος
Imperfect,	ἐτυπτόμην					
Perfect,	τέτυμμαι	τέτυψο			τετύφθαι	τετυμμένος
Pluperfect,	ἐτετύμμην					
Future 1.	τυφθήσομαι			τυφθησοίμην	τυφθήσεσθαι	τυφθησόμενος
Aorist 1.	ἐτύφθην	τύφθητι	τυφθῶ	τυφθείην	τυφθῆναι	τυφθείς
Future 2.	τυπήσομαι			τυπησοίμην	τυπήσεσθαι	τυπησόμενος
Aorist 2.	ἐτύπην	τύπηθι	τυπῶ	τυπείην	τυπῆναι	τυπείς
Future 3.	τετύψομαι			τετυψοίμην	τετύψεσθαι	τετυψόμενος

MIDDLE.

	Indic.	Imper.	Subj.	Opt.	Infin.	Part.
Future 1.	τύψομαι		τύψωμαι	τυψοίμην	τύψεσθαι	τυψόμενος
Aorist 1.	ἐτυψάμην	τύψαι		τυψαίμην	τύψασθαι	τυψάμενος
Future 2.	ἀγγελοῦμαι			ἀγγελοίμην	ἀγγελεῖσθαι	ἀγγελούμενος
Aorist 2.	ἐτυπόμην	τυποῦ	τύπωμαι	τυποίμην	τυπέσθαι	τυπόμενος

* Or ἀγγελοίην.

56. *Terminations (combined with the*

TENSES.		MOODS.				
		Indicative.			Imperative.	
PRESENT and FU-TURE (the *Future* without *Imperat.* and *Subj.*).	S. P. D.	ω ομεν 	εις ετε ετον	ει ουσι(ν) ετον	ε ετε or όντων* ετον [Sing. 2. orig. ε-θι]	έτω έτωσαν έτων
FUTURE 2.	S. P. D.	ῶ οῦμεν 	εῖς εῖτε εῖτον	εῖ οῦσι(ν) εῖτον	None.	
Imperfect and *Aorist* 2.	S. P. D.	ον ομεν 	ες ετε ετον	ε ον έτην	Aorist 2	
PERFECT 1 and 2.	S. P. D.	ᾰ ᾰμεν 	ᾰς ᾰτε ᾰτον	ε ᾱσι ᾰτον	Like	
Aorist 1. [Obs. Aor. Imper. ον.]	S. P. D.	ᾰ ᾰμεν 	ᾰς ᾰτε ᾰτον	ε ᾰν ᾰτην	ον ατε or άντων* ατον	άτω άτωσαν άτων
Pluperfect 1 and 2.	S. P. D.	ειν ειμεν 	εις ειτε mostly εσαν ειτον	ει εισαν έσαν είτην		

REMARKS.—The Principal Tenses and Subj. have 3 dual in *ον*, 3 plur. in *σι*.—The Historical Tenses and the Optat. have 3 dual in *ην*, 3 plur. in *ν*.

---

* The *dissyllabic* termination of the *Imperat.* 3 *plur.* is the more common in Attic Greek, though the longer form is not *uncommon.* Care must be taken not to mistake it for the *gen. plur.* of a participle.

‡ Together with this ending, another is in use (called the *Æolic Aor.*) in *εια.* It is rare in the *first* person: but in the *second* and *third sing.* and *third plur.* it is far more common than the other form,— *ειας, ειε.*—plur. *ειαν.*

§ The *old* Attic has also an ending, *η, ης,* which is contracted from the Ionic form *εα, εας.* Thus *ἐβεβουλεύκη* for *ἐβεβουλεύκειν*

Mood-Vowels) of the Active Voice.

MOODS.			
Subjunctive.	*Optative.*	*Infinitive.*	*Participle.*

ω   ης   η
 ωμεν ητε ωσι
     ητον ητον
 [η in *sing.* sub-
script.]
	οιμι οις οι
	 οιμεν οιτε οιεν
	     οιτον οίτην
		ειν	ων ουσα ον
			 οντος 'ούσης οντος

None.	οἶμι† οἶς οἶ οἶμεν οῖτε οἶεν οῖτον οίτην	εἶν	ῶν ουσα οῦν οῦντος ούσης οῦντος
like	Present.	Aor. 2. εῖν	Aorist 2. ών ουσα όν όντος ούσης όντος
the	Present.	έναι	ώς υῖα ός ότος υίας ότος
Like the Pre- sent.	αιμι‡ αις αι αιμεν αιτε αιεν αιτον αίτην	αι	ᾶς ᾶσα ἄν αντος άσης αντος
			.

For ACCENTUATION, see pp. 206–208.

† Together with this ending the Optative of the Fut. 2. has also the termination οίην (e. g. φανοίην), which is a common Optative ending of *contracted verbs*. The *Futurum Atticum* has usually this Optative;[1] which is also occasionally found in the *Perf. Optat.* (especially that of *Perf.* 2; πεποιθοίην, ἐκπεφευγοίην, προεληλυθοίην); and in σχοίην, Aor. 2. Opt. from ἔχω.—

     οίην, οίης, οίη,—οίημεν, οίητε, οίησαν,—οίητον, οιήτην,

        or οἶμεν,   οἶτε,   οἶεν,   οἶτον, οίτην.

[1] The *Opt.* of ἐπιτελῶ (for instance), *Fut. Att.* for ἐπιτελέσω, is either ἐπιτελοίην or ἐπιτελέσοιμι᾽ never ἐπιτελοῖμι.

57. Terminations (combined with the Mood-

TENSES.		MOODS.			
		Indicative.			Imperative.
PRESENT and FUTURE.	S. P. D.	ομαι ομεθα† ομεθον†	η (ει)* εσθε εσθον	εται ονται εσθον	ου*　εσθω εσθε　εσθωσαν or εσθων‡ εσθον εσθων (*Future*, none.)
PERFECT.	S. P. D.	μαι μεθα μεθον	σαι σθε σθον	ται νται} σθον	σο　σθω σθε　σθωσαν or σθων σθον σθων
Pluperfect.	S. P. D.	μην μεθα μεθον	σο σθε σθον	το ντο} σθην	
Imperfect and Aor. 2. Mid.	S. P. D.	ομην ομεθα ομεθον	ου* εσθε εσθον	ετο οντο εσθην	Aor. 2.
Aor. 1. Mid. [Obs. Imper. αι.]	S. P. D.	αμην αμεθα αμεθον	ω* ασθε ασθον	ατο αντο ασθην	αι　ασθω ασθε　ασθωσαν or ασθων ασθον ασθων
FUT. 2. MID.	S. P. D.	οὖμαι ούμεθα ούμεθον	ῇ (εἰ) εἰσθε εἰσθον	εἶται οὖνται εἰσθον	None.
Pass. Aorists. [conjugated without *mood-vowels*.]	S. P. D.	ην ημεν	ης ητε ητον	η ησαν ητην	ηθι (Aor. 1. ητι) ητω ητε　ήτωσαν ητον ήτων

REMARKS.—The *Principal Tenses* and *Subj.* have 3 dual in ον, 3 plur. in ται; the *Historical Tenses* and *Optat.* have 3 dual in ην, 3 plur. in το. The dual -μεθον is very rare: the 1st pl. -μεθα being used instead of it.—ηθι (Aor. Imper.) becomes ητι when the η is preceded by an *aspirated mute* (hence always in Aor. 1): τύφθητι.

---

* The second persons from μαι, μην, are properly σαι, σο. But when these were appended to the root by a connecting vowel, the σ was thrown away; and εσαι, for instance, contracted into η, Atticè ει, which is the only termination for βούλει, ὄψει, οἴει (*you choose, will see, think*). [Kühner says, that ει is the regular form in *Aristophanes*, but is avoided by the *Tragic* writers; that it is used by *Thucyd.* and *Xen.*; but that *Plato* and the *Orators* use both forms.]—So ου is for εσω; ω (Aor. 1. Mid.) for ασω; η in *Subj.* for ησαι; οιο in *Optat.* for οισο.

Vowels) of the Passive and Middle Voice.

MOODS.				
Subjunctive.		**Optative.**	**Infin.**	**Participle.**
ωμαι η* ηται ώμεθα ησθε ωνται ώμεθον ησθον ησθον (*Future*, none.)		οἰμην οιο* οιτο οἰμεθα οιοθε οιντο οἰμεθον οιοθον οἰσθην	εσθαι	όμενος η ον
			σθαι	μένος μένη μένον
as		**Present.**	**Aor. 2.** έσθαι	**As Present.**
Like Present.		αἰμην αιο αιτο αἰμεθα αιοθε αιντο αἰμεθον αιοθον αἰσθην	ασθαι	άμενος η ον
None.		οἰμην οἰο οἰτο οἰμεθα οἰοθε οἰντο οἰμεθον οἰσθον οἰσθην	εἰσθαι	ούμενός η ον
ὦ ῇς ῇ ὦμεν ῆτε ὦσι ῆτον ῆτον		εἰην εἰης εἰη εἰημεν εἰητε εἰησαν or·εἰεν‖ εἰητον εἰήτην	ῆναι	εἰς εἰσα εν έντος εἰσης έντος

For ACCENTUATION, see pp. 206–208.

---

† The 1 *dual* and *plural* had each an extended form, μεσθον, μεσθα: they are used even by Attic *poets.*

‡ The shortened form of the 3 pl. *Imperative* is very common: the Epic poets use no other form. It is identical with 3rd dual.

§ The terminations νται, ντο, are unmanageable, except from pure roots. The *Ionic* forms in αται, ατο (before which the *p* and *k* sounds are aspirated), are also found in the *older* and *middle* Attic writers: λελείφαται, τετάχαται, ἐφθάραται, κεχωρίδαται [χωρίζω]. A periphrasis with partcp. (λελειμμένοι εἰσί) is generally used.

‖ εἰεν is more common than εἰησαν. Similar forms for the 1st and 2nd persons (εἰμεν, εἰτε) are found in the Attic dialect, principally in the poets, but also in prose.

58. Regular Verb in ω.
THE ACTIVE.

	Indicative.	Subjunctive.	Optative.	Imperative.
Pres. S.	λύ-ω	λύ-ω	λύ-οιμι	
	λύ-εις	λύ-ῃς	λύ-οις	λῦ-ε
	λύ-ει	λύ-ῃ	λύ-οι	λυ-έτω
P.	λύ-ομεν	λύ-ωμεν	λύ-οιμεν	
	λύ-ετε	λύ-ητε	λύ-οιτε	λύ-ετε
	λύ-ουσι(ν)	λύ-ωσι(ν)	λύ-οιεν	λυ-έτωσαν or λυ-όντων
D.	λύ-ετον	λύ-ητον	λύ-οιτον	λύ-ετον
	λύ-ετον	λύ-ητον	λυ-οίτην	λυ-έτων

Imperf. S. ἔ-λυ-ον P. ἐ-λύ-ομεν D. ———
ἔ-λυ-ες ἐ-λύ-ετε ἐ-λύ-ετον
ἔ-λυ-ε(ν) ἔ-λυ-ον. ἐ-λυ-έτην

	Indicative.	Subjunctive.	Optative.	Imperative. (very rare.)*
Perf. S.	λέ-λῠ-κᾰ	λε-λύ-κω	λε-λύ-κοιμι	(λέ-λυ-κε)
	λέ-λυ-κᾰς	like the	like the	like the
	λέ-λυ-κε(ν)	Present.	Present.	Present.
P.	λε-λύ-καμεν			
	λε-λύ-κατε			
	λε-λύ-κασι(ν)			
D.	λε-λύ-κατον			
	λε-λύ-κατον			

Plupf. S. ἐλε-λύ-κειν P. ἐλε-λύ-κειμεν D. ———
ἐλε-λύ-κεις ἐλε-λύ-κειτε ἐλε-λύ-κειτον
ἐλε-λύ-κει (ἐλε-λύ-κεισαν) ἐλε-λυ-κείτην
ἐλε-λύ-κεσαν

	Indicative.	Subjunctive.	Optative.	Imperative
Fut.	λύσω like the Present.	none	λύ-σοιμι like the Present.	none
Aor. S.	ἔ-λῡ-σᾰ	λύ-σω	λύ-σαιμι	
	ἔ-λυ-σᾰς	like the	λύ-σαις, -σειας	λῦ-σον
	ἔ-λυ-σε(ν)	Present.	λύ-σαι, -σειε(ν)	λυ-σάτω
P.	ἐ-λύ-σαμεν		λύ-σαιμεν	
	ἐ-λύ-σατε		λύ-σαιτε	λύ-σατε
	ἔ-λυ-σᾰν		λύ-σαιεν, -σειαν	λυ-σάτωσαν or λυ-σάντων
D.	ἐ-λύ-σατον		λύ-σαιτον	λύ-σατον
	ἐ-λυ-σάτην		λυ-σαίτην	λυ-σάτων

Infin. Pr. λύειν; Fut. λύσειν; Aor. λῦσαι; Perf. λελυκέναι.
Partcp. Pr. λύων, λύουσα, λῦον; Fut. λύσων, λύσουσα, λῦσον;
  Aor. λύσᾱς, λύσᾱσα, λῦσᾰν; Perf. λελῠκώς, υῖα, ός,
  G. κότος, κυίας, κότος

* From a few words whose *Perf.* has a *present* meaning; e. g
κεχήνετε (Kr.).—The usual form is Imper. of εἰμί with *perf. partcp.*

THE PASSIVE.

	Indicative.	Subjunctive.	Optative.	Imperative.
Pres. S.	λύ-ομαι	λύ-ωμαι	λυ-οίμην	
	λύ-η, -ει	λύ-η	λύ-ριο	λύ-ου
	λύ-εται	λύ-ηται	λύ-οιτο	λυ-έσϑω
P.	λυ-όμεϑα	λυ-ώμεϑα	λυ-οίμεϑα	
	λύ-εσϑε	λύ-ησϑε	λύ-οισϑε	λύ-εσϑε
	λύ-ονται	λύ-ωνται	λύ-οιντο	λυ-έσϑωσαν
				or λυ-έσϑων
D.	[λυ-όμεϑον]	[λυ-ώμεϑον]	[λυ-οίμεϑον]	
	λύ-εσϑον	λύ-ησϑον	λύ-οισϑον	λύ-εσϑον
	λύ-εσϑον	λύ-ησϑον	λυ-οίσϑην	λυ-έσϑων

	Singular.	Plural.	Dual.
Imperfect.	ἐ-λυ-όμην	ἐ-λυ-όμεϑα	[ἐ-λυ-όμεϑον]
	ἐ-λύ-ου	ἐ-λύ-εσϑε	ἐ-λύ-εσϑον
	ἐ-λύ-ετο	ἐ-λύ-οντο	ἐ-λύ-εσϑην
Perf. Indic.	λέ-λῦ-μαι	λε-λύ-μεϑα	[λε-λύ-μεϑον]
	λέ-λυ-σαι	λέ-λυ-σϑε	λέ-λυ-σϑον
	λέ-λυ-ται	λέ-λυ-νται	λέ-λυ-σϑον
Perf. Imper.	λέ-λυ-σο	λέ-λυ-σϑε	λέ-λυ-σϑον
	λε-λύ-σϑω	λε-λύ-σϑωσαν	λε-λύ-σϑων
		or λε-λύ-σϑων	
Pluperfect.	ἐλε-λύ-μην	ἐλε-λύ-μεϑα	[ἐλε-λύ-μεϑον]
	ἐλέ-λυ-σο	ἐλέ-λυ-σϑε	ἐλέ-λυ-σϑον
	ἐλέ-λυ-το	ἐλέ-λυ-ντο	ἐλε-λύ-σϑην

[On the Subj. and Opt. of the Perfect, see Pdm. 55.]

	Indicative.	Subjunctive.	Optative.	Imperative.
Fut.	λυ-ϑήσομαι	none	λυ-ϑησοίμην	none
First Aor.				
S.	ἐ-λύ-ϑην	λυ-ϑῶ	λυ-ϑείην	
	ἐ-λύ-ϑης	λυ-ϑῇς	λυ-ϑείης	λύ-ϑητι
	ἐ-λύ-ϑη	λυ-ϑῇ	λυ-ϑείη	λυ-ϑήτω
P.	ἐ-λύ-ϑημεν	λυ-ϑῶμεν	λυ-ϑείημεν, -ϑεῖμεν	
	ἐ-λύ-ϑητε	λυ-ϑῆτε	λυ-ϑείητε, -ϑεῖτε	λύ-ϑητε
	ἐ-λύ-ϑησαν	λυ-ϑῶσι(ν)	λυ-ϑείησαν, -ϑεῖεν	λυ-ϑήτωσαν
D.	ἐ-λύ-ϑητον	λυ-ϑῆτον	λυ-ϑείητον, -ϑεῖτον	[λυ-ϑέντων ?]
	ἐ-λυ-ϑήτην	λη-ϑῆτον	λυ-ϑειήτην, -ϑείτην	λύ-ϑητον
Fut. 3.				λυ-ϑήτων
	λε-λύ-σομαι	none	λε-λυ-σοίμην	none

Infinitive. Pres. λύεσϑαι; Perf. λελύσϑαι; Aor. λυϑῆναι; Future, λυϑήσεσϑαι; Future 3. λελύσεσϑαι.

Participle. Pres. λυόμενος, η, ον; Perf. λελυμένος, η, ον; Aor. λυϑείς, εῖσα, έν, G. έντος, είσης, έντος; Fut. λυϑησόμενος, η, ον; Fut. 3. λελυσόμενος, η, ον.

THE MIDDLE.

Indicative.	Subjunctive.	Optative.	Imperative.
ɪ ιt. λύ-σομαι	none	λυ-σοίμην	none
First Aor.			
2. ἐ-λυ-σάμην	λύσωμαι	λυ-σαίμην	
ἐ-λύ-σω	λύσῃ	λύ-σαιο	λῦ-σαι
ἐ-λύ-σατο	λύ-σηται	λύ-σαιτο	λυ-σάσθω
P. ἐ-λυ-σάμεθα	λυ-σώμεθα	λυ-σαίμεθα	
ἐ-λύ-σασθε	λύ-σησθε	λύ-σαισθε	λύ-σασθε
ἐ-λύ-σαντο	λύ-σωνται	λύ-σαιντο	λυ-σάσθωσαν
			or λυ-σάσθων
D. [ἐ-λυ-σάμεθον	λυ-σώμεθον	λυ-σαίμεθον]	
ἐ-λύ-σασθον	λύ-σησθον	λύ-σαισθον	λύ-σασθον
ἐ-λυ-σάσθην	λύ-σησθον	λυ-σαίσθην	λυ-σάσθων

Infinitive.   Future, λύσεσθαι   Aor. λύσασθαι

Participle.   Future, λυσόμενος, η, ον.   Aor. λυσάμενος, η, ον.

     Verbal Adjective, λῠ-τός, ή, όν· λυ-τέος, α, ον.

Tempora Secunda.

(φεύγω, flee; βάλλω, throw; κόπτω, hew.)

Perf. 2.	πέφευγα, &c.	Plupf.	ἐπεφεύγειν, &c.
Aor. 2. Act. Ind.	ἔβαλον	Imper.	βάλε
Subj.	βάλω	Infin.	βαλεῖν
Optat.	βάλοιμι	Part.	βαλών, οὖσα, ὅ
Aor. 2. Mid. Ind.	ἐβαλόμην	Imper.	βαλοῦ
			βαλέσθω
			βάλεσθον
			βαλέσθων
			βάλεσθε
			βαλέσθωσαν
			or βαλέσθων
Subj.	βάλωμαι	Infin.	βαλέσθαι
Optat.	βαλοίμην	Part.	βαλόμενος
Aor. 2. Pass. Ind.	ἐκόπην	Imperf.	κόπηθι, κόπητω, &c.
Fut. 2. Pass. Ind.	κοπήσομαι		

A. ACCENTUATION OF THE ACTIVE VOICE.

☞ With respect to accentuation, the terminations αι, οι are considered *long* in the *Optative*. With this exception, the termination αι is considered short in verbs, as αι, οι are, as the termination of *substantives*.

a) The *general* rule is, that the accent is as *far from the end* of the word as possible.

b) But *Infin. Aor.* 1. *Act.* is always accented on the *penult.*
[*Infin.* κωλῦσαι, φυλάξαι.]

c) *Infin.* of *Aor.* 2. *Act.* is perispomenon; its *Partcp.* oxytone.
[βαλεῖν, βαλών.]

d) The *Infin.* of *Perf. Act.* is paroxytone, *Partcp.* oxytone.
[τετυφέναι, τετυφώς.]

e) The *Imperatives* εἰπέ, εὑρέ, ἐλθέ, and (in *Attic*) λαβέ, ἰδέ, are oxytone.—But in their compound forms, the accent is thrown back. [ἔξελθε, ἀπόλαβε.]

f) In the Indicative of an *augmented tense*, the accent is never moved nearer to the beginning than the *augment*:

εἶχον, προσεῖχον· ἔσχον, παρέσχον. ἴκται, ἀφῖκται.

—But λεῖπε, κατάλειπε in the *Imperative*. So also if the augment is rejected by poetic license: ἔκφευγον for ἐξέφευγον.

g) The accent *helps* us to distinguish the three following forms, which but for that are identical.

Aor. 1. Act.		Aor. 1. Mid.
Infin.	*3rd sing. Opt.*	*2nd sing. Imperative.*
φυλάξαι	φυλάξαι	φύλαξαι
ποιῆσαι	ποιῆσαι	ποίησαι

In *dissyllable* verbs these forms are not distinguished by the accent, unless the penult of Aor. 1. Act. is long by nature: e. g. λῦσαι (Inf. Aor. 1. Act.; Imper. of Aor. 1. Mid.): λύσαι (3 s. Opt. Aor. 1. Act.): but τρέσαι, λέξαι, in all the forms.

h) *Participles* have in all their forms the same *tone-syllable* as the *nom. masc.*, unless the general rules make a change necessary.

φυλάττων	φυλάττουσα	φυλάττον
τετυφώς	τετυφυῖα	τετυφός
βαλών	βαλοῦσα	βαλόν
παιδεύων	παιδεύουσα	παιδεῦον

B. Accentuation of the Passive and Middle Voice.

Accent as far from the end of the word as possible.

a) But *Infin.* of *Aor. 2. Mid.* is *paroxytone.*   [συμβαλέσθαι.]

b) *Infin.* and *Partcp.* of Perf. Pass. have accent on *penult.*
   [πεπαιδεῦσθαι· λελύσθαι.—πεπαιδευμένος.]

c) *Infinitives* in ναι have always accent on penúlt [λυθῆναι].
   Cf. A. *d.*

d) The *Participles of Pass. Aorists* are *oxytone.*   [λυθείς.]

e) The *Subj.* of the *Pass. Aorists* (ῶ being contracted from ἐω)
   is *perispomenon* through the sing., and *properispomenon* in
   dual and plur.

f) In *Imper.* of *Aor. 2. Mid.* ου is *perispomenon* (λαβοῦ)   The
   other persons conform to the general rule.

g) For the *participles* see A, *h.*

| λυθείς | λυθεῖσα | λυθέν | Dat. pl. *m.* and *n.* |
| λυθέντος | λυθείσης | λυθέντος | εῖσι (not εσι). |

59. TABLE OF

(ACTIVE.)

A) PRES.		τομ-		φιλ-		χρυσ-	
Indic.	S.	ἀω,	-ῶ,	ἐω,	-ῶ,	ὁω,	-ῶ,
		ἀεις,	-ᾷς,	ἐεις,	-εῖς,	ὁεις,	-οῖς,
		ἀει,	-ᾷ,	ἐει,	-εῖ,	ὁει,	-οῖ,
	P.	ἀομεν,	-ῶμεν,	ἐομεν,	-οῦμεν,	ὁομεν,	-οῦμεν,
		ἀετε,	-ᾶτε,	ἐετε,	-εῖτε,	ὁετε,	-οῦτε,
		ἀουσι,	-ῶσι,	ἐουσι,	-οῦσι,	ὁουσι,	-οῦσι,
	D.	ἀετον,	-ᾶτον,	ἐετον,	-εῖτον,	ὁετον,	-οῖτον,
		ἀετον,	-ᾶτον.	ἐετον,	-εῖτον.	ὁετον,	-οῦτον.
Imp.	S.	αε,	-α,	εε,	-ει,	οε,	-ου,
		αέτω,	-άτω,	εέτω,	-είτω,	οέτω,	-ούτω,
	P.	ἀετε,	-ᾶτε,	ἐετε,	-εῖτε,	ὁετε,	-οῦτε,
		αέτωσαν,	-άτωσαν,	εέτωσαν,	-είτωσαν,	οέτωσαν,	-ούτωσαν
	D.	ἀετον,	-ᾶτον,	ἐετον,	-εῖτον,	ὁετον,	-οῦτον,
		αέτων,	-άτων.	εέτων,	-είτων.	οέτων,	-ούτων.
Subj.	S.	ἀω,	-ῶ,	ἐω,	-ῶ,	ὁω,	-ῶ,
		ἀῃς,	-ᾷς,	ἐῃς,	-ῇς,	ὁῃς,	-οῖς,
		ἀῃ,	-ᾷ,	ἐῃ,	-ῇ,	ὁῃ,	-οῖ,
	P.	ἀωμεν,	-ῶμεν,	ἐωμεν,	-ῶμεν,	ὁωμεν,	-ῶμεν,
		ἀητε,	-ᾶτε,	ἐητε,	-ῆτε,	ὁητε,	-ῶτε,
		ἀωσι,	-ῶσι,	ἐωσι,	-ῶσι,	ὁωσι,	-ῶσι,
	D.	ἀητον,	-ᾶτον,	ἐητον,	-ῆτον,	ὁητον,	-ῶτον,
		ἀητον,	-ᾶτον.	ἐητον,	-ῆτον.	ὁητον,	-ῶτον.
Opt.		ἀοιμι,	-ῷμι,	ἐοιμι,	-οῖμι,	ὁοιμι,	-οῖμι,
		ἀοις,	-ῷς,	ἐοις,	-οῖς,	ὁοις,	-οῖς,
		ἀοι,	-ῷ,	ἐοι,	-οῖ,	ὁοι,	-οῖ,
		ἀοιμεν,	-ῷμεν,	ἐοιμεν,	-οῖμεν,	ὁοιμεν,	-οῖμεν,
		ἀοιτε,	-ῷτε,	ἐοιτε,	-οῖτε,	ὁοιτε,	-οῖτε,
		ἀοιεν,	-ῷεν,	ἐοιεν,	-οῖεν,	ὁοιεν,	-οῖεν.
		ἀοιτον,	-ῷτον,	ἐοιτον,	-οῖτον,	ὁοιτον,	-οῖτον,
		αοίτην,	-ῴτην.	εοίτην,	-οίτην.	οοίτην,	-οίτην.
Prt		ων,	-ῶν,	ἐων,	-ῶν,	ὁων,	⌐
		ουσα,	-ῶσα,	ἐουσα,	-οῦσα,	ὁουσα,	⌐
		ον,	-ῶν.	ἐον,	-οῦν.	ὁον,	⌐

CONTRACTED VERBS.
(PASSIVE.)

					χρυσ-	
S.	ἀόμαι,	-ῶμαι,	ἐόμαι,	-οῦμαι,	ὀόμαι,	-οῦμαι,
	ἀῃ,	-ᾷ,	ἐῃ	-ῇ,	ὀῃ,	-οῖ,
	ἀέται,	-ᾶται,	ἐέται,	-εῖται,	ὀέται,	-οῦται,
P.	ἀόμεθα,	-ώμεθα,	ἐόμεθα,	-ούμεθα,	ὀόμεθα,	-ούμεθα,
	ἀέσθε,	-ᾶσθε,	ἐέσθε,	-εῖσθε,	ὀέσθε,	-οῦσθε,
	ἀόνται,	-ῶνται,	ἐόνται,	-οῦνται,	ὀόνται,	-οῦνται,
D.	ἀόμεθον,	-ώμεθον,	ἐόμεθον,	-ούμεθον,	ὀόμεθον,	-ούμεθον,
	ἀέσθον,	-ᾶσθον,	ἐέσθον,	-εῖσθον,	ὀέσθον,	-οῦσθον,
	ἀέσθον.	-ᾶσθον.	ἐέσθον.	-εῖσθον.	ὀέσθον.	-οῦσθον.

ἀόυ,	-ῶ,	ἐόυ,	-οῦ,	ὀόυ,	-οῦ,
ἀέσθω,	-ᾶσθω,	ἐέσθω,	-είσθω,	ὀέσθω,	-ούσθω,
ἀέσθε,	-ᾶσθε,	ἐέσθε,	-εῖσθε,	ὀέσθε,	-οῦσθε,
ἀέσθωσαν,	-ᾶσθωσαν,	ἐέσθωσαν,	-είσθωσαν	ὀέσθωσαν,	-ούσθωσαν,
ἀέσθον,	-ᾶσθον,	ἐέσθον,	-εῖσθον,	ὀέσθον,	-οῦσθον,
ἀέσθων.	-ᾶσθων.	ἐέσθων,	-εῖσθων.	ὀέσθων,	-ούσθων.

ἀώμαι,	-ῶμαι,	ἐώμαι,	-ῶμαι,	ὀώμαι,	-ῶμαι,
ἀῃ,	-ᾷ,	ἐῃ,	-ῇ,	ὀῃ,	-οῖ,
ἀῆται,	-ᾶται,	ἐῆται,	-ῆται,	ὀῆται,	-ῶται,
ἀώμεθα,	-ώμεθα,	ἐώμεθα,	-ώμεθα,	ὀώμεθα,	-ώμεθα,
ἀῆσθε,	-ᾶσθε,	ἐῆσθε,	-ῆσθε,	ὀῆσθε,	-ῶσθε,
ἀῶνται,	-ῶνται,	ἐῶνται,	-ῶνται,	ὀῶνται,	-ῶνται,
ἀώμεθον,	-ώμεθον,	ἐώμεθον,	-ώμεθον,	ὀώμεθον,	-ώμεθον,
ἀῆσθον,	-ᾶσθον,	ἐῆσθον,	-ῆσθον,	ὀῆσθον,	-ῶσθον,
ἀῆσθον.	-ᾶσθον.	ἐῆσθον.	-ῆσθον.	ὀῆσθον,	-ῶσθον.

ἀοίμην,	-ῴμην,	ἐοίμην,	-οίμην,	ὀοίμην,	-οίμην,
ἀοιο,	-ῷο,	ἐοιο,	-οῖο,	ὀοιο,	-οῖο,
ἀοιτο,	-ῷτο,	ἐοιτο,	-οῖτο,	ὀοιτο,	-οῖτο,
ἀοίμεθα,	-ῴμεθα,	ἐοίμεθα,	-οίμεθα,	ὀοίμεθα,	-οίμεθα,
ἀοισθε,	-ῷσθε,	ἐοισθε,	-οῖσθε,	ὀοισθε,	-οῖσθε,
ἀοιντο,	-ῷντο,	ἐοιντο,	-οῖντο,	ὀοιντο,	-οῖντο,
ἀοίμεθον,	-ῴμεθον,	ἐοίμεθον,	-οίμεθον,	ὀοίμεθον,	-οίμεθον,
ἀοισθον,	-ῷσθον,	ἐοισθον,	-οῖσθον,	ὀοισθον,	-οῖσθον,
ἀοίσθην.	-ῴσθην.	ἐοίσθην,	-οίσθην.	ὀοίσθην,	-οίσθην.

-ώμενος,	ἐόμενος,	-ούμεν	
-ωμένη,	ἐομένη,	-ουμέν	
-ώμενον.	ἐόμενον,	-ούμεν	

(Imperfect Active.)

B) Impf.		ἐτίμ-		ἐφιλ-		ἐχρύσ-	
Indic.	S.	αον,	-ων,	εον,	-ουν,	οον,	-ουν,
		αες,	-ας,	εες,	-εις,	οες,	-ους,
		αε,	-α,	εε,	-ει,	οε,	-ου,
	P.	άομεν,	-ῶμεν,	έομεν,	-οῦμεν,	όομεν,	-οῦμεν,
		άετε,	-ᾶτε,	έετε,	-εῖτε,	όετε,	-οῦτε,
		αον,	-ων,	εον,	-ουν,	οον,	-ουν,
	D.	άετον,	-ᾶτον,	έετον,	-εῖτον,	όετον,	-οῦτον,
		αέτην,	-άτην.	εέτην,	-είτην.	οέτην,	-ούτην.

60.

Verbs in μι.

τίθημι, place ; ἵστημι, make to stand ; δίδωμι, give ; δείκνυμι, show

(Formed from simpler roots, θε, στα, δο, δεικ.)

MOODS OF THE ACTIVE VOICE.

Indic.	Imperat.	Subj.	Opt.	Infin.	Part.
Pres. τίθημι	(τίθετι) τίθει	τιθῶ (ῇς, ῇ)	τιθείην	τιθέναι	τιθείς
ἵστημι	(ἵστᾰθι) ἵστη	ἱστῶ, (ῇς, ῇ)	ἱσταίην	ἱστάναι	ἱστάς
δίδωμι	(δίδοθι) δίδου	διδῶ (ῷς, ῷ)	διδοίην	διδόναι	διδούς
δείκνυμι	(δείκνυθι) δείκνῠ			δεικνῠναι	δεικνύς
Aor. 2. ἔθην	θές .	θῶ (ῇς, ῇ)	θείην	θεῖναι	θείς
ἔστην	στῆθι	στῶ (ῇς, ῇ)	σταίην	στῆναι	στάς
ἔδων	δός	δῶ (ῷς. ῷ)	δοίην	δοῦναι	δούς

TENSES OF THE ACTIVE VOICE.

Indicative.

Present.

S.	τίθημι	ἵστημι	δίδωμι	δείκνυμι
	τίθης	ἵστης	δίδως	δείκνυς
	τίθησι(ν)	ἵστησι(ν)	δίδωσι(ν)	δείκνυσι(ν)
P.	τίθεμεν	ἵστῐμεν	δίδομεν	δείκνυμεν
	τίθετε	ἵστᾰτε	δίδοτε	δείκνυτε
	τιθέᾱσι(ν)	ἱστᾶσι(ν)	διδόᾱσι(ν)	δεικνύᾱσι(ν)
D.	τίθετον	ἵστᾰτον	δίδοτον	δείκνυτον
	τίθετον	ἵστᾰτον	δίδοτον	δείκνυτον

(Imperfect Passive.)

B) Impf.		ἐτιμ-		ἐφιλ-		ἐχρυσ-	
Indic.	S.	αόμην,	-ώμην,	εόμην,	-ούμην,	οόμην,	-ούμην,
		άου,	-ῶ,	έου,	-οῦ,	όου,	-οῦ,
		άετο,	-ᾶτο,	έετο,	-εῖτο,	όετο,	-οῦτο,
	P.	αόμεϑα,	-ώμεϑα,	εόμεϑα,	-ούμεϑα,	οόμεϑα,	-ούμεϑα,
		άεσϑε,	-ᾶσϑε,	έεσϑε,	-εῖσϑε,	όεσϑε,	-οῦσϑε,
		άοντο,	-ῶντο,	έοντο,	-οῦντο,	όοντο,	-οῦντο,
	D.	αόμεϑον,	-ώμεϑον,	εόμεϑον,	-ούμεϑον,	οόμεϑον,	-ούμεϑον,
		άεσϑον,	-ᾶσϑον,	έεσϑον,	-εῖσϑον,	όεσϑον,	-οῦσϑον,
		αέσϑην,	-άσϑην.	εέσϑην,	-είσϑην.	οέσϑην,	-ούσϑην.

Imperfect [Cf. p. 218, e].

S.	ἐτίϑην	ἵστην	[ἐδίδων]*	ἐδείκνῦν
	(ἐτίϑης)	ἵστης	[ἐδίδως]	ἐδείκνῦς
	(ἐτίϑη)	ἵστη	[ἐδίδω]	ἐδείκνῦ
P.	ἐτίϑεμεν	ἵστᾰμεν	ἐδίδομεν	ἐδείκνῦμεν
	ἐτίϑετε	ἵστᾰτε	ἐδίδοτε	ἐδείκνῦτε
	ἐτίϑεσαν	ἵστᾰσαν	ἐδίδοσαν	ἐδείκνῦσαν
D.	ἐτίϑετον	ἵστᾰτον	ἐδίδοτον	ἐδείκνῦτον
	ἐτιϑέτην	ἱστάτην	ἐδιδότην	ἐδεικνύτην

2nd Aorist.

S.	[ἔϑην]	ἔστην	[ἔδων]	(none)
	[ἔϑης]	ἔστης	[ἔδως]	
	[ἔϑη]	ἔστη	[ἔδω]	
P.	ἔϑεμεν	ἔστημεν	ἔδομεν	
	ἔϑετε	ἔστητε	ἔδοτε	
	ἔϑεσαν	ἔστησαν	ἔδοσαν	
D.	ἔϑετον	ἔστητον	ἔδοτον	
	ἐϑέτην	ἐστήτην	ἐδότην	

Subjunctive.
Present.

S.	τιϑῶ	ἱστῶ	διδῶ	from δεικνύω
	τιϑῇς	ἱστῇς	διδῷς	
	τιϑῇ	ἱστῇ	διδῷ	
P.	τιϑῶμεν	ἱστῶμεν	διδῶμεν	
	τιϑῆτε	ἱστῆτε	διδῶτε	
	τιϑῶσι(ν)	ἱστῶσι(ν)	διδῶσι(ν)	
D.	τιϑῆτον	ἱστῆτον	διδῶτον	
	τιϑῆτον	ἱστῆτον	διδῶτον	

* The forms in use are: ἐδίδουν, ἐδίδους, ἐδίδου, p. 218, e. ἐδίδων
only Xen. An. 5, 8, 4. (as Od. τ. 367.)

2nd Aorist.

S. θῶ   στῶ   δῶ   (none)
θῇς   στῇς   δῷς

The Terminations as in the Present.

Optative.
Present.

S. τιθείην   ἱσταίην   διδοίην   from δεικνύω
τιθείης   ἱσταίης   διδοίης
τιθείη   ἱσταίη   διδοίη
P. τιθείημεν   ἱσταίημεν   διδοίημεν
τιθεῖμεν   ἱσταῖμεν   διδοῖμεν
τιθείητε   ἱσταίητε   διδοίητε
τιθεῖτε   ἱσταῖτε   διδοῖτε
(τιθείησαν)   (ἱσταίησαν)   (διδοίησαν)
τιθεῖεν   ἱσταῖεν   διδοῖεν
D. τιθείητον   ἱσταίητον   διδοίητον
τιθείτον   ἱσταῖτον   διδοῖτον
τιθειήτην   ἱσταιήτην   διδοιήτην
τιθείτην   ἱσταίτην   διδοίτην

2nd Aorist.

S. θείην   σταίην   δοίην   (none)

Terminations as in the Present.

Imperative.
Present.

S. [τίθετι]   [ἵστᾰθι]   [δίδοθι]   [δείκνῡθι]
τίθει   ἵστη   δίδου   δείκνῡ
τιθέτω   ἱστάτω   διδότω   δεικνύτω
P. τίθετε   ἵστᾰτε   δίδοτε   δείκνῠτε
[τιθέτωσαν]   [ἱστάτωσαν]   [διδότωσαν]   [δεικνύτωσαν]
τιθέντων   ἱστάντων   διδόντων   δεικνύντων
D. τίθετον   ἵστᾰτον   δίδοτον   δείκνῠτον
τιθέτων   ἱστάτων   διδότων   δεικνύτων

2nd Aorist.

S. θές*   στῆθι†   δός*   (none)
θέτω   στήτω   δότω

Terminations as in the Present.

* The compounds throw the accent back on the preceding syllable: περίθες, ἀπόδος, ἀπόδοτε.
† In the compounds στᾰ: παράστᾰ, ἀπόστᾰ.

Infinitive.
Present.

| τιθέναι | ἱστάναι | διδόναι | (δεικνΰναι) |

2nd Aorist.

| θεῖναι | στῆναι | · δοῦναι | (none) |

Participle.
Present.

Masc.	τιθείς	ἱστάς	διδούς	δεικνύς
	G. -έντος	-άντος	-όντος	-ύντος
Fem.	τιθεῖσα	ἱστᾶσα	διδοῦσα	δεικνῦσα
Neut.	τιθέν	ἱστάν	διδόν	δεικνύν

2nd Aorist.

θείς, θεῖσα, θέν,   στάς, στᾶσα, στάν,   δούς, δοῦσα, δόν,   (none)

61.

PASSIVE AND MIDDLE.

Moods of the Passive and Middle.

Pres. Indic.	Imper.	Subj.	Opt.	Infin.	Part.
τίθ-εμαι	εσο (ου)	ῶμαι	είμην	εσθαι	έμενος
ἵστ-ᾰμαι	ασο (ω)	ῶμαι	αίμην	ασθαι	άμενος
δίδ-ομαι	οσο (ου)	ῶμαι	οίμην	οσθαι	όμενος
δείκν-ῠμαι	ῠσο	——	——	υσθαι	ύμενος

Aor. 2.	Imper.	Subj.	Opt.	Infin.	Part.
ἐθέμην	(θέσο) θοῦ	θῶμαι	θείμην	θέσθαι	θέμενος
[ἐστάμην not found]					
ἐπτάμην flew	(πτάσο) πτῶ	πτῶμαί	πταίμην	πτάσθαι	πτάμενος
ἐδόμην	(δόσο) δοῦ	δῶμαι	δοίμην	δόσθαι	δόμενος

TENSES OF THE PASSIVE AND MIDDLE.

Indicative.

Present.

Sing.	τίθεμαι	ἵστᾰμαι	δίδομαι	δείκνῠμαι
	τίθεσαι	ἵστᾰσαι	δίδοσαι	δείκνῠσαι
	‘ [τίθῃ]	[ἵστᾳ]		
	τίθεται	ἵστᾰται	δίδοται	δείκνῠται
Plur.	τιθέμεθα	ἱστάμεθα	διδόμεθα	δεικνύμεθα
	τίθεσθε ‘	ἵστασθε	δίδοσθε	δείκνυσθε
	τίθενται	ἵστανται	δίδονται	δείκνυνται
Dual.	[τιθέμεθον]	[ἱστάμεθον]	[διδόμεθον]	[δεικνύμεθον]
	τίθεσθον	ἵστασθον	δίδοσθον	δείκνυσθον
	τίθεσθον	ἵστασθον	δίδοσθον	δείκνυσθον

Imperfect.

Sing.	ἐτιθέμην	ἱστάμην	ἐδιδόμην	ἐδεικνύμην
	ἐτίθεσο	ἵστασο	ἐδίδοσο	ἐδείκνυσο
	[ἐτίθου]	[ἵστω]	[ἐδίδου]	
	ἐτίθετο	ἵστατο	ἐδίδοτο	ἐδείκνυτο
Plur.	ἐτιθέμεθα	ἱστάμεθα	ἐδιδόμεθα	ἐδεικνύμεθα
	ἐτίθεσθε	ἵστασθε	ἐδίδοσθε	ἐδείκνυσθε
	ἐτίθεντο	ἵσταντο	ἐδίδοντο	ἐδείκνυντο
Dual.	[ἐτιθέμεθον]	[ἱστάμεθον]	[ἐδιδόμεθον]	[ἐδεικνύμεθον]
	ἐτίθεσθον	ἵστασθον	ἐδίδοσθον	ἐδείκνυσθον
	ἐτιθέσθην	ἱστάσθην	ἐδιδόσθην	ἐδεικνύσθην

2nd Aorist Middle.

Sing.	ἐθέμην	[ἐστάμην]	ἐδόμην	(none)
	ἔθου	[ἔστω]	ἔδου	
	ἔθετο	[ἔστατο]	ἔδοτο	

Terminations the same as those of the Imperfect.

Subjunctive.   [Cf. p. 218, c.]

Present.

Sing.	τιθῶμαι	ἱστῶμαι	διδῶμαι	from δεικνύω
	τιθῇ	ἱστῇ	διδῷ	
	τιθῆται	ἱστῆται	διδῶται	
Plur.	τιθώμεθα	ἱστώμεθα	διδώμεθα	
	τιθῆσθε	ἱστῆσθε	διδῶσθε	
	τιθῶνται	ἱστῶνται	διδῶνται	
Dual.	[τιθώμεθον]	[ἱστώμεθον]	[διδώμεθον]	
	τιθῆσθον	ἱστῆσθον	διδῶσθον	
	τιθῆσθον	ἱστῆσθον	διδῶσθον	

2nd Aorist Middle.*

Sing.	θῶμαι	[στῶμαι]·	δῶμαι	(none)
	θῇ	[στῇ]	δῷ	

Terminations the same as those of the Present.

Optative.

Present.

Sing.	τιθείμην	ἱσταίμην	διδοίμην	from δεικνυω
	τιθεῖο	ἱσταῖο	διδοῖο	
	τιθεῖτο	ἱσταῖτο	διδοῖτο	
Plur.	τιθείμεθα	ἱσταίμεθα	διδοίμεθα	
	τιθεῖσθε	ἱσταῖσθε	διδοῖσθε	
	τιθεῖντο	ἱσταῖντο	διδοῖντο	
Dual.	[τιθείμεθον]	[ἱσταίμεθον]	[διδοίμεθον]	
	τιθεῖσθον	ἱσταῖσθον	διδοῖσθον	
	τιθείσθην	ἱσταίσθην	διδοίσθην	

* Here too the accentuation of the compounds is often thrown back: ἐπιθῶμαι (or ἐπιδῶμαι)· πρόσθηται.

2nd Aorist Middle.

Sing. Ͽείμην [σταίμην] δοίμην (none)

Terminations the same as those of the Present.

Imperative.
Present.

Sing.	τίϿεσο	ἵστᾱσο	δίδοσο	δείκνῡσο
	[τίϿου]	(ἵστω)	[δίδου]	
	τιϿέσϿω	ἱστάσϿω	διδόσϿω	δεικνύσϿω
Plur.	τίϿεσϿε	ἵστασϿε	δίδοσϿε	δείκνυσϿε
	τιϿέσϿωσαν	ἱστάσϿωσαν	διδόσϿωσαν	δεικνύσϿωσαν
or	τιϿέσϿων	ἱστάσϿων	διδόσϿων	δεικνύσϿων
Dual.	τίϿεσϿον	ἵστασϿον	δίδοσϿον	δείκνυσϿον
	τιϿέσϿων	ἱστάσϿων	διδόσϿων	δεικνύσϿων

2nd Aorist Middle.

Sing. Ͽοῦ* [στάσο, στῶ] δοῦ* (none)
ϿέσϿω [στάσϿω] ϿόσϿω

Terminations the same as in the Present.

Infinitive.
Present.

τίϿεσϿαι ἵστασϿαι δίδοσϿαι δείκνυσϿαι

2nd Aorist Middle.

ϿέσϿαι [στάσϿαι] δόσϿαι (none)

Participle.
Present.

τιϿέμενος ἱστάμενος διδόμενος δεικνύμενος

2nd Aorist Middle.

Ͽέμενος [στάμενος] δόμενος (none)

62.

The remaining tenses are formed from the original roots: of τίϿημι, ἵστημι, δίδωμι, δείκνυμι (orig. roots, Ͽε, στα, δο, δεικ), they are these:

Future.

Act.	Ͽήσω	στήσω	δώσω	δείξω
Mid.	Ͽήσομαι	στήσομαι	δώσομαι	δείξομαι
Pass.	τεϿήσομαι	σταϿήσομαι	δοϿήσομαι	δειχϿήσομαι

Aorist.

Ac.	ἔϿηκα	ἔστησα	ἔδωκα	ἔδειξα
Mid.	[ἐϿηκάμην]	ἐστησάμην	[ἐδωκάμην]	ἐδειξάμην
Pass.	ἐτέϿην	ἐστάϿην	ἐδόϿην	ἐδείχϿην

* In the compounds the accent is thrown back: but not that of the 2nd sing., unless the prep. is a dissyllable: ἀπόδου. προσϿοῦ: ἀπό-ϿεσϿε, πρόσϿεσϿε.

10

Perfect.

Act.	τέθεικα	ἕστηκα	δέδωκα	δέδειχα
Pass.	τέθειμαι	(ἕσταμαι)	δέδομαι	δέδειγμαι

Pluperfect.

Act.	ἐτεθείκειν	εἱστήκειν ἑστήκειν	ἐδεδώκειν	ἐδεδείχειν
Pass.	ἐτεθείμην	(ἱστάμην)	ἐδεδόμην	ἐδεδείγμην

On the syncopated forms of the Perf. ἕστηκα, see Pdm. 65. For ἵημι, see Pdm. 67.

a) A fut. ἑστήξω (*stabo*) was formed fr. Perf.—ἑστήξομαι later. —The Aorists ἔθηκα, ἔδωκα are used only in the sing. Indic.; the forms of the 2nd Aor. in dual and pl.; in the other moods; and in the participle. Ἐθηκάμην, ἐδωκάμην are *un-Attic*.

b) The peculiarity of κα, as termination of Aor. 1, belongs to ἔθηκα, ἔδωκα, ἧκα (ἵημι).

c) The *Opt.* and *Subj.* of the *Pres. Pass.* from τίθημι, δίδωμι, and ἵημι, are usually conjugated as if from τίθω, δίδω, ἵω, the accent being thrown back: thus τίθωμαι, δίδωμαι, &c.; τιθοίμην, διδοίμην (δίδοιο, δίδοιτο, &c.). So in Aor. 2. Mid. ἀπόθωμαι, ἀπόδοιτο, &c.

d) This analogy, as far as regards the *accent*, is followed by δύναμαι (*am able*), and ἐπίσταμαι (*know how*).

Thus: ἐπίστωμαι -ῃ -ηται | δυναίμην -αιο -αιτο
(But ἱστῶμαι -ῇ -ῆται) | ἱσταίμην -αιο -αιτο
So also ὀναίμην ὄναιο ὄναιτο.

e) In the *Imperf. Active* the singular of τίθημι and ἵημι is often, that of δίδωμι regularly, formed as if from τιθέω, διδόω: ἐτίθουν is not found; but ἐτίθεις, ἐτίθει, are far commoner than ἐτίθης, ἐτίθη: ἐδίδουν, ἐδίδους, ἐδίδου. In Attic poetry the forms of the Present τιθεῖς, τιθεῖ, and (from ἵημι) ἱεῖς, ἱεῖ are also found.

63. *Verbs with 2nd Aorist like Verbs in μι.*

2nd Aorist.

ἀποδιδράσκω, I run away.	ῥέω, I flow.	γιγνώσκω, I know.	φύω, I put forth naturally (Aor. 2. intrans.).
Indicative.			
S. ἀπέδραν	ἐρρύην	ἔγνων	ἔφῡν
ἀπέδρας	ἐρρύης	ἔγνως	ἔφῡς
ἀπέδρα	ἐρρύη	ἔγνω	ἔφῡ
P. ἀπέδραμεν	ἐρρύημεν	ἔγνωμεν	ἔφῡμεν
ἀπέδρατε	ἐρρύητε	ἔγνωτε	ἔφῦτε
ἀπέδρασαν	ἐρρύησαν	ἔγνωσαν	ἔφῦσαν
D. ἀπέδρατον	ἐρρύητον	ἔγνωτον	ἔφῦτον
ἀπεδράτην	ἐρρυήτην	ἐγνώτην	ἐφύτην

Subjunctive.   2nd Aorist.

S. ἀποδρῶ   ῥυῶ   γνῶ   φύω (prob. ῠ)
   ἀποδρᾷς   ῥυῇς   γνῷς   φύῃς
   ἀποδρᾷ   ῥυῇ   γνῷ   φύῃ
P. ἀποδρῶμεν   ῥυῶμεν   γνῶμεν   φύωμεν
   ἀποδρᾶτε   ῥυῆτε   γνῶτε   φύητε
   ἀποδρῶσι(ν)   ῥυῶσι(ν)   γνῶσι(ν)   φύωσι
D. ἀποδρᾶτον   ῥυῆτον   γνῶτον   φύητον
   ἀποδρᾶτον   ῥυῆτον   γνῶτον   φύητον

Optative.

S. ἀποδραίην   ῥυείην   γνοίην   φύοιμι or φύην
   ἀποδραίης   ῥυείης   γνοίης   φύοις or φύης
   ἀποδραίη   ῥυείη   γνοίη   φύοι   or φύη
   &c.   &c.   &c.   &c.

Imperative.

S. ἀπόδραϑι   ῥυῆϑι   γνῶϑι   (φῦϑι)
   ἀποδράτω   ῥυήτω   γνώτω   (φύτω)
   &c.   &c.   &c.   &c.

Infinitive.

   ἀποδρᾶναι   ῥυῆναι   γνῶναι   φῦναι

Participle.

   ἀποδράς   ῥυείς, εῖσα, έν γνούς,   φυς, φῦσα, φῠν
   ᾶσα, άν   γνοῦσα, γνόν

64. The following are additional examples of this formation :—

	Aor. 2.	Imp.	Subj.	Opt.	Infin.	Partic.
ἀλίσκομαι (am taken)	ἥλων, (was taken) ἑάλων (Att.)	—	ἀλῶ (ῷς, ῷ)	ἀλοίην	ἀλῶναι	ἀλούς [ᾰex· cept in Ind.]
βαίνω, go	ἔβην (went)	βῆϑι	βῶ (ῇς, ῇ)	βαίην	βῆναι	βάς
βιόω, live	ἐβίων (lived)	—	βιῶ (ῷς, ῷ)	βιῴην	βιῶναι	βιούς (οῦσα, οῦν)
πέτομαι, fly	ἔπτην(flew)†	—	(πτῶ ?)	πταίην	πτῆναι	πτάς
σκέλλω, dry	ἔσκλην (wi- thered)	—	—	—	σκλῆναι	
δύω	ἔδυν (went into)	δῦϑι	δύω (ης, η)	[δύην Hom.]	δῦναι	δύς (ῦσα)
φϑάνω (come before, anticipate)	ἔφϑην	—	φϑῶ (ῇς, ῇ)	φϑαίην	φϑῆναι	φϑάς

---

* φύην for φυίην. Hippocrates has Aor. 2. ἐφύην (φυῆναι, &c.), like ἐρρύην. This is the usual form in later writers; and the Subj. φυῶ (Plat.) must be referred to this, not to ἔφυν. (Buttmann.)

† Late: ἐπτόμην the usual form.

65. *Syncopated Perfect.*

	Sing.	Plural.	Dual.
Indicative	ἕστηκα	ἕστᾰμεν	—
	ἕστηκας	ἕστᾰτε	ἕστᾰτον
	ἕστηκε(ν)	ἑστᾶσι(ν)	ἕστᾰτον
Subjunctive	ἑστῶ		
Optative	ἑσταίην, ἑσταίης, &c.		
Imperative	ἕστᾰϑι, ἑστᾰτω, &c.		
Infinitive	ἑστάναι		
Participle	ἑστώς, ῶσα, ώς or ός, Gen. ἑστῶτος, ώσης, ῶτος.		

Pluperfect.

Sing.	Plural.	Dual.
ἑστήκειν or εἰστήκειν	ἕστᾰμεν	—
ἑστήκεις or εἱστήκεις	ἕστᾰτε	ἕστᾰτον
ἑστήκει or εἱστήκει	ἕστᾰσαν	ἑστάτην

a) These syncopated forms are only found in the *Dual* and *Plural*. The regular forms of ἕστηκα are sometimes met with, though the shorter forms are the commoner in the best authors, especially for the *Plural.*—ἑστηκέναι rare in Attic (*Kr.*).

b) In the Pluperf. of ἵστημι, ἕστασαν is the form of this kind that principally occurs.

c) The Participle arises by contraction from αώς. The ω (as arising from αο) is retained through the oblique cases : but the neuter ἑστός has better authority than ἑστώς.

66. (*Other Syncopated Perfects.*)

δείδω (Hom.), *fear*, δέδια (rare in Sing.) Pl. δέδῐμεν, δέδῐτε, δεδίᾱσιν. Part. δεδιώς. Imperf. δέδῐϑι. Subj. δεδίω. Opt. δεδιείην. Impf. δεδιέναι. Pluperf. 3rd Plur. ἐδέδισαν or ἐδεδίεσαν.

ϑνήσκω, *die* τέϑνηκα (-ας, -ε), τέϑνᾰμεν, τέϑνᾱτε, τέϑνᾶσι. Imperat. τέϑνᾰϑι. Opt. τεϑναίην. Inf. τεϑνά-ναι. Part. τεϑνεώς (-εῶσα, -εώς).

The Perfects τέϑνηκα and δέδια are the only Perfects besides ἕστηκα whose syncopated forms are in common use in *prose*, the Partcp. βεβώς (from βαίνω) forming a partial exception. Of τέϑνηκα, it is only the Infin. and Partcp. that are common in *Attic prose :* the Participle is τεϑνεώς, with the (Ionic) intercalation of ε.

Δέδια occurs *throughout*: the longer form, δέδοικα, occurs only in the *Indicat.* of Perf. and Pluperf. (where it is commoner in the *Singular* than the abridged forms), in the Infin. in the Dramatic writers, and in the Participle.

67. ῞Ιημι,—εἰμί and εἶμι,—φημί.

It is very important that the pupil should acquire a thorough familiarity with the forms of ἵημι, εἰμί and εἶμι, which, from the resemblance of some to others, are often hard to distinguish: indeed some forms (especially in the compounds) are *identical*, and can only be distinguished by the sense. ῞Ιημι occurs principally in its compounds, ἀφίημι, μεθίημι, &c. The ι is usually *long* in Attic Greek [as *short*, it occurs principally in the *participle*].

(ἵημι. Root, ἑ.)

Active.

	Ind.	Imper.	Subj.	Opt.	Inf.	Partcp.
Pres.	ἵημι	ἵει	ἱῶ	ἱείην	ἱέναι	ἱείς, ἱεῖσα, ἱέν
		ἱέτω, &c.				
Impf.	ἵην					
Perf.	εἷκα					
Plup.	εἵκειν					
Aor. 1.	ἧκα					
Aor. 2.	[ἧν] }	ἕς, ἕτω,	ὧ	εἵην	εἷναι	εἷς, εἷσα, ἕν
Pl.	εἷμεν	&c.				
	εἷτε					
	εἷσαν					
Fut.	ἥσω					

Passive.

Pres.	ἵεμαι (as τίθεμαι). [On *Subj.* and *Opt.* see p. 218, c.]					
Impf.	ἱέμην					
Perf.	εἷμαι	εἷσο			εἷσθαι	εἱμένος
Plup.	εἵμην					
Aor.	εἵθην	ἕθητι	ἑθῶ	ἑθείην	ἑθῆναι	ἑθείς
Fut. 1.	ἑθήσομαι					
Fut. 3.	(none)					

Middle.

Aor. 1.	(ἡκάμην)					
Aor. 2.	εἵμην	οὗ	ὧμαι	εἵμην	ἕσθαι	ἕμενος
Fut.	ἥσομαι					

Verbal Adjective, ἑτός, ἑτέος.

As a general rule, ἵημι is conjugated like τίθημι.

a) The 3rd *Plur.* of the *Present Indic. Act.* is ἱᾶσι(ν) only, for ἱέᾱσι(ν).

b) The *Imperf.* ἵην is doubtful in the singular: ἵουν, ἵεις, ἵει are undoubted, and it seems that ἵειν also was used as 1st sing.*

c) From ἀφίημι the *Imperf.* appears with a double augment: ἠφίει· ἠφίεσαν. But ἀφίει, and especially ἀφίεσαν, have more and better authority.

d) The *Aor.* 1. ἧκα, which is not found except in the *Indicative*, was in general use in the *singular*. In the *plural* it is *rarely* used by any Attic writers. Of ἧν the *singular of the Indicative* is no where found.

e) What is here said of ἧκα, ἧν, applies also to ἔδωκα, ἔθηκα: ἔδων, ἔθην. In *Aor.* 1. *Mid.* ἡκάμην is *sometimes*, but ἐδωκάμην, ἐθηκάμην, never found in Attic writers.

f) The *Dual* and *Plur.* of 2nd *Aor. Act.*; the *Indic.* of *Aor.* 2. *Mid.* and *Aor.* 1. *Pass.* are found in the common language (also in Herodotus); but always *with* the augment. Hence ἀφίοιτε, ἀφίοιεν, ἔμεν, ἔτε, ἔσαν, ἔθην, ἔμην, never occur.

g) Whether εἷμεν, εἷτε, εἵμην are *Indic.* or *Opt.* can only be determined by the *context*.

h) In the compounds of ἵημι the accent of the *Imperative* ἕς is thrown back: ἄφες. But οὗ retains it, even in compounds, in *this form*, not in the others: προοῦ; but πρόεσθε.

i) Of forms conjugated like barytone verbs (besides the Subj. and Opt. of Pres. Pass. and Aor. 2. Mid.; cf. p. 218, *c*), ἀφίοιτε, ἀφίοιεν, are found as *Pres. Opt.*; and ἵω is sometimes accented as a *barytone* Subj. (for ἰῶ).

68. (Εἰμί, εἶμι.)

☞ Εἰμί (am) has root ἐς· εἶμι (ibo) root ἰ.

(1) εἰμί, *I am*; εἶμι, *I shall go* (Pres. mostly with *Fut.* meaning).

	Imperat.			Subj.	Opt.	Infin.	Partcp.
Moods	εἰμί,	ἴσθι,	(ἔστω, &c.)	ὦ	εἴην	εἶναι	ὤν ʼ(am)
	εἶμι,	ἴθι,	(ἴτω, &c.)	ἴω	ἴοιμι	ἰέναι	ἰών (go)

* This and the following remarks are from *Krüger.*

	INDICATIVE. Present.		SUBJ. of *to be.*	SUBJ. of *to go.*

S.	εἰμί, *I am*
	εἶ
	ἐστί(ν)
		εἶμι, *I will go*
		εἶ
		εἶσι(ν)
			S. ὦ
			  ᾖς
			  ᾖ
				ἴω
				ἴῃς
				ἴῃ

P.	ἐσμέν
	ἐστέ
	εἰσί(ν)
		ἴμεν
		ἴτε
		ἴᾶσι(ν)
			P. ὦμεν
			  ἦτε
			  ὦσι(ν)
				ἴωμεν
				ἴητε
				ἴωσι(ν)

D.	ἐστόν ἐστόν	ἴτον ἴτον	D. ἦτον ἦτον	[ἴητον ?] [ἴητον ?]

IM S.	ἴσθι
	
	  ἔστω
	P. ἔστε
	  ἔστωσαν
	  and ἔστων
	  (ὄντων
	  Plat.)
	D. ἔστον
	  ἔστων
		ἴθι (πρόσιθι :
		 seld. πρόσει)
		ἴτω (προσίτω)
		ἴτε
		ἴτωσαν or
		ἰόντων (ἴτων
		Æsch. E. 32.)
		ἴτον
		ἴτων
			Opt. S. εἴην
			  εἴης
			  εἴη
			P. εἴημεν. εἶμεν
			 εἴητε [εἶτε]
			 εἴησαν, εἶεν
			D. [εἴητον, εἶτον]
			 εἰήτην, εἴτην
			INF. εἶναι
			PART. ὤν, οὖσα, ὄν
			 G. ὄντος, οὔσης
				ἴοιμι or ἰοίην
				ἴοις
				ἴοι
				ἴοιμεν
				ἴοιτε
				ἴοιεν
				[ἴοιτον ?]
				[ἰοίτην ?]
				
				ἰέναι
				ἰών, ἰοῦσα, ἰόν
				ἰόντος, ἰούσης

IMPERFECT.

S.	ἦν, *I was* ἦσθα ἦν (from ἦε-ν)	ᾔειν; old Attic, ᾖα, *I went.* ᾔεις, usu. ᾔεισθα ᾔει	
P.	ἦμεν ἦτε (ἦστε) ἦσαν	ᾔειμεν, us. ᾖμεν ᾔειτε — ᾖτε ᾔεσαν	
D.	ἦστον [ἦτον] ἦστην [ἤτην]	ᾔειτον, — ᾖτον ᾐείτην, — ᾔτην	

_ *Ful.* ἔσομαι, *I shall be,* ἔσῃ or ἔσει, ἔσται (for the poet. ἔσεται),
&c. Opt. ἐσοίμην. Inf. ἔσεσθαι. Partc. ἐσόμενος.

The *Middle* form (ἴεμαι, ἴεσαι or ἴῃ, ἴεται, &c., Imp. ἴεσο, Inf.
ἴεσθαι, Partcp. ἰέμενος, Impf. ἰέμην, ἴεσο, &c.), signifying *to
hasten,* ought probably to be written with the rough breathing
(a supposition which is mostly confirmed by the manuscripts),
and referred to ἵημι. Verbal adj. ἰτός is found in compounds :
ἰτέος is more common than ἰτητέος (*Kr.*).

a) Εἰμί, *to be* (with the exception of εἶ), is *enclitic* in Pres. Indic.
[See Rules for *Enclitics*]. In compounds, the accent is on

the preposition, if the general rules of accentuation will allow it to be so far back, e. g. πάρειμι, πάρει, πάρεστι, &c., Imp. πάρισθι; but παρῆν on account of the augment; παρέσται (= παρέσεται); παρ-εῖναι from the general rule for infinitives in ναι; subj. παρῶ, -ῇς, ῇ, &c., on account of the contraction; and Opt. παρεῖμεν, &c. = παρείημεν, &c. The accentuation of the Partcp. in the compounds should be particularly noted; e. g. παρών, Gen. παρόντος, so also παριών, Gen. παριόντος.

b) With reference to *accentuation*, the compounds of εἶμι, *ibo*, follow the same rules as those of εἰμί, *sum* (Göttling says, Inf. ἰέναι); hence several forms of these two verbs are the same in compounds, e. g. πάρειμι, πάρει and πάρεισι (third sing. of εἶμι, and 3rd plur. of εἰμί).

c) Εἶεν, esto, *be it so, good*, 3rd *plur.* Opt. (=εἴησαν).—The first person Impf. is often ἦ in Attic poets, sometimes in Plato; ἤμην (which occurs in no other person) is very rare in Attic Greek. (Xen.) The *un-Attic* form of the second person Impf. ἦς is found frequently in the later writers, and now and then in lyric passages of the Attic poets. The dual forms with σ (ἤστον, ἤστην) are preferred; but in the 2*nd* pl., ἦτε seems to have been exclusively in use (*Kr.*). Ἔστων is less common than ἔστωσαν.

d) From εἶμι, the third pers. sing. Impf. ἤειν instead of ἤει is found in *the Attic poets* only before vowels, προσῄειν. [Before a consonant, Pl. Crit. 114.]

e) The Pres. of εἶμι, *to go*, has, in Attic prose, almost always a Future meaning. Ἰέναι and ἰών occur both as *Present* and as *Future*. So also the Optative. (*Kr.*)

69. Φημί, *to say*. [οὐ φημι = *nego; say ... not*].

(*Moods:* φημί, φάθι or φαθί, φῶ, φαίην, φάναι, φάς.)

Present.	Singular.	Plural.	Dual.
	φημί	φαμέν	
	φῄς (φής?)	φατέ	φατόν
	φησί(ν)	φασί(ν)	φατόν
Imperfect.	ἔφην	ἔφαμεν	
	(ἔφης) ἔφησθα	ἔφατε	ἔφατον
	ἔφη	ἔφασαν	ἐφάτην

Fut. φήσω. Aor. ἔφησα. Verbal Adjective, φατός, φατέος.

a) The second sing. φῄς is quite anomalous both in *accent* and in the ι subscript. (Göttling and Krüger print φής.) The compounds retain, in *this* form, the accent on the ultima, e. g. ἀντιφῄς, but σύμφημι, σύμφασι, &c.

b) This verb has two significations, (a) *to say* in general, (b) *to affirm, to assert*, &c. (aio). The Fut. φήσω, however, has only the last signification.—Φῶ, φαίην *often* and φάναι *usually* relate to the *past*. The Participle φάς does not belong to *Attic prose*.

c) With φημί the verb ἠμί, *inquam*, may be compared. The Imperfect ἦν, ἦ is used in the phrases ἦν δ᾽ ἐγώ, said I, ἦ δ᾽ ὅς, *said he* (inserted parenthetically), in relating a conversation.

The pres. φημί (with the exception of φῄς) is *enclitic*. [See Rules for Enclitics.]

70. Οἶδα.

Οἶδα (*novi*) is properly a Perf. 2. from root εἰδ- [*vid-ēre*]; but it passes over to the forms of a verb in μι: having second sing. -θα (as ἔφησθα, ἦσθα have from φημί, εἰμί).

Moods:

οἶδα | ἴσθι (ἴστω) | εἰδῶ | εἰδείην | εἰδέναι | εἰδώς, υἶα, ός.

Present.

Sing.		Plur.	Dual.
	οἶδα	ἴσμεν	
	οἶσθα	ἴστε	ἴστον
	οἶδε(ν)	ἴσᾶσι(ν)	ἴστον

Imperfect.

Sing.		Pl.	Dual.
ᾔδειν, Att. ᾔδη		ᾔδειμεν	
ᾔδεισθα, } Att. { ᾔδησθα		ᾔδειτε	ᾔδειτον
ᾔδεις, } { ᾔδης			
ᾔδει, Att. ᾔδειν, ᾔδη		ᾔδεσαν [ᾔδεισαν]	ᾔδείτην

Fut. εἴσομαι. Verbal Adjective, ἰστέον.

a) Though the *sing.* forms ᾔδη, &c. are usually called *Attic*, the forms ᾔδειν, &c. occur even in the best Attic writers.— In the *Dual* and *Plur.* of *Imperf.*, ᾖστην, ᾖσμεν, -τε, -σαν are also found in the poets.

b) *Fut.* εἴσομαι, and the *Subj.* [*Opt.*] and *Infin.* of the *Present* have also the meaning of *to understand*.

10*

71. Κεῖμαι (jaceo), ἧμαι (sedeo).

Κεῖμαι, according to Krüger, is from κείομαι = κέομαι: according to Buttmann, a *Perfect* for κέκειμαι.

a) The Infin. is accented like a *Perf. Infin.*, and retains this accent in compounds: κεῖσθαι, κατακεῖσθαι.

b) But κατάκειμαι, κατάκεισαι throw back the accent.

᾽Ημαι (in Attic prose κάθημαι is the usual form) is in form a *Passive Perfect.*

Present.

Ind.	Subj.	Opt.	Imperfect.
κεῖμαι	[κέωμαι]	[κεοίμην]	ἐκείμην
κεῖσαι	[κέῃ]	[κέοιο]	ἔκεισο
κεῖται	κέηται	κέοιτο	ἔκειτο
κείμεθα			ἐκείμεθα
κεῖσθε			ἔκεισθε
κεῖνται	κέωνται	κέοιντο	ἔκειντο
[κείμεθον]			[ἐκείμεθον]
κεῖσθον			ἔκεισθον
κεῖσθον			ἐκείσθην

Imper. κεῖσο, κεῖσθω, &c. Infin. κεῖσθαι. Partcp. κείμενος. Fut. κείσομαι. No Aorist.

a) Present, ἧμαι, ἧσαι, ἧσται, &c. 3 plur. ἧνται.

　　Imper. ἧσο, ἧσθω, &c. Infin. ἧσθαι. Partcp. ἥμενος.

　　Imperf. ἥμην, ἧσο, ἧστο, &c. 3 plur. ἧντο.

b) Present, κάθημαι, κάθησαι, κάθηται, &c.

　　Subj. καθῶμαι. 3. καθῆται. Plur. 1. καθώμεθα. 3. καθ-ῶνται.

　　Opt. καθοίμην [καθήμην ?] 3. καθοῖτο [καθῆτο ?].

　　Imper. κάθησο [κάθου]. Inf. καθῆσθαι. Partcp. καθήμενος.

　　Imperf. ἐκαθήμην (καθήμην.) 3. ἐκάθητο, καθῆστο (καθῆτο).

　　　　　　3 plur. ἐκάθηντο, καθῆντο.

The Imperf. of κάθημαι often prefixes the Syll. Augment to the preposition (but not in the Tragic poets) in ἐκαθήμην: but also καθῆσο, καθῆτο are found (more commonly καθῆστο, καθῆντο) where the Augment is *compensated for* by the accentuation. So also καθῆσθε, whereas κάθησθε is the *Present.* In the Subj. καθῶμαι is more regular than κάθωμαι: so also καθοῖτο, Opt., for which, *perhaps,* καθήμην, καθῆτο (but only in these forms) were used (*Kr.*).

72. Anomalous Verbs.

It is an anomaly of *meaning* when the *Future Middle* (in form) has a Passive sense.

FUTURE MIDDLE with PASSIVE sense.

ἀδικήσομαι, *shall be injured*
ἄξομαι, *shall be led*
θρέψομαι, *shall be nourished* (also *Mid.*).
οἰκήσομαι, *shall be inhabited*
τιμήσομαι, *shall be honoured*

} In these the *Pass.* meaning is pretty steady.

ζημιώσομαι, *shall be punished*
στερήσομαι, *shall be deprived*
φοβήσομαι, *shall be feared*
ὠφελήσομαι, *shall be benefited*

} In these, usage fluctuates between these forms and those in -θήσομαι; those in -θήσομαι denoting rather a *continued* action. (*Herm.*)

So, ἄρξομαι (*shall be ruled*, and [*Mid.*] *shall begin*), εἴρξομαι (*shall be restrained*), βλάψομαι (*shall be hurt*), ταράξομαι (*shall be disturbed*), τρίψομαι (*shall be rubbed*), φυλάξομαι (*shall be guarded*), are all found in good Attic writers.

73. *Futura Media* of *regular* verbs, which in classical writers are the quite or nearly exclusive forms.

ἀκούσομαι (-ούω), *shall hear.*
ἀλαλάξομαι (-άζω), *shall shout.*
ἀπαντήσομαι (-άω), *shall meet.*
ἀπολαύσομαι (-αύω), *shall derive* (from any thing).
βαδιοῦμαι (-ίζω), *shall walk.*
βοήσομαι (-άω), *shall shout.*
γελάσομαι (-άω), *shall laugh.*
κωκύσομαι (-ύω), *shall wail.*
οἰμώξομαι (-ώζω), *shall wail, lament.*

ὀλολύξομαι (-ύζω), *shall cry aloud* (to the gods).
πηδήσομαι (-άω), *shall leap.*
σιγήσομαι (-άω), *shall be silent.*
σιωπήσομαι (-άω), *shall hold my tongue.*
σπουδάσομαι (-άζω), *shall make haste, be busy.*
συρίξομαι (-ίζω), *shall pipe.*
τωθάσομαι (-άζω), *shall jeer.*

Futura Media of regular verbs whose *Future Active* is a less common form :

ᾄσομαι, ᾄσω (-δω), *will sing.*
ἁρπάσομαι, -άσω (-άζω), *shall snatch.*
βλέψομαι, -ψω (-πω), *shall look.*
γηράσομαι, -άσω (α[σκ]ω), *shall grow old.*
διώξομαι, ξω (-κω), *shall pursue.*
ἐγκωμιάσομαι, -άσω (-άζω), *shall panegyrize.*
ἐπαινέσομαι, -έσω (-έω), *shall praise.*

ἐπιορκήσομαι, -ήσω (-έω), *shall forswear myself.*
θαυμάσομαι, -άσω (-άζω), *shall wonder.*
κλέψομαι, -ψω (-πτω), *shall steal.*
ῥοφήσομαι, -ήσω (-έω), *shall sup up.*
σκώψομαι, -ψω (-πτω), *shall mock.*
χωρήσομαι, -ήσω (-έω), *shall retire.*

Θηράσομαι and 3ηρεύσομαι, *will chase*, and κολάσομαι, *will chas-tise*, do not belong here; for the *Middle Form* of *other tenses* is found as *Active* (implying that the action is done *for the agent's own satisfaction*), and the Futures in -σω are also in use. So ἑψήσομαι (Plat.) = mihi *coquam*. The *Regular* Fut. is ἑψήσω.

74. *Deponents Passive* (i. e. that have a *Passive Aorist*.)

ἠδυνήϑην or ἐδυνήϑην; ἐδυνάσϑην, was able (δύναμαι).

ἠράσϑην, loved (ἔραμαι).

ηχϑέσϑην, was vexed at (ἄχϑομαι).

ἐβουλήϑην, ἠβουλήϑην, wished; chose (βούλομαι).

ἐδεήϑην, begged (δέομαι).

ἥσϑην, was delighted; was pleased (ἥδομαι).

ᾠήϑην, thought (οἴομαι).

ἐσέφϑην,* reverenced (σέβομαι).

ἐφαντάσϑην, likened myself (φαν-τάζομαι).

διελέχϑην, conversed with (διαλέ-γομαι).

ἐπεμελήϑην, cared for (-[ἐ]ομαι).

ἐνεϑυμήϑην, considered

προεϑυμήϑην, was eager

ἐνενοήϑην, considered, intended

διενοήϑην, thought over; intended

ἀπενοήϑην, was beside myself; was desperate

} (-εομαι).

ἠναντιώϑην, opposed (-οομαι).

εὐλαβήϑην, shunned scrupulously (-εομαι).

ἐφιλοτιμήϑην, was ambitious (-εο-μαι).

I. Verbs in ω, with collateral forms in εω or εομαι.

Present.	Future.	Perfect.	Aorist.
ἀλέξω, ward off	[ἀλεξήσω]		[ἤλεξα]
Middle	ἀλεξήσομαι		ἠλεξάμην
βόσκω, feed	βοσκήσω		
(ἐ)ϑέλω, will	(ἐ)ϑελήσω	ἠϑέληκα	ἠϑέλησα
ἔρρω, take oneself off	ἐρρήσω	ἤρρηκα	ἤρρησα
εὕδω, sleep	εὑδήσω	(none)	(none)
ἕψω, boil	ἑψήσω (Pdm. 73)	?	ἥψησα
Passive		ἥψημαι	ἡψήϑην
Middle	ἑψήσομαι		ἡψησάμην
μέλει, curæ est	μελήσει	μεμέληκεν	ἐμέλησεν
μέλλω, am going	μελλήσω	?	ἐμέλλησα
μένω, remain	μενῶ	μεμένηκα	ἔμεινα
νέμω, distribute	νεμῶ	νενέμηκα	ἔνειμα
Passive		νενέμηναι	ἐνεμήϑην
ὄζω, smell of	ὀζήσω	[ὄδωδα]	ὤζησα
ὀφείλω, owe (ought)	ὀφειλήσω	ὠφείληκα	ὠφείλησα
τύπτω, beat	τυπτήσω	?	(ἔτυπον)
Passive	τυπτήσομαι	τέτυμμαι	ἐτύπην
χαίρω, rejoice	χαιρήσω	κεχάρηκα (ημαι)	ἐχάρην
ἄχϑομαι, am vexed (at)	ἀχϑέσ(ϑήσ)ομαι	?	ἠχϑέσϑην

* Plat. Phædr. 254.

Present.	Future.	Perfect.	Aorist.
βούλομαι, *will; choose*	βουλήσομαι	βεβούλημαι	ἐβουλήθην
[ἔρομαι], *ask*	ἐρήσομαι	(none)	ἠρόμην
μάχομαι, *fight*	μαχοῦμαι	μεμάχημαι	ἐμαχεσάμην
μέλομαι, *care for*	μελήσομαι	μεμέλημαι	ἐμελήθην
οἴομαι, *think*	οἰήσομαι	(none)	ᾠήθην
οἴχομαι, *am gone*	οἰχήσομαι	[ᾤχημαι]	(none)

II. Verbs in εω, with a collateral form in ω.

Present.	Future.	Perfect.	Aorist.
γαμέω, *marry*	γαμῶ	γεγάμηκα	ἔγημα
Middle	γαμοῦμαι	γεγάμημαι	ἐγημάμην
δοκέω, *seem*	δόξω	δέδογμαι	ἔδοξα
ὁιπτέω, ῥίπτω, *throw.*	ῥίψω	ἔρριφα	ἔρριψα
Passive		ἔρριμμαι	ἐρρίφ(θ)ην
ὠθέω, *thrust*	ὤσω (ὠθήσω)	(ἔωκα)	ἔωσα
Passive	ὠσθήσομαι	ἔωσμαι	ἐώσθην
Middle	ὤσομαι		ἐωσάμην

III. Verbs in ἄν-ω, ἄν-ομαι; i. e. whose roots are formed by αν appended to the simpler root. (With some in νω, ίνω, αύνω, αίνο μαι, νέομαι.)

Present.	Future.	Perfect.	Aorist.
ἁμαρτάνω, *miss; sin*	ἁμαρτήσομαι	ἡμάρτηκα	ἥμαρτον
Passive		ἡμάρτημαι	ἁμαρτηθῆναι
αὔξ(άν)ω, *increase*	αὐξήσω	ηὔξηκα	ηὔξησα
Passive.	αὐξη(θή)σομαι	ηὔξημαι	ηὐξήθην
βλαστάνω, *bud*	βλαστήσω	(β)εβλάστηκα	ἔβλαστον
δαρθάνω, *sleep*	δαρθήσομαι (?)	δεδάρθηκα	ἔδαρθον
ὀλισθάνω, *slip*	ὀλισθήσω (?)	(ὠλίσθηκα)	ὤλισθον
αἰσθάνομαι, *perceive*	αἰσθήσομαι	ᾔσθημαι	ᾐσθόμην
ἀπεχθάνομαι, *become hat-*	ἀπεχθήσομαι	ἀπήχθημαι	ἀπηχθόμην
τίνω, *pay*　　　[*ed*	τίσω	τέτικα	ἔτισα, τῖσαι
Passive		τέτισμαι	ἐτίσθην
Middle			ἐτισάμην
φθάνω, *come before*	φθήσομαι	ἔφθακα	ἔφθασα, ἔφ-
δάκνω, *bite*	δήξομαι	?	ἔδακον [θην
Passive	δηχθήσομαι	δέδηγμαι	ἐδήχθην
κάμνω, *become weary*	καμοῦμαι	κέκμηκα	ἔκαμον
τέμνω, *cut*	τεμῶ	τέτμηκα	ἔτεμον
Passive	τετμήσομαι	τέτμημαι	ἐτμήθην
βαίνω, *go*	βήσομαι	βέβηκα	ἔβην
ἐλαύνω, *drive*	ἐλῶ	ἐλήλακα	ἤλασα
Passive		ἐλήλαμαι	ἠλάθην
Middle			ἠλασάμην
ὀσφραίνομαι, *smell*	ὀσφρήσομαι	[ὤσφρημαι]	ὠσφρόμην
ἱκνέομαι, *come*	ἵξομαι	ἷγμαι	ἱκόμην

IV. Verbs in άνω, άνομαι, whose *short root* was strengthened by *ν*₁ before *αν* was_appended : ληϑ-, λαϑ- ; λανϑ-, λανϑ-άν-ω.

Present.	Future.	Perfect.	Aorist.
λανϑάνω, *am hid*	λήσω	λέληϑα	ἔλαϑον
Middle	λήσομαι	λέλησμαι	ἐλαϑόμην
μανϑάνω, *learn*	μαϑήσομαι	μεμάϑηκα	ἔμαϑον
λαμβάνω, *take*	λήψομαι	εἴληφα	ἔλαβον
Passive	ληφϑήσομαι	εἴλημμαι	ἐλήφϑην
Middle			ἐλαβόμην
ϑιγγάνω, *touch*	ϑίξομαι (-ω ?)	?	ἔϑιγον
λαγχάνω, *receive by lot*	λήξομαι	εἴληχα	ἔλαχον
Passive		εἴληγμαι	ἐλήχϑην
τυγχάνω, *hit a mark*	τεύξομαι	τετύχηκα	ἔτυχον
πυνϑάνομαι, *inquire*	πεύσομαι	πέπυσμαι	ἐπυϑόμην

V. Verbs in σκω appended to the simpler root.

Present.	Future.	Perfect.	Aorist.
γηρά(σκ)ω, *grow old*	γηράσομαι(σω)	γεγήρᾱκα	ἐγήρᾱσα
ἡβά(σκ)ω, *pubescere*	ἡβήσω	ἤβηκα	ἤβησα
ἀρέσκω, *please*	ἀρέσω	(ἀρήρεκα)	ἤρεσα
εὑρίσκω, *find*	εὑρήσω	εὕρηκα	εὗρον
Passive	εὑρεϑήσομαι	εὕρημαι	εὑρέϑην
ἀνᾱλίσκω, *spend*	ἀναλώσω	ἀνάλωκα	ἀνάλωσα
		ἀνήλωκα	ἀνήλωσα
Passive	ἀναλωϑήσομαι	ἀνάλωμαι	ἀναλώϑην
		ἀνήλωμαι	ἀνηλώϑην
ἀμβλίσκω, *miscarry*	(ἀμβλώσω)	ἤμβλωκα	ἤμβλωσα
ϑνήσκω, *die*	ϑανοῦμαι	τέϑνηκα	ἔϑανον
ἱλάσκομαι, *propitiate*	ἱλάσομαι		ἱλασάμην
Passive		(ἵλασμαι)	ἱλάσϑην
ἁλίσκομαι, *am taken*	ἁλώσομαι	ἑάλωκα	ἑάλων
		ἥλωκα	ἥλων

VI. Verbs in σκω appended to a *simpler* root reduplicated :
βρω-, βιβρωσκ-.

Present.	Future.	Perfect.	Aorist.
βιβρώσκω, *eat*	[βρώσομαι]	βέβρωκα	[ἔβρωσα]
Passive	(βρωϑήσομαι)	βέβρωμαι	ἐβρώϑην
γιγνώσκω, *know*	γνώσομαι	ἔγνωκα	ἔγνων
Passive	γνωσϑήσομαι	ἔγνωσμαι	ἐγνώσϑην
τιτρώσκω, *wound*	τρώσω	?	ἔτρωσα
Passive	τρωϑήσομαι	τέτρωμαι	ἐτρώϑην
μιμνήσκω, *put in mind*	μνήσω		ἔμνησα
Passive (=remember)	μνησϑήσομαι	μέμνημαι	ἐμνήσϑην
	μεμνήσομαι		

Present.		Future.	Perfect.	Aorist.
διδράσκω, *run away*		δράσομαι	δέδρᾱκα	ἔδρᾱν
πιπράσκω, *buy*			πέπρᾱκα	
Passive		πεπράσομαι	πέπρᾱμαι	ἐπρά3ην

VII. Verbs that supply their tenses from other roots.

Present.	Borrowed Root.	Future.	Perfect.	Aorist.
αἱρέω, *take*,	ἑλ-	αἱρήσω	ᾕρηκα	εἷλον
		αἱρε3ήσομαι	ᾕρημαι	ᾑρέ3ην
εἰπεῖν, *say*,	ἐρ-	ἐρῶ	εἴρηκα	εἶπον, (-α)
Passive		ῥη3ήσομαι	εἴρημαι	ἐρρή3ην
		εἰρήσομαι		
ἔρχομαι, *go*,	ἐλευ3-	ἐλεύσομαι	ἐλήλῡ3α	ἦλ3ον
ἐσ3ίω, *eat*,	ἐδ-, φαγ-	ἔδομαι	ἐδήδοκα	ἔφαγον
Passive			ἐδήδεσμαι	(ἠδέσ3ην)
ἔχω, *have*,	σχ, σχε	ἕξω, σχήσω	ἔσχηκα	ἔσχον
Passive		[μαι	ἔσχημαι	[ἐσχέ3ην]
Middle		ἕξομαι, σχήσο-		ἐσχόμην
ὁράω, *see*,	ὀπ-, ἰδ-,	ὄψομαι	ἑώρᾱκα	εἶδον
Passive		ὀφ3ήσομαι	ἑώρᾱμαι, ὦμμαι	ὤφ3ην
Middle				εἰδόμην
πάσχω, *suffer*,	πη3-, πεν3-	πείσομαι	πέπον3α	ἔπα3ον
πίνω, *drink*,	πε-, πο-	πίομαι	πέπωκα	ἔπιον
Passive		πο3ήσομαι	πέπομαι	ἐπό3ην
πίπτω, *fall*,	πετ-, πετο-	πεσοῦμαι	πέπτωκα	ἔπεσον
τρέχω, *run*,	δραμ-	δραμοῦμαι	δεδράμηκα	ἔδραμον
Passive			δεδραμῆσ3αι	
φέρω, *bear*,	ἐνεκ-, οἰ-	οἴσω	ἐνήνοχα	ἤνεγκον
Passive		{ ἐνεγ3ήσομαι	ἐνήνεγμαι	ἠνέχ3ην
		{ οἰσ3ήσομαι		
Middle		οἴσομαι		ἠνεγκάμην

VIII. Verbs in μι whose original root ends in α (like ἵστημι).

Present.	Future.	Perfect.	Aorist.	Root.
κίχρημι (1), *lend*	χρήσω	κέχρηκα	ἔχρησα	χρα-
Mid. *borrow*	χρήσομαι		*ἐχρησάμην	
ὀνίνημι (2), *benefit*	ὀνήσω		ὤνησα	ὀνα-
ὀνίναμαι, Mid. *to*	ὀνήσομαι		{ ὀνήμην,	
derive advantage.			(ησο, &c.)	
			{ ὠνάμην,	
			later	
			ὠνή3ην	
ass.				
πίμπλημι (3), *fill*	πλήσω	πέπληκα	ἔπλησα	πλα-
Mid. {			ἐπλησάμην	(π.λη3-
			ἐπλήμην	*for*
Pass. { πίμ-			(poet.)	*other*
πλᾰμαι	πλησ3ήσο-	πέπλησ-	ἐπλήσ3ην	*tenses*)
	μαι	μαι		

Present.	Future.	Perf.	Aorist.	Root.
πίμπρημι (4), *burn*	πρήσω	πέπρηκα	ἔπρησα	πρα-
Mid. ⎰ πίμ- Pass. ⎱ πραμαι	πρησθήσο- μαι πεπρήσομαι	πέπρησ- μαι	ἐπρήσθην	(πρηθ- for other tenses)
[τλῆμι] (5) *endure*	τλήσομαι	τέτληκα	ἔτλην	τλα-

On φημί, see Pdm. 69.

Other forms :

(1) Inf. κιχράναι.　　* ἐχρησάμην = '*I borrowed*,' *un-Attic.*

(2) Inf. Pr. ὀνινάναι.—Aor. Imper. ὄνησο. Opt. ὀναίμην. part ὀνήμενος (*Hom.*)　[The rest supplied by ὠφελεῖν.]

(3) The μ in the reduplication of this and the following verb is usually omitted in composition, when a μ precedes the reduplication ; e. g. ἐμπίπλαμαι, but ἐνεπιμπλάμην.

Inf. Pr. πιμπλάναι.　Impf. ἐπίμπλην.　Inf. Pr. Mid. πίμπλασθαι. Impf. ἐπιμπλάμην.

(4) Exactly like πίμπλημι.　Xen. has πιμπράω.

(5) ἔτλην, τλῆθι, τλῶ, τλαίην, τλῆναι, τλάς.　The word is rare in Attic prose.

(Deponents.)

Present.	Future.	Perf.	Aorist.
ἄγαμαι, *wonder*	ἀγάσομαι (*Ep.*).		ἠγάσθην ἠγασάμην (*Ep.* once *Dem.*).
δύναμαι (1), *can*	δυνήσομαι	δεδύνημαι	ἐδυνήθην ἠδυνήθην ἐδυνάσθην (*Ion.* and *Xen.*).
ἐπίσταμαι (2),* *understand*	ἐπιστήσομαι		ἠπιστήθην
ἔραμαι, *love*	ἐρασθήσομαι		ἠράσθην

(ἐράω is the prose form).

κρέμαμαι (see κρεμάννυμι, Table X).

Other forms :

(1) Moods of Pres. δύν-ασο, -ωμαι, -αίμην, -ασθαι, -άμενος. [δύν ωμαι, *accentu retracto*.]　Imperf. ἐδυνάμην or ἠδυνάμην.

* Properly *to stand upon* (i. e. as having *mastered* it).

(2) Moods of Pres. ἐπίστ-ω (less commonly -ασο), -ωμαι, -αίμην, -ασθαι, -άμενος. Impf. ἠπιστάμην, 2 sing. ἠπίστω (less commonly -ασο). ☞ ἐπίστωμαι, accentu retracto.

To these must be added :

(1) χρή, oportet, ἔχρην, or χρῆν, oportebat, χρήσει, oportebit (R. χρα- or χρε-).

	Imper.	Subj.	Opt.	Infin.	Partcp.
	χρή	(none)	χρῇ	χρείη	χρῆναι	τὸ χρεών

(2) ἀπόχρη, sufficit, Inf. ἀποχρῆν [or -χρῆν], Part. ἀποχρῶν. Imperf. ἀπέχρη, Fut. ἀποχρήσει, Aor. ἀπέχρησε(ν). It also takes some personal forms (as from ἀποχράω), ἀποχρῶσιν, ἀποχρήσουσι(ν). In Mid. ἀποχρῆσθαι (= to have enough) is conjugated like χράομαι.

(3) ἐπριάμην, to buy (used by the Attics as Aorist to ὠνέομαι).

Imper.	Subj.	Opt.	Infin.	Partcp.
ἐπριάμην	πρίω	πρίωμαι	πριαίμην	πρίασθαι	πριάμενος

IX. Verbs in νυμι appended to an *impure* original root.

Present.	- Future.	Perfect.	Aorist.
ἄγνυμι, break	ἄξω	ἔᾱγα	ἔαξα
Passive		[ἔαγμαι]	(ἐάγην)
δείκνυμι, show (Pdm. 60)			
ζεύγνυμι, bind	ζεύξω	?	ἔζευξα
Passive		ἔζευγμαι	ἐζύγην (ἐζεύχθην)
Middle	ζεύξομαι		ἐζευξάμην
μίγνυμι, mix	μίξω	(μέμιχα)	ἔμιξα
Passive	μιχθήσομαι	μέμιγμαι	ἐμίχθην, ἐμίγην
οἴγνυμι, οἴγω, open	οἴξω	ἔῳχα	ἔῳξα, οἶξαι
Passive (= am open)		ἔῳγμαι	ἐῴχθην, οἰχθῆναι
ὀμόργνυμι, wash off		?	ὤμορξα
Passive		?	ὠμόρχθην
Middle	ὀμόρξομαι		ὠμορξάμην
πήγνυμι, fix, fasten		πέπηγα (*284)	ἔπηξα
ῥήγνυμι, tear	ῥήξω	ἔῤῥωγα (*283)	ἔῤῥηξα
Passive	ῥαγήσομαι		ἐῤῥάγην
Middle			ἐῤῥηξάμην
ὄμνυμι, swear	ὀμοῦμαι	ὀμώμοκα	ὤμοσα
		ὀμωμόσθαι	ὀμο(σ)θῆναι
ὄλλυμι, destroy	ὀλῶ	ὀλώλεκα	ὤλεσα
Middle	ὀλοῦμαι	ὄλωλα (perii)	ὠλόμην

X. Verbs in ννυμι appended to a *pure* original root.

Present.	Future.	Perfect.	Aorist.
ἀμφιέννυμι, *put on* (*clothes*)	ἀμφιῶ	(none)	ἠμφίεσα
Middle	ἀμφιέσομαι	ἠμφίεσμαι	
κορέννυμι, *satisfy*	(κορέσω)	[κεκόρηκα]	ἐκόρεσα
Passive		κεκόρεσμαι	ἐκορέσθην
σβέννυμι, *extinguish*	σβέσω		ἔσβεσα
Passive	σβεσθήσομαι	ἔσβεσμαι	ἐσβέσθην
Intransitive	σβήσομαι	ἔσβηκα ·	ἔσβην
στορέννυμι, *strew, spread*	στορῶ	· (none)	ἐστόρεσα
(Comp. στρώννυμι)		ἐστόρεσμαι	[ἐστορέσθην]
κεράννυμι, *mix*	κεράσω (?)	κέκρᾱκα (?)	ἐκέρᾱσα
Passive		{ κέκρᾱμαι	{ ἐκρᾱθην
		{ κεκέρασμαι	{ ἐκεράσθην
Middle			ἐκερασάμην
κρεμάννυμι, *hang* (trans.)	κρεμῶ	?	ἐκρέμᾰσα
Passive		(κεκρέμαμαι)	ἐκρεμάσθην
κρέμαμαι, *hang* (intrans.)	κρεμήσομαι		
πετάννυμι, *spread out;*	{ πετάσω,	[πεπέτᾰκα]	ἐπέτᾰσα
extend	{ Att. πετῶ		
Passive		πέπτᾰμαι	ἐπετάσθην
σκεδάννυμι, *scatter*	σκεδῶ		ἐσκέδᾰσα
Passive		ἐσκέδασμαι	ἐσκεδάσθην ·
ζώννυμι, *gird* ·	ζώσω	[ἔζωκα]	ἔζωσα
Passive		ἔζωσμαι	
Middle	·		ἐζωσάμην
ῥώννυμι, *strengthen*	ῥώσω	?	
Passive	ῥωσθήσομαι	ἔρρωμαι	ἐρρώσθην
στρώννυμι, *strew*	στρώσω		ἔστρωσα
Passive		ἔστρωμαι	ἐστρώθην
Middle		•	ἐστρωσάμην
χρώννυμι, *color*		?	ἔχρωσα
Passive		κέχρωσμαι	ἐχρώσθην

LIST OF NUMERALS.

CARDINALS.		ORDINALS.	
1	α΄ εἷς, μίᾰ, ἕν	1	ὁ πρῶτος, η, ον
2	β΄ δύο	2	δεύτερος, α, ον
3	γ΄ τρεῖς, τρία	3	τρίτος, η, ον
4	δ΄ τέσσαρες, τέσσαρα	4	τέταρτος, η, ον
5	ε΄ πέντε	5	πέμπτος, &c.
6	ς΄ ἕξ	6	ἕκτος
7	ζ΄ · ἑπτά	7	ἕβδομος
8	η΄ ὀκτώ	8	ὄγδοος
9	θ΄ ἐννέα	9	ἔνατος (ἔνναmore)
10	ι΄ δέκα	10	δέκατος
11	ια΄ ἕνδεκα	11	ἑνδέκατος
12	ιβ΄ δώδεκα	12	δωδέκατος
13	ιγ΄ τρισκαίδεκα	13	τρισκαιδέκατος
14	ιδ΄ τεσσαρακαίδεκα	14	τεσσαρακαιδέκατος
15	ιε΄ πεντεκαίδεκα	15	πεντεκαιδέκατος
16	ις΄ ἑκκαίδεκα	16	ἑκκαιδέκατος
17	ιζ΄ ἑπτακαίδεκα	17	ἑπτακαιδέκατος
18	ιη΄ ὀκτωκαίδεκα	18	ὀκτωκαιδέκατος
19	ιθ΄ ἐννεακαίδεκα	19	ἐννεακαιδέκατος
20	κ΄ εἴκοσι(ν)	20	εἰκοστός
21	κα΄ εἴκοσιν εἷς, μία, ἕν	21	εἰκοστὸς πρῶτος
22	κβ΄ εἴκοσι δύο	22	εἰκοστὸς δεύτερος
23	κγ΄ εἴκοσι τρεῖς, τρία	23	εἰκοστὸς τρίτος
24	κδ΄ εἴκοσι τέσσαρες, ρα	24	εἰκοστὸς τέταρτος
25	κε΄ εἴκοσι πέντε	25	εἰκοστὸς πέμπτος
26	κς΄ εἴκοσιν ἕξ	26	εἰκοστὸς ἕκτος
27	κζ΄ εἴκοσιν ἑπτά	27	εἰκοστὸς ἕβδομος
28	κη΄ εἴκοσιν ὀκτώ	28	εἰκοστὸς ὄγδοος
29	κθ΄ εἴκοσιν ἐννέα	29	εἰκοστὸς ἔνατος
30	λ΄ τριάκοντα*	30	τριακοστός

* ☞ τριᾱκοντᾰ· τεσσαρᾱκοντᾰ.

CARDINALS.		ORDINALS.	
31	λα΄ τριάκοντα εἷς	31	τριακοστὸς πρῶτος
32	λβ΄ τριάκοντα δύο	32	τριακοστὸς δεύτερος
to	to	to	to
39	λθ΄ τριάκοντα ἐννέα	39	τριακοστὸς ἔννατος
40	μ΄ τεσσαράκοντα	40	τεσσαρακοστός
50	ν΄ πεντήκοντα	50	πεντηκοστός
60	ξ΄ ἑξήκοντα	60	ἑξηκοστός
70	ο΄ ἑβδομήκοντα	70	ἑβδομηκοστός
80	π΄ ὀγδοήκοντα	80	ὀγδοηκοστός
90	ϙ ἐνενήκοντα	90	ἐνενηκοστός
100	ρ΄ ἑκατόν	100	ἑκατοστός
200	σ΄ διᾱκόσιοι, αι, α	200	διακοσιοστός
300	τ΄ τριᾱκόσιοι	300	τριακοσιοστός
400	υ΄ τετρᾱκόσιοι [τεσσερ.]	400	τεσσαρακοσιοστος
500	φ΄ πεντᾱκόσιοι	500	πεντακοσιοστός
600	χ΄ ἑξᾱκόσιοι	600	ἑξακοσιοστός
700	ψ΄ ἑπτᾱκόσιοι	700	ἑπτακοσιοστός
800	ω΄ ὀκτᾱκόσιοι	800	ὀκτακοσιοστός
900	ϡ ἐνᾱκόσιοι (ἐννᾱκ.)	900	ἐνακοσιοστός (ἐννακοσ.)
1000	͵α χίλιοι, αι, α	1000	χιλιοστός
2000	͵β δισχίλιοι	2000	δισχιλιοστός
3000	͵γ τρισχίλιοι	3000	τρισχιλιοστός
4000	͵δ τετρᾱκισχίλιοι	4000	τετρακισχιλιοστός
5000	͵ε πεντᾱκισχίλιοι	5000	πεντακισχιλιοστός
6000	͵ϛ ἑξᾱκισχίλιοι	6000	ἑξακισχιλιοστός
7000	͵ζ ἑπτᾱκισχίλιοι	7000	ἑπτακισχιλιοστός
8000	͵η ὀκτᾱκισχίλιο.	8000	ὀκτακισχιλιοστός
9000	͵ϡ ἐνᾱκισχίλιοι	9000	ἐνακισχιλιοστός (ἐννακισ-
10,000	͵ι μύριοι	10,000	μυριοστός [χιλιοστός)
20,000	͵κ δισμύριοι	20,000	δισμυριοστός
to	to	to	to
100,000	͵σ δεκακισμύριοι	100,000	δεκακισμυριοστός

DIFFERENCES OF IDIOM, GRAMMATICAL HINTS, &C.

A. PREPOSITIONS.

1. About.

To be employed *about* any thing.	ἀμφί τι ἔχειν or εἶναι.
About = nearly (of *numerical* approximation), ἀμφί or περί with *acc.* ; ὡς (*conjunct.*).	στρατιώτας ἔπεμψαν ἀμφὶ τοὺς διακοσίους, or ὡς διακοσίους.
About (of approximate time).	περὶ μέσην τὴν ἡμέραν.
About noon.	ἀμφὶ μέσον ἡμέρας.

2. Above (ὑπέρ).

(1) *Above* = *more than,* ὑπέρ, c. acc. ; πλέον ἤ.

Above 100.	πλείους [= πλείονες] or πλείω (neut.) τῶν ἕκατον.
Men who are *above* 50 years old.	ἄνδρες πλεῖόν τι ἢ πεντήκοντα ἔτη γεγονότες ἀπὸ γενεᾶς.
The raven lives *above* 200 years.	ὁ κόραξ ὑπὲρ τὰ διακόσια ἔτη ζῇ.

(2) *Above* = beyond (of degree). See *Beyond.*

3. After.

To see any body *after* a long time.	ἰδεῖν τινα διὰ χρόνου.

4. Against.

To avail *against* any thing.	ἰσχύειν πρός τι.
To assist any body *against* any body.	βοηθεῖν τινι ἐπί τινα.

5. Amidst, Amongst.

Amongst the enemy.	ἐν μέσοις τοῖς πολεμίοις.
To be (have fallen) *amongst* robbers.	ἐν λῃσταῖς εἶναι.
Amongst men.	ἐν ἀνθρώποις.

6. AROUND, ROUND.   περί.—ἀμφί (= on both sides).

To sit *round* any thing.	κύκλῳ περικαϑῆσϑαί τι.
To throw a cloak *round* one.	περιβάλλεσϑαι or ἀμπέχεσϑαι ἱμάτιον.
To go *round* the city.	(κύκλῳ) περιιέναι τὴν πόλιν.

7. AT.

At intervals of five days (= every five days).	διὰ πέντε ἡμερῶν.
To look *at* one object.	εἰς ἓν βλέπειν.
To discharge arrows, &c. *at* an object.	πρός τι ἀφιέναι τὰ βέλη.

8. BEFORE.   ἐξ ἐναντίας (gen.).—ἐν (dat.).—πρός, εἰς (acc.).—ἐπί (gen.).—πρός (gen.).

(1) *Locally,* πρό (*gen.*).—ἔμπροσϑεν or ἐπίπροσϑεν (gen.).—ἐνώπιον (= in the presence of a *person*).—ἐναντίον (= in the presence of).—πρὸ τῆς πολέως (ϑύρας, &c.).—ἔμπροσϑεν τῆς ϑύρας (πρὸς τῇ ϑύρᾳ = close to it).

To stand *before* any body.	στῆναι ἔμπροσϑέν τινος : προστῆναί τινος, στῆναι ἐνώπιόν τινος, πρός τινος.
To stand *before* a glass.	ἐξ ἐναντίας τοῦ κατόπτρου στῆναι.
To speak *before* the people.	λέγειν ἐν τῷ δήμῳ (πρὸς or εἰς τὸν δῆμον).

= In the presence of.]

Before many witnesses.	ἐναντίον πολλῶν μαρτύρων.
To come *before* you (with reference to an assembled body *amongst* whom a person comes).	εἰς ὑμᾶς εἰσιέναι.

(2) *Temporally,* πρό (*gen.*).—πρότερον (*gen.*).

Before the war.	πρὸ τοῦδε τοῦ πολέμου.
A year *before* the taking of ——.	ἐνιαυτῷ πρότερον τῆς ἁλώσεως.
Before sunrise.	πρὸ (or πρότερον) ἡλίου ἀνιόντος or ἀνίσχοντος.

(πρὶν with Infin.)

Before day-break.	πρὶν ἡμέραν γίγνεσϑαι.

(If '*before*' introduces a *sentence*.)

9. BEHIND. ὄπισθεν, gen. (only of *place*).—κατόπιν, gen. (of *place* or *time*).—μετά, acc.—ἐπί, dat. *place* or *time*.—ὑπό (dat.) and ἀντί (only of *place*).

To stand *behind* a tree.	ἀντὶ δένδρου, or ὑπὸ δένδρῳ ἑστηκέναι (the former = facing it ; the latter *under it* for protection).
To be *behind* any thing.	ὄπισθεν γίγνεσθαί τινος.
To place oneself *behind* any thing.	ἔμπροσθεν ποιεῖσθαί τι (i. e. to cause it to be *before* one).

10. BELOW. ὑπό, gen. and dat.—κατά, gen. (so that the object *envelopes* or covers us). See *Under*.

To be *below* any body.	ἥττω (acc. m.) εἶναί τινος.
To think any thing *below* (beneath) one.	ἀπαξιοῦν τι.
This thing is *below* them.	ἀνάξιον αὐτῶν τοῦτ' ἐστι.

11. BENEATH. See *Below, Under*.

12. BESIDE. παρά (*dat.* of person ; *acc.* of thing).

To shoot *beside* the mark.	παραμαρτάνειν τοῦ σκοποῦ.

13. BETWEEN. μεταξύ (gen.), ἐν μέσῳ (gen.), ἐν (dat.).

Between ourselves.	ὡς ἐν ἡμῖν εἰρῆσθαι. ὡς πρὸς σέ (if *one* person only is addressed).

14. BEYOND. παρά, ὑπέρ (both acc.), μεῖζον ἤ.

Above (beyond) my power.	παρὰ (ὑπὲρ) δύναμιν.
That is *above* the power of man.	τὸ ἔργον ἐστὶ μεῖζον ἢ κατ' ἄνθρωπον (= the Lat. *major quam pro* ——).

15. BY (of *agent*): = BESIDE, vid. πρός, dat. = *close by*. τῇ πόλει, &c.

Day *by* day (daily) ; year *by* year (every year), yearly.	καθ' ἡμέραν : κατ' ἔτος.
To judge a person *by* any thing.	μετρεῖν (metiri) τινα ἔκ τινος.
To stand *by* any body.	παραστῆναί τινα.

(By = NEAR, vid.)

To implore any body *by* the gods.	πρὸς τῶν Θεῶν.
By the father's side.	πρὸς πατρός.

16. DOWN, κατά, gen. = down into; under.

In compos. κατά: To *fall* down, καταπίπτειν. To *run* down, κατατρέχειν, καταθεῖν.

Down (the) hill.	κατὰ (or κάτω) τοῦ ὄρους.

17. FOR.

To fight, brave dangers, &c. *for* any thing.	μάχεσθαι (κινδυνεύειν, &c.) ὑπέρ τινος (= on behalf of).
A remedy *for* any thing.	A *remedy* of *any thing* (objective, gen.).
Laws drawn up *for* this purpose (= to secure these objects.)	νόμοι ἐπὶ τούτοις τεταγμένοι.

18. FROM.

To receive any thing *from* any body.	λαμβάνειν τι παρά τινος.
To take an estimate of a person *from* any thing.	μετρεῖν (= metiri) τινα ἔκ τινος.

FROM (denoting a *cause*). Thus; From thinking so and so, τῷ νομίζειν.

    (1) dat.
    (2) διά with acc.
    (3) ἐκ with gen.

To remove any body from a magistracy.	παύειν τινα τῆς ἀρχῆς.

19. IN.

To exceed (surpass, excel) any body *in* any thing.	διαφέρειν (= *to differ, to be distinguished*), τινός τινι (dat. of *thing in which* one excels —).
To delight *in* any thing.	ἥδεσθαί τινι.
To end *in* any thing.	τελευτᾶν εἴς τι.
I am poor, rich *in* any thing.	ἐνδεής εἰμί (πλουτῶ) τινος.
To inquire, &c. *in what way* any thing may be done.	πυνθάνεσθαι τίνα τρόπον —.
To be shut up *in* a place.	To be shut up *into* (εἰς, *acc.*) a place.

20. INTO. εἰς (acc.).

With verbs of motion, ἐν with the dat. is found instead of εἰς with the Acc. ; "but only with the *Perf.* and *Pluperf.* in Attic writers. The ἐν denotes the point to which the motion is directed as *reached :* οἱ ἐν τῷ Ἡραίῳ καταπεφευγότες [but ἐς τὸ Ἡρ̅ κατέφυγον]. It is only with τιθέναι and the like, that ἐν occurs (though also εἰς) with all the forms, to denote *rest* as a *result* of the motion." *Kr.* Ἐν χερσὶ λαβεῖν.

21. NEAR. ἐγγύς (gen.). πλησίον (gen.).

To be *near* any body.	ἐγγὺς or πλησίον εἶναί τινος.
To put any thing *near* any body.	πλησίον ποιεῖν τί τινος.

22. OF.

To die *of* disease.	νόσῳ τελευτᾶν.

23. OFF.

I am *off.*	οἴχομαι.
To be three stadia *off.*	τρεῖς σταδίους ἀπέχειν (e. g. τῆς πόλεως).
To take one's clothes *off.*	ἀποδύεσθαι (e. g. *shoes).*—ἐκδύεσθαι (a garment from which one has to *come out).*
To take any body's clothes *off.*	ἐκδύειν τινά τι.

24. OUT (of). ἐκ (gen.).

Dat.—also = *cause, motive.* ἐκ (less commonly ἀπό) c. gen.— ὑπό (gen.).—διά, acc.

Out of kindness.	εὐνοίᾳ.—ὑπ᾽ εὐνοίας.

25. ON, UPON.

To spend money *upon* any body.	χρήματα ἀναλίσκειν εἴς τινα.
To sow *upon* stones.	εἰς λίθους σπείρειν (a proverb; sowing usually consisting of putting seed *into* the earth).
On the wing (of an army).	ἐπὶ κέρως.
To look *on* the ground.	εἰς γῆν ὁρᾶν.
All depends *on* you.	ἐν σοὶ πᾶν τὸ πρᾶγμα.

26. OVER. ὑπέρ (gen.).

11

27. THROUGH.

(1) Of direction from one extremity *through* to the other, διά with gen.

To wound any body *through* his breastplate.   διὰ τοῦ θώρᾱκος τιτρώσκειν τινά.

To flow *through* the country.   ῥεῖν διὰ τῆς γῆς.

(2) Of extension *over* all parts of a surface : διά (gen.), ἀνά (acc.).

Through the whole country.   ἀνὰ πᾶσαν τὴν χώραν.

(3) OCCASION, CAUSE, &c.   See *Out of.*
(In composition, διά.)

28. TILL, UNTIL, μέχρι, gen.

Till sunset.   μέχρι ἡλίου δυσμῶν (or δύνοντος).
Till death.   μέχρι θανάτου.
Till morning.   εἰς τὴν ἔω.

As a temporal conjunction with a sentence : ἕως, ἔστε, μέχρι (οὗ),—πρίν (prius).

29. TO, UNTO.

To conduct *to* — mankind.   ἄγειν (τινὰ) εἰς ἀνθρώπους.
Any thing is good for nothing *to*   πρός with *acc.*
    (= compared with) another.
To look *to* any thing (i. e. to   βλέπειν πρός τι.
    consider it, make it an object).
To be brought *to* any body.   ἐνεχθῆναι παρά τινα.
To come or go back again *to* the   αὖθις ἐπὶ τὴν ἀρχὴν ἰέναι πάλιν.
    beginning.
To go in *to* any body.   εἰσιέναι παρά τινα.

30. TOWARDS.

To be harsh *towards* any body.   χαλεπὸν εἶναί τινι.

31. UNDER.

ὑπό (c. *acc.*), to denote motion   ὑπὸ δένδρον καταστῆναι.
    towards an object that is above
    us. — ὑπό (dat.), of *rest* be-
    neath (ὑπὸ ἱματίῳ ἔχειν τι).

κατά (c. gen.), if we *sink* into it.   κατὰ γῆς καταδῦναι.

καταδύεσθαι κατὰ τοῦ ὕδατος.

Under = *in less* than, *ἐντός* (within : c. gen.).

Under twenty years.   ἐντὸς εἴκοσι ἐτῶν.

Under fifty years old.   ἀνὴρ οὔπω πεντήκοντα ἔτη γεγονὼς ἀπὸ γενεᾶς.

ἀνὴρ ἔλασσόν τι ἢ πεντήκοντα ἔτη
γεγονὼς (= *somewhat* under).

Under = *in subjection* to.   εἶναι ὑπό τινι or ἐπί τινι.

Under these circumstances.   ὧδ᾽ ἐχόντων τῶν πραγμάτων.—
οὕτως ἐχόντων.—ὅτε ταῦθ᾽ οὕ-
τως ἔχει.—ἐκ τούτων τοιούτων
ὄντων.

To be *under* arms.   ἐν ὅπλοις εἶναι.

32. WITH.

To build houses *with* the saw.   οἰκίας ποιεῖν ἀπὸ πρίονος.

To be angry *with* any body.   ὀργίζεσθαί τινι (ἐν ὀργῇ ἔχειν ᾽ϛ
ποιεῖσθαί τινα).

33. WITHIN.]   ἐντός, Gen. (of *time*. See UNDER).

34. WITHOUT.]   ἄνευ (Gen.).   χωρίς (Gen.).   ἔξω (Gen.).

Without transgressing the laws.   σὺν τοῖς νόμοις.

Without friends.   φίλων ἔρημος.

Without any right.   παρὰ πάντα τὰ δίκαια.

Without any body's knowledge.   κρύφα or λάθρα τινός.   ἀγνοοῦν-
τός τινος, or by circumlocution
with λανθάνειν τινά.

Often by a negative with particip. ; or by a negative compound.

Without laughing.   οὐ (or μὴ) γελάσας : ἀγελαστί.

B. MISCELLANEOUS.

35. Words that modify a substantive (i. e. *attributive* notions) **are** usually inserted between the article and its substantive, or after the substantive, the article being repeated.

a) Thus : *the men in the town,* would be, in Greek, ' *the in the town men,*' or ' *the men the in the town.*'

b) In this way the Greeks often use *long attributive notions* where *we* should use a relative clause : e. g.

Eng. Those *who are* in the enjoyment of all earthly blessings, &c.

Greek. The in the enjoyment of all earthly blessings (persons).

c) The substantive is here usually omitted, when it is *men, things,* &c. ; so that the article *often stands alone,* in connection with a substantive governed by a preposition, &c. : e. g. οἱ ἐν τῇ γῇ (*the in the land* =) the inhabitants of the country. οἱ ἐπὶ τῷ τείχει, the men on the wall.

Hence in translating, when an article is followed by some word or words with which it does not *agree, read on till you find a substantive with which the article can agree,* connecting the intermediate notions, attributively or otherwise, with this substantive. *If there is no substantive of the kind,* understand *men* or *things,* &c.

36. The girl has beautiful hair.   The girl has the hair beautiful.

37. The article is used when a substantive denotes a *class.* Thus *horses, poets,* &c. (when a truth is asserted of the *class ;* of *any* horse, &c.), are οἱ ἵπποι, οἱ ποιηταί.

38. It is not possible to —   οὐχ οἶόν τε (sc. ἐστίν), with *infin.*
I am not able to —   οὐχ οἷός τε (sc. εἰμί), with infin. (οἷος is ' *such* '). Hence οὐκ εἰμὶ οἷος ποιεῖν τι = I am not such a one (as) to do it. The τε = *que* is a remains of the old mode of affixing τε as a connecting particle to relatives, &c.

39. The dual is not *always* used for two; but very often δύο with plural.

40. *a)* 'Ο ποιῶν = he who does.

'Ο ποιήσας = he who has done, &c.

b) The participle may, of course, be resolved, as in Latin, (1) by a relative clause (with *who, which, that*); or (2) by an *adverbial one*, whether *conditional* (if), *adversative* (though), *temporal* (when, after, &c.) :—and often (3) by the *participial substantive* with *in, by,* &c. [λῃζόμενοι ζῶσιν, *they live* by plundering; *raptu* vivunt], and (4) by a *finite verb* connected with the principal verb by *and,* &c. ['*having fallen sick,* he died' = '*he* fell sick, *and died*'].

c) Hence conversely, *relative clauses, adverbial clauses,* the *participial substantive* (with *in, by,* &c.), a verb preceding another verb, and connected with it by *and,* may often be translated by a *participle.*

41. *a)* When two opposed notions are connected by an *unemphatic but* (δέ), the first usually takes μέν. Hence prefix μέν to the first of such *opposed* notions, although the English has no *indeed.*

b) Also place the *opposed notions* at the head of their clauses. For instance: arrange '*I like honey, but not wine,*' thus: '*Honey indeed I like, but wine not*' [in Greek it must be: *wine but* (οἶνον δέ), because δέ follows its word].

42. With three others. *Himself the fourth,* τέταρτος αὐτός.

43. This' (with emphasis). τοῦτό γε (γέ enclit.). This γέ *emphasizes* the preceding word: it may sometimes be rendered *at least, quite,* &c.

Diagoras. Διαγόρας γε or δή.

44. θεοὺς ἡγεῖσθαι or νομίζειν = deos esse credere, to believe in the existence of the gods.

τοὺς θεοὺς ἡγεῖσθαι or νομίζειν, credere deos esse, quos esse credi solet.

δίκην νομίζειν = to *observe* or *practise* justice; to acknowledge there is such a thing.

45. (To have) any thing *a foot long* (broad, deep) ; or, *of a foot in length* (breadth, depth).

(*To have any*) *thing* (the) *length,* breadth, depth of a foot.

46. With A *not* B.

'*With A* but not (ἀλλ' οὐ) B' (but often καὶ οὐ or οὐ only).

47. A, B, C, D, and E.

(1) A, *and* B, *and* C, *and* D, *and* E.

(2) *both* (καί) A, *and* B, *and* C, *and* D, *and* E.

(3) A, B, C, D.
That 's, in Greek the '*and*' is not placed *only* between the *two last* terms of a series.

48. *a)* He *evidently* desires.

a) *He is evident* desiring, &c. (δῆλός ἐστιν ἐπιθῡμῶν).—So φανερός ἐστιν.

b) It is *just* (*fair*, &c.) that he should bear the blame of this.

b) *He is just* (*fair*, &c.) to bear the blame of this. δίκαιός ἐστι τούτου τὴν αἰτίαν φέρειν. So ἄξιός ἐστιν (e. g. τοῦ γεγενημένου ἀπολαῦσαί τι ἀγαθόν).

49. To come *with* twenty hoplites.
To walk *with* a stick.

To come *having* (ἔχων) twenty hoplites.
To walk *bearing* (φέρων) a stick.

50. I am come *to do it.*

I am come *about to do it* (ποιήσων).

I send a man *to do it.*

I send [τὸν] ποιήσοντα.

51. A sort of prophets.

μάντεις τινές.

52. Many great men.

Many *and* great men.

53. I *say* that it is *not* —.
I *think* it does *not* —.
I *pretend* it is *not* —.

οὔ φημι — εἶναι.
οὐκ οἴομαι — εἶναι.
οὐ προσποιοῦμαι — εἶναι.

54. I should like to (behold).

ἡδέως ἂν θεασαίμην.

55. I *naturally* desire.
It is my nature to desire.
I desire by reason of a natural inclination.

πέφῡκα ἐπιθῡμεῖν = (*ita naturâ comparatus sum, ut — concupiscam*).

56. *Who, whom, what* are often *indefinite:* == *any person who, whom; any thing that.* They are then to be translated by ὃς ἄν with *Subj.* after *Pres.* or *Fut.*; by ὅς with *Optative* after the historical tenses (cf. 295).

So, *whatever* = ὃ ἄν, ἃ ἄν, ὅσα ἄν with Subj. after a principal tense; ὅ, ἅ, ὅσα with Opt. after an historical tense.

57. The *Aorist* is often translated into English by the *Perfect.* Especially,

a) The *Aor. Infin.* after *verba putandi et declarandi* has the force of a præteritum; and is often translated by the Perfect:

$$\phi\eta\sigma\grave{\imath}\ \pi o\iota\hat{\eta}\sigma a\iota = \begin{cases} \text{he says that he } \textit{did} \text{ it.} \\ \text{he says that he } \textit{has done} \text{ it.} \end{cases}$$

b) In the statement of *general* truths founded on frequent experience (especially with ἤδη), the *Aor.* is often translated by the *Perfect.*

Men have often been compelled.   ἤδη πολλοὶ ἠναγκάσθησαν

58. The *Aorist* has often the force of the *Pluperfect.*

a) The Aor. is *regularly* used (the Pluperf. comparatively seldom) after ἐπεί, ἐπειδή, &c.

b) The Aor. Infin. is used after an historical tense of a *verbum declarandi et putandi*:

$$\check{\epsilon}\phi\eta\ \pi o\iota\hat{\eta}\sigma a\iota. = \begin{cases} \text{he said that he } \textit{did} \text{ it.} \\ \text{he said that he } \textit{had done} \text{ it.} \end{cases}$$

59. Too wise to —.   σοφώτερος ἢ ὥστε c. infin. (In Latin, *sapientior quam ut* —).

MEANINGS OF PREPOSITIONS.

☞ For convenience sake, as well as for clearness, the Prepositions are here collected together: they are divided, according to their construction, into

a) Prepositions with the *gen.*, ἀντί, ἀπό, ἐκ, πρό.
b)   "   "   *dat.*, ἐν, σύν.
c)   "   "   *acc.*, ἀνά, εἰς, ὡς.
d)   "   "   *gen.* and *acc.*, διά, κατά, ὑπέρ.
e)   "   "   *gen.*, *dat.*, and *acc.*, ἀμφί, περί, ἐπί μετά, παρά, πρός, and ὑπό.

ἀμφί, about, for, on; around; (of time and number) about.

ἀνά, up, on, up to, upon.

ἀντί, over against, opposite, instead of.

ἀπό, from, away from, with, by, at; (as adv.) forth, off, away, quite.

διά, through, after, by; on account of, by reason of.

εἰς and ἐς, into; to, at, for; until, towards, on.

ἐκ and ἐξ, out of, from, according to, after, to, by.

ἐν, in, among, at, by, near, during, with.

ἐπί, upon, on, by, in the case of. in presence of, during, towards, after; upon, at, by, against; on, over, towards, for, into.

κατά, from above, down, concerning, against, opposite, in, according to, by.

μετά, in midst, with, in conformity with, among; after, next after, since.

παρά, by, close by, by the side of; along, near, beyond, besides, through, by means of, within.

περί, all around, round, for, about, with reference to; near; above.

πρό, before, for, forwards.

πρός, before, in presence of, towards, in the opinion of, for advantage of, by, near, besides; with, against, towards, according to, on account of, in conformity with.

σύν, with, by, together with.

ὑπέρ, over (super), for, for the good of, beyond, contrary to.

ὑπό, under (sub), out from under, for, on account of; towards; during; by, with.

ὡς, to (used only with persons and personified objects, to denote direction).

INDEX I.

GREEK AND ENGLISH.

☞ The Roman numerals refer to the Lists of Irregular Verbs, pp. 228–234.—Adjectives in *os* that are followed by 2, are of *two terminations;* i. e. the form in *os* is also used for the feminine.

A.

Αβλάβεια (ἀ. βλαβ, short root of βλάπτειν, to hurt), innocence.

{ ἀγαϑόν (neut. adj.), advantage.
{ ἀγαϑός, good, brave.

ἄγαν (*nimis*), too much; too.

ἀγαπᾶν (= ά-ειν), to love; (with dat. or acc.) to be contented (*or* satisfied) with.

ἄγγελος, ὁ, messenger.

{ ἄγε (Imperat. of ἄγειν =), *age,* come now.
{ ἄγειν, to lead, carry. ἄγειν ἡσυχίαν, to keep quiet.

ἀγεννής, -ές (ἀ. γεν, root of verbs relating to *production, origin,* &c.), ignoble, low-bred.

ἄγηρως, -ων (ἀ. γῆρας, old age), not growing old; immortal, imperishable.

ἀγκών, -ῶνος, ὁ, (bend of · the) elbow.

ἄγνυμι, I break (pf. ἔαγα). IX.

ἀγορά, ἡ, market-place (ἀγείρειν, to assemble).

ἄγραφος (ἀ. γράφειν, to write), unwritten.

ἀγρός, ὁ, a field.

ἀγρυπνεῖν (= έ-ειν), to keep awake, to forego sleep (ἀ. ὕπνος, sleep).

ἀγχίνους 2, shrewd, clever, quick-witted (ἄγχι, near. νοῦς, mind).

ἀγώγιμες (ἄγειν), that may be conveyed *or* imported amongst: —hence *current* (of foreign money).

ἀγών, ἀγῶν-ος, ὁ, contest.

ᾄδειν (ἀείδειν), to sing.

{ ἀδελφή, ἡ, sister.
{ ἀδελφός, ὁ, brother.

{ ἀδικεῖν (= έ-ειν), to commit injustice; to do wrong.—c. acc. to wrong (ἀ, not. δίκη, justice).
{ ἀδίκημα, τό, wrong, unjust act.
{ ἀδικία, ἡ, injustice.
{ ἄδικος 2, unjust.

{ ἀδυνατεῖν (=έ-ειν), to be unable.
{ ἀδύνατος 2, impossible.

ἀεί, always.

ἀεικής, -ές, unseemly, disgraceful.

ἀετός, ὁ, eagle.

ἀηδών, ἀηδόν-ος, ἡ, nightingale.

ἀϑάνατος 2, immortal (ἀ. ϑάνατος, death).

{ 'Αϑηνᾶ, Athene (Minerva).
{ 'Αϑῆναι, -ῶν, αἱ, Athens.
{ 'Αϑηναῖος, Athenian.

{ ἄϑλιος, miserable.
{ ἀϑλίως, miserably.

ἆϑλον, τό, prize.

ἀϑυμεῖν (=έ-ειν), to be dispirited (ἀ, not. ϑυμός, spirit).

Αἰακός, ὁ, Æacus.

11*

Αἰγύπτιος, Egyptian.
Αἴγυπτος, ἡ, Egypt.
αἰδεῖσθαι (= ἐ-εσθαι,) to reverence.
αἰδώς, ἡ, shame, reverence.
Αἰήτης, Æetes (king of Colchis).
αἰθήρ, -έρος, ὁ, ether, pure air.
αἷμα, αἵματ-ος, τό, blood.
αἴξ, αἰγ-ός, ὁ, ἡ, goat.
αἱρεῖν (= ἐ-ειν), to take. VII.
αἴρειν, to raise.
αἰσθάνεσθαι, αἰσθήσομαι, &c., to perceive. III.
αἴσθησις, εως, ἡ, sensation, perception.
αἴσχιστος, superl. of αἰσχρός.
αἰσχροκερδής, pursuing gain by base means (αἰσχρός, base. κέρδος, gain).
αἰσχρός, disgraceful, base.
αἰσχρῶς, disgracefully.
αἰσχύνειν, to shame. MID. αἰσχύνεσθαι, to be ashamed.
αἰτεῖν (= ἐ-ειν), (τινά τι), to ask.
αἰτιᾶσθαι (= ά-εσθαι,), to accuse, charge, blame, &c.; τινά τι (rare), ὅτι —.
αἰχμάλωτος, ον, prisoner of war.
αἶψα, quickly.
ἀκάθαρτος, uncleansed, impure (ά. καθαίρειν, purificare).
ἀκμή, point. ω ἡλικίας, the full vigor (or flower) of one's age.
ἀκοή, hearing (ἀκούειν)
ἀκόλαστος, intemperate; prop. unchastised, unchastened (ά, non. κολάζειν, castigare).
ἀκούειν, to hear, to listen to; Fut. ἀκούσομαι; Pass. with σ.
ἀκούσιος, involuntary.
ἄκρα, ἡ, summit.
ἀκρατής, -ές, intemperate, immoderate (ά. κράτος, strength).
ἀκριβής, -ές, accurate.
ἀκροᾶσθαι (= ά-εσθαι), to hear, listen to.
ἀκροατής, -οῦ, ὁ, auditor.

ἀκρό-πολις, -εως, ἡ, citadel.
ἄκρος, highest.
ἄκων, -ουσα, -ον, unwilling.
ἀλγεῖν (= ἐ-ειν), to feel pain.
ἀλγεινός, painful.
ἄλγος, -ους, τό, pain.
ἀλείφειν, to anoint, rub.
ἀλεκτρυών, -όνος, ὁ, a cock.
Ἀλέξανδρος, ὁ, Alexander.
ἀλήθεια, ἡ, truth.
ἀληθεύειν, to speak the truth.
ἀληθής, -ές, true.
ἀληθῶς, truly.
ἅλις, enough.
ἁλίσκεσθαι, to be taken. V.
ἀλκή, ἡ, strength.
Ἀλκιβιάδης, -ου, ὁ, Alcibiades.
ἀλλά, but.
ἀλλήλων, of one another.
ἄλλοθεν, from another place.
ἄλλος, -η, -ο, another, alius.
ἀλλότριος (= alienus), others', another's.
ἄλλως, otherwise. ἄλλως τε καί, especially.
ἀλογία, unreasonableness, absurdity (ά. non. λόγος, ratio).
ἄλογος (ά. λόγος, ratio), irrational, senseless (2 terminations).
ἅλς, ἁλός, salt; pl. ἅλες. Note 9.
ἄ-λύπως, without grief or sorrow.
ἀλώπηξ, ἀλώπεκ-ος, ἡ, fox.
ἅλως, ἡ, halo.
ἅλωσ-ις, -εως, ἡ (ἁλο-, simpler root of ἁλίσκ-ομαι), taking, capture.
ἅμα (simul), at the same time: also used as a prep. with dat., together with: ἅμα τῇ ἕῳ (at the same time with the dawn =) at day-break; ἅμα τῷ σίτῳ ἀκμάζοντι, &c.
ἀμαθία, ἡ (ά, non. μαθ, short root of μανθάνειν, discere), ignorance.
ἄμαξα, ἡ, wagon.

{ ἁμαρτάνειν (1) *errare*, to miss (with gen.) ; (2) *peccare*, to sin, commit a fault, err.

ἁμάρτημα, ἁμαρτήματος, τό, error, fault.

ἁμαρτία, ἡ, offence.

ἀμαυροῦν (= ό-ειν), to darken.

ἀμείνων, better (ἄμεινον as adv.).

{ ἀμέλεια, ἡ, carelessness.

{ ἀμελεῖν (= έ-ειν), to neglect (gen.—ἀ. μέλει, *curæ est*).

ἀμοιβή, exchange, return (ἀμείβεσθαι).

ἄμπελος, ἡ, vine.

ἀμύνειν, to ward off; *Mid.* to ward off from myself ; also, to revenge myself on any body (*acc.*) ; for any thing, ὑπέρ τινος.

ἀμφι-έννυμι, I put on; I clothe. x.

ἄμφω, both.

ἄν, with Subj., = ἐάν, if. This ἄν, which has ā, and can stand as the first word of a clause, must not be confounded with ἄν with ă, the *modal* particle, explained in 279.

ἀνα-γιγνώσκειν, to read. VI.

{ ἀναγκάζειν, to compel.

{ ἀναγκαῖος, necessary.

{ ἀνάγκη, necessity.

ἀναίδεια, ἡ, shamelessness.

ἀν-αλίσκειν, to spend. v.

ἀνα-μένειν, to wait.

ἀνά-παυσις, -εως, ἡ, rest (ἀναπαύεσθαι).

ἀν-αιρεῖν (= έ-ειν), to take up, take away, destroy (aor. ἀνεῖλον). VII.

ἀναρχία (ἀ. ἀρχή), anarchy, licentiousness, ungoverned licence.

ἀνάστατος 2, ruined, laid waste (of cities and countries) : ἀνάστατον ποιεῖν, to destroy utterly, to lay waste (properly, to make the inhabitants *rise up* and quit.—ἀνά, up. στα-, simpler root of ἵστημι).

ἀνα-τίθημι, ἀνα-τιθέναι, to put up, offer.

ἀναχώρησις, retreat (ἀνά. χωρεῖν, *cedere*).

{ ἀνδρεία, ἀνδρία, ἡ, bravery.

{ ἀνδρεῖος, brave (ἀνήρ, man).

{ ἀνδρείως, adv., bravely.

ἀνδρίας, -άντος, ὁ, image *or* statue (of a man.—ἀνήρ, ἀνδρ-ός).

Ἀνδρόγεως, -ω, ὁ, Androgeus.

ἄνεμος, ὁ, wind.

ἄνευ (gen.), without.

ἀνήρ, ἀνδρ-ός, ὁ, a man. Pdm. 19.

ἄνθος· τό, a flower.

{ ἀνθρώπινος, human ; to which humanity is subject : hence (of *faults*) venial.

{ ἄνθρωπος, ὁ, man.

ἀν-ίστημι, -ιστάναι, to set up.

{ ἀνόητος, unintelligent, silly (ἀ not. νοεῖν, to understand).

{ ἄνοια, ἡ, want of sense, stupidity, folly.

ἀν-οιγνύναι, ἀν-οίγειν, to open. IX.

{ ἀνομία (ἀ. νόμος, law), lawlessness.

{ ἄνομος 2. lawless.

ἄνους (= ἄνοος), -ουν, senseless, imprudent (ἀ. νοῦς, mind).

ἀντι-λέγειν, to contradict.

ἄνω, above, more inland, beyond (gen.).

ἀνώγεων, τό, upper floor, diningroom (ἄνω, above. γῆ, earth).

{ ἀξιό-λογος, worth mentioning.

{ ἄξιος, worthy (gen.).

{ ἀξιοῦν (= ό-ειν), to think worthy, claim, expect.

{ ἀξίωμα, ἀξιώματ-ος, τό, consideration, reputation, dignity, rank (ἄξιος).

ἀοιδή, song (ἀείδειν).

ἀπ-άγειν, to lead away.

ἀπαίδευτος 2, uneducated (ἀ. παιδεύειν, to educate. παιδ, root of παῖς, boy).

ἀπ-αλλάττειν, to set free from ; *Mid.* to depart from.

ἅπαξ, once.

ἅπας, all, whole, altogether.

⎰ ἀπειϑεῖν (έ-ειν), to disobey (dat.).
⎱ ἀπειϑής, disobedient (ἀ. πεί-
⎱ ϑειν, to obey).

ἀπ-εικάζειν, to copy.

ἅπ-ειμι, Inf. ἀπ-εῖναι, to be absent.

ἅπ-ειμι, Inf. ἀπ-ιέναι, to go away
(Pres. with meaning of Fut.).

ἄπειρος 2 (gen.), unacquainted
with, inexperienced (ἀ. πεῖρα,
attempt).

ἀπ-έρχεσϑαι, to go away. VII.

⎰ ἀπ-έχειν, to keep off; to be
⎱ distant from. VII.
⎱ ἀπ-έχεσϑαι (gen.), to abstain
⎱ from. VII.
⎱ ἀπιστεῖν (= έ-ειν), to disbe-
⎱ lieve, distrust.
⎱ ἄπιστος 2, unfaithful, faithless.
⎱ —suspected (by) (ἀ. πιστός,
⎱ faithful).

ἁπλόος, -οῦς, simple.

ἀπο-βαίνειν, to disembark; to go
away. III.

ἀποβάλλειν, to cast away; to
shed (horns).

ἀπο-βλέπειν, to look upon.

ἀπο-δείκνυμι, ἀπο-δεικνύναι, to
show; to appoint.

ἀπο-δέχεσϑαι, to receive, accept.

ἀπο-δίδωμι, ἀπο-διδόναι, to give
back, to give, allot.

ἀποϑαν-. See ἀποϑνήσκ-ειν.

ἀπο-ϑνήσκειν (-ϑανοῦμαι, -τέϑνηκα,
-έϑανον), to die. V.

ἀπο-κάμνειν, Fut. -καμοῦμαι, -κέ-
κμηκα, -έκαμον (c. partcp.), to
grow weary. In Aor., to be
wearied. 317.

ἀποκόπτειν, to cut off.

ἀπο-κρίνεσϑαι, to answer.

ἀπο-κρύπτειν, to conceal.

ἀπο-κτείνειν, to kill (κτείνω. f. κτε-
νῶ. pf. ἔκτονα : later ἔκτακα).

ἀπο-λείπειν, to leave, to quit.

ἀπ-όλλυμι, ἀπ-ολλύναι, to ruin, to
destroy. IX.

Ἀπόλλων, -ωνος, ὁ, Apollo.

ἀπο-λύειν, to dissolve ; to acquit

⎰ ἀπορεῖν (= έ-ειν), to be in
⎱ want.
⎱ ἄπορος 2, difficult (ἀ, not. πό-
⎱ ρος, passage through).
⎱ ἀποῤῥεῖν (= έ-ειν), to flow
⎱ from. ›
⎱ ἀποῤῥοή, a flowing off, an efflu-
⎱ ence ὸr emanation.

ἀπο-σπᾶν (= ά-ειν), to draw away.

ἀπο-στερεῖν (= έ-ειν), to deprive
of.

ἀπο-στρέφειν, to turn away.

ἀπο-σφάττειν, to cut (a man's)
throat; to slay.

ἀπο-τίϑημι, ἀπο-τιϑέναι, to put
away ; Mid. take off; lay
aside.

ἀπο-φαίνειν, to show ; to make ;
to appoint : Mid. declare.

ἀπο-ψύχειν, to dry up.

ἀπρόσβατος 2, inaccessible (ἀ.
πρός, to. βα-, simpler root of
βαίνειν, to go).

ἅπτεσϑαι, to touch (gen.).

ἆρα ; (interrogative.)

ἄρα, igitur, therefore.

ἀργαλέος, troublesome.

⎰ ἀργύρεος, (made) of silver;
⎱ silver (adj.).
⎱ ἀργύριον, τό, silver money; mo-
⎱ ney.
⎱ ἄργυρος, ὁ, silver.

Ἄρειος πάγος, Mars' hill (the
hill on which the court of the
Areopagus sat) ; the hill of the
Areopagus.

ἀρετή, ἡ, virtue.

ἀριϑμός, ὁ, number.

ἄριστος, best.

ἄρκτος, ὁ, ἡ, a bear.

ἅρμα, ἅρματ-ος, τό, chariot.

ἀρνεῖσϑαι (= έ-εσϑαι,) Dep. Pass.,
to deny.

ἁρπάζειν, to seize, plunder, carry
off.

ἄῤῥην, -εν, male.

ἀρτί, just now.

ἄρτιος, -α, -ον, even (opp. *odd*) ; of an even number.

{ ἀρτοπώλης, breadseller, baker (ἄρτος, bread, loaf. πωλεῖν, to sell).

ἄρτος, ὁ, bread.

ἄρχειν (gen.), to rule over, to be master of ; to begin.

ἄρχεσθαι (gen.), to begin.

ἀρχή, ἡ, beginning, commencement ; commencing-point.

{ ἀσέβεια, ἡ, impiety.

{ ἀσεβεῖν (= έ-ειν), to be guilty of impiety (σέβειν, *venerari*).

{ ἀσέβημα, τό, an impiety, *or* impious act.

{ ἀσθένεια, ἡ, weakness.

{ ἀσθενεῖν (== έ-ειν), to be weak, to be ill.

{ ἀσθενής, -ές, weak (ἀ. σθένος, strength).

ἀσκεῖν (= έ-ειν), to practise.

ἀσπάλαθος, ὁ, the aspalathus (a prickly shrub).

ἀσπίς, ἀσπίδ-ος, ἡ, shield.

{ ἀστραπή, ἡ, lightning.

{ ἀστράπτειν, to lighten.

ἄστρον (*astrum*), star.

ἄστυ, τό, city.

ἀ-σύνετος 2, stupid.

ἀσφαλής, -ές, firm (ἀ. σφάλλεσθαι, to stumble).

ἀτέλεια (ἀτελής), exemption (from public burdens : *immunitas*.—ἀ. τελεῖν, to pay).

{ ἀτιμάζειν, to despise (ἀ. τιμή, honor).

{ ἀτιμία, ἡ, dishonor.

Ἀττίκη, ἡ, Attica.

{ ἀτυχεῖν (= έ-ειν), to be unsuccessful *or* unfortunate (ἀ. τυχ, short root of τυγχάνειν, *to hit* [a mark, &c.], to obtain. τύχη, fortune).

{ ἀτύχημα, τό, misfortune.

{ ἀτυχής, -ές, unfortunate.

{ ἀτυχία, ἡ, misfortune.

{ αὖ, again ; on the other hand.

{ αὖθις, again.

αὐλός, ὁ, flute.

αὖος, dry.

αὐτός, -ή, -ό, self : but αὐτοῦ, -ῷ, -όν, *ejus, ei, eum*.—So in pl.

αὐχήν, αὐχέν-ος, ὁ, neck.

ἀφ-αιρεῖσθαι (= έ-εσθαι) τινά τι, to deprive of, take away. Cf. αἱρεῖν in VII.

{ ἀφανής, -ές, unseen, unknown. (ἀ. φαν, short root of φαίνειν, to show).

{ ἀφανίζειν, to cause to disappear. ω τὴν γῆν, to cover it.

ἄφθονος (ἀ. φθόνος, envy), abundant (there being so much, that none need *envy* another).

ἀφ-ίημι, ἀφ-ιέναι, to let go.

ἀφ-ικνεῖσθαι (= έ-εσθαι), to come. III.

ἀφ-ίστημι, ἀφ-ιστάναι, to put away, to turn aside from.—Aor. 2, ἀπόστηναι (*deficere*), to revolt from, desert from.—Aor. 1, ἀποστῆσαι = to make to revolt.

ἄ-φρων, foolish.

ἀχάριστος 2, ungrateful (ἀ. χάρις, *gratia*).

ἄχθεσθαι, to be indignant.

Ἀχιλλεύς, -έως, ὁ, Achilles.

ἄχρηστος 2, useless (ἀ. χρά-εσθαι = χρῆσθαι).

B.

{ Βάθος, -ους, τό, depth.

{ βαθύς, -εῖα, -ύ, deep.

βαίνειν, to go. III.

βαλανεῖον, bath, public bath (*i. e.* bathing-room).

βάλλειν, to throw. 317. 371.

βάπτ-ειν, to dip.

βάρβαρος, barbarian.

{ βασιλεύειν, to be a king, to reign.

{ βασιλεύς, -έως, ὁ, king.

{ βασιλισσᾰ, ἡ, queen.

βέβαιος 3 and 2, firm.
{ βέλτιστος, best.
{ βελτίων, ον, better.
βία, ή, violence.
{ βιβλίον, τό, book.
{ βιβλιο-πώλης, bookseller (πω-
　λεῖν, to sell).
{ βίος, ό, life.
{ βίοτος, livelihood.
{ βιοῦν (= ό-ειν), to live.
{ βλαβερός, injurious.
{ βλάβη, ή, injury.
{ βλάπτειν, to injure, to hurt.
βλέπειν, to look at.
{ βυήθεια, ή, help.
{ βοηθεῖν (= έ-ειν), to help (dat.).
{ βοηθητικός, ready or able to help.
βομβεῖν (= έ-ειν), to hum, buzz.
Βορρᾶς, -ᾶ, ό, Boreas, the north
　wind.
{ βόσκειν, to feed.
{ βόσκημα, τό (βόσκειν), fed or
　fattened beast: pl. cattle (as
　fed for the butcher).
{ βούλεσθαι, to wish.
{ βουλεύειν, to deliberate, ad-
　vise; Mid. to advise oneself.
{ βουλή, ή, advice, council, se-
　nate.
βοῦς, ό, ή, ox. Pdm. 29.
βραδύς, -εῖα, -ύ, slow.
βροντᾶν (= ά-ειν), to thunder.
βροτός, mortal.
βωμός, ό, altar.

Γ.

Γάλα, τό, milk. Note 9.
γαλῆ, weasel.
{ γαμεῖν (= έ-ειν), to marry.
{ γάμος, ό, marriage.
γάρ, for (stands after the first
　word of the sentence).
γαστήρ, ή, belly. 183. Pdm. 19.
γαυροῦν (=ό-ειν), to make proud;
　Mid. exult in, be proud of.

γέ (quidem, certe), at least.—Often only adds emphasis to the
word it follows.
γεγραμμένος, written (perf. part.
of γράφειν).
{ γελᾶν (= ά-ειν), to laugh.
{ γέλως, -ωτος, ό, laughter.
{ γενναῖος, of noble birth.
{ γενναίως, with spirit, bravely,
　nobly; with fortitude.
{ γένος, γένους, τό, kind, race.
{ γέρας, τό, honorary privilege,
　reward.
{ γέρων, -οντος, ό, old man.
γενειν, to cause to taste; Mid.
to taste (gen.).
{ γεωμέτρης, -ου, ό, geometer
　(γῆ, earth. μετρεῖν, to mea-
　sure).
{ γῆ, ή, the earth.
{ γήϊνος, of earth, of brick.
{ γῆρας, τό, old age. 192.
{ γηράσκειν, γηρᾶν (= ά-ειν),
　to grow old.
γίγνεσθαι* (fieri), to become, to
be formed.
γιγνώσκειν, to know. VI.
γλυκύς, -εῖα, -ύ, sweet.
γλῶττα, ή, tongue.
γνώμη, ή, opinion, mind.
{ γόης, ητος, juggler.
{ γοητεύ-ειν, to juggle.
γονεύς, ό, parent (γεν, root of verbs
denoting procreation, origin).
{ γράμμα (for γράφ-μα), τό, let-
　ter; pl. (literæ), a letter.
{ γραμματεύς, έως, ό, scribe.
{ γράφειν, to write, to draw up
　(a law).
{ γραφεύς, έως, ό, painter.
Γρύλλος, ό, Gryllus.
{ γυμνάζειν, to exercise (γυμνός,
　naked).
{ γυμναστική (fem. adj.: under-
　stand τέχνη, ars), gymnas-
　tics.

---

* γίγνομαι, γενήσομαι, { γεγένημαι } , ἐγενόμην.
　　　　　　　　　　　 { γέγονα

γυναικεῖος, belonging to women.
γυνή, ἡ, woman. R. γυναικ-.
Note 9.

Δ.

Δαίμων, δαίμον-ος, ὁ, ἡ, deity, divinity.

δάκνειν, to bite. III.

δακρύειν, to weep.
δάκρυον, τό, a tear.

δακτύλιος, ὁ, ring.

δέ (autem), but (stands after the first word of the sentence).

δεῖ (oportet), it is necessary.

δείδειν, to fear [Perf. δέδοικα and δέδια; Aor. ἔδεισα].

δειλία, cowardice, timidity.
δειλός, timid, cowardly.

δεῖν (= έ-ειν), to want; to need: to bind. Δέω, I bind (not δέω, I want) mostly contracts εο and εω into ου, ω.

δεινός (δείδ-ειν, to fear), fearful, terrible, dreadful.
δεινῶς, terribly.

δεῖσθαι (= έ-εσθαι), to want, need (gen.).

δέκα, ten.

δέλεαρ, δελέατ-ος, τό, bait.

Δελφοί, Delphi.

δένδρον, τό, tree. Note 9.

δέον, τό (id quod oportet, sc. facere), duty.

δεσπότης, -ου, ὁ, master.

δεῦρο, hither.

δέχεσθαι, Dep. Mid., to receive; also, of receiving.

δή, with an imperative, emphasizes it, = pray, I beg. It also occurs with numerals, pronouns, adverbs, &c. πολλοὶ δή, νῦν δή, &c.

δῆθεν, namely, scilicet.

δῆλος, evident. δῆλός εἰμι ποιῶν τι, I manifestly do something.
δηλοῦν (= ό-ειν), to make evident.

δημαγωγός (δῆμος, people. ἄγειν, to lead), demagogue.

δημοκρατία, ἡ, democracy (δῆμος. κρατεῖν, to be strong; to rule).

δῆμος, ὁ, people, democratical constitution.

Δημο-σθένης, -ους, ὁ, Demosthenes.

δημοσίᾳ, in one's public character or life.

δημιουργός, ὁ. See Vocab. 22.

δήπου (opinor), I imagine, I suppose.

δῆτα, certainly.

δι-άγειν, to carry through; live.

διάδημα, τό, diadem (διά. δεῖν, to tie).

δια-λέγεσθαι, to converse (dat.).

δια-λύειν, to dissolve.

δια-μένειν, to remain.

δια-νέμειν, to distribute.

διάπλους, ὁ, a passage (across) (διά. πλεῖν, navigare).

δια-πράττειν, to effect.

δι-άρθρωσις, -εως, ἡ, articulation (of a joint.—ἄρθρον, joint).

δια-σπείρειν, to scatter.

δια-τελεῖν (= έ-ειν), to complete, to continue.

δια-τίθημι, δια-τιθέναι, to put in order, to dispose (a person).

δια-φέρειν, to differ (from any thing or person, τινός); hence to excel, to surpass (gen.) VII.
δια-φορά, ἡ, difference (of colors, shade): also, difference = dispute, &c.

δια-φθείρειν, to corrupt, to destroy.

διαφωνεῖν (= έ-ειν), to sound apart; hence, to dissent from, disagree (διά. φωνή, voice).

διδακτόν (διδάσκειν), capable of being taught, that can be taught.

διδάσκαλος, ὁ, teacher.

διδάσκειν, to teach.

διδράσκειν, to run away. VI.

δίδωμι, διδόναι, to give.

διηγεῖσθαι (ἐ-εσθαι), to go through relate, narrate (διά, through. ἡγεῖσθαι, to lead).

δι-ίστημι, δι-ιστάναι, to separate.

δίκαιος, just.
δικαιοσύνη, ἡ, justice.
δικαίως, justly.
δικαστής, -οῦ, ὁ, judge, juror.
δίκη, ἡ, justice, a cause or trial.

Διογένης, -ους, ὁ, Diogenes.

Διόνυσος, ὁ, Bacchus.

· δι-ορύττειν (lit. to dig through =) to break into (a house).

διπλόος, -οῦς, double; double-minded.

δίς, bis, twice.

δίσκος, m. quoit, discus.

δισ-μύριοι, twenty thousand.

δίχα (gen.), apart from.

διψῆν (= ά-ειν), to be thirsty, to thirst. 346.

διώκειν, to pursue.

δοκεῖν (=ἐ-ειν), to seem, think.
δοκεῖ, (1) videtur; (2) placet, visum est.

δοκιμάζειν, to test, to prove.

δολοῦν (= ό-ειν), to deceive, entrap (δόλος, trick, deceit).

δόξα, opinion, credit, honor, glory.

δουλεύειν, to be the slave of, be willing.
δοῦλος, ὁ, slave.
δουλοῦν (= ό-ειν), to enslave; Mid. to subject to myself.

δρᾶν (= ά-ειν), to do, act.

δρόμος, ὁ, running, race-course.
δρόμῳ θεῖν (of a charge of infantry =) to charge at double quick time; to rush to the charge (θεῖν = currere).

δύναμις, ἡ, power.
δύνασθαι (δύναμαι), posse. πολὺ, τοσοῦτον, &c. δύνασθαι (= multum, tantum, &c. posse), to have much (so much, &c.) power.
δυνατός, possible, powerful.

δύσνοος, -ους, ill-disposed (to any body); disaffected (to —, or towards —). (δύς, ill. νοῦς, mind).

δυσόργητος, passionate (δύς, ill. ὀργή, anger).

δυστυχεῖν (= ἐ-ειν), to be unfortunate (δύς, ill. τυχ, shor. root of τυχεῖν, to hit [a mark]).
δυστυχία, misfortune.

δῶρον, τό, gift.

E.

Ἐάγοτ-, see ἄγνυμι.

ἐάν (with Subj.), if.

ἐᾶν (= ά-ειν), to permit.

ἔαρ, ἔαρος, τό, spring.

ἐγγύθεν, from near, near.
ἐγγύς, near.

ἐγείρειν, to awaken.

ἔγκλημα, τό, charge, accusation (ἐγ-καλεῖν).

ἐγκράτεια, self-control.
ἐγκρατής, -ές, continent (ἐν, in. κράτος, strength. κρατεῖν, to be strong.)

ἐγρήγορα, I am awake. Cf. 388.

ἐγχειρίζειν (ἐν. χείρ, hand), to put into the hands; (τί τινι) to hand over.

ἔγχελυς, -υος, ἡ, eel.

ἐγχώριος, national, native (ἐν. χώρα, country).

ἐγώ, I. Pdm. 41.

ἐθέλειν, to wish, be willing.

ἐθίζειν, to accustom.

ἔθνος, -ους, τό, nation.

ἔθος, -ους, τό, custom.

εἰ, if; (in a question), whether.

εἶδος, εἴδους, τό, form.

εἴθε (with Opt.), O that.

εἰκάζειν, to liken.

εἴκειν, to yield.

εἰκῆ, rashly, inconsiderately.

εἰκότως, adv., naturally.

εἰκών, εἰκόν-os, ἡ, statue.
εἱλον. See αἱρεῖν (=έ-ειν). VII.
εἰμί, εἶναι, to be.
εἰμι, ἰέναι, to go. Pres. = I will go.
εἰργειν (gen.), to shut out.
εἰσ-βάλλειν, (1) to throw into; (2) intrans. to fall into. 317. 371.
εἰσ-ειμι, εἰσ-ιέναι, to go into.
εἶτα, then, and then.—next.
εἶτε—εἶτε, sive—eive, whether—or.
εἴωϑα, I am accustomed.—έϑί-
ἑκάς (gen.), far. [ζειν. *384.
ἕκαστος, -η, -ον, each.
ἑκατέρωϑεν, on both sides.
ἐκ-βάλλειν, to throw out. See βάλλειν.
ἐκ-δίδωμι, -διδόναι, to put forth, to publish (a book).
ἐκεῖνος, -η, -o, that, he.
ἐκκλησία, ἡ, assembly (ἐκ. καλεῖν, to call: root κλα, κλη).
ἐκ-κόπτειν, to cut out; cut off.
ἐκ-πέμπειν, to send out.
ἐκτός, without (gen.).
Ἑκτωρ, -ορος, ὁ, Hector.
ἑκών, -οῦσα, -όν, willing.
ἔλαιον, oil.
ἐλάττων, less, fewer.
ἐλαύνειν, to drive. III.
ἔλαφος, ἡ, s'ag.
ἐλάχιστος, least, shortest.
ἐλέγχειν, to examine, correct.
{ ἐλευϑερία, ἡ, freedom, liberty.
  ἐλεύϑερος, free.
  ἐλευϑεροῦν (= ό-ειν), to make free, liberate.
ἐλέφας, ὁ, elephant.
ἐλϑεῖν (ἦλϑον, Aor. of ἔρχομαι). VII.
ἑλκύειν and ἕλκειν, to draw [Fut. ἕλξω; Aor. εἵλκυσα, Inf. ἑλκύσαι; Aor. Pass. εἱλκυσϑην; Perf. Mid. or Pass. εἵλκυσμαι].
{ Ἑλλάς, -άδος, ἡ, Hellas.
  Ἑλλην, -ηνος, ὁ, a Greek.
  Ἑλλησ-ποντος, ὁ, the Hellespont.

{ ἐλπίζειν, to hope, expect.
  ἐλπίς, -ίδος, ἡ, hope.
ἐμ-βάλλειν, to throw or fling in; (2) (intrans.), to fall in or upon = to charge. 317. 371.
ἐμ-βιοῦν (ό-ειν), to live in or at.
ἐμβροχίζω, to catch in a noose.
ἐμ-μένειν (lit. to remain in); to abide by (treaties); to observe, or not to transgress (laws).
ἔμπεδος, firm, lasting, secure (ἐν, in. πέδον, solid ground).
ἔμ-πλεως, n. ων, full (gen.).
ἐμποδών (ἐν, in. πούς, ποδός, foot), adv. in the way of (dat.). ∞ εἶναί τινι, to be in the way of (or a hindrance to) any thing.
ἐμ-ποιεῖν, to cause. ∞ τί τινι, to cause any thing to any body, or in any body.
ἐμ-πόριον, the mart; (at Athens) the custom-house (ἐν, in. πόρος, passage.—ἔμπορος, merchant).
ἐμ-φράττειν, to block up, to bar
{ ἐμ-φύειν, to implant. [(a port).
  ἐμ-φυτεύειν, to implant.
ἐναντίος, opposite.
{ ἐναντιοῦσϑαι (= ό-εσϑαι), to oppose, Dep. Pass.
ἔνδεια, ἡ, want (ἐν. δέω, I need).
ἐν-δείκνυμι, ἐν-δεικνύναι, to show.
ἐν-δύειν, to put on.
ἐν-εδρεύειν, to lie in wait for, plot against (acc.—ἐν. ἕδρα, seat).
ἔνεκα, (propter) for the sake of; on account of (gen.).
{ ἔνϑα, there.
  ἐνϑάδε, hither.
  ἔνϑεν, whence.
ἐνϑυμεῖσϑαι (= έ-εσϑαι), Dep. Pass., to consider, think (ἐν. ϑυμός, mind).
ἐνιαυτός, ὁ, year.
{ ἔνιοι, some.
  ἐνιότε, sometimes.
ἐν-ίστημι, ἐν-ιστάνα:, to put into.
{ ἔννατος, ninth.
  ἐννέα, nine.

258 FIRST GREEK BOOK.

ἐνταῦθα, here, hither (also, *in eum locum*).

ἐν-τέλλειν, -εσθαι, to commission, command, enjoin.

ἐν-τίθημι, ἐν-τιθέναι, to put in, instil.

ἔντομον, insect (ἐν, in. τεμ, root of τέμνειν, to cut).

ἐντός, within (gen.).

ἐν-τυγχάνειν, to fall in with (dat.); to meet. IV.

> ἐνυπνιάζ-ειν (ἐν. ὕπνος), to dream.
> ἐνύπνιον, τό, dream.

ἐξ-άγειν, to carry further out, extend.

ἐξ-αλείφειν, to wipe off, expunge.

ἐξ-αμαυροῦν (= ό-ειν), to obscure utterly.

ἐξ-απατᾶν (= ά-ειν), to deceive utterly (completely).

ἐξ-εῖναι, *licere*, ἔξ-εστι, *licet*, it is lawful, in one's power, one may.

ἔξ-ειμι, ἐξ-ιέναι, to go out.

ἐξ-εῖπον (Aor.), ἐξ-ειπεῖν, to utter.

ἐξ-ετάζειν, to examine.

ἐξῆς, in order.

ἐξ-ισοῦν (= ό-ειν), to make equal (ἴσος, equal).

ἔοικα, I am like. 384.

ἐπ-άγειν, to bring on.

> ἐπ-αινεῖν (= έ-ειν), to praise.
> ἔπ-αινος, ὁ, praise.

Ἐπαμινώνδας, -ου, ὁ, Epaminondas.

ἐπάν (ἐπήν), = ἐπεὶ ἄν, c. subj., when, after.

ἐπεί, when, since, after: = else, otherwise.

ἐπειδάν (= ἐπειδὴ ἄν), c. subj., when, after.

ἐπειδή, since, because, when.

ἕπειν, to be busily engaged in; in prose only in comp. (περιέπειν, διέπειν, &c.); Aor. Act. ἔσπον not used in Att. prose]; Mid. ἕπομαι, to follow [Impf. εἱπόμην; Fut. ἕψομαι; Aor. ἑσπόμην, ἐφεσπόμην; Inf. σπέσθαι; Imp. σποῦ, ἐπίσπου].

ἔπειτα, then.

ἐπ-έρχεσθαι, to come to. VII.

ἐπι-βοηθεῖν (= έ-ειν), to come to the assistance of (dat.).

ἐπι-βουλεύειν, to plot against; have a design against (dat.).

ἐπι-γράφειν, to inscribe.

ἐπι-δείκνυμι, ἐπι-δεικνύναι, to show boastfully; show off for display.

ἐπι-διώκειν, to pursue.

ἐπι-εικής, -ές, fair, equitable, reasonable.

> ἐπιθυμεῖν (= έ-ειν), to desire (ἐπί. θυμός, mind).
> ἐπιθυμία, ἡ, desire.

ἐπιλανθάνεσθαι, to forget. IV.

> ἐπιμέλεια, ἡ, care (ἐπί. μέλει, *curæ est*).
> ἐπιμέλεσθαι, -εῖσθαι, to care for (gen.).
> ἐπιμελητής, superintendent, inspector: οἱ τοῦ ἐμπορίου ἐπιμεληταί, the custom-house officers.

ἐπίνοια, ἡ, device (ἐπί. νοῦς).

> ἐπιορκεῖν (= έ-ειν), to swear falsely (ἐπί. ὅρκος, oath).
> ἐπίορκος, ὁ, perjured.

ἐπι-πίπτειν, to fall upon. VII.

ἐπίρρυτος 2, flowing in or to; well watered.

ἐπί-σημος, distinguished, famous.

ἐπι-σκοπεῖν (= έ-ειν), to look upon.

> ἐπ-ίστασθαι, to know how; to understand.
> ἐπιστήμη, ἡ, knowledge.
> ἐπιστήμων 2 (gen.), acquainted with.

ἐπιστολή, ἡ, epistle (ἐπί. στέλλειν, to send).

ἐπι-τάττειν, to entrust to.

ἐπι-τελεῖν (= έ-ειν), to accomplish.

ἐπι-τίθημι, ἐπι-τιθέναι, to put upon.

ἐπι-τρέπειν, (1) to entrust to (2) to permit, to give up to.

ἐπιχειρεῖν (= έ-ειν), c. dat., to put the hand to something (ἐπί. Χείρ, hand).

ἐπιχείρημα (ἐπιχειρήματ-ος), τό, attempt.

ἕπομαι. Comp. ἕπω.

ἐπ-όμνυμι, to swear by. IX.

ἔπος,-ους,τό, word: pl. epic poetry.

ἐπωάζειν (ἐπί, on. ᾠόν, egg), to sit; to be sitting.

ἐρᾶν (= ά-ειν), to love.

ἐργάζεσθαι, to work, perform.
ἐργαστήριον, τό, workshop.
ἐργάτης, laborer, cultivator.
ἔργον, τό; work, action.

ἐρείδειν, to prop; to lean against.

ἔρεσθαι. I.

ἐρίζειν. to contend with.
ἔρις, -ιδος, ἡ, contention.

ἕρμαιον, a windfall, a godsend: a lucky discovery (supposed to be sent by Hermes).

ἑρμηνεύς, interpreter.
Ἑρμῆς, -οῦ, ὁ, Hermes, Mercury.

ἐρρωμένος, strong.

ἔρυμα, -ατος, τό, defence.

ἔρχεσθαι, to go, come. VII

ἔρως, -ωτος, ὁ, love.

ἐρωτᾶν (= ά-ειν), to ask.

ἐσήγησις, ἡ, introduction (ἐς. ἡγεῖσθαι, to lead).

ἐσθής, -ῆτος, ἡ, dress.

ἐσθίειν, to eat.

ἐσθλός, noble, good.

ἔσπλους (= ἔσπλοος), ὁ, the entrance to a harbor (ἐς. πλεῖν, navigare).

ἔστε, until.

ἔσχατος, last, extreme.

ἕτερος, the other; alter.

ἔτι, besides, moreover, still.

ἔτος, -ους, τό, year.

εὖ, well. εὖ πράττειν, to be doing well; to be prosperous. εὖ ποιεῖν, to confer benefits on (benefacere, prodesse).

Εὔβοια, ἡ, Euboea.

εὐ-γενής, of high birth.

εὐδαιμονεῖν (= έ-ειν), to be fortunate (εὐ. δαίμων, deity).
εὐδαιμονία, ἡ, happiness.
εὐδαιμονίζειν, to account happy.
εὐδαιμόνως, fortunately.
εὐδαίμων, -ονος, fortunate, happy.

εὐδοκιμεῖν (= έ-ειν), to be celebrated, honored, popular (εὐ. δοκ-, root of δοκεῖν, videri).

εὐεργεσία, ἡ, beneficence.
εὐεργετεῖν (= έ-ειν), to benefit, confer benefits on (εὐ. ἔργον, work).

εὐήθης, simple, foolish (εὐ, well. ἦθος, character).

εὐθύς, adv., immediately.

εὔκλεια, ἡ, fame, good report.

εὐ-λαβεῖσθαι (= έ-εσθαι), Dep. Pass., to be cautious, to beware of;—to reverence (εὐ, well. λαβ, short root of λαμβάνειν, to take).

εὐμενῶς, in a friendly way; kindly.

εὔνοος, εὔνους 2, well-disposed; kind; kindly-disposed (to a person). (εὐ, well. νοῦς).

εὐπετῶς, adv., easily (εὐ, well. πετ-, root of πίπτειν = πιπέτ-ειν, to fall).

Εὐριπίδης, -ους, ὁ, Euripides.

εὑρίσκειν, to find. V.

εὐρύς, -εῖα, -ύ, broad.

εὐσεβεῖν (= έ-ειν), to reverence (εὐ. σέβειν, venerari).
εὐσεβής, -ές, pious.

εὐτυχεῖν (= έ-ειν), to be fortunate or prosperous.
εὐτυχής, -ές, fortunate (εὐ, well. τύχη, fortune).
εὐτυχία, ἡ, good fortune.

εὔχ-εσθαι, to pray.
εὐχή, ἡ, prayer, request.

εὐψυχία, spirit, courage (εὐ, well. ψυχή, spirit.

ἐφόδιον, τό, travelling money. (ἐπί, for. ὁδός, road).

ἔχειν, to have; c. inf., to be able. ἔχω has root ἐχ-; the rough breathing is changed into the smooth, whilst the χ remains; but *returns*, when it disappears: hence *fut.* ἕξ-ω (with *aspirate*). οὕτως ἔχειν (= *ita se habere*), to be so affected *or* disposed; εὖ *or* καλῶς ἔχειν (= *bene se habere*), to be well; to be well off: for any thing, τινός. VII.

ἔχθρος, hostile: used *substantively*, = an enemy.

ἕως, as long as; until.

ἕως, -ω, ἡ, dawn, morning.

Z.

Ζῆν (= ἀ-ειν), to live. 346.

ζηλοῦν (= ό-ειν), to emulate; to pursue emulously (ζῆλος, emulation).

ζημία, ἡ (*damnum*), hurt, loss, injury, calamity.

ζημιοῦν (= ό-ειν), to punish.

ζητεῖν (= έ-ειν), to seek.

ζωή, ἡ, life.

ζῶον, τό, animal.

ζωοτόκος, viviparous (τεκ, τοκ, short roots of τίκτειν, to give birth to).

ζωός, alive.

H.

Ἦ (in questions), cf. K. 344. 5.

ἤ, or, than; ἤ—ἤ, aut—aut.

ἥβη, ἡ, youth.

ἡγεῖσθαι (= έ-εσθαι), to lead, to think.

ἡγεμών, όνος, ὁ, ἡ, leader.

ἥδεσθαι, to rejoice:

ἡδέως, *adv.* pleasantly, gladly.

ἡδονή, ἡ, pleasure.

ἡδύς, -εῖα, -ύ, sweet, pleasant.

ἤδη, already, at once; before now.

ἦθος, -ους, τό, habit, character, disposition.

ἥκιστα, least of all.

ἥκω, I am come; ἥξω, will come.

ἠλιθιότης, (-τητος), ἡ, silliness.

ἡλικία, ἡ, age.

ἡλίκος, as great as.

ἥλιος, ὁ, sun.

ἡμέρα, ἡ, day.

ἡμεροδρόμος, ὁ, courier (δραμ, root used to supply the tenses of τρέχω, *curro*).

ἡμερότης, ἡμερύτητος, ἡ, tameness.

ἤν, c. subj., if. (= ἐάν.)

ἡνίκα, when.

Ἥρα, ἡ, Hera *or* Juno.

Ἡρακλῆς, -έους, ὁ, Hercules (201).

ἥρως, -ωος, ὁ, hero.

ἧσθαι, to sit. Pdm. 71.

ἧσσον (later Att. ἧττον), less.

ἡσυχάζειν, to be quiet, still.

ἡσυχία, quietness, &c. ἡσυχίαν ἔχειν *or* ἄγειν, to remain quiet, to keep quiet.

ἥσυχος 2, quiet.

ἧττα, ἡ, defeat.

ἡττᾶσθαι (= ά-εσθαι), to be defeated; to be inferior to (gen.).

Θ.

Θάλασσα, Θάλαττα, ἡ, sea.

Θάλλειν, to bloom.

Θάνατος, ὁ, death.

Θάπτειν, to bury.

Θαρραλέως, *adv.*, boldly.

Θαρρεῖν (= έ-ειν), to be of good courage; Θ. τινι, to have confidence in; Θ. τινα, not to be afraid of a person; Θ. τι, to endure (not to fear) something.

Θαρρούντως, confidently.

Θᾶττον, more quickly (neut. of compar. adj.). 391.

Θαυμάζειν, to wonder, wonder at, admire, be surprised at. Θ. τινά *or* τι = to admire: τινός, to be surprised or wonder at (mostly with blame).

Θεά, ἡ, goddess.
Θεᾶσθαι (= ά-εσθαι), Dep. Mid., to behold.
Θεῖν (= έ-ειν), to run.
  Θεῖον, τό, deity.
  Θεῖος, godlike, divine.
Θέλγειν, to charm, soothe.
Θεμέλιον, τό, foundation (Θε, short root of τίθημι).
Θεμιστοκλῆς, -έους, ὁ, Themistocles (201).
Θεός, ὁ, God.
  Θεραπεία, ἡ, care.
  Θεραπεύειν, to honor, pay court to.
  Θερίζειν, to reap.
  Θέρος, -ους, τό, summer.
Θεσσαλός, Thessalian.
Θῆβαι, αἱ, Thebes.
Θήγειν, to whet, to sharpen.
Θῆλυς, -εια, -υ, female.
  Θήρ, -ός, ὁ, wild beast.
  Θήρα, chase, hunting. Θήραν ποιεῖσθαι, to hunt.
  Θηρεύειν, to hunt.
  Θηρίον, (any) wild beast: also, τὰ Θηρία = game, any beast that is hunted.
  Θηριώδης (Θηρίον. εἶδος), brutish.
Θής, Θητ-ός, ὁ, paid laborer.
Θησαυρός, ὁ, treasure.
Θησεύς, -έως, ὁ, Theseus.
Θνητός, mortal (Θνα, root of Θνήσκειν).
Θρίξ, τριχός, ἡ, hair.
Θυγάτηρ, -τρος, ἡ, daughter. 183.
  Θύειν, to sacrifice.
  Θῦμα (Θυματ-ος), τό, sacrifice, offering.
Θυμός, ὁ, mind.
Θύρα, ἡ, door.
Θύρσος, ὁ, a thyrsus.
Θυσία, ἡ, sacrifice (Θύειν).

Ἰᾶσθαι (= ά-εσθαι), Dep. Mid., to heal, cure.
ἰατρός, ὁ, physician.
ἰδέα, ἡ, appearance.
  ἰδίᾳ, privately; in one's private character or life.
  ἴδιος, one's own.
ἱδρύειν, to build.
ἱδρώς, -ῶτος, ὁ, sweat.
  ἱέρεια, ἡ, priestess.
  ἱερεύς, -έως, ὁ, priest.
  ἱερόν, τό, victim, temple.
  ἱερός, sacred to (gen.).
ἵημι, ἱέναι, to send forth; to emit; to utter. Pdm. 67.
  ἱκανός, sufficient, able.
  ἱκανῶς, sufficiently, adequately.
  ἱκέτης, -ου, ὁ, suppliant.
  ἱκνεῖσθαι (= έ-εσθαι). See ἀφικνεῖσθαι.
ἰκτῖνος, ὁ, kite.
ἵλεως, -ων, merciful, propitious.
ἱμάτιον, τό, garment; *especially* the outer garment, *pallium*.
ἵνα, (1) where; (2) in order that; that.
  ἱππεύς, -έως, ὁ, horseman, horse-soldier.
  ἵππος, ὁ, horse; ἡ, cavalry.
ἴσος, equal.
ἵστημι, ἱστάναι, to place. For the meaning cf. 396.
  ἰσχύειν, to be strong, to avail.
  ἰσχυρός, strong.
  ἰσχυρῶς, severely.
ἰχθύς, -ύος, ὁ, fish.
ἴχνος, -ους, τό, track, trace.

K.

Καθαίρειν, to purify.
καθ-έζεσθαι, to sit down. Fut. καθεδοῦμαι.
καθ-εύδειν, to sleep.
καθ-ῆσθαι, to sit down. Pdm. 71.

καϑ-ίστημι, -ιστάναι, to establish.
καί, and, even : καί—καί, both— and (et—et).
καινός, new.
καιρός, the right time, season : εἰς καιρόν, at the right time ; opportunely.
κακία, ἡ, vice, flaw.
κακίζειν, to worst (κακός, bad).
κάκιον, worse (as adv.) : neut. adj. from κακίων, comp. of κακός.
κακός, bad, wicked, cowardly.
κακότης, ἡ, wickedness.
κακουργεῖν (= έ-ειν), acc., to do evil to ; to harm ; to ravage.
κακοῦργος, ὁ, evil-doer.
κακοῦν (= ό-ειν), to treat ill, hurt ; to injure or ravage (a country).
κακῶς, adv., badly, ill.
καλεῖν (= έ-ειν), to call, name.
Καλλίας, -ου, ὁ, Callias.
κάλλος, -ους, τό, beauty.
καλοκἀγαϑία, ἡ, rectitude, honorableness (καλοκἀγαϑός = καλὸς καὶ ἀγαϑός).
καλός, beautiful, honorable, good.
καλῶς, adv., well, honorably.
καλύπτ-ειν, to cover, hide, &c.
κάμηλος, ὁ, ἡ, camel.
κάμνειν (= laborare), to toil ; to be suffering or ill. III.
κἄν, even if = καὶ ἐάν.
καρδία, ἡ, heart.
καρπός, ὁ, fruit ; wrist.
κάρτα, very.
καρτερία, ἡ, endurance ; patience.
Καρχηδών, -όνος, ἡ, Carthage.
κατα-γελᾶν (= ά-ειν), to laugh at (gen.).
κατα-δύειν, to go down.
κατα-κλαίειν, to bewail.
κατα-κλείειν, to shut.
κατα-κρύπτειν, to hide.
κατα-λείπειν, to leave behind.
κατα-λύειν, to loosen, dissolve, destroy.

κατα-μεϑύσκ-ειν, to make drunk Fut. -μεϑύσω.
κατα-μένειν, to remain behind (in a country).
κατα-νοεῖν (= έ-ειν), to perceive, to discover.
κατα-πηδᾶν (= ά-ειν), to leap down.
κατα-πλήττειν, to astonish.
κατα-σκάπτειν, to dig down.
κατα-σκευάζειν, to prepare.
κατα-στρέφ-εσϑαι, to overthrow (for oneself) ; to subdue, to conquer.
κατα-τείνειν, to stretch tight.
κατα-τίϑημι, -τιϑέναι, to lay down.
κατα-φλέγειν, to burn up.
κατα-φρονεῖν (= έ-ειν), to despise (gen.).
κατα-φυγή, ἡ, refuge.
κατ-έχειν, to restrain.
κατηγορεῖν (= έ-ειν), to accuse.
κατήγορος, ὁ, accuser (κατά. ἀγορά, assembly, marketplace).
κάτω, below.
κεῖμαι, κεῖσϑαι, to lie down ; (of a law) κεῖσϑαι = to be enacted. Pdm. 71.
κελεύειν, to order, bid.
κενοδοξία, vain-glory ; vanity (κενός, empty. δόξα, opinion, glory).
κενός, empty, groundless, vain.
κέντρον, τό, prick, sting.
κεράννυμι, κεραννύναι, to mix.
κέρας, τό, horn. Pdm. 20.
κερδαίνειν, to gain ; [Perf. κεκέρδακα.]
κέρδος, -ους, τό, gain.
κεφαλή, ἡ, head.
κήδεσϑαι, to care for (gen.).
κῆπος, ὁ, garden.
κηρός, ὁ, wax.
κῆρυξ, -υκος, ὁ, herald.
κηρύττειν, to proclaim (by a herald).

GREEK AND ENGLISH INDEX. 263

{ κινδυνεύειν, to be in danger ; to incur *or* brave danger.
κίνδυνος, ὁ, danger.

κισσός, κιττός, ὁ, ivy.

κλαίειν, to weep.

{ κλείειν, to shut (Perf. pass. κέκλεισμαι and κέκλειμαι).
κλεῖθρον, bolt, bar.

κλέπτειν, to steal (Fut. κλέψω and κλέψομαι ; κέκλοφα. Aor. 2. Pass. ἐκλάπην).

κλίνειν, to bend.

κοῖλος, hollow.

{ κοινός, common : τὸ κοινόν, commonwealth.
κοινωνία, ἡ, communion, participation (τινός).

κόκκος, ου (granum), the seed (of a pomegranate, &c.).

κόκκυξ, κόκκῡγ-ος, ὁ, cuckoo.

κολάζειν, to chastise, punish.

{ κολακεύειν, w. acc., to flatter.
κόλαξ, κόλακ-ος, ὁ, flatterer.

κόλπος, ὁ, bosom.

κομίζειν, to bring.

κόπτειν, to cut.

κόραξ, κόρακ-ος, ὁ, crow *or* raven.

κόρη, damsel.

Κορίνθιος, ὁ, Corinthian.

κοσμεῖν (= έ-ειν), to adorn, to order *or* arrange (harmoniously).

κοῦφος, light.

κράζειν, to cry out [Fut. κεκράζομαι], κέκρᾱγα.

κράνος, -ους, τό, helmet.

{ κρατεῖν (= έ-ειν), gen., to have power over ; to prevail, conquer.
κράτος, -ους, τό, strength.

κρέας, τό, flesh.

κρείσσων or (later) κρείττων, more powerful, better. Note 13.

{ κρίνειν, to judge.
κριτής, -οῦ, ὁ, judge.

Κροῖσος, ὁ, Crœsus.

κρόταφος, ὁ, temple.

κρύπτειν, to conceal, hide.

κτᾶσθαι (= ά-εσθαι), to acquire ; κέκτημαι = possideo.

κτείνειν, to kill ; usually ἀποκτείνειν.

κτείς, κτενός, ὁ, comb.

κτῆμα, -ατος, τό (κτᾶσθαι), possession.

κτίζειν, to found.

{ κυβευτής, -οῦ, dicer, gambler.
κύβος, ὁ, a die, cube.

κύκλος, circle.

κύπελλον, τό, goblet.

κυριεύειν, to be master of (gen.)

Κυρῖνος, Quirinus.

κύριος, having authority. κύριός εἰμι ποιεῖν τι, I have a right to do it.

κυρίττειν, to butt.

Κῦρος, ὁ, Cyrus.

κύων, κυνός, ὁ, ἡ, dog. Note 9

κωλύειν, to hinder.

κωφός, dumb.

Λ.

Λαγώς, -ώ, ὁ, hare.

Λακεδαιμόνιος, ὁ, Lacedæmonian

λακτίζειν (fut. ίσω), to kick (at).

{ λαλεῖν (= έ-ειν), to talk.
λάλος 2, talkative.

λαμβάνειν, to take, receive. iv.

{ λαμπρός, brilliant, bright.
λαμπρύνειν, to brighten ; Mid., to brighten (something of my own).

λανθάνειν, to be concealed from. iv.

λάρναξ, λάρνακ-ος, ἡ, chest, coffin.

λέαινα, ἡ, lioness.

λέγειν, (1) to say, tell,—call. (2) to collect.—Aor. Pass. ἐλέχθην and ἐλέγην : also to read (what is written) out to another.

λειμών, λειμῶν-ος, ὁ, meadow.

λείπειν, to leave ; leave behind [Aor. ἔλιπον : Perf. λέλοιπα].

λέων, λέοντ-ος, ὁ, lion.

λεώς, ὁ, people. *Att. decl.*

λήθη, obliviousness, forgetfulness.

{ ληρεῖν (= έ-ειν), to talk nonsense.

λῆρος, (mere) talk, (mere) nonsense; after which πρός =
to, i. e. in comparison of. }

λῃστής, -οῦ, ὁ, robber.

λίαν, very.

λίθος, ὁ, stone.

λίμην, ἡ, marsh, lake.

λῑμός, ὁ, hunger.

λόγος, ὁ, word, speech, reason.

λοιδορεῖν (= έ-ειν), to scold, rail
at (Mid. c. dat.).

λοιμός, ὁ, plague, pestilence.

λοιπός (λείπ-ειν), remaining.

λού-ειν, to wash; Mid., to wash
(myself or some one belonging
to me).

λουτρόν, bath.

λόφος, ὁ, crest.

λυγρός, sad.

λύειν, to loose, dissolve; ·repeal
(a law); break (a truce); dis-
miss (an assembly).

λύκος, ὁ, wolf.

Λυκοῦργος, ὁ, Lycurgus.

λυμαίνεσθαι (acc.), to abuse, maltreat.

{ λῡπεῖν (= έ-ειν), to distress.
λύπη, ἡ, sorrow, grief. }

λυσιτελεῖν (= έ-ειν), dat., to be
useful to (λύειν, to solve. τέλος, end, object).

λωποδύτης, ου, cutpurse, footpad
(properly a filcher of clothes.
λῶπος, or -η, robe, mantle. δύ-
ειν, to get into).

λῴων, better. Note 13.

M.

{ Μάθημα, τό, thing learnt, lesson
(μαθ-, short root of μανθάνειν, discere).

μαθητής, οῦ, ὁ, a disciple, pupil. }

μάκαρ, -αρος, happy.

Μακεδονία, ἡ, Macedonia.

Μακεδονικός, Macedonian.

Μακεδών, -όνος, ὁ, a Macedonian:

μακρός, long.

μαλακός, soft.

{ μάλιστα, most, especially.
μᾶλλον, more, rather (potius). }

μανθάνειν, to learn. IV.

μανία, ἡ, madness.

μάντις, -εως, ὁ, prophet.

{ μαρτυρεῖν (= έ-ειν), μαρτύρε-
σθαι, to bear testimony.
μάρτυς, -τυρος, ὁ, witness. }

{ μάχαιρα, hunting-knife; cutlass (short sword).

μάχεσθαι, to fight. Fut. μαχοῦμαι (= μαχέσομαι). Aor.
ἐμαχεσάμην. Perf. μεμάχη-
μαι.

μάχη, ἡ, battle. }

{ μέγας, -άλη, -α, great.

μέγεθος, -ους, τό, greatness;
magnitude.

μέγιστος, sup. of μέγας, great. }

μέθη, ἡ, drunkenness.

μεθ-ίημι, μεθ-ιέναι, to let go.

μεθύειν, to be drunk.

μείζων, comp. of μέγας, great.
Note 13.

μειράκιον, τό, boy, lad (of about
fourteen).

μέλας, -αινα, -αν, black.

μέλει, it concerns; curae est (dat.
of pers., gen. of thing).

{ μέλι, -ιτος, τό, honey.
μέλιττα, ἡ, a bee. }

μέλλειν, to be about (or, be going)
to.

μέλος, -ους, τό, limb; song.

μέμφεσθαι, c. acc. to blame; c.
dat. to reproach.

μέν—δέ (indeed),—but.

μένειν, to remain; c. acc. to a-
wait; wait for.

{ μερίζειν, to divide.

μέριμνα, ἡ, care.

μέρος, -ους, τό, part. }

μεσημβρία, ἡ, mid-day (μέσος, middle. ἡμέρα, day).
μέσος, middle.

μεστός, full (gen.).

μετα-βάλλειν, tŏ change.
μετα-βολή, ἡ, change.

μετα-δίδωμι, -διδόναι, to give a share of (gen.).

μεταξύ, between (gen.).

μετα-πέμπεσθαι, to send for.

μετα-τίθημι, -τιθέναι, to change; transpose.

μετ-έχειν, to share in, take part in (gen.).

μέτοικος, ὁ, resident-foreigner.

μετρεῖν (= έ-ειν), to measure.
μετρίως, adv., moderately.
μέτρον, τό, measure.

μέχρι, until; as prep. up to.

μή, not. On μή, μὴ οὐ, after expressions of fear, cf. K. 318. 7.

μηδαμοῦ, nowhere; μ. εἶναι, to be of no value.

μηδαμῶς (nequaquam), by no means.

Μήδεια, ἡ, Medea.

μηδείς, -εμία, -έν, no (one), nobody.

μηδέποτε, never.

μήν, -νός, ὁ, mouth.

μήποτε, never.

μήπω, not yet.

μηρός, thigh.

μήτε—μήτε, neither—nor.

μήτηρ, -τρος, ἡ, mother. 183.

μηχανᾶσθαι (= ά-εσθαι), Dep. Mid., to contrive, devise.
μηχανή, contrivance.

μιαίνειν, to pollute.
μιᾰρός, unclean, impure, abominable (of persons).

μικρός, small; μικρῷ (by) a little: μικροῦ, within a little; almost.

μιμεῖσθαι (= έ-εσθαι), to imitate.
μιμητής, οῦ, ὁ, imitator.

Μίνως, -ω, ὁ, Minos.

μισεῖν (= έ-ειν), to hate.

μισθός, ὁ, reward; pay.
μισθωτός (mercenarius), hireling; a mercenary.

μνᾶ, ᾶς, ἡ, mina.

μνημεῖον, monument.
μνήμων, -ονος, of retentive memory.

μοῖρα, ἡ, fate; share.

μόλις, with difficulty.

μοναρχία, ἡ, monarchy (μόνος, only. ἀρχή, government).
μόνον, only.
μόνος, alone.

μόριον, part, portion.

Μοῦσα, ἡ, a Muse.
μουσική, ἡ, music (sc. τέχνη).

μυελός, ὁ, marrow.

μῦθος, ὁ, tale, legend.

μυκτήρ, μυκτῆρ-ος, ὁ, nostril, trunk (of elephant).

μυρίος, innumerable.

μωρός, foolish, a fool.

N.

Ναυμαχία, ἡ, sea-fight (μάχη, battle).
ναῦς, ἡ, ship.
ναύτης, ου, sailor.
ναυτικός, nautical: ναυτικόν, a fleet; a navy.

νεανίας, -ου, ὁ, a youth.

νέμειν, to divide, distribute, or allot [Fut. νεμῶ and νεμήσω: Aor. ἔνειμα: Perf. νενέμηκα: Aor. Pass. ἐνεμήθην and -έθην].

νέμεσις, εως, ἡ, just - resentment; hence, avenging-fate.

νέος, young.

νεοττεύειν (or νεοσσεύειν), to hatch its young; to breed. (We may translate it *to build its nest*, since *we* should rather refer to that *preparatory act*.)

νεόττιον, young bird (pl. **young** ones).

νεώς, -ώ, ὁ, temple.
νή. yes, by — (in swearing).
νῆιτος, ἡ, island.
{ νικᾶν (= ά-ειν), to conquer.
{ νική. ἡ, victory.
νίφει, it snows.
νόησις, -εως, ἡ, intellectual faculty, intellect (νοεῖν, to perceive).
{ νομίζειν, to think.
{ νόμισμα, τό, coin, money.
{ νομοθετεῖν (= έ-ειν), to legislate ; to make laws.
{ νομοθέτης, ου, ὁ, lawgiver (νόμος, law. ?ε-, original root of τιθέναι, ponere).
{ νόμος. ὁ, law.
νόος = νοῦς, ὁ, reason ; intelligence ; mind : ἐν νῷ ἔχειν (in animo habere), to purpose, intend.
{ νοσεῖν (= έ-ειν), to be sick.
{ νόσος, ἡ, disease.
νύκτωρ (adv.), by night.
νῦν, νυνί, now.
νύξ, νυκτ-ός, ἡ, night.

Ξ.

Ξένος, ὁ, stranger, guest, host.
Ξενοφῶν, -ῶντος, ὁ, Xenophon.
ξίφος, -ους, τό, sword.

O.

Ὀβολός, οῦ, ὁ, an obolus (a small coin).
ὅδε. ἥδε, τόδε, this.
ὁδός, ἡ. way, road.
ὁδούς, ὀδόντ-ος, ὁ, tooth.
ὀδύρεσθαι, tò mourn.
ὅθεν, whence.
οἷ, whither.
οἶδα (= novi), I know. Pdm. 70.
οἴεσθαι, to think.

οἰκεῖν (= έ-ειν), to dwell.
οἰκεῖος, belonging to ; own ; intimate.
οἰκέτης, -ου, ὁ, domestic ; servant.
οἴκησις, -εως, ἡ, dwelling.
οἰκία, ἡ, house ; family.
οἰκίδιον, small house, house.
οἰκίζειν, to colonize.
οἰκοδομεῖν (= έ-ειν), to build (a house). (δέμειν, to build).
οἶκος, ὁ, house.
οἰκτείρειν, w. acc., to pity.
οἶμαι, I think. It is used instead of the longer form οἴομαι: principally when inserted parenthetically ; = opinor, credo. See οἴεσθαι.
οἶνος. ὁ, wine.
ὄϊς, ὄϊος, ὁ, ἡ, sheep.
οἴχεσθαι, to depart : οἴχομαι = abii.
{ ὀλιγαρχία, oligarchy (ἀρχή, government).
{ ὀλίγος, little. ὀλίγοι, few.
ὄλλυμι, ὀλλύναι, to destroy. IX.
ὅλος, whole, complete, perfect.
ὀλοφύρεσθαι, to pity.
ὅλως (omnino), at all ; altogether — in general.
Ὅμηρος, ὁ, Homer.
{ ὁμῑλεῖν (= έ-ειν), c. dat., to associate with.
{ ὁμιλία, ἡ, intercourse with.
ὀμνύειν, to swear. See ὄμνυμι, IX.
ὁμοίως, in like manner.
{ ὁμολογεῖν (= έ-ειν), to agree with, admit (ὁμός [poet.], same. λέγειν. λόγος).
{ ὁμολογία, confession, concession.
ὁμόνοια (ὁμός. νοῦς), concord, unity.
{ ὀνειδίζειν, Fut. -σω, to reproach (τί τινι).
{ ὄνειδος, -ους, τό, reproach.

Ὀνήτωρ, Onêtor, prop. name.

ὀνίνημι, ὀνινάναι, to benefit.

ὄνομα, -ατος, τό, name.
ὀνομάζειν, to name.

ὄνος, ὁ, ἡ, ass.

ὄντως, really (ὀντ-, root of ὤν, being).

ὄνυξ, ὀνυκ-ος, ὁ, claw, talon.

ὀξύρροπος (ὀξύς. ῥέπειν, vergere), quick.
ὀξύς, -εῖα, -ύ, sharp, sour; quick, hasty.

ὄπη, whither, where.

ὀπίσω, back.

ὁπλή, hoof.

ὁπλίτης, -ου, ὁ, heavy-armed soldier, hoplite.
ὅπλον, τό, weapon.

ὅποι, whither.

ὁποῖος, qualis, of what sort.

ὁποσονοῦν, how great soever, how long soever. [Since it means of what magnitude soever, it may sometimes mean however short.]
ὁπόσος, quantus, as great as.

ὁπόταν, c. subj., when.

ὁπότε, when, since.

ὅπου, where.

ὅπως, how, that.

ὁρᾶν (= ά-ειν), to see, look.

ὀργή, ἡ, anger.
ὀργίζεσθαι, Dep. Pass., to be angry (dat.).

ὄρεξις, -εως, ἡ, a longing after; a yearning for (ὀρέγεσθαι, to seek for; to desire).

Ὀρέστης, ου, ὁ, Orestes.

ὀρθός, straight, right.
ὀρθοῦν (= ό-ειν), to make straight.

ὁρίζειν, to fix, limit, define.

ὅρκος, ὁ, oath.

ὁρμᾶν (= ά-ειν), to rush.

ὀρνιθο-θήρας, -α, ὁ, bird-catcher (θηρᾶν, to chase).
ὄρνις, -ιθος, ὁ, ἡ, bird.

ὄρος, -ους, τό, mountain.

ὄρυγ-μα, τό, pit (fovea).
ὀρύττειν, to dig [Fut. ὀρύξω: Perf. ὀρώρυχα (with Att. redupl.): Perf. Mid. or Pass. ὀρώρυγμαι].

ὅσιος, holy.

ὅσος, as great as, as much as; after demonstratives, as.

ὀστέον, -οῦν, τό, bone.　　[who.

ὅστις, ἥτις, ὅ τι, or ὅ,τι, whoever,

ὄσφρησις, -εως, ἡ, (sense of) smell (ὀσφρε, shorter root of ὀσφραίνεσθαι, to smell).

ὅταν, c. subj., when (= ὅτε ἄν).

ὅτε, when.

ὅτι, that, because.

οὐ, not.

οὗ, where.

οὐδαμῇ, nowhere.

οὐδέ, not even (ne—quidem).

οὐδείς, -εμία, -έν, no (one).

οὐδέποτε, never.

οὐκ, not.

οὐκέτι, no longer.

οὖν, therefore, then.

οὔποτε, οὐδέποτε, never.

οὔπω, never yet.

οὐρά, ἡ, tail.

οὐρανός, heaven.

οὖς, ὠτός, τό, ear.

οὐσία, possession (ουσ-, root of fem. participle of εἶναι).

οὔτε—οὔτε, neither—nor.

οὔτω(ς), thus, so.

οὐχ, not.

ὀφείλειν, to owe.

ὀφθαλμός, ὁ, eye.

ὀφλισκάνειν, to owe. ὀφλισκάνειν μωρίαν = to incur the imputation of folly. ὀφλήσω. ὤφληκα. —ὤφλον.

ὄχλος, ὁ, a crowd, mob; the common people (plebs).

ὀχυροῦν (= ό-ειν), to make-fast, bar, &c.

ὀψέ, late.

ὄψις, -εως, ἡ, (power of) sight visage.

Π.

Πάγκακος, thoroughly bad (πᾶς. κακός).

πάγος, ὁ, hill.

{ παιάν, -ᾶνος, ὁ, war-song.
{ παιανίζ-ειν, to sing the Pæan.

{ παιδεύειν, to educate, train, instruct (παιδ, root of παῖς, boy).
{ παιδίον, τό, little child.
{ παιδονόμος, ου, ὁ, the inspector of the boys (a magistrate at Sparta.—νόμος, law).

παίειν, to strike.

{ παίζειν, to play.
{ παῖς, -δός, ὁ, ἡ, child, boy.

{ πάλαι, formerly, long ago.   οἱ πάλαι, the ancients.
{ παλαιός, ancient.   οἱ π., the men of old.

πάλιν, again.

Παλλάδιον, Palladium.

πάμπολυ, very much indeed (πᾶς. πολύς).

παντάπᾶσι(ν), wholly, quite.

πανταχοῦ, πανταχῆ, every where, in all respects.

παντελῶς, perfectly (πᾶς, omnis. τέλος, finis).

παντοδαπός, of every kind.

πάντως, wholly.

πάνυ, altogether, quite, very

παρα-βαίνειν, to transgress.

παρ-αγγέλλειν, to order.

παρ-αινεῖν (= έ-ειν), dat., to advise, to exhort.

παρα-καλεῖν (= έ-ειν), to call to ; to exhort.

παρά-νομος 2, contrary to law.

παρα-πλήσιος, like.

παρα-σκευάζειν, to prepare ; Mid. provide any thing (for myself).

παρα-τίθημι, -τιθέναι, to place beside, provide ; to place on the table (apponere).

πάρδαλις, -εως, ἡ, pard, panther.

πάρ-ειμι, Inf. παρ-εῖναι, to be present : πάρεστι(ν), it is lawful ; in one's power.

πάρ-ειμι, Inf. παρ-ιέναι, to go by near.

παρ-έρχεσθαι, to go by. VII.

παρ-έχειν, to offer, grant.

παρ-ίημι, -ιέναι, to let pass, neglect.

παρ-ίστημι, -ιστάναι, to place beside.

παρ-οξύνειν, to encourage, incite (ὀξύς, acer).

{ παρρησία, ἡ, frankness ; boldness of speech (παρά. ρε, root of the obsol. present ρέω, dico ; whence εἴ-ρη-κα. ρη-θείς, &c.).
{ παρρησιάζ-εσθαι, to use frankness or boldness of speech.

παρών = præsens. Partcp. of παρεῖναι.

πᾶς, πᾶσα, πᾶν, in sing.   (1) without article : every ; all manner of : hence sometimes all imaginable ; extreme. (2) with article : πᾶς ὁ — = the whole : sometimes ὁ πᾶς —.   In plur. πάντες (οἱ) —, all.   οἱ πάντες, in all.

πάσχειν, to suffer. VII.

{ πατήρ, -τρός, ὁ, father. 183.
{ πατρίς, -ίδος, ἡ, (native) country.

παύειν, to cause to cease, stop, put an end to ; Mid. to cease [Aor. Pass. ἐπαύσθην ; Perf. Mid. or Pass. πέπαυμαι, tr cease ; Third Fut. πεπαύσομαι will cease].

πεδίον, τό, a plain.

πεζός (pedes), foot-soldier.

{ πείθειν, to persuade ; πείθομαι, I am persuaded, I obey (dat.) [Aor. ἐπείσθην, I obeyed].
{ πειθώ, -οῦς, ἡ, persuasiveness, persuasion, obedience.

πεινῆν (= ά-ειν), to hunger. be hungry. On the contraction into η, cf. 346.

πειρᾶσθαι (= ά-εσθαι), Dep. Pass. to try, endeavor.

πέλεκῦς, -εως, ὁ, hatchet, axe, battle-axe.

⎰ Πελοποννησιακός, Peloponnesian.
⎱ Πελοπόννησος, ἡ, Peloponnesus.

πελταστής, ὁ, targeteer.

πέμπειν, to send.

⎰ πένεσθαι, to be poor.
⎱ πένης, -ητος, ὁ, ἡ, poor.

πενθεῖν (= έ-ειν), to grieve.

πενία, ἡ, poverty.

πέντε (indecl.), five.

πέρδιξ, πέρδῐκ-ος, ὁ, ἡ, partridge.

περι-βάλλειν, to throw round. Mid. to throw round oneself; to surround oneself with; ∽ τάφρον, to entrench themselves (or their position).

περιβόητος (περί, about. βοᾶν. clamare), talked-about : ∽ εἶναι, to be the common talk.

περίβολος, ὁ, circuit (of walls, &c.). (περί, round. βάλλω, throw).

Περικλῆς, -έους, ὁ, Pericles.

περι-ορᾶν (= ά-ειν), to overlook, permit, allow.

περίπλοος, -ους, ὁ, voyage round (περί. πλεῖν, to sail).

περιῤῥεῖν (= έ-ειν), to flow round (ῥεῖν, to flow).

περι-τίθημι, -τιθέναι, to put or set round.

περιττός, beyond the usual number, more than sufficient.

πέτρα, ἡ, rock.

πῆ ; where ? whither ?

πήγνυμι, to fix, make firm (πέπηγα, I am fixed).

πῆχυς, -εως, ὁ, elbow, fore-arm, cubit.

πιαίνειν, to fatten.

πίνειν, to drink. VII.

πιπράσκειν, to sell.

πίπτειν, to fall. VII.

πίσσᾰ, Att. πίττᾰ, pitch.

⎰ πιστεύειν, to trust, believe.
⎱ πιστός, trustworthy, faithful.

πλάσσειν, to form.

Πλάταια, ἡ, Platæa : better Πλαταιαί, Platææ.

πλάτος, -ους, τό, breadth.

πλέγ-μα, τό, thing woven : hence snare, gin (πλέκ-ειν).

πλεῖν (= έ-ειν), to sail. πλεύσομαι. πέπλευκα.—ἔπλευσα.

⎰ πλεῖστος, most. ⎱ Note 13.
⎱ πλείων, more. ⎰

πλέκειν, to knit, weave.

⎰ πλεονέκτης, -ου, avaricious (πλέον, neut., more. ἔχειν, to have).
⎱ πλεονεξία, ἡ, avarice.

πλεύσας, partcp. Aor. 1. from πλεῖν.

πληγή, ἡ, a blow, stroke, wound.

πλῆθος, -ους, τό, multitude, constitution (in a démocracy).

πλήν (gen.), except.

⎰ πλήρης, -ες, full, satisfied with (gen.).
⎱ πληροῦν (= ό-ειν), to fill.

πλησιάζειν, to approach, draw near.

πλήττειν, to strike ; [Pf. πέπληγα, I have struck ; Aor. Pass. ἐπλήγην : but in composition ἐπλάγην, e. g. ἐξεπλάγην.]

πλόος = πλοῦς, ὁ, voyage (πλεῖν, to sail).

⎰ πλούσιος, rich.
⎰ πλουτίζειν, to enrich.
⎱ πλοῦτος, ὁ, riches.

πνεῖν (= έ-ειν), to breathe, blow. πνεύσομαι, &c. like πλεῖν.

πόα, herbage, grass.

πόθεν ; whence ?

ποιεῖν (= έ-ειν), to make, do, render : εὖ ποιεῖν τινα, to confer a benefit on any body.

ποιεῖσθαί τι περὶ ἐλάττονος ἤ, to think any thing of less importance than : περὶ πολλοῦ ποιεῖσθαι, to attach great importance to, &c. See Vocab. 29.

ποίημα, τό (= thing made), poem.

ποίησις, -εως, (ἡ), the making or composition. See ἔπος (ποιεῖν).

ποιητής, -οῦ, ὁ, poet.

ποικίλλειν, to variegate, decorate.

ποικίλος, variegated.

ποιμήν, -ένος, ὁ, shepherd.

ποῖος ; of what kind ?

πολεμεῖν (= έ-ειν), to carry on (wage) war (dat.).

πολεμικός, warlike.

πολέμιος, hostile ; as subst., an enemy.

πόλεμος, ὁ, war.

πολιορκεῖν (= έ-ειν), to besiege.

πόλις, -εως, ἡ, city.

πολιτεία, ἡ. constitution ; a commonwealth.

πολιτεύειν, to govern the state ; Mid., to live as a citizen, to govern the state.

πολίτης, -ου, ὁ, citizen.

πολλάκις, often.

πολύς, much ; πολλοί, many.

πολυσχιδής, -ές, much divided, branching.

πολυτελής, -ές, costly (τέλος, end, price).

πολυφιλία, ἡ, multitude of friends (φίλος, friend).

πολυχειρία, ἡ, multitude of hands, of workmen (χείρ, hand).

πομπή (πέμπειν), procession.

πονεῖν (= έ-ειν), to toil.

πονηρός, wicked.

πόνος, ὁ, toil.

πορεύ-εσθαι, to set out (proficisci) ; to march (of an army).

Ποσειδῶν, -ωνος, ὁ, Poseidon, Neptune.

πόσις, -εως, ἡ, drinking (πο, root used to supply the tenses of πίνειν).

πόσος ; how great ?

ποταμός, ὁ, river.

ποτέ, at any time, ever : in questions (= tandem), in the world ; ever.

πότερος, which of two.

ποτόν, τό, drink (πο, root used to supply the tenses of πίνειν).

πούς, ποδός, ὁ, foot.

πρᾶγμα, -ατος, τό, an action, affair (πράττειν, to do).

πρᾶξις, -εως, ἡ, an action.

πρᾶος, mild.

πραότης (πραότητ-ος),mildness. gentleness.

πράττειν, to do, perform : εὖ πράττειν, to be doing well. (πράττεσθαι, to exact [money, &c., with two accusatives]).

πρέπει, it is becoming (dat.). πρέπειν, to be becoming (decere).

πρεσβεία, ἡ, embassy.

πρέσβεις, οἱ, ambassadors.

πρεσβευτής, -οῦ, ὁ, ambassador.

πρέσβυς, -εια, -υ, old.

πρεσβύτερος, elder, aged person.

πρίασθαι, to buy.

πρίν, before ; c. indic. or inf.: πρὶν ἄν, c. subj.

πρίων, πρίον-ος, ὁ, saw (?).

προ-άγειν, to move (or march) forward ; to advance.

πρόβατον, τό, sheep (πρό, forward. βα, short root of βαίνειν, to go ; from the animal's going steadily forward to graze).

{ προ-δίδωμι, -διδόναι, to betray.
{ προ-δότης, -ου, ὁ, betrayer.

προ-εῖπον (Aor.), 1 said before, ordered, proclaimed. VII.

προ-έρχεσθαι, to go before. VII.

{ προθυμία, ἡ, willingness, eagerness.
{ πρόθυμος 2, willing (θυμός, mind, *animus*).
{ προθύμως, adv., willingly.

πρόνοια, ἡ, foresight (πρό. νοῦς. mind).

προσ-βλέπειν, to look at.

προσ-δοκᾶν (= ά-ειν), to expect.

πρόσ-ειμι, Inf. προσ-εῖναι, to be present. Pdm. 68.

πρόσ-ειμι, Inf. προσ-ιέναι, to go to. Pdm. 68.

προσ-έρχεσθαι, to come to. VII.

προσ-έχειν τὸν νοῦν (*animum applicare ad* —), to pay attention to ; attend to.

προσήκων, belonging to ; becoming (πρός, to. ἥκειν, to have come).

πρόσθεν, before (gen.).

προσμίσγειν, to put in at, land at.

προσ-τάττ-ειν (Fut. -ξω), to command, enjoin.

προσ-τίθημι, -τιθέναι, to add.

προ-τίθημι, -τιθέναι, to put before, set out for show *or* sale.

προφητεύειν, to prophesy (πρό, forth, before. φη, root of φημί).

πρῶτος, first.

πτωχός very poor.

πύκτης, ου, ὁ, boxer, pugilist (πύξ, with the fist).

πύλη, ἡ, gate.

πυνθάνεσθαι, to ask, to inquire. Aor., to learn by inquiry ; to be informed ; to have heard, *or* to hear. IV.

πῦρ, πυρός, τό, fire.

πώ (enclitic), yet.

πωλεῖν (= έ-ειν), to sell.

πώποτε, ever.

πῶς ; how ?

P.

{ Ῥᾴδιος, easy.
{ ῥᾳδιουργεῖν (= έ-ειν) [to take it easily. ῥᾴδιος, easy. ἔργον, work], to be idle ; to shirk work.
{ ῥᾳδίως, adv., easily.
{ ῥᾳθυμεῖν (= έ-ειν), to be indolent, apathetic, lazy (ῥᾴων, more easy. θυμός, mind).

ῥεῖν (= έ-ειν), to flow.

ῥήγνυμι, -νύναι, to tear, break. IX.

ῥήτωρ, -ορος, ὁ, orator (ῥέω, obsol. in Pres.).

ῥίζα (*not* ῥῖζα), ἡ, root.

ῥίπτειν, to throw.

ῥίψ, ῥιπός, bundle of reeds, rushes, &c.

ῥοία, ἡ, pomegranate.

(ῥόος =) ῥοῦς, ὁ, stream (ῥεῖν, to flow).

Ῥωμαῖος, Roman.

ῥώννυμι, ῥωννύναι, to strengthen.

Σ.

{ Σάλπιγξ, -ιγγος, ἡ, trumpet.
{ σαλπίζειν, to blow a trumpet.

Σάμιος, ὁ, Samian.

Σαρδανάπᾱλος, ὁ, Sardanapalus.

Σάρδεις, -εων, αἱ, Sardis.

σάρξ, σαρκ-ός, ἡ, flesh.

{ σαφής, -ές, clear.
{ σαφῶς, clearly.

σβέννυμι, σβεννύναι, to quench. X.

σέβεσθαι, to honor.

σελήνη, ἡ, the moon.

{ σημαίνειν, to give a sign.
{ σημεῖον, τό, sign.

{ σιγᾶν (= ά-ειν), to be silent. Fut. σιγήσομαι.
{ σιγή, ἡ. silence.

{ σιδηρεος, -οῦς, of iron, iron (adj.) ; *iron-hearted*.
{ σιδηρεύς, ὁ, smith, blacksmith.
{ σίδηρος, ὁ, iron.

σῖτος, ὁ, corn.

σιωπᾶν (= ά-ειν), to be silent, to hold one's tongue. Fut. σιω-πήσομαι.

σκεδάννυμι, σκεδαννύναι, to scatter. x.

σκηνή, ἡ, tent.

σκῆπτρον, τό, sceptre.

σκληρός, dry.

σκοπεῖν, -εῖσθαι, to behold, consider.

σκύμνος, ὁ, young animal, cub, whelp. οἱ σκύμνοι, the young (ones).

σκώπτειν, to scoff, jeer (τινά or εἴς, πρός τινα).

{ σοφία, ἡ, wisdom.
{ σοφιστής, -οῦ, ὁ, sophist.
{ σοφός, wise.

Σοφοκλῆς, -έους, ὁ, Sophocles.

{ Σπάρτη, ἡ, Sparta.
{ Σπαρτιάτης, -ου, ὁ, Spartan.

σπείρειν, to sow [Pf. ἔσπορα: Aor. Pass. ἐσπάρην].

σπεύδειν, to hasten; to exert oneself.

σπονδαί (prop. libations. σπένδειν), a truce, a treaty.

σποράδην (σπείρειν), dispersedly; in a scattered way, not in collected masses.

{ σπουδάζειν, to hasten, to be zealous, in a hurry.
{ σπουδαῖος, earnest, serious: in character = sterling, good.
{ σπουδαίως, adv., zealously.
{ σπουδή, ἡ, zeal, earnestness (σπεύδειν, to exert oneself).

στάδιον, τό (pl. also οἱ στάδιοι), stadium.

{ στασιάζειν, to revolt, to be divided by factions, at variance.
{ στάσις, -εως, ἡ, faction (στα, root of ἵστημι).

στέλλειν, to send.

στέργειν, with acc., to love; with dat. (and also acc.), to be contented with.

στερεῖν (= έ-ειν) τινά τινος, to deprive one of something (in Pass. also c. acc. rei).

στερεός, solid.

στέρεσθαι, to be without (τινός).

στέφανος, ὁ, crown, garland.

στολή, ἡ, robe, dress (στέλλειν to equip).

στόμα, -ατος, τό, mouth.

στοχάζεσθαι (gen.), to aim at.

{ στρατεύειν, to serve; to bear arms; to make an expedition.
{ στρατεύεσθαι, to serve, to march (of soldiers).
{ στράτευμα, -ατος, τό, army.
{ στρατηγός, ὁ, a general (ἄγειν).
{ στρατία, ἡ, army.
{ στρατιώτης, -ου, ὁ, soldier.
{ στρατοπεδεύεσθαι, to encamp.
{ στρατόπεδον, τό, encampment, encamped army.
{ στρατός, ὁ, army.

στρέφειν, to turn, twist [Aor. Pass. ἐστράφην, ἐστρέφθην].

συγ-γιγνώσκειν (VI), to think with, agree with; σ. ἐμαυτῷ, to be conscious; σ. τινί, to pardon.

συγ-κόπτειν, to knock to pieces, batter.

συγ-κυκᾶν (= ά-ειν), to confound.

{ συκῆ, ἡ, fig-tree.
{ συκοφάντης· ου, propr. common or vexatious informer. Sycophant; but not in our sense (said to be from σῦκον, fig. φαίνειν, to denounce, to inform against: = one who accused a man of exporting figs against the Attic law).
{ συκοφαντία, sycophancy, vexatious information (see συκο-φάντης).

συλᾶν (= ά-ειν) τινά τι, to rob, pillage, rob one of something.

συλ-λαμβάνειν, to take with, seize: —to help. IV.

συλ-λέγειν, to collect.

συμ-βουλεύ-εσθαί τινι (Mid.), to consult with him.
συμ-βουλεύειν, to advise (dat.).
σύμβουλος, ὁ, adviser.
συμμαχία, ἡ, alliance, aid.
σύμμαχος, ὁ, ally (σύν, with. μάχη, battle).
σύμ-πας, all together, whole.
συμ-πονεῖν (= έ-ειν), to work with.
συμ-φέρει, it is expedient. τὸ συμφέρον = the expedient.
συμ-φέρειν (lit. to bring with ; hence, to contribute =) to be profitable, useful, or expedient (c. dat.).
συμφορά, ἡ, an event, calamity.
σύν-ειμι, Inf. συν-εῖναι, to be with. Pdm. 68.
σύν-ειμι, Inf. συν-ιέναι, to come or assemble with. Pdm. 68.
σύν-εξ-ομοιοῦν (= ό-ειν), to make equal or like (ὁμοῖος, like).
σύνεσις, -εως, ἡ, understanding, intelligence (σύν, with, together. έ, short root of ἰέναι, to send, to put. συνιέναι [to put together =] to understand).
συνετός, sensible.
συνεχῶς (σύν. ἔχω), continually.
συνθηκη, ἡ, treaty (σύν. τιθέναι, Aor. ἔ-θηκ-α, to place).
συν-ίστημι, -ιστάναι, to put together.
σύν-οιδα, συν-ειδέναι, to know with ; σ. ἐμαυτῷ, to be conscious. Pdm. 70.
Σύρος, ὁ, a Syrian.
σῦς, συός, ὁ, ἡ, boar, sow.
σφαῖρα, ἡ, ball.
σφόδρα, very, excessively.
σφοδρός, violent.
σχεδόν τι, almost.
σώζειν, to save [Perf. Mid. or Pass. σέσωσμαι : Aor. Pass. ἐσώθην].
Σωκράτης, -ους, ὁ, Socrates.
σωτηρία, ἡ, safety, preservation.

σωφρονεῖν (= έ-ειν), to be of sound mind.
σωφροσύνη, ἡ, modesty ; temperance ; sobriety of mind ; self-restraint.
σώφρων, wise, temperate. μὴ σώφρων, intemperate (σῶς, safe. φρήν, mind).

T.

Τάλαντον, τό, talent (a weight)
τάλας, -αινα, -αν, wretched.
Ταξίαρχος, ὁ, a Taxiarch.
ταπεινός, low, base.
ταπεινοῦν (= ό-ειν), to bring low, to humble.
Τάρας, -αντος, ὁ, Tarentum.
ταράττειν, to throw into confusion.
τάσσειν or τάττειν, to arrange, appoint ; to order.
ταῦρος, ὁ, bull.
ταύτῃ (dat. fem. of οὗτος, used adverbially), here.
τάφος, burial ; tomb.
τάφρος, ἡ, trench.
τάχα, quickly, probably, perhaps.
ταχέως, quickly.
ταχύ, quickly, at once.
ταώς, ταώ, ὁ, peacock.
τέ—καί, both—and.
τείνειν, to stretch [Pf. τέτακα].
τειχίζειν (τεῖχος, wall), to surround with a wall, to fortify.
τεῖχος, -ους, τό, wall.
τέκνον, τό, child, young one (τεκ, root of τίκτειν [Aor. ἔ-τεκ-ον], parĕre).
τελεῖν (= έ-ειν), to accomplish.
τελευταῖος, last.
τελευτᾶν (= ά-ειν), to end, to die.
τελευτή, ἡ, end, death.
τέλος, -ους, τό, end.
τέρας, -ατος, τό, wonder, portentous monster.

12*

τέρπειν, to delight.

τετράπους, n. -πουν, gen. -ποδος, four-footed (τέσσαρες, τέτταρες, four. πούς, foot).

τέχνη, ἡ, art.

Τηλέμαχος, ὁ, Telemachus.

-ηλικοῦτος, so large.

Γίγρης, Τίγρητ-ος, ὁ, the Tigris.

τίθημι, τιθέναι, to place : νόμους θεῖναι (of the legislator), θέ-σθαι (of the people : seld. of the legislator), to enact, pass, make laws.

·ίκτειν, to beget, bear [Fut. τέξο-μαι : Aor. ἔτεκον : Perf. τέτοκα].

τιμᾶν (= ά-ειν), to honor.

τιμᾶσθαι (= τιμά-εσθαι) πρὸ πολλῶν χρημάτων, lit. to value above much money ; to give a great deal (if a thing were so).

τιμή, ἡ, honor.

τιμωρεῖν (= έ-ειν), to help.

τιμωρεῖσθαι (= έ-εσθαι), to punish, revenge oneself on.

τιμωρία, ἡ, punishment.

τίνειν, to expiate, pay.

τιτρώσκειν, to wound. VL.

τοί, assuredly, indeed.

τοίνυν, hence, therefore.

τοῖος, of such a nature.

τοιοῦτος, such.

τοῖχος, ὁ (= paries), wall of a house (or room, or court).

τολμᾶν (= ά-ειν), to dare.

τόπος, ὁ, place.

τοσοῦτος, so great.

τότε, then.

τράγος, ὁ, goat.

τραγ-ῳδία, ἡ, tragedy.

τραῦμα, τραύματ-ος, τό, wound.

τράχηλος, ὁ, neck, throat.

τρέπειν, to turn ; Mid., to turn myself ; (2) for myself, i. e. to put to flight [Aor. ἔτρεψα : Mid. -άμην : Pass. ἐτρέφθην : ἔτραπον, -όμην, ἐτράπην : Perf. Act. τέτροφα : Perf. Mid. or Pass. τέτραμμαι].

τρέφειν, to nourish [Fut. θρέψω Aor. ἔθρεψα : Perf. τέτροφα : Perf. Mid. or Pass. τέθραμμαι : Aor. Pass. ἐτράφην (seldom ἐτρέφθην)].

τρίβειν, to rub, pound.

τρίβων, -ωνος, ὁ, a worn cloak.

τριήρης, -ήρους, ἡ, trireme.

τρόπαιον, τό, trophy.

τρόπος, ὁ, way, manner, character.

τροφή, nourishment, food (τρέφειν).

τροφός, ἡ, nurse.

τρυγών, τρυγόν-ος, the turtle-dove.

Τρωϊκός, Trojan.

τυγχάν-ειν (τεύξομαι. τετύχηκα. ἔτυχον), to hit (a mark), obtain, attain to ; to chance c. partcp. ἔτυχον παρών = I chanced to be present : but often not to be translated τυγχάνω ὤν (I chance to be), having little more force than I am.

τύμβος, ὁ, tomb.

τύπτειν, to strike.

τύραννος, ὁ, tyrant, despot.

τυφλοῦν (= ό-ειν), to make blind, to blind.

τυφλός, blind.

τύχη, ἡ, fortune.

Υ.

Ὑβρίζειν, to be haughty towards one, to maltreat, insult. εἴς τινα, πρός τινα : also τινά τι.

ὕβρις, -εως, ἡ, insolence, assault. ὕβρεως νόμος = the law of assaults.

ὕδωρ, τό, G. ὕδατος, water.

ὕει, it rains.

υἱδοῦς, grandson.

υἱός, ὁ, son.

ὑπ-άρχειν, to be at hand, to be ; to belong to.

ὑπερ-βάλλειν, to throw beyond, exceed.

ὑπερ-ήφανος 2, haughty.

ὑπερ-ορᾶν (= ά-ειν), to look over, to despise.

ὑπηνέμιος. ὑπηνέμιον ᾠόν, a wind-egg (ὑπό = sub. ἄνεμος, wind).

ὑπηρετεῖν (= έ-ειν), to aid, serve (dat.).

ὑπισχνεῖσθαι (= έ-εσθαι), to promise. ὑποσχήσομαι. ὑπέσχημαι.—Aor. ὑπεσχόμην.

ὕπνος, ὁ, sleep.

ὑπο-δέχ-εσθαι, to receive.

ὑπό-δημα, -ατος, τό, sandal, shoe (δεῖν, to bind).

ὑπο-μένειν, to await, endure (acc.).

ὑπο-φέρειν, to endure. VII.

ὗς, ὑός (ὁ, ἡ), sus : ⁊ ἄγριος, wild boar.

ὑστεραῖος, following.

ὑψηλό-φρων, high-minded.

Φ.

Φάγειν, see ἐσθίειν.

φαίνειν, to show.
φαίνεσθαι (apparēre), to be seen ; to be (c. partcp.) ; to appear.
φανερός, evident.

φάρμακον, τό, drug, poison, remedy.

φαῦλος, bad, evil, worthless.

φείδεσθαι, Dep. Mid., to spare (gen.).

φέρειν, to bear. VII.

Φερεκύδης, -ους, ὁ, Pherecydes.

φεύγειν, to flee ; also = to be an exile.

φημί, φάναι, to say. Pdm. 69.

φθέγγ-εσθαι, to sound.

φθείρειν, to destroy.

φθονεῖν (= έ-ειν), to envy (dat.).
φθόνος, ὁ, envy.

φιάλη, shallow cup ; bowl (= patera).

φιλεῖν (= έ-ειν), to love.

φιλία, ἡ, friendship.

φιλο-κερδής, -ές, fond of gain.

φίλος (adj.), friendly, dear.

φίλος, ὁ, friend.

φιλο-σοφεῖν (= έ-ειν), to philosophize.

φιλο-σοφία, ἡ, philosophy.

φιλό-τῑμος (φίλος. τιμή,) ambitious.

φλέψ, φλεβός, ἡ, vein.

φονεύειν, to murder, slay.
φονεύς, -έως, ὁ, murderer.
φόνος, ὁ, murder.

φράζειν, to say, tell.

φοβεῖν (= έ-ειν), to frighten ; Mid. to fear.
φόβος, ὁ, fear.

φρήν, φρενός, ἡ (φρένες), mind.

φρονεῖν (= έ-ειν), to think ; to be sensible, prudent, wise.

φροντίζειν, to care for (gen.).
φροντίς, -ίδος, ἡ, concern.

φύειν, to bring forth, put forth.

φυλακή, ἡ, guard, watch.
φυλάττειν, to guard ; Mid. c. acc., to guard against something. ⁊ ποιεῖν τι, to anxiously avoid doing it.

φυσικός (physicus), a natural philosopher.
φύσις, -εως, ἡ, nature.

φυτεύειν, to plant.

φωνή, ἡ, voice.

X.

Χαῖρε, hail.
χαίρειν, to rejoice.
χαλεπός, troublesome.
χαλεπῶς, adv., with difficulty.

χαλινός, ὁ, bridle.

χάλκεος, -οῦς, brazen.
χαλκύς, ὁ, brass.
χαλκο-τύπος, brazier, coppersmith (τύπτειν, to beat).

χαρίεις, graceful.
χαριέντως, gracefully.
χαρίζεσθαι, to gratify (dat.).
χάρις, -ιτος, ἡ, favor. χάριν ἀποδιδόναι, *gratiam reddere*; to repay or return a favor.
χάριν ἔχειν, *gratiam habere*.

χειμών, -ῶνος, ὁ, winter; stormy weather.

χεῖν (= έ-ειν), to pour.

χείρ, χειρός, ἡ (d. pl. χερσί), hand.

χειροῦσθαι (= ό-εσθαι), to subdue.

χελιδών, -όνος, ἡ, swallow.

χθές, yesterday.

χθών, χθονός, ἡ, the earth.

χίλιοι, a thousand.

χιών, χιόνος, ἡ, snow.

χόλος, ὁ, anger.

χόρτος, ὁ, fodder.

χρῆσθαι (= ά-εσθαι), to use.

χρή, *oportet*; one (we) ought to; it is necessary.

χρῄζειν, to be in want (gen.).

χρῆμα, χρήματος, τό, a thing, property. *Pl.* money.

χρηματίζ-εσθαι, to enrich oneself by trade; to trade for profit (χρήματα).

χρόνος, ὁ, time.

χρυσός, ὁ, gold.
χρύσεος· (οῦς), -έᾱ (ῆ), -εον (οῦν), golden, of gold.

χρῶμα, χρώματος, τό, color (of the skin), plumage, &c.

χυμός, juice, taste [χεῖν (= ό ειν)].

χώρα, ἡ, country, region.

χωρίς (gen.), separately, apart from, without.

Ψ.

Ψέγειν, to blame.

ψεύδειν, to deceive; Mid. σθαι, to be disappointed of it.
ψευδής, -ές, false.
ψεύστης, -ου, ὁ, liar.

ψήφισμα, -ατος, τό, decree.

ψυχή, ἡ, the soul; the mind.

Ω.

Ὠνεῖσθαι (= έ-εσθαι), to buy.

ᾠόν (ὠϜόν = *ovum*), egg.

ὡς, as, when, how, because: ὡς τάχιστα, as soon as possible; with indefinite numbers = *about*;—as final particle = that; in order that.

ὥρα (*hora*), time.

ὥσπερ, as, just as.

ὥστε, so that.

ὠφέλεια, ἡ, advantage, profit, benefit.
ὠφελεῖν (= έ-ειν), to benefit (acc.).
ὠφέλιμος 2, useful.

INDEX II.

ENGLISH AND GREEK.

A.

Abide by, παραμένειν, ἐμμένειν (dat.).

able, to be, δύνασθαι (δύναμαι): οἷός τέ εἰμι : ἔχω.

abode, οἴκησις, εως, ἡ.

about, περί, ἀμφί.

absence of government, anarchy, ἀναρχία, ἡ.

absent, ἀπών, partcp. of ἀπεῖναι.

abundant, ἄφθονος, ον.

abusive, φιλολοίδορος.

accept, ἀποδέχεσθαι.

accompany, ἕπεσθαι (dat.).

accomplish, ἐξεργάζεσθαι : τελεῖν (= έ-ειν).

according to, in accordance with, κατά (acc.).

account of, on, διά (acc.), ἕνεκα (gen.).

account, on this, διὰ τοῦτο.

accurate, ἀκριβής, -ές.

accuse (of), κατηγορεῖν (= έ-ειν) (gen. of charge).

accustom, ἐθίζειν.

Achilles, Ἀχιλλεύς, -έως, ὁ.

acquainted with, to be, οἶδα, εἰδέναι. Pdm. 70. ἐπίστασθαι.

acquit, ἀπολύειν.

Acropolis, Ἀκρόπολις, -εως, ἡ.

act, an, πρᾶξις, -εως, ἡ. πρᾶγμα, τό : = work, ἔργον, τό.

action, see Act.

act-unjustly, ἀδικεῖν (= έ-ειν).

accuse (any body), ἐγκαλεῖν τινι : αἰτιᾶσθαι (= ά-εσθαι), = to lay the blame on, c. acc.

adhere to (a confession, &c.), ἐμμένειν (dat.).

admire, θαυμάζειν.

admirer, ἐπαινέτης, ου (= laudator : ἐπαινεῖν).

adorn, κοσμεῖν (= έ-ειν).

advantage, ὠφέλεια, ἡ.

advantage, an, ἀγαθόν, τό.

advantageous, χρήσιμος 2 or 3, ὠφέλιμος 2.

advise, βουλεύειν : συμβουλεύειν τινί.

Æschines, Αἰσχίνης, -ου, ὁ.

Ætolia, Αἰτωλία, ἡ.

affair, πρᾶγμα, τό.

affirm, φημί, φάναι. Pdm. 69.

afford, παρ-έχειν, παρ-έχεσθαι. VII.

afraid, to be, φοβεῖσθαι (= έ-ε-σθαι).

after, μετά (acc.).

again, αὖθις, πάλιν.

age, ἡλικία, ἡ.

age, old, γῆρας, -ως, τό.

aged person, πρεσβύτερος (= senior).

agreeable, ἡδύς, -εῖα, υ.

aid, βοηθεῖν (= έ-ειν), dat., ὑπηρετεῖν (dat.).

alas ! οἴμοι, φεῦ.

Alcibiades, Ἀλκιβιάδης, -ου, ὁ.

alike, ὁμοίως.

all, πᾶς, ἅπας.

alliance, συμμαχία, ἡ.

allot, νέμειν.

allow, ἐᾶν (= ά-ειν). I am allowed to do any thing, ἔξεστί (= licet) μοι ποιεῖν τι. I was allowed to —, ἐξῆν μοι —.

allowable, to be, ἔξεστι (dat.).

almost, σχεδόν (τι).

alone, μόνος : adv. μόνον.

already, ἤδη.

also, καί.

altar, βωμός, ὁ.

although, κἄν or καὶ ἐάν (subj.).

always, ἀεί.

am (to be), εἶναι (εἰμί), ὑπάρχειν, ἔχειν (with adverbs).

ambassador, πρεσβευτής, -οῦ, ὁ.

ambassadors, πρέσβεις, οἱ.

amid, ἐν (dat.).

among, ἐν, παρά.

ancient, παλαιός.

and, καί. τέ (enclit.).

Androgeus, Ἀνδρόγεως, ὁ.

anger, ὀργή, ἡ.

angry, to be, ὀργίζεσθαι, or χαλεπαίνειν (c. dat.), ἐν ὀργῇ ἔχειν or ποιεῖσθαι (acc.). ἄχθεσθαι (dat.).

animal, ζῶον, τό.

announce, ἀγγέλλειν.

anoint, ἀλείφειν, χρίειν.

another, ἄλλος.

any one, τὶς (enclit.).

any thing, τὶ (enclit.).

any where, πού (enclit.) : in a sentence with a negative, οὐδαμοῦ.

appear, φαίνεσθαι.

appetite, ὄρεξις, -εως, ἡ.

appoint, τάσσ-ειν : fut. ξω = determine, &c. ; ἀπο-δείκνυμι, ἀποδεικνύναι = declare a man, e. g. general, &c.

archer, τοξότης, -ου, ὁ.

argument, λόγος, ὁ.

Aristodemus, Ἀριστόδημος.

Aristotle, Ἀριστοτέλης, -ους, ὁ.

arms (weapons), ὅπλα, τά.

army, στρατιά, ἡ. στρατός, ὁ.

arrow (missile), βέλος, τό.

art, τέχνη, ἡ.

artfully, more, τεχνικώτερον.

Artemis, Ἄρτεμις, -ιδος, ἡ.

articulation of a joint, διάρθρωσις, ἡ.

as, ὡς, ὥσπερ.

as long as, ἕως.

as much. τοσοῦτος.

as soon as, ὡς τάχιστα.

as well — as, καί — καί.

ashamed to be, αἰδεῖσθαι (= ε-εσθαι), αἰσχύνεσθαι.

Asia, Ἀσία, ἡ.

ask, ἐρωτᾶν (= ά-ειν), [a question, ἔρεσθαι], αἰτεῖν (= έ-ειν), ask-for. I asked, ἠρόμην.

asleep, to be, καθεύδειν.

ass, ὄνος.

assault, ὕβρις, -εως (prop. insolence).

assert, φημί, φάναι. Pdm. 69.

assist, παραστῆναι (dat.).

assistant, ὑπηρέτης, ου (= minister).

Assyrian, Ἀσσύριος, ὁ.

Athēne (= Minerva), Ἀθηνᾶ, ἡ.

Athenian, Ἀθηναῖος, ὁ.

Athens, Ἀθῆναι, αἱ.

attack, to, ἐπιτίθεσθαι (dat.).

attain-to, τυχεῖν (gen.), 2nd Aor. of τυγχάνειν.

attempt, to, πειρᾶσθαι (= ά-εσθαι) : ἐπιχειρεῖν (= έ-ειν), to take in hand (dat. ἐπί. χείρ).

attend (= follow upon), ἕπ-εσθαι (dat.).

attend to, φροντίζειν, τὸν νοῦν προσέχειν.

attendant, ὑπηρέτης, ου (= minister).

attention. To pay ∽ to, τὸν νοῦν προσέχειν (animum applicare), dat. of thing.

Attica, Ἀττική, ἡ.

attire, στολή.

avail, ἰσχύειν.

avoid, φεύγειν.

awake, to be, ἐγρηγορέναι, Perf. 2. of ἐγείρειν.

awaken, ἐγείρειν. ἀνίστημι, -ιστάναι.

away, to lead, ἀπάγειν.

axe, πέλεκυς, -εως, ὁ.

B.

Back, ὀπίσω.

bad, κακός, πονηρός, φαῦλος.

bad, the (abstract), κακόν, τό.

badness, φαυλότης, -ότητος, ἡ.

ball, σφαῖρα, ἡ.

bar, v., ἐμφράττειν, -ξω.

bar, s., κλεῖθρον.

barbarian, a, βάρβαρος, ὁ.

base, ταπεινός, ἡ, όν.

battle, μάχη, ἡ.

be, to, εἶναι (εἰμί).

be seen, φαίν-εσθαι.

be with, συνεῖναι (σύνειμι), dat.

bear (carry), φέρειν. VII. To bear false witness, μαρτυρεῖν τὰ ψευδῆ (= testify the things that are false).

beast (wild), θηρίον, τό.

beautiful, καλός.

beautiful, the, καλόν, τό.

beautifully, καλῶς.

because, ὅτι.

because of, διά (acc.).

become, γίγνεσθαι (γενήσομαι, γεγένημαι and γέγονα.—ἐγενόμην).

becomes, it, προσήκει, πρέπει.

becoming, προσήκων.

becoming, it is, προσήκει.

before, πρό (gen.).

begin, ἄρχεσθαι.

beginning, ἀρχή, ἡ.

beguile, ψεύδειν.

behalf of, in, ὑπέρ (gen.).

behave insolently, ὑβρίζ-ειν.

behold, θεᾶσθαι (= ά-εσθαι).

believe = trust, πείθεσθαι : = think, ἡγεῖσθαι (= έ-εσθαι), νομίζειν.

believed, to be, πιστεύεσθαι.

belly, γαστήρ, γαστρός, ἡ.

beloved, to be, see To love.

benefactor, εὐεργέτης, -ου, ὁ.

benefit, to, ὠφελεῖν (acc.).

benefit, εὐεργέτημα, τό. εὐεργεσία, ἡ. To confer a —, εὐεργετεῖν (= έ-ειν), acc.

besides, ἔτι.

besiege, πολιορκεῖν (= έ-ειν).

best, ἄριστος.

betray, προδιδόναι (προδίδωμι).

better. See ἀγαθός in Note 9.—

Adv. βέλτιον.

between, μεταξύ (gen.).

beware of, φυλάττεσθαι (acc.) : εὐλαβεῖσθαί (= έ-εσθαι) τι.

beyond, prep., ὑπέρ.

bid, κελεύειν (c. acc. and inf.).

bind, δεῖν (= έ-ειν).

bird, ὄρνις, -ιθος, ὁ, ἡ.

bite, δάκνειν (List III.)

bitter, πικρός.

black, μέλας : as subst., τὸ μέλαν.

blame, to, αἰτιᾶσθαι (= ά-εσθαι, acc.).

blessing, a, ἀγαθόν, τό.

blood, αἷμα, τό.

blow, πληγή, ἡ.

Bœotia, Βοιωτία, ἡ.

boldly, θαρρῶν. See Vocab. 23.

bonassus, βόνασσος.

bookseller, βιβλιοπώλης.

born, to be, φῦναι (πέφυκα = I am by nature, &c.).

both, ἄμφω.

both—and, καί—καί, τέ—καί.

bow, τόξον, τό.

bowl, φιάλη.

boy, παῖς, ὁ. παιδίον, τό.

branching (of horns), πολυσχιδής.

brass, χαλκός, ὁ.

brass (as adj.) : brazen, χάλκεος, -οῦς.

brave, ἀνδρεῖος, γενναῖος.

brave-dangers, κινδυνεύειν.

bravely, ἀνδρείως, γενναίως.

bravery, ἀνδρία, ἡ. ἀρετή, ἡ.

bread, ἄρτος, ὁ.

breadth, πλάτος, τό.

break (a peace, &c.), λύειν : (a limb), κατάγνυμι, -αγνύναι. List IX.

brighten, λαμπρύνειν.

brilliant, λαμπρός.

bring, ἄγειν.

bring up (= educate), παιδεύειν.
brother, ἀδελφός, ὁ.
build, ἱδρύειν, κτίζειν, οἰκοδομεῖν.
bull, ταῦρος, ὁ.
burn, καίειν (καύσω, &c.). Att.
Impf. ἔκαον. Aor. ἔκηα.
burn down, κατακαίειν (see the
preceding word).
bury, ϑάπτειν.
business, ἔργον, τό. πρᾶγμα, τό.
but, δέ, ἀλλά.
but also, ἀλλὰ καί.
butt, to, κυρίττειν.
buying a horse, ἱππωνεία, ἡ.
by, ὑπό, παρά, πρός (gen.) : in
swearing, νή (= yes, by), (οὐ)
μά (= no, by), acc.

C.

Call, to, καλεῖν (= έ-ειν), ἀπαγο-
ρεύειν, λέγειν. = name, ὀνομάζειν.
camel, κάμηλος, ὁ, ἡ.
camp, στρατόπεδον.
can (be able), δύνασϑαι.
care, to, care for, take care for,
ἐπιμέλεσϑαι, φροντίζειν (gen.).
carry, φέρειν. VII.
carry on war, πολεμεῖν (= έ-ειν),
dat.
carry out (to sea), ἀποφέρειν (ἐς
τὸ πέλαγος) : [to be carried out
to sea, cf. Sea]. On φέρειν,
see List VII.
cart, ἄμαξα.
Carthage, Καρχηδών, -όνος, ἡ.
cast, to, ῥίπτειν.
cast away, ἀποβάλλειν.
castle, ἄκρα, ἡ.
catch, ϑηρεύειν, ἀγρεύειν.
cavalry, οἱ ἱππεῖς (pl. of ἱππεύς)
= equites. ἵππος, ἡ (collec-
tively).
cease, παύεσϑαι, διαλείπειν. See
Vocab. 23.
censure any thing, μέμφεσϑαί τι.
Ceres, Δημήτηρ, ἡ.

chance, τύχη, ἡ.
change, μετα-στρέφειν (= turn
backwards) : μετα-βάλλειν.
character, ἦϑος, -ους, τό.
charge, ἐμβάλλειν εἰς (lit. to cast
into).
chariot, ἅρμα, τό.
chastise, κολάζ-ειν (Fut. -σομαι
or -σω).
cheat, ψεύδειν.
chest, λάρναξ, -ακος, ἡ.
child, παῖς, ὁ. ἡ. τέκνον, τό.
choice, αἵρεσις, -εως. ἡ.
choose, αἱρεῖσϑαι (= έ-εσϑαι) :
= will, βουλεύεσϑαι, ἐϑέλειν.
chorus, χόρος, ὁ.
circle, κύκλος, ὁ.
citizen, πολίτης, ὁ.
city, πόλις, ἡ. ἄστυ, τό.
cleave, to, ἔχεσϑαι (gen.).
clerk, γραμματεύς, -εως, ὁ.
clever, ἀγχίνους. See 136.
cleverness, σοφία.
cloud, νεφέλη.
collect (in a heap), ἀϑροίζειν (e. g.
manure).
colonize, οἰκίζειν.
color, χρῶμα, -ατος, τό.
combat, μάχη, ἡ.
come, ἔρχεσϑαι. VII. I am come,
= am present, ἥκω.
command (military), στρατηγία.
command, to, κελεύειν, ἐπιτάττειν
προστάττειν : (of generals)
παραγγέλλειν.
commander, στρατηγός.
commend, ἐπαινεῖν (= έ-ειν).
commit injustice, ἀδικεῖν (= έ-
ειν).
common, κοινός.
companion, ἑταῖρος, ὁ.
compel, ἀναγκάζειν.
complete, διατελεῖν.
compulsion, ἀνάγκη, ἡ.
conceal, ἀποκρύπτειν, κατακρύ-
πτειν, κεύϑειν, καλύπτειν.
concerns, it, μέλει (c. dat. pers.
gen. rei : sts nom. rei).

condemn, κρίνειν : ∞ to death, Sανάτου.

conduct, ἄγειν.

confer benefits, εὖ ποιεῖν (= έ-ειν) τινα, εὐεργετεῖν (= έ-ειν) τινα.

confession, ὁμολογία, ἡ.

conquer, νικᾶν (= ά-ειν), κρατεῖν (= έ-ειν), gen.

consider, σκοπεῖν (= έ-ειν), (= reckon), νομίζειν.

consult with, συμβουλεύεσθαί τινι.

consume, ἀναλίσκειν. v.

contemplate, Sεωρεῖν (= έ-ειν), σκοπεῖν (= έ-ειν).

contest, μάχη, ἡ.

continually, συνεχῶς.

continue, διατελεῖν (= έ-ειν), διάγειν.

contradict, ἀντιλέγειν (τινί).

converse with, διαλέγεσθαί τινι.

convert - into - blood, ἐξ-αιματοῦν (= ό-ειν).

copper, χαλκός, ὁ.

copy, ἀπεικάζειν.

Corcyræans, Κερκυραῖοι.

corpse, νεκρός, ὁ.

correct, ἐπανορθοῦν (= ό-ειν), lit. to make straight again.

count, ἀριθμεῖν (= έ-ειν).

country, χώρα, γῆ, ἡ : one's country, πατρίς, -ίδος, ἡ.

courage, ἀρετή, ἡ. ἀνδρία, ἡ. Sυμός, ὁ.

courageously, ἀνδρείως.

court, Sεραπεύειν (= pay court to), acc.

cover, καλύπτειν : (of snow, &c.), ἀφανίζειν (i. e. cause to disappear).

cow, βοῦς, ἡ.

cowardice, ἀνανδρία, ἡ.

credit to, πείθεσθαι (dat.).

Cretan, Κρής, -ητός.

Crete, Κρήτη. ἡ.

crown, a, στέφανος, ὁ.

cuckoo, κόκκυξ, -υγος, ὁ.

cultivate (= practise a habit), ἀσκεῖν (= έ-ειν) [exerceo].

cup, κύπελλον, τό.

custom, ἔθος : it is an established custom, νόμος ἐστί.

cutlass, μάχαιρα, ἡ.

cut-off, ἀποκόπτ-ειν : ἐκ-κόπτειν (= cut-out, e. g. a vice, bad custom, &c.).

Cyrus, Κῦρος, ὁ.

D.

Danger, κίνδυνος, ὁ : to incur —, κινδυνεύειν.

dare, τολμᾶν (= ά-ειν).

Darius, Δαρεῖος, ὁ.

daughter, Sυγάτηρ, Sυγατρός, ἡ.

dawn, ἔως, ἡ (acc. ἔω).

day, ἡμέρα, ἡ.

daybreak, at, ἅμα ἔῳ, ἅμα ἡμέρᾳ.

dead, the, οἱ νεκροί : to be dead, τεθνηκέναι.

dear, φίλος.

death, Sάνατος, ὁ.

deathless, ἀγήρως.

deceive, ψεύδ-ειν, ἐξαπατᾶν (= ά-ειν).

declare, ἀποφαίνεσθαι (e. g. one's opinion, γνώμην).

decree, a, ψήφισμα, τό.

deed, ἔργον, τό.

deem, νομίζειν : to be deemed worthy, ἀξιοῦσθαι (= ό-εσθαι).

deep, βαθύς.

defend, φυλάττειν.

define, ὁρίζειν (ὅρος, boundary, limit) ; hence the horizon = boundary line of earth and air.

deliberate, βουλεύεσθαι : ∞ with another, συμβουλεύεσθαι (dat.).

delight in, χαίρειν (dat.), ἥδεσθαι, τέρπεσθαι. ἀγάλλεσθαι.

delightful, ἡδύς (sweet).

deliverance (= safety), σωτηρία, ἡ.

Delphi, Δελφοί, -ῶν.

demagogue, δημαγωγός, -οῦ.

demand, to, (= ask), αἰτεῖν (= έ-ειν).

Demeter (Ceres), Δημήτηρ, -τρος, ἡ.

Demosthenes, Δημοσθένης, -ους, ὁ.

deny, ἀρνεῖσθαι (= έ-εσθαι).

depart, ἀπιέναι (ἄπειμι), ἀπαλλάττεσθαι, ἀπέρχεσθαι. VII.

deplore, κλαίειν, κλαύσομαι. Pf. Pass. κέκλαυμαι : seld. -σμαι.

deprive, στέρειν (= έ-ειν), ἀφαιρεῖσθαι (= έ-εσθαι).

deserve, ἄξιον εἶναι.

deserving, ἄξιος.

desire, a, ἐπιθυμία, ἡ.

desire, to, ἐπιθυμεῖν (= έ-ειν), gen.

desirous, to be (= wish), ἐθέλειν.

despise, καταφρονεῖν (= έ-ειν), gen.

destitute, ἐρῆμος, -η, -ον.

destroy, φθείρειν, διαφθείρειν, καταλύειν, ἀπολλύναι. IX.

destroy (a form of government), λύ-ειν (= dissolvere).

determined, it is, δοκεῖ (c. aat. pers.).

device, ἐπίνοια, ἡ.

devise, μηχανᾶσθαι (= ά-εσθαι) = machinari.

die, s., κύβος, ὁ.

die, to, θνήσκειν, ἀποθνήσκειν, V. τελευτᾶν (ά-ειν).

differ (from), διαφέρειν (gen.).

dig down, κατασκάπτειν.

diligently, σπουδαίως.

din, κτύπος, ὁ.

dine, δειπνεῖν (= έ-ειν).

dinner, δεῖπνον, τό (= cœna).

Diodorus, Διόδωρος, ὁ.

Diogenes, Διογένης, -ους, ὁ.

dip, βάπτ-ειν.

disaffected, δύσνοος, -ους.

disagree, διαφωνεῖν.

disappear, ἀφανίζεσθαι, c. Aor. Pass.

disappoint, ψεύδειν (τινά τινος). To be disappointed of —, ψεύδεσθαι (c. gen.).

disciple, μαθητής, -οῦ.

discreet, φρόνιμος.

discus, δίσκος, ὁ.

disease, νόσος, ἡ.

disembark, ἀπο-βαίνειν. III.

disgraceful, αἰσχρός.

disgracefully, αἰσχρῶς.

disobey, ἀπειθεῖν (= έ-ειν), dat.

dispirited, to be, ἀθυμεῖν (= έ-ειν).

display (= show off), ἐπιδεικνύσθαι.

disposed, kindly, εὔνους 2.

dissatisfied, μεμψίμοιρος.

dissolve, λύειν.

distinguish oneself; be distinguished for, διαφέρειν.

disturb, κῑνεῖν (= έ-ειν), movere. ταράττειν, συγκεῖν (= έ-ειν).

divine, θεῖος.

do, πράττειν, ποιεῖν (= έ-ειν), δρᾶν (= ά-ειν).

do good to, εὖ ποιεῖν (= έ-ειν), acc. ; εὐεργετεῖν (= έ-ειν), acc.

dog, κύων, κυνός, ὁ, ἡ.

door, θύρα, ἡ.

draw, ἀπεικάζειν (= take a likeness of).

drain away, ἀποσπᾶν.

draw up (of an army), τάττειν.

dream, ἐνυπνιάζειν.

drink, to, πίνειν. VII.

drug, φάρμακον, τό.

dwell, οἰκεῖν (= έ-ειν).

E.

Each other, ἀλλήλων, -οις, -ους.

eagerness, σπουδή (σπεύδειν).

eagle, ἀετός, ὁ.

ear, οὖς, ὠτός, τό. Note 9.

earnest, σπουδαῖος, α, ον.

earth, the, γῆ, ἡ.

easily, ῥᾳδίως.

eat, ἐσθίειν. VII.

educate, παιδεύειν.

educated, πεπαιδευμένος.

education, παιδεία, ἡ.

egg, ᾠόν (ᾠϝόν = ovum)

Egypt, Αἴγυπτος, ἡ.

Egyptian, Αἰγύπτιος, ὁ.

either—or, ἤ—ἤ.

elbow, ἀγκών, ὁ.

elephant, ἐλέφας, -αντος, ὁ.

employ, χρῆσθαι (= ά-εσθαι), dat.

empowered, I am, κύριός εἰμι (ποιεῖν τι).

emulate, ζηλοῦν (= ό-ειν).

emulation, ζῆλος.

enact laws, τιθέναι (Aor. θεῖναι) νόμους.

encampment, στρατόπεδον, τό.

end, τέλος, -ους, τό.

endeavor, to, πειρᾶσθαι (= ά-εσθαι), Dep. Pass.

endure, ὑπομένειν.

enemy, πολέμιος, ὁ (hostis). ἐχθρός, ὁ.

enjoin upon, ἐντέλλειν.

enslave, δουλοῦν (= ό-ειν), καταδουλοῦν (= ό-ειν). Mid. 'for oneself or to oneself.'

enter, εἰσιέναι (εἶμι, ibo).

entrance (of a port), εἴσπλους or ἔσπλους, ὁ.

entreat, ἱκετεύειν.

entrust to, ἐπιτρέπειν.

envious, φθονερός.

envy, φθόνος, ὁ.

envy, to, φθονεῖν (= έ-ειν), dat.

Eretria, Ἐρέτρια, ἡ.

err, ἁμαρτάνειν. III.

especially, μάλιστα.

esteem = value much, ποιεῖσθαι (= έ-εσθαι) περὶ πολλοῦ : = consider, think, νομίζειν.

ether, αἰθήρ, αἰθέρος, ὁ.

Eucles, Εὐκλῆς (-οῦς).

Europe, Εὐρώπη, ἡ.

even, of an even number, ἄρτιος, ά, ον.

even, after or before not, οὐδέ (= ne — quidem), the not to be untranslated.

even if, even though (καὶ ἐάν =) κἄν (subj.).

ever (= always), ἀεί : not ever, οὔποτε, μήποτε, or οὐ—ποτέ, μὴ—ποτε (ποτέ, enclit.).

every, πᾶς : = quisque, ἕκαστος.

every thing, πᾶν.

every where, πανταχοῦ.

evident, δῆλος.

evidently. To be translated by δῆλός ἐστι (ἦν, &c.) with partcp. He evidently loves —, δῆλός ἐστι φιλῶν . . .

evil, κακός. To speak evil of, κακῶς λέγειν (acc. personæ).

evil, an, κακόν, τό. κακία, ἡ.

evil-doer, κακοῦργος, ὁ.

examine, ἐξετάζειν.

examine-by-torture, βασανίζειν.

example (= instance), παράδειγμα, τό.

excellence, ἀρετή, ἡ (virtus).

excellent, ἀγαθός, κάλλιστος.

excellently, ἄριστα (neut. adj. used adverbially).

exclude, εἴργειν.

exercise, to, ἀσκεῖν (= έ-ειν) : = make trial of, πειρᾶσθαι (= ά-εσθαι).

expect (= hope), ἐλπίζειν : = claim, ἀξιοῦν (= ό-ειν) : = look for, ὑποπτεύειν, προσδοκᾷν (= ά-ειν).

expedition, to make an, στρατεύειν.

expensive, πολυτελής.

experience, ἐμπειρία, ἡ.

expunge, to, ἐξαλείφειν (blot-out).

extend, ἐξάγειν.

external, ὁ (ἡ, τό) ἔξω (adv.).

extreme, ἔσχατος, η, ον.

eye, ὀφθαλμός, ὁ. ὄμμα, τό.

F.

Face, πρόσωπον.

fair (= beautiful), καλός.

faithful, πιστός.

faithlessness, ἀπιστία.

false, ψευδής.

falsely, to swear, ἐπιορκεῖν (= έ-ειν).
fate, μοῖρα, ἡ.
father, πατήρ, πατρός, ὁ.
fear, φόβος, ὁ.
fear, to, φοβεῖσθαι (= έ-εσθαι). δεδοικέναι (δέδοικα) or δεδιέναι. Pdm. 66.
fearful, δεινός : to be —, φοβεῖσθαι (= έ-εσθαι).
feel pain, ἀλγεῖν.
female, θῆλυς, -εῖα, υ.
few, ὀλίγοι, -αι, -α.
fight, to, μάχεσθαι. I.
fig-tree, συκῆ, ἡ.
find, εὑρίσκειν. v.
fine (= beautiful), καλός.
fire, πῦρ, πυρός, τό.
first; πρῶτος : adv. πρῶτον. τ·ῶ-τα, τά.
fit, ἱκανός.
fix (= to make firm), πηγνύναι (List ix).
flatter, κολακεύειν (acc.).
flatterer, κόλαξ, κόλἅκος, ὁ.
flee, φεύγειν.
flee away from, ἀποφεύγειν (acc.).
fling, ῥίπτειν. ∞ into, ἐμ-βάλλειν.
flute, αὐλός.
fly (= flee), φεύγειν.
fodder, χόρτος, ὁ.
follow, ἕπεσθαι (dat.).
fond of gain, φιλοκερδής, ές.
food, τροφή, ἡ.
foot, πούς (or better πούς), ποδός, ὁ.
foot-soldier, πεζός, ὁ.
force, military, δύναμις, -εως, ἡ.
force (violence), βία, ἡ.
foreign, ἀλλότριος.
form (= species), εἶδος, τό.
fortune, τύχη, ἡ.
fortune, good, εὐτυχία, ἡ.
fortunate, εὐδαίμων, -ονος. εὐτυχής, -ές.

fortunate, to be, εὐτῠχεῖν (= ε ειν), εὐδαιμονεῖν (= έ-ειν).
found, to, κτίζειν. ἱδρύειν.
foundation, θεμέλιον, τό.
fountain, πηγή. ἡ. κρήνη, ἡ.
fox, ἀλώπηξ. -εκος, ἡ.
free, ἐλεύθερος.
free, to, λύειν, ἐλευθεροῦν(=ό-ειν).
freedom, ἐλευθερία, ἡ.
friend, φίλος, ὁ.
friendship, φιλία, ἡ.
from, ἀπό, ἐκ, παρά (gen.).
fruit, καρπός, ὁ.
full, μεστός, πλήρης, -ες (gen.), ἔμπλεως.
future, τὸ μέλλον.

G.

Gain, κέρδος, -ους, τό. ὠφέλεια.
gain, to, κερδαίνειν.
game, τὰ θηρία (= small wild animals).
garden, κῆπος, ὁ.
garland, στέφανος, ὁ.
garment, ἐσθής, ἐσθῆτ-ος, ἡ.
gate, πύλη, ἡ.
Geloni (the), Γελωνοί.
general, a, στρατηγός, ὁ
geometer, γεωμέτρης, ου, ὁ.
geometry, γεωμετρία.
giant, γίγας, γίγαντ-ος.
gift, δῶρον, τό : = act of giving, δόσις, εως, ἡ.
give, διδόναι (δίδωμι).
give back, ἀποδιδόναι.
give one a share of any thing, μεταδιδόναι (μεταδίδωμί) τινί τινος.
give over, λήγειν (c. partic.).
gladly, ἄσμενος (adj.).
glory, δόξα, ἡ.
go, ἔρχομαι* βαίνειν (ΙΙΙ.), πορεύεσθαι.

* εἶμι (= I will go) is more common than the fut. of ἔρχομαι; the moods of εἶμι, than the moods of the pres. of ἔρχομαι; and imperf. ᾔειν than ᾐρχόμην.—Βαίνω is used of going on foot (gradior).

goal, αἴξ, αἰγ-ός, ἡ.

go away, ἀπιέναι (ἄπειμι), ἀπέρ-χεσθαι (VII.), ἀπαλλάττεσθαι (= get off, come off).

go - on - an - expedition, στρατεύ-εσθαι.

goblet, κύπελλον, τό.

God, a god, θεός, ὁ.

goddess, θεά, ἡ.

gold, χρυσός, ὁ. χρυσίον, τό.

golden, gold (as adj.), χρυσέος, -οῦς.

good, ἀγαθός, ἐσθλός, καλός : οἱ ἀγαθοί, the good : τὸ ἀγαθόν, the good (abstract) : = a good thing, ἀγαθόν. Very good, ἄριστος. βέλτιστος, κράτιστος (Note 13).

good for nothing, οὐδενὸς ἄξιος.

good will, εὔνοια, ἡ.

govern, κρατεῖν (= έ-ειν), gen. ; ἄρχειν (gen.).

government, πολιτεία, ἡ.

governor, ἄρχων, ἄρχοντ-ος (pro-perly a partcp. *ruling*).

gracious, ἵλεως.

grant, to, διδόναι (δίδωμι).

grass, πόα, ἡ.

gratitude, χάρις, -ιτος, ἡ.

grave, θήκη (τίθημι).

great, μέγας. Very ∞, μέγιστος.

Grecian. Ἑλληνικός

Greece, Ἑλλάς, Ἑλλάδος, ἡ.

Greek, a, Ἕλλην, Ἕλληνος, ὁ.

grief, λύπη, ἡ.

grieve, λυπεῖσθαι (= έ-εσθαι).

grow old, to. γηράσκειν.

Gryllus, Γρύλλος.

guard, to, φυλάττειν, διαφυλάτ-τειν.

guard : to be on one's guard against, φυλάττεσθαι (acc.).

Gylippus, Γύλιππος.

H.

Halo, ἅλως, ἡ.

hand, χείρ, χειρός, ἡ (d. pl χερσί).

hand-over, ἐγχειρίζειν (τί τινι).

happiness, εὐδαιμονία, ἡ.

happy, εὐδαίμων.

hard (difficult), χαλεπός.

hardship, πόνος, ὁ.

hare, λαγώς, -ώ, ὁ.

harsh, χαλεπός.

hatch (its) young ; breed, νεοττεύ-ειν (wh. see).

hate, to, μισεῖν (= έ-ειν).

have, ἔχειν. VII.

head, κεφαλή. ἡ.

heal, ἰᾶσθαι (= ά-εσθαι).

healthy, ὑγιής, -ές.

hear, ἀκούειν.

heaven, οὐρανός, ὁ.

Hellas, Ἑλλάς, -άδος, ἡ.

Hellenes, Ἕλληνες, οἱ.

Hera (Juno), Ἥρα, ἡ.

herald, κήρυξ, -υκος, ὁ.

Hercules, Ἡρακλῆς. -έους, ὁ.

Hermes (Mercury), Ἑρμῆς, -οῦ, ὁ.

hide, κρύπτειν, ἀποκρύπτειν.

highly, to esteem more, περὶ μεί-ζονος ποιεῖσθαι (= έ-εσθαι). To reverence or prize highly, περὶ πολλοῦ ποιεῖσθαι (= έ-εσθαι).

hinder, κωλύειν.

him, αὐτόν.

hireling, μισθωτός, ὁ.

his,* αὐτοῦ (*ejus*).

his own,* ἑαυτοῦ or αὐτοῦ (*ipsius, suus*).

hit, τυγχάνειν (Aor. τυχεῖν), gen.

hither, δεῦρο.

hold-in-estimation, τιμᾶν (ά-ειν).

hold-office, ἄρχειν.

hollow, κοῖλος.

holy, ἱερός, ὅσιος.

home, οἶκος, ὁ.

---

* *His* father (acc.), τὸν πατέρα αὐτοῦ or αὐτοῦ τὸν πατέρα. **His own** father, τὸν ἑαυτοῦ πατέρα or τὸν πατέρα τὸν ἑαυτοῦ.

honey, μέλι, -ιτος, τό.
honorary-privilege, γέρας, τό.
honor, τιμή, ἡ.
honor, to, τιμᾶν (= ά-ειν).
hoof, ὁπλή, ἡ.
hope, ἐλπίς, ἐλπῐδ-ος, ἡ.
hope, to, ἐλπίζειν.
hoplite, ὁπλίτης.
horn, κέρας, τό.
horse, ἵππος, ὁ: = cavalry, ἵππος, ἡ.
horseman, ἱππεύς, ὁ.
host, ξένος, ὁ.
hostile, πολέμιος, ἐχϑρός.
house, οἶκος, ὁ. οἰκία, ἡ.   Small
   house, οἰκίδιον.
how ? πῶς ; (in an indirect question), ὅπως (or πῶς) ; how
   much, ὅσος.
human, ἀνϑρώπινος.
hunger, λιμός, ὁ.
hungry, to be, πεινῆν (= ά-ειν).
hunt, to, ϑηρεύειν.
hurl, ῥίπτειν.
hurtful, βλαβερός.
husbandman, γεωργός (γῆ. ἔργον,
   work).

I.

I, ἐγώ. Pdm. 41.
idleness, ῥᾳϑυμία, ἡ (= sluggish
   indifference, laziness).
idle-talk, λῆρος, ὁ.
if, εἰ.—ἐάν, ἤν, ἄν (subj.).
ignoble, ἀγεννής, -ές.
ignorant, ἀμαϑής, -ές.
ill, to be, νοσεῖν (= έ-ειν), ἀσϑε-
   νεῖν (= έ-ειν).
ill-affected, δύσνους (σ-ος).
illness, νόσος, ἡ.
imitate, μιμεῖσϑαι (= έ-εσϑαι).
immediately, εὐϑύς, παραχρῆμα.
immoveable, ἀκίνητος.
implant, ἐμφυτεύειν.
impossible, ἀδύνατος 2.
in, ἐν.
in order to, by Fut. Partcp., or a
   final conjunction, as ἵνα, ὡς.

in the way of, ἐμποδών (dat.).
indeed, μέν: indeed—but, μέν—δέ.
indisposed, to be, κακῶς διατεϑῆ-
   ναι, &c.
injure, βλάπτειν (acc.), ἀδικεῖν
   (= έ-ειν), acc.
injurious, βλαβερός.
injury, βλάβη, ἡ. ζημία, ἡ.
innocence, ἀβλάβεια.
insatiably-desirous, ἄπληστος (lit.
   not to be filled), c. gen.
insect, ἔντομον.
insolence, ὕβρις, -εως, ἡ.
insolently, see To behave.
inspector of boys (at Sparta), παιδονόμος, ὁ.
instil, ἐντιϑέναι (ἐντίϑημι).
instruct, παιδεύειν, διδάσκειν.
instruction, παιδεία, ἡ. διδαχή.
insult, ὑβρίζειν (ὕβρις).
intellect, νόησις, ἡ.
intelligence, σύνεσις, -εως, ἡ.
intemperate, ἀκρᾱτής, ἀκόλαστος.
intend to, μέλλειν: also by Fut.
   Partcp.
interest (= gain to oneself) ὠφέλεια.
interpreter, ἑρμηνεύς, ὁ.
intimate (of friends), οἰκεῖος.
into, εἰς.
intoxication, μέϑη, ἡ.
invasion of a country, ἐσβολή (εἰς
   γῆν τινα).
investigate, ζητεῖν (= έ-ειν), quæ-
   rere.
invite, καλεῖν (= έ-ειν), vocare
   (followed by ἐπί c. acc).
iron (of), σιδήρεος, -οῦς.

J.

Judge, a, κρῐτής, -οῦ, ὁ. δικαστής,
   -οῦ, ὁ.
judge, to, κρίνειν.
juggle, to, γοητεύ-ειν (γόης, juggler).
juice, χυμός, ὁ.
Juno, Ἥρα, ἡ.

Jupiter, Ζεύς. Note 9.
just, δίκαιος.
justice, δικαιοσύνη, ἡ (as habit).
δίκη, ἡ : court of —, δικαστή-
ριον, τό.
justly, δικαίως.

K.

Keep, ἔχειν (VII.) : τρέφειν (nutrire, of keeping animals).
keep an oath, ἐμμένειν τῷ ὅρκῳ.
keep silence, κατασιωπᾶν (= ά-
ειν).
kick, λακτίζειν.
kill, ἀποκτείνειν : = murder, φονεύειν.
kind, s., γένος, τό.
kind of —, τὶς (enclit.), in agreement. A kind of disease, νόσος τις, &c. This kind of —.
ὁ τοιοῦτος —. This kind of
thing, τὸ τοιοῦτον.
kindly-disposed, εὔνους, -ουν.
kindness, εὐεργεσία, ἡ : = favor,
χάρις, -ιτος, ἡ.
king, βασιλεύς, -έως, ὁ.
kite, ἰκτῖνος, ὁ.
know, γιγνώσκειν (VI.), ἐπιστά-
σθαι, εἰδέναι (οἶδα).
know how, ἐπίστασθαι.
known, to make, δηλοῦν (= ό-
ειν).

L.

Labor, πόνος, ὁ.
labor, to (= work), ἐργάζεσθαι :
with toil, πονεῖν (= έ-ειν).
laborer, ἐργάτης, -ου. (Paid) laborer, θής, θῆτ-ος, ὁ.
Lacedæmonian, Λακεδαιμόνιος, ὁ.
land (opp. sea), γῆ.
land (region), γῆ (ἡ), χώρα, ἡ.
language, διάλεκτος, ἡ.
law, νόμος, ὁ : by law, κατὰ νόμον.
lawgiver, νομοθέτης, -ου, ὁ.
lay eggs, to, ᾠὰ τίκτ-ειν.

laziness, ῥᾳθυμία, ἡ. To be lazy,
ῥᾳδιουργεῖν.
lead, to, ἄγειν.
lead away, ἀπάγειν.
leader, ἡγεμών, ἡγεμόνος.
leap-down, καταπηδᾶν (= ά-ειν).
learn, μανθάνειν. IV.
least, ἥκιστα.
leave, λείπειν.
leave behind, καταλείπειν.
leave off, παύεσθαι.
legend, μῦθος, ὁ.
leisure, to be at, to have, σχολά-
ζειν.
less (adv.), ἧττον.
lest, after a word denoting fear,
μή : = that not, by ἵνα (ὅπως,
or ὡς) μή.
let (permit), ἐᾶν (= ά-ειν).
letters, γράμματα, τά.
liar, ψεύστης, -ου, ὁ.
liberty, ἐλευθερία, ἡ.
lie, a, ψεῦδος.
lie in wait for, ἐνεδρεύειν (acc.).
life, βίος, ὁ. ζωή, ἡ.
like, ὅμοιος, ἴσος, παραπλήσιος.
like, I am, ἔοικα (perf.), with dat.
like. I should like to —, ἡδέως
ἄν, with Optative (= I would
with-pleasure do it).
limb, μέλος, τό.
lion, λέων, λέοντ-ος, ὁ.
little, ὀλίγος : adv. μικρόν : less,
μεῖον.
live, βιοῦν (= ό-ειν), ζῆν (= ά-
ειν).
live-in, tn, ἐμβιοῦν (= ό-ειν).
long, μακρός : = much, πολύς.
look (at), βλέπειν, προσβλέπειν.
lose, to, ἀπολλύναι (ἀπόλλυμι). IX
love, ἔρως, -ωτος, ὁ.
love, to, φιλεῖν (= έ-ειν), ἀγαπᾶν
(= ά-ειν), στέργειν : = ar-
dently, ἐρᾶν (= ά-ειν).
lover, ἐραστής, -ου. ὁ.
low-estate, ταπεινότης, ταπεινότητ-
ος, ἡ.
Lycurgus, Λυκοῦργος, ὁ

M.

Mad, to be, μαίνεσθαι. Like a dog, λυττᾶν (= ά-ειν).

magistracy, ἀρχή.

maiden, κόρη, ἡ.

maintain (affirm), φάναι, φημί. Pdm. 69.

make, ποιεῖν (= έ-ειν) : make one something, ἀποδεικνύναι (= appoint) : place, τιθέναι.

make-fast, ὀχυροῦν (= ό-ειν).

make an expedition, στρατεύειν.

make use of, χρῆσθαί (= ά-εσθαι) τινι.

man, ἄνθρωπος, ὁ. ἀνήρ, ἀνδρός, ὁ.

mane, χαίτη.

manifest, φανερός, δῆλος.

mankind, ἄνθρωποι (οἱ).

manure (dung), κόπρος, ὁ.

many, πολλοί, -αί, -ά.

march, to, against (ἐπί), στρατεύεσθαι, πορεύεσθαι.

mark, σκοπός.

marrow, μυελός, ὁ.

marry, γαμεῖν (= έ-ειν).

mart, ἐμπόριον, τό.

master, δεσπότης, -ου, ὁ : =teacher, διδάσκαλος.

master of, to be, ἄρχειν (gen.).

measure, μετρεῖν (= έ-ειν).

meat (i. e. flesh-meat), pl. of κρέας, τό.

meet, to, ἀπαντᾶν (= ά-ειν) : = fall in with, ἐντυγχάνειν (dat.).

merciful, ἵλεως.

mere-nonsense, λῆρος, ὁ (= idle-talk).

messenger, ἄγγελος, ὁ, ἡ.

Midas, Μίδας, gen. ου.

middle, middle of, μέσος.

mina, μνᾶ, ἡ.

mind, νοῦς. ὁ. φρήν, -ενός.

Minerva, Ἀθηνᾶ.

Minos, Μίνως (Gen. Μίνωος and Μίνω), ὁ.

misfortune, a, συμφορά, ἡ.

mode of examination (i. e. by torture, &c.), ἔλεγχος, ὁ.

monarchy, μοναρχία (μόνος, on.y. ἀρχή, government).

money, χρήματα, τά. τὸ ἀργύριον νόμισμα, -ατος, τό.

month, μήν, μηνός, ὁ.

monument, μνημεῖον, τό.

moon, σελήνη, ἡ.

morals, ἤθη, τά.

more, πλεῖον, πλέον, plus ; μᾶλλον, magis (comp. much).

mortal, θνητός.

most, πλεῖστος.

most [of all] (especially), μάλιστα.

mother, μήτηρ, μητρ-ός, ἡ.

motion, to be in, κινεῖσθαι (= έ εσθαι) w. Pass. Aor.

move, κινεῖν (= έ-ειν).

moved, to be, κινεῖσθαι (= έ-εσθαι).

much, πολύς.

multitude of hands, πολυχειρία.

Munychia, Μουνυχία.

music, μουσική, ἡ.

must, one, δεῖ, χρή (oportet).

N.

Name, ὄνομα, τό.

native land or country, πατρίς, -ίδος, ἡ.

natural disposition, φύσις, εως, ἡ.

natural philosopher, φυσικός, ὁ.

nature, φύσις, εως, ἡ.

nearly, σχεδόν τι.

necessary, ἀναγκαῖος.

necessary, to be, δεῖ, χρή (w. acc. and inf.).

necessity, ἀνάγκη, ἡ.

neck, αὐχήν, -ένος, ὁ. δέρη, ἡ

need, to, δεῖσθαι (= έ-εσθαι /, gen. ; χρῄζειν (gen.).

neglect, to, ἀμελεῖν (=έ-ειν), gen.

neighbor, ὁ πέλας (= the near person. πέλας. adv.).

Neptune, Ποσειδών, -ῶνος, ὁ.

never, οὔποτε, οὐδέποτε, μήποτε, μηδέποτε (mostly of ful.)—οὐδεπώποτε, μηδεπώποτε (only of past).
nevertheless, ὅμως.
night, νύξ, νυκτός, ἡ.
nightingale, ἀηδών, -όνος, ἡ.
Nile, Νεῖλος, ὁ.
no, no one, none, οὐδείς, μηδείς: by no means, οὐδαμῶς, ἥκιστα: no longer, οὐκέτι (μηκέτι).
nobly, γενναίως.
nobody, οὐδείς, μηδείς.
north-wind, βορρᾶς, -ᾶ, ὁ.
not, οὐ (οὐκ, οὐχ): with the Imp., μή: not only, οὐ μόνον: not the less, οὐδὲν ἧττον: not even, οὐδέ (μηδέ).
not one, οὐδείς.
not yet, never yet, οὔπω, οὐδεπώποτε.
nothing, οὐδέν (μηδέν).
nourish, τρέφειν.
now, νῦν.
nurse, τρόφος, ἡ.

O.

O that, εἴθε w. opt.
oath, ὅρκος, ὁ.
obedient, εὐπειθής, κατήκοος 2, (gen.).
obey, πείθεσθαι (dat.), ὑπακούειν, πειθαρχεῖν (= ἑ-ειν), dat.
obliged, to be (necessary), δεῖ w. acc. and inf., ἀναγκαῖός εἰμί.
obscurity, ἀδοξία.
observe (a law), see Vocab. 19.
obtain, κτᾶσθαι (= ἁ-εσθαι), λαμβάνειν (IV.), τυγχάνειν (IV.), gen.
Œnoe, Οἰνόη, ἡ.
offer (as a gift to a divinity), ἀνατιθέναι: (= propose to give), pres. and imperf. of δίδωμι.
offering, θῦμα, τό.
office (in the state), ἀρχή, ἡ.
often, πολλάκις.
oil, ἔλαιον, τό.

old, never growing, ἄγηρως.
old age, γῆρας, τό.
old man, γέρων, γέροντ-ος.
oligarchy, ὀλιγαρχία, ἡ.
once, ἅπαξ: at once (= at the same time), ἅμα.
one, εἷς, μία, ἕν.
one another (of), ἀλλήλων.
only, μόνον: (adj.) μόνος.
opinion, an, γνώμη, ἡ.
opponents, οἱ ἐναντίοι.
opposite, ἐναντίος.
orator, ῥήτωρ, ῥήτορ-ος, ὁ.
oratory, ῥητορική, ἡ. See Vocab. 22.
Orestes, Ὀρέστης, ου, ὁ.
other, the (= alter), ἕτερος: = alius, ἄλλος.
otherwise, ἄλλως.
ought, δεῖ, χρή (oportet), προσήκει = decet.

P.

Pain, ἄλγος, -ους, τό: = grief, λύπη, ἡ: severe ω, ὀδύνη, ἡ.
painter, γραφεύς, -έως, ὁ.
Palladium, Παλλάδιον, τό.
panegyric, ἔπαινος, ου, ὁ (praise).
pardon, to, συγγιγνώσκειν (dat.). VI.
parent, γονεύς, -έως, ὁ.
part, a, μέρος, -ους, τό: take part in, μετέχειν (gen.).
participation, participating, κοινωνία.
passion, πάθος, τό: = angry passions, ὀργαί (pl.): = evil desire, ἐπιθυμία, ἡ.
path, ὁδός, ἡ.
patience, καρτερία, ἡ.
pay, μισθός, ὁ.
pay attention (to), τὸν νοῦν προσέχειν (= animum applicare); or προσέχειν only, τὸν νοῦν being understood.
peace, εἰρήνη.
peacock, ταώς, -ώ, ὁ.

13

Peloponnesus, Πελοπόννησος, ἡ.

people, δῆμος, ὁ.

perceive, κατανοεῖν.

perform, πράττειν, ἐργάζεσθαι.

perhaps, ἴσως.

Pericles, Περικλῆς, -έους.

peril, κίνδυνος.

perish, ἀπόλλυσθαι. ἀπόλωλα = perii.

permit, ἐᾶν (= ά-ειν): it is permitted, ἔξεστι.

Persian, Πέρσης, -ου, ὁ.

persuade, πείθειν (acc.).

persuasion, πειθώ, -οῦς, ἡ.

phalanx, φάλαγξ, -γγος, ἡ.

Philip, Φίλιππος, ὁ.

philosopher, φιλόσοφος, ὁ.

philosophy, φιλοσοφία, ἡ.

Phoenicians, Φοίνικες, οἱ.

physician, ἰατρός, ὁ.

piety, εὐσέβεια, ἡ.

pillage, συλᾶν (= ά-ειν).

pious, εὐσεβής, -ές.

Piraeus, Πειραιεύς, -έως, ὡς.

pitch, πίττα, ἡ.

place, τόπος, ὁ.

place, to, τιθέναι (τίθημι). ∾ before, προτιθέναι.

plant, to, ἐμφυτεύειν.

Platæa, Πλάταια, ἡ: or pl. Πλαταιαί.

Plato, Πλάτων, -ωνος, ὁ.

pleasant, ἡδύς, -εῖα, -ύ.

pleasantly, ἡδέως.

please, ἀρέσκειν (dat.): = choose, βούλεσθαι.

pleasure, ἡδονή, ἡ.

plot against, ἐνεδρεύειν (insidiari, acc.).

poet, ποιητής, -οῦ, ὁ.

poetry, epic, ποίησις ἐπῶν, τὰ ἔπη.

poison, φάρμακον (drug).

pollute, μιαίνειν.

poor, πένης, -ητος. ἐνδεής, πτωχός.

poor, to be, πένεσθαι.

poorly (badly), κακῶς.

portentous monster, τέρας, -ατος, τό.

Poseidon (Neptune), Ποσειδῶν, -ῶνος, ὁ.

possess, ἔχειν (VII.) Also Perf. κέκτημαι (= I have acquired).

possession, κτῆμα, τό.

possible, δυνατός.

pound, τρίβειν (rub).

power, δύναμις: to be in the — of, γίγνεσθαι ἐπί τινι.

power, it is in one's (possible), ἔξεστι.

power, to have much, πολλὰ δύνασθαι (cf. multum valere or posse).

practise, to, μελετᾶν (= ά-ειν), ἀσκεῖν (= έ-ειν).

praise, ἔπαινος, ὁ.

praise, to, ἐπαινεῖν (= έ-ειν).

pray, εὔχεσθαι: = entreat, ἱκετεύειν.

prayer, εὐχή, ἡ.

prefer, αἱρεῖσθαι (= έ-εσθαι). VII.

prepare, παρασκευάζ-ειν.

prepare oneself, παρασκευάζεσθαι: for something, εἴς τι.

present, παρών.

present, δόσις, -εως (= act of giving).

present, to be, παρεῖναι (πάρειμι). Pdm. 68.

preservation, σωτηρία.

priest, ἱερεύς, -έως, ὁ.

priestess, ἱερεία, ἡ.

prisoner (of war), αἰχμάλωτος, ἡ.

privilege, γέρας, τό.

profess, ἐπαγγέλλεσθαι. ὁμολογεῖν (= έ-ειν, to allow).

profit, ὠφέλεια.

profit, to, ὠφελεῖν (= έ-ειν), acc.

prone (to), ὀξύῤῥοπος, -ον.

properly, ὀρθῶς (recte).

property, χρήματα, τά.

prophet, μάντις, ὁ.

propitious, ἵλεως.

proportion, λόγος, ὁ.

propose, προτιθέναι (προτίθημι).

prosperity, εὐτυχία, ἡ.

prosperous, to be, εὐτυχεῖν, εὖ πράττειν.

prove, ἀποδεικνύναι (ἀποδείκνυμι).
prove (= test), δοκιμάζειν.
provided that, εἰ, ἐάν.
prudence, σωφροσύνη, ἡ.
prudent, φρόνιμος.
public, δημόσιος : in a public capacity, δημοσίᾳ.
punish, κολάζειν, τιμωρεῖσθαι (= ἐ-εσθαι) (= revenge oneself or requite), acc.: ἀποτίνεσθαι : to punish (by a fine), ζημιοῦν (= ό-ειν). •
punishment, τιμωρία, ἡ : (as a fine), ζημία, ἡ.
pupil, μαθητής, -οῦ, ὁ.
pursue, διώκειν.
pursuing gain by base means, αἰσχροκερδής, -ές.
put into the hands, ἐγχειρίζειν.
put on, ἀμφιεννύναι (ἀμφιέννυμι). X.
put to death, ἀποκτείνειν.
put to flight, τρέπεσθαι.

Q.

Queen, βασίλισσα, ἡ.
quick, ὀξύς (= sharp in intellect).
quietness, ἡσυχία, ἡ.
Quirinus, Κυρῖνος.
quoit, δίσκος, ὁ.

R.

Race, γένος, -ους, τό : human —, ἀνθρώπων γένος.
rail-at, λοιδορεῖσθαι (= ἐ-εσθαι), dat.
raised-in-price, to be, ἐπιτιμᾶσθαι (= ά-εσθαι).
rather, μᾶλλον.
raven, κόραξ, -ἄκος, ὁ.
read, ἀναγιγνώσκειν. VI.
ready, to be (willing), ἐθέλειν.
readiness, προθυμία, ἡ.
reality, in, ἀληθῶς.
reap, θερίζειν.
reason, λόγος, ὁ: with —, δικαίως.

reasonable, ἐπιεικής, -ές.
receive, λαμβάνειν (III.), δέχεσθαι
reed, a, ῥίψ, ὁ.
reign over, βασιλεύειν (gen.).
rejoice, χαίρειν (dat.), ἥδεσθαι (dat.).
relate, διηγεῖσθαι.
relation, συγγενής, -ές (σύν, with. γένος, race, family) ; prop. an adj.
rely upon (trust), πιστεύειν.
remain, μένειν, διαμένειν.
remedy, φάρμακον.
remember, μεμνῆσθαι (perf. μέμνημαι), gen.
remove any body (from a command, magistracy, &c.), παύειν τινὰ (στρατηγίας, ἀρχῆς, &c.).
render (= make), ποιεῖν.
repay, ἀποδιδόναι (ἀποδίδωμι).
repent, μεταμέλεσθαι : or impers. μεταμέλει τινί τινος.
report, a, λόγος, ὁ.
reproach, ὀνειδίζειν (ὄνειδος), acc. rei; dat. personæ (cf. exprobrare alicui ignaviam).
request, to, αἰτεῖν (= ἐ-ειν), δεῖσθαι (= ἐ-εσθαι).
requite a favor, ἀποδιδόναι χάριν.
resident-foreigner, μέτοικος, ὁ.
resolve, γιγνώσκειν (VI.), δοκεῖ τινι.
respect, αἰδώς : with — to, περί.
rest, the, ἄλλος : = reliquus, λοιπός.
restore, ἀποδιδόναι (ἀποδίδωμι).
retail-trader, to be, καπηλεύειν.
retentive memory, of a, μνήμων, -ονος.
retreat, ἀναχώρησις, ἡ.
return, ἀναχωρεῖν (= ἐ-ειν).
revenge oneself on or upon, τιμωρεῖσθαι (= ἐ-εσθαι), acc., ἀμύνεσθαι (τινὰ ὑπέρ τινος).
reverence, αἰδώς, -οῦς, ἡ.
revile, λοιδορεῖν (= ἐ-ειν), acc.
revolt, to cause to, ἀφιστάναι (Aor. inf. ἀποστῆσαι). Mid., to revolt. So Aor. 2. act. ἀπέστην.

reward, ἆθλον, τό.

rich, πλούσιος : be or become rich, πλουτεῖν (= έ-ειν).

riches, πλοῦτος.

right (just), δίκαιος.

rightly, ὀρθῶς.

rise up, ἀνίστασθαι.

river, ποτάμός, ὁ.

road, ὁδός, ἡ.

rob, ἁρπάζειν : = deprive of, ἀφαιρεῖσθαί (= έ-εσθαι) τινά τι : συλᾶν (= ά-ειν).

robber, λῃστής, -οῦ, ὁ.

rock, πέτρα, ἡ.

root, ῥίζα, ἡ.

Roman, 'Ρωμαῖος.

rose, ῥόδον, τό.

royal, βασίλειος.

rub, τρίβειν.

rudder, πηδάλιον.

ruin, to, ἀπολλύναι. IX.

ruined, ἀνάστατος, -ον.

rule, rule over, to, ἄρχειν (gen.), βασιλεύειν (gen.).

ruler, ἄρχων, -οντος, ὁ.

run, τρέχειν (VII.) : run to, προστρέχειν.

run away, ἀποδιδράσκειν (acc.). VI.

rush, to, ὁρμᾶν (= ά-ειν).

S.

Sacrifice, θυσία, ἡ. θῦμα, τό.

sacrifice, to, θύειν.

sadness, λύπη, ἡ.

safe, ἀσφαλής, -ές.

safely, ἀσφαλῶς.

safety, σωτηρία, ἡ.

sail, πλεῖν (= έ-ειν).—πλεύσομαι. πέπλευκα. Aor. ἔπλευσα.

sail, ἱστίον.

sail away, ἀποπλεῖν (= έ-ειν).

sake of, for the, ἕνεκα, περί (gen.).

same, the, ὁ αὐτός.

Samian, Σάμιος, ὁ.

satisfied, to be, ἀγαπᾶν (= ά-ειν) [lit. to love] with acc. or dat.

saw, a, πρίων, ὁ.

say, λέγειν, φάναι (Pdm. 69), εἰπεῖν (= έ-ειν). VII.

sceptre, σκῆπτρον, τό.

scoff at, σκώπτειν.

scribe, γραμματεύς, ὁ.

Scythian, Σκύθης.

sea, θάλασσα, θάλαττα, ἡ : by sea, κατὰ θάλατταν : to be carried out to sea, ἀποφέρεσθαι ἐς τὸ πέλαγος (-ους).

season, καιρός, ὁ. See Vocab. 24.

secretly, κρύφα.

secure, ἀσφᾰλής. -ές : firm, βέβαιος.

securely, ἀσφαλῶς.

see, ὁρᾶν (= ά-ειν). VII.

seek, seek for, ζητεῖν (= έ-ειν).

seem, δοκεῖν (= έ-ειν), φαίνεσθαι.

seize, ἁρπάζ-ειν.

self, αὐτός.

self-government, αὐτονομία (αὐτός, ipse. νόμος, lex).

sell, πωλεῖν (= έ-ειν), ἀποδίδοσθαι.

send, πέμπειν, ἀποστέλλειν.

send back, ἀποπέμπειν.

senselessness, ἄνοια.

sensible, συνετός.

sensual pleasures, αἱ περὶ τὸ σῶμα ἡδοναί.

separate, to, διιστάναι (διίστημι).

sepulchre, τάφος, ὁ.

serve (= be a slave), δουλεύειν.

set-down, τιθέναι (= hold it to be).

set off (on a journey), set out, πορεύεσθαι.

set upon (place), ἐπιτιθέναι : = attack, ἐπιτίθεσθαι.

shame, αἰδώς, -οῦς, ἡ.

shameful, αἰσχρός.

shameless, ἀναιδής.

sharpen, θήγ-ειν.

sheep, πρόβατον, τό.

shepherd, ποιμήν, ποιμένος, ὁ.

shield, ἀσπίς, ἀσπίδος, ἡ.

ship, ναῦς, νεώς, ἡ.

shoot, ἀφιέναι, ἀφίημι (= let fly). Pdm. 67.

short, βραχύς, -εῖα, ύ.

show, to, δεικνύναι (δείκνυμι), δηλόειν.

show-off, ἐπιδεικνύναι.

shut, κλείειν (perf. pass. -σμαι or -μαι) : ∞ in or up, κατακλείειν.

Sicily, Σικελία, ἡ.

sick, ἀσθενής, -ές.

sick, to be, νοσεῖν (= έ-ειν), ἀσθενεῖν (= έ-ειν).

sight, ὄψις, ἡ.

sign, σημεῖον, τό.

silliness, ἠλιθιότης (-ητος).

silver, ἄργυρος, ὁ.

silver (adj.), ἀργύρεος, -οῦς.

sin, ἁμάρτημα, -ατος, τό.

sin, to, ἁμαρτάνειν. III.

since (because), ὅτε, ἐπεί.

sing, to, ᾄδειν.

sister, ἀδελφή, ἡ.

sit, to (of a bird), ἐπωάζειν.

slaughter, φονεύ-ειν.

slaughter, φόνος.

slave, δοῦλος, ὁ. οἰκέτης (= famulus) : to be the slave of, δουλεύειν (c. dat.).

slavery, δουλεία, ἡ.

slay, φονεύειν.

sleep, ὕπνος, ὁ.

sleep, to, εὕδειν, καθεύδειν.

slow, βραδύς (also of intellect).

small, μικρός, ὀλίγος.

smelling, ὄσφρησις, ἡ.

snatch at, ἁρπάζ-ειν.

snow, χιών, χιόνος, ἡ.

so, οὕτως· = this, τοῦτο.

so great, τοσοῦτος.

so long (adj.), τοσοῦτος.

so that, ὥστε.

sober-minded, σώφρων, -ονος.

sobriety of mind, σωφροσύνη.

Socrates, Σωκράτης, -ους, ὁ.

soldier, a, στρατιώτης, -ου, ὁ.

solid, στερεός.

some, ἔνιοι (often indef.), τινές.

some—others, οἱ μὲν ... οἱ δέ.

son, υἱός, ὁ.

soon, τάχα.

Sophocles, Σοφοκλῆς, -έους, ὁ.

soul, ψυχή, ἡ.

sound, φωνή (vox).

sow, to, σπείρειν.

spare, to, φείδεσθαι (gen.).

Sparta, Σπάρτη, ἡ.

Spartan, a, Σπαρτιάτης, -ου, ὁ.

speak, λέγειν.

speak ill of —, κακῶς λέγειν (c. acc. personæ).

spear, δόρυ, τό. Note 9.

spend (one's life), διάγειν (τὸν βίον).

sphere, σφαῖρα.

spirit, νοῦς, νοῦ, ὁ.

spirit (= courage), high-mindedness, courage, εὐψυχία (εὐ. ψυχή). φρόνημα, τό.

spring, ἔαρ, ἔαρ-ος, τό.

stadium, στάδιον, τό.

stag, ἔλαφος, ὁ, ἡ.

star, ἄστρον, τό.

state, a, πόλις, -εως, ἡ.

statue, ἀνδριάς, -άντος, ὁ.

stay, μένειν.

steal, κλέπτειν : steal away, ἁρπάζειν.

still (yet), ἔτι.

stillness, ἡσυχία, ἡ.

stir (move), to, κινεῖν (= έ-ειν).

stone, λίθος, ὁ.

straight, ὀρθός, ή, όν.

stranger, ξένος, ὁ.

strength, ἰσχύς, -ύος, ἡ.

strike, τύπτειν : παίειν.

strive (= endeavor), πειρᾶσθαι (= ά-εσθαι).

strong, ἰσχυρός.

study, a, μάθημα, τό.

subjugate, χειροῦσθαι (= ό-εσθαι), δουλοῦν (= ό-ειν).

such, τοιοῦτος or ὁ τοιοῦτος, the article when the particular class or kind is to be made prominent.

such as, οἷος.

sudden, αἰφνίδιος.
suffering, to be, κάμνειν.
sufficient, ἱκανός.
sufficiently, ἱκανῶς.
summer, θέρος, -ους, τό.
sun, ἥλιος. ὁ.
superintendent, ἐπιμελητής, ὁ.
supply, bestow, παρέχεσθαι.
suppose, ἡγεῖσθαι (= ἑ-εσθαι),
νομίζειν.
supreme (of laws), κύριος.
surpass, νικᾶν (= ά-ειν), τινά,
διαφέρειν (gen.) = to be distinguished from him.
swallow, χελιδών, -όνος, ἡ.
swear, ὀμνύναι (ὄμνυμι). IX.
sweat, ἱδρώς, -ῶτος, ὁ.
sweet, ἡδύς.
sweetmeats, τραγήματα.
swift, ταχύς.
sword, ξίφος, τό.
sycophant, συκοφάντης, -ου.
Syracuse, Συράκουσαι, αἱ.

T.

Tail, οὐρά, ἡ.
take = capture, αἱρεῖν (= ἑ-ειν).
List VII.
take care, ἐπιμέλεσθαι (gen.).
take hold of, ἅπτεσθαι (gen.).
take place (be done), γίγνεσθαι.
taken, to be, ἁλίσκεσθαι. VII.
tale, λόγος, ου. μῦθος, ὁ.
talk, to, λαλεῖν (= ἑ-ειν).
talked-about, περιβόητος, ον.
talk nonsense, ληρεῖν.
talon, ὄνυξ, -υχος, ὁ.
taste, to, γεύεσθαι (c. gen.).
teach, διδάσκειν τινά τι. παιδεύειν
(= educate).
eacher, διδάσκαλος.
tear, a, δάκρυον, τό.
tell, λέγειν, φράζειν.
temperate, ἐγκρατής, -ές.
tempest-tossed, to be, χειμάζε-
σθαι.
temple, νεώς, -εώ, ὁ.

tell, λέγειν.
terrible, δεινός.
Thales, Θαλῆς, ὁ (G. Θάλεω, D. ῃ,
A. ῆν) : Thales and his school,
οἱ ἀμφὶ Θαλῆν.
than, ἤ : Gen. after a comparative.
that, in order, ἵνα, ὡς, ὅπως.
Theban, Θηβαῖος, ὁ.
Thebes, Θῆβαι, αἱ.
them, αὐτούς.
Themistocles, Θεμιστοκλῆς, -έους,
ὁ.
themselves. See Pdm. 45.
then, τότε.
there, ἐκεῖ. I was there, παρῆν
(= I was present).
therefore, οὖν.
Thermopylæ, Θερμοπύλαι, αἱ.
Thessalian, Θετταλός, ὁ.
thief, κλέπτης, -ου, ὁ.
thigh, μηρός, ὁ.
thing, πρᾶγμα, τό.
think, ἡγεῖσθαι (= ἑ-εσθαι), νομίζειν, οἴεσθαι.
thirst, δίψος, -ους, τό.
thirst, to, or be thirsty, διψῆν (=
ά-ειν).
this, οὗτος. See Pdm. 47.
this (emphatic, the accent being
used to mark the emphasis),
οὗτός γε (τοῦτό γε, &c.).
thou, σύ. Pdm. 42.
though, κἄν (= καὶ ἐάν).
through, διά.
throughout, adv., διόλου.
throw, ῥίπτειν.
throw away, to, ἀπο-βάλλ-ειν.
thus, οὕτω(ς).
time, χρόνος, ὁ : right —, καιρός, ὁ.
Tissaphernes, Τισσαφέρνης, -ους,
ὁ.
together with, ἅμα (w. dat.)
toil, to, κάμνειν.
tongue, γλῶσσα (γλῶττα), ἡ.
tooth, ὀδούς, -όντος, ὁ.
torture, βασανίζειν.
touch, to, ἅπτεσθαι (gen.).

town, πόλις, -εως, ἡ.
train, to, παιδεύειν: (to — any thing, πρός τι).
travel, to, πορεύεσθαι.
travelling-money, ἐφόδιον, τό.
treason, προδοσία, ἡ.
treaty, συνθήκη, ἡ. σπονδαί, αἱ.
tree, δένδρον, τό.
trial : to make — of, πειρᾶσθαι (= ά-εσθαι), gen.
Trojan, Τρωϊκός.
trophy, τρόπαιον, τό.
trouble, πόνος, ὁ. ˋ
truce, σπονδαί (pl.), -ῶν (lit. libations).
true, ἀληθής, -ές.
truly (really), ἀληθῶς.
trunk (of an elephant), μυκτήρ, -ῆρος, ὁ.
trust, to, πείθεσθαι, πιστεύειν (dat.).
truth, ἀλήθεια, ἡ.
truth, to speak the, λέγειν τἀληθῆ (= τὰ ἀληθῆ).
tunic (a small), χιτώνιον, τό.
turn, to, στρέφειν (trans.) ; = devote oneself to, τρέπεσθαι.
twice, δίς.
tyrant, τύραννος. See Vocab. 28.

U.

Ulysses, Ὀδυσσεύς, -έως ὁ.
unbearable, ἀφόρητος.
under, ὑπό.
understand, ἐπίστασθαι, εἰδέναι (οἶδα).
understanding, νοῦς, ὁ. φρένες, αἱ.
undertaking, ἔργον, τό.
undying, ἀγήρως.
unexpected, ἀπροσδόκητος [ἀ. προσδοκᾶν (= ά-ειν)].
unfortunate, to be, δυστυχεῖν (= έ-ειν). κακῶς πράττειν (= to be doing ill).
ungrateful, ἀχάριστος 2.
unjust, ἄδικος 2.
unseen, ἀόρατος, ον.

unsparingly, ἀφειδῶς : most ce, ἀφειδέστατα.
unsworn, ἀνώμοτος, ὁ, ἡ.
unwritten, ἄγραφος, ον.
up, ἀνά : lay up, κατατιθέναι.
us, ἡμᾶς.
use, to, χρᾶσθαι (= ά-εσθαι).
use, to be of, συμφέρειν (dat.).
useful, χρήσιμος 2, ὠφέλιμος 2.
useful, to be, ὠφελεῖν (= έ-ειν).
utter, to, λέγειν: (= emit as a sound), ἀφιέναι (ἀφίημι). Pdm. 67.
utterly-deceive, ἐξαπατᾶν (= ά-ειν).

V.

Variegate, ποικίλλειν.
vegetables, λάχανα, τά.
very, λίαν, σφόδρα, πάνυ : also by the Sup. of the adjective.
vexatious-information, συκοφαντία, ἡ.
victory, νίκη, ἡ.
vine, ἄμπελος, ἡ.
violence, βία, ἡ.
violently, σφόδρα, λίαν
virtue, ἀρετή, ἡ.
viviparous, ζωοτόκος. **See Vocab. 24.**
voice, φωνή.
void, ἔρημος (gen.).
vulture, γύψ, γυπ-ός, ὁ.

W.

Wagon, ἄμαξα.
wait, μένειν.
waking (of a waking person, &c.), ἐγρηγορικός.
wall, τεῖχος (-ους).
want, to, δεῖν (= έ-ειν).
war, πόλεμος, ὁ.
war, to carry on, πολεμεῖν (= έ-ειν).
ward off, ἀμύνειν. See Vocab. 29.

warrior, στρατιώτης, -ου, ὁ.
war-song, παιάν, παιᾶν-ος, ὁ.
wash, λούειν.
water, ὕδωρ, ὕδατος, τό.   Note 9.
wax, κηρός, ὁ.
way (road, journey), ὁδός, ἡ : (= manner), τρόπος, ὁ.
we, ἡμεῖς.
weak, ἀσθενής, -ές.
weakness, ἀσθένεια, ἡ.
wealth, πλοῦτος, ὁ. χρήματα, τά.
weary, to be, κάμνειν.
weave (a garland), πλέκ-ειν.
weep, to, κλαίειν.
well, καλῶς, εὖ : do well to, εὖ
  ποιεῖν (= έ-ειν), εὐεργετεῖν
  (= έ-ειν), acc. : to be well, εὖ
  ἔχειν : to be doing well, εὖ
  πράττειν.
well - appointed,   κεκοσμημένος
  (partcp. perf. pass. from κοσμεῖν [= έ-ειν], to adorn, arrange beautifully).
well-disciplined, εὐπειθής (= obedient).
well-disposed, εὔνοος, -ους.
well-ordered, τεταγμένος (perf.
  pass. partcp. from τάσσειν).
what? τίς; τί;
what kind of, ποῖος.   See Vocab.
  25.
whatever, ὅστις, ὅσπερ.
when, ὅτε, ἐπεί.
whence, ἐξ οὗ.
whenever, ὅταν (subj.).
where, οὗ, ὅπου: where? πῆ;
wherever, ὅπου ἄν (subj.).—οὗ,
  ὅπου (w. opt.).
whet, θήγ-ειν.
whether, πότερον.
which? (of two), πότερος.
white, λευκός : as subst., τὸ λευκόν.
whither? πῆ;
who, which, ὅς: interrog. τίς;
whoever, ὅστις, ὅσπερ.
whole, πᾶς, ἅπας, σύμπας, ὅλος.
wicked, κακός, πονηρός.

wife, γυνή, γυναικ-ός, ἡ.
wild beast, θηρίον, τό.
willing, ἑκών, -οῦσα, -όν.
willing, to be, βούλεσθαι, ἐθέλειν.
willingly, ἡδέως. Most —, ἑκών,
  see Willing.
wind, ἄνεμος, ὁ.
wine, οἶνος, ὁ.
wing, πτερόν, τό. πτέρυξ, -γος, ἡ.
wing (of an army), κέρας, τό.
winter, χειμών.
wisdom, σοφία.
wise, σοφός : to be —, φρονεῖν
  (= έ-ειν), prudentem esse.
wish, to, βούλεσθαι, ἐθέλειν.
with, σύν (dat.), μετά (gen.).
within, ἐντός (gen.).
without, ἄνευ (gen.).
woman, γυνή, γυναικ-ός, ἡ.
woman, old, γραῦς, γρᾶός, ἡ.
wonder, to, to wonder at, θαυμάζειν.
wonderful, θαυμαστός.
wont, to be, ἐθίζειν.
word, λόγος, ὁ.
work, ἔργον, τό.
write, γράφειν.
worst, to, ἡττᾶσθαι (= ά-εσθαι),
  κακίζειν.
would that —, εἴθε.
wound, τραῦμα, -ατος, τό.
wrist, καρπός, ὁ.
wrong, to do, ἀδικεῖν (= έ-ειν).
wrought, εἰργασμένος (ἐργάζεσθαι.

X.

Xenophon, Ξενοφών, -ῶντος, ὁ.
Xerxes, Ξέρξης, -ου, ὁ.

Y.

Year, ἔτος, -ους, τό. ἐνιαυτός, ὁ.
yesterday, χθές.
yet, ἔτι, πώ.
yield, εἴκειν.
you, ὑμᾶς.

young, νέος.
young animal, σκύμνος, ὁ.
young bird, νεοττός (Attice for νεοσσός).

young man, νεανίας, -ου.
yourself, αὐτός, in nom.; σεαυτοῦ (σαυτοῦ) in oblique cases Pl. yourselves, ὑμεῖς αὐτοί.

THE END.

A First Greek Book and Introductory Reader.

BY PROF. A. HARKNESS, PH. D.,

OF BROWN UNIVERSITY, AUTHOR OF "ARNOLD'S FIRST LATIN BOOK," ETC.,

12mo. 276 pages. $1 00.

This work embraces, in one small volume, the leading features of the author's two Latin books. It is designed to conduct the pupil in a series of Lessons and Exercises through the Forms and Syntax of the language, and to give him sufficient practice in translating, first classified sentences and then easy connected discourses in the form of fables, anecdotes, and legends, to prepare him to enter with ease and success upon the consecutive study of such a work as the Anabasis of Xenophon.

A Greek Grammar
FOR SCHOOLS AND COLLEGES.

BY JAMES HADLEY,

PROFESSOR IN YALE COLLEGE

12mo. 366 pages. $1 50.

Professor Hadley's long-expected Grammar is presented to the public in the confident belief that it will, in every respect, meet the wants of Academies and Colleges. It displays a thorough acquaintance with the labors of English and German critics, while the original researches of its author, with special reference to the wants of American students, impart to it a peculiar value. Its masterly treatment of the Greek particles, as variously construed with the different moods and tenses of the verb, is worthy of particular attention. It will be found clear in its language, accurate in its definitions, judicious in its arrangement, and sufficiently comprehensive for all purposes, while it is free from that cumbrous array of details so repulsive to the student.

Virgil's Æneid.

WITH EXPLANATORY NOTES.

BY HENRY S. FRIEZE,

PROFESSOR OF LATIN IN THE STATE UNIVERSITY OF MICHIGAN.

12mo. Illustrated. 598 pages. $1 50.

The appearance of this edition of Virgil's Æneid will, it is believed, be hailed with delight by all classical teachers. Neither expense nor pains have been spared to clothe the great Latin epic in a fitting dress. The type is unusually large and distinct, and errors in the text, so annoying to the learner, have been carefully avoided. The work contains eighty-five engravings, which delineate the usages, costumes, weapons, arts, and mythology of the ancients with a vividness that can be attained only by pictorial illustration. The great feature of this edition is the scholarly and judicious commentary furnished in the appended Notes. The author has here endeavored, not to show his learning, but to supply such practical aid as will enable the' pupil to understand and appreciate what he reads. The notes are just full enough, thoroughly explaining the most difficult passages, while they are not so extended as to take all labor off the pupil's hands. Properly used they cannot fail to impart an intelligent acquaintance with the syntax of the language. In a word, this work is commended to teachers as the most elegant, accurate, interesting, and practically useful edition of the Æneid that has yet been published.

From JOHN H. BRUNNER, *Pres. Hiwassee Coll.*

The typography, paper, and binding of Virgil's Æneid, by Prof. Freize, are all that need be desired; while the learned and judicious notes appended, are very valuab indeed.

From PRINC. OF PIEDMONT (Va.) ACADEMY.

I have to thank you for a copy of Prof. Frieze's edition of the Æneid. I have bee exceedingly pleased in my examination of it. The size of the type from which the text is printed, and the faultless execution leave nothing to be desired in these respect The adherence to a standard text throughout, increases the value of this edition.

From D. G. MOORE, *Princ. U. High S. Rutland.*

The copy of Frieze's "Virgil" forwarded to me was duly received. It is so evidently superior to any of the other editions, that I shall unhesitatingly adopt it in m classes.

Lightning Source UK Ltd.
Milton Keynes UK
UKHW020259261118
332889UK00007B/450/P